The Individual Investor's Guide to No-Load Mutual Funds
Sixth Edition

D1291824

The Individual Investor's Guide to No-Load Mutual Funds

Sixth Edition

American Association of Individual Investors

International Publishing Corporation
Chicago

The American Association of Individual Investors is an independent, non-profit corporation formed for the purpose of assisting individuals in becoming effective managers of their own assets through programs of education, information and research.

ISBN 0-942-641-00-0
Library of Congress Catalog Card Number: 87-80864

Published by: International Publishing Corporation

Data in this guide were gathered from company releases. Factual material is not guaranteed but has been obtained from sources believed to be reliable.

Preface

Finding the appropriate no-load mutual funds for your investment portfolio requires preparation and organization. The mutual fund selection process has become a bit more difficult because of the ever-expanding universe of funds to choose from. There are many more funds available and a proliferation of investment approaches. Comparing the funds means getting useful information and establishing an effective, uniform evaluation plan.

The goals of this guide are to gather data on no-load mutual funds, insure that the information is correct and comparable, and to present the information in a format that makes the mutual fund investment decision an efficient one for the individual investor. The guide simplifies the task of data gathering and organization so that the individual can concentrate time and effort on the mutual fund choice.

We have reported on all no-load mutual funds that were carried in the NASD list appearing in most major newspapers at the end of December 1986. Not all funds that are listed as no-load in the financial press met our definition of a no-load fund. Any load, whether small or not, precluded entry of the fund into our guide. Any fund that was previously a no-load and instituted a load last year was eliminated from detailed coverage in this guide. A fund that has a redemption fee that does not disappear after six months was considered to be effectively loaded and was also excluded from the guide. Funds that have closed, have unusually high minimum initial deposits, are restricted to special groups, or failed to provide information, were also excluded from analysis but are noted at the end of the guide. However, funds that have closed but otherwise meet our criteria for inclusion in the guide are included in our historical performance rankings. Since funds with 12b-1 plans fall in a grey area of charges, we have not excluded any but have instead provided information on the charges.

In this guide there are 316 no-load funds with comprehensive share data, returns, levels of diversification, up and down market performance, investment objectives, portfolio composition, shareholder services and telephone numbers and addresses. There are also an additional 25 funds that were new in 1986 and lack a full year of data. For these funds, we have only provided detailed descriptions.

All return and risk calculations were made by AAII staff with data that we feel is reliable. We verified our figures on net asset values, income distributions and capital gains distributions with the funds whenever discrepancies were found.

Our standard is full disclosure; we have strived to provide you with pertinent information while avoiding subjective evaluations. We hope we have given you the basis for an informed financial decision.

In this edition, William H. Anderson, Jr. supervised all the data collection activities and produced the return, risk and ranking statistics. Maria Crawford Scott and her staff provided editorial assistance. Marie Anderson assisted in the data collection.

Chicago
June 1987

John Markese, Ph.D.
Vice President
Director of Research

Table of Contents

Introduction vii
  Diversification viii
  Why No-loads? viii
  Sorting Out Charges ix
  Investing in No-Load Funds xi

CHAPTER 1: Mutual Fund Categories 1
  Aggressive Growth Funds 1
  Growth Funds 2
  Growth & Income Funds 3
  Balanced Funds 4
  Bond Funds and Tax-Exempt Bond Funds 4
  Precious Metals Funds 5
  International Funds 6
  Other Funds 7

CHAPTER 2: Understanding Mutual Fund Statements 9
  The Prospectus 9
  Statement of Additional Information 14
  Annual, Semiannual and Quarterly Reports 15
  Marketing Brochures 15
  Account Statements 16

CHAPTER 3: Mutual Fund Recordkeeping and Taxes 17
  Recordkeeping 17
  Taxes 17

CHAPTER 4: A Systematic Approach to Fund Selection 23
  Important Considerations 23
  Life Cycles 24
  Beta: A Closer Look at Risk 25

CHAPTER 5: An Explanation of the Mutual Fund Statistics 29
  Individual Funds 30
  Other Lists 34

CHAPTER 6: Mutual Fund Performance Rankings 35
  Top 20 and Bottom 20 Funds in 1986 36
  Top 50 Funds Over 5 Years 37
  Aggressive Growth Funds 38

Growth Funds 40
Growth & Income Funds 42
Balanced Funds 43
Bond Funds 44
Tax-Exempt Bond Funds 46
International Funds 48
Precious Metals Funds 48
Closed Funds 49

CHAPTER 7: Mutual Fund Data Summaries 51
(alphabetical listing by fund name)

CHAPTER 8: Tax-Exempt Bond Funds 309
(alphabetical listing by fund name)

New Funds 341
(alphabetical listing by fund name)

Funds Not Listed in Data Pages 351
(alphabetical listing by fund name)

Mutual Fund Families 355
(alphabetical listing by fund family)

Index of Mutual Funds 365

Introduction

A mutual fund is an open-ended investment company that pools investors' money to invest in securities. It is open-ended because it continuously issues new shares when investors want to invest in the fund, and it redeems shares when investors want to sell. A mutual fund trades directly with its shareholders, and the share price of the fund represents the underlying value of the securities that the fund holds.

There are several unique advantages that mutual funds offer individual investors. They provide:

- Professional investment management at a very low cost,
- A diversified group of securities that only a large portfolio can provide,
- Information through prospectuses and annual reports that facilitates fund comparisons,
- Special services, such as checkwriting, dividend reinvestment plans, telephone switching, periodic withdrawal and investment plans, etc.,
- Recordkeeping statements that make it easy to track the value of one's own holdings and that ease the paperwork at tax time.

Many individuals feel that they can invest their own money more cheaply and with better results by doing it themselves. Whether this is true for you is a question only you can answer. Many individual investors do not measure their own performance accurately or do not make a valid comparison of their results versus a mutual fund. Mutual fund performance figures, in contrast, are easily available from sources such as this guide.

If you can do better than the average mutual fund—consistently, over a relatively long time period—then individual stock selection makes financial sense. The next question is, can you do it as cheaply? Successful investing takes time. Investors must spend a considerable amount of time searching for opportunities and monitoring each investment.

Yet, professional investment management comes cheaply with mutual funds. The typical adviser charges about 0.5% annually for managing a fund's assets. For an individual making a $10,000 investment, that comes to only $50 a year. If you value your time, you can see that your money might be well spent by paying someone else to do the work.

Of course, mutual fund investing does not preclude investing in securities on your own. One useful strategy would be to invest in mutual funds and individual securities. The mutual funds would insure your participation in overall market moves and lend diversification to your portfolio while the individual securities would provide you with the opportunity to beat the market.

Diversification

If there is one ingredient to successful investing that is universally agreed upon, it is the benefits of diversification. The concept is so commonsensical that it is a piece of folk wisdom: "Don't put all your eggs in one basket." It is also a concept that is backed up by a great deal of research.

The benefit that diversification provides is risk reduction. Risk to investors is frequently defined as volatility of return—in other words, by how much each year an investment's returns vary. Investors prefer returns that are relatively predictable, and thus less volatile. On the other hand, they want returns that are high. Diversification eliminates some of the risk, without reducing potential returns.

Mutual funds, because of their size, provide investors with a significant amount of diversification that might be difficult for an individual to duplicate. This is true not only for common stock funds, but also for bond funds, municipal bond funds, gold funds, international funds—in fact, for almost all mutual funds. Even the sector funds offer diversification within an industry. The degree of diversification will vary among funds, but most will provide investors with some amount of diversification.

Why No-Loads?

This book is dedicated to no-load mutual funds. Investors have learned that:

- A load is a sales commission that goes to whoever sells fund shares to an investor;

- The load does not go to anyone responsible for managing the fund's assets, and does not serve as an incentive for the fund manager to perform better;
- Funds with loads, on average, consistently underperform no-load funds when the load is taken into consideration in performance calculations.
- For every high-performing load fund, there exists a similar no-load fund that can be purchased instead;
- Loads understate the real commission charged because they reduce the total amount being invested: $10,000 invested in an 8.5% front-end load fund results in an $850 sales charge and only a $9,150 investment in the fund. The load actually represents 9.3% of the net funds invested;
- If a load fund is held over a long time period, the effect of the load is not diminished as quickly as many people believe because the load is paid upfront; if that money had been working for you, as in a no-load fund, it would have been compounding over the whole time period.

The bottom line in any investment is how it performs for you, the investor. There may be some load funds that will do better, even factoring in the load, but you have no way of finding that fund in advance. The only guide you have is historical performance, which is not necessarily an indication of future performance. With a load fund, you are starting your investment with a loss—the load. Start even. Stick with no-loads.

Sorting Out Charges

Although it is best to stick with no-loads, they are becoming more difficult to distinguish from load funds. On the one hand, full front-end load funds have declined in popularity, and some are now turning to other kinds of charges.

On the other hand, some no-load funds have found that to compete, they must market themselves much more aggressively. To do so, they have introduced charges of their own.

The result has been the introduction of low loads, redemption fees and 12b-1 plans. Low loads are simply upfront sales charges that are lower than the traditional 8.5% rate, which used to be the standard. Some low loads are as little as 1%.

Redemption fees are effectively back-end loads: You pay when you get out. Some funds have sliding scale redemption fees, so that the longer you remain invested, the lower the charge when you leave.

The most confusing charge involves the 12b-1 plan. The adoption of a 12b-1 plan by a fund permits the adviser to use fund assets to pay for distribution costs, including advertising, distribution of fund literature such as prospectuses and annual reports, and commissions paid to brokers. Some funds use 12b-1 plans as masked load charges: They levy very high rates on the fund, and use the money to pay brokers to sell the fund. Since the charge is annual and based on the value of the investment, this can result in a total cost to a long-term investor that exceeds the old 8.5% upfront sales load, yet it allows the fund still to be classified as a no-load. Other funds use money from 12b-1 plans to pay only distribution costs, and still others have 12b-1 plans but don't use them to levy charges against fund assets. In some instances, the fund advisor may use the 12b-1 plan to pay distribution expenses from his own pocket. A careful reading of the distribution plan section of the prospectus is required to sort out the impact of a 12b-1 plan.

In this guide, we include mutual funds that have 12b-1 plans if there is no front-end or back-end load. For some funds, however, their plans may result in charges equivalent to low loads. How can you analyze this?

One solution is to convert the annual percentage 12b-1 charge into an equivalent front-end load. Figure 1 allows you to do that. For instance, a 0.25% 12b-1 charge is equivalent to a 1% front-end load, if you remain invested in the fund for four years. The comparison depends upon an assumed investment time horizon, since

Figure 1
Front-End Equivalent of 12b-1 Charges

Holding Period (Years)	12b-1 Charge (%)					
	0.10%	0.25%	0.50%	0.75%	1.00%	1.25%
1	0.10	0.25	0.50	0.75	1.00	1.25
2	0.20	0.50	1.00	1.50	2.00	2.50
3	0.30	0.75	1.50	2.25	3.00	3.75
4	0.40	1.00	2.00	3.00	4.00	5.00
5	0.50	1.25	2.50	3.75	5.00	6.25
10	1.00	2.50	5.00	7.50	10.00	12.50
20	2.00	5.00	10.00	15.00	20.00	25.00
30	3.00	7.50	15.00	22.50	30.00	37.50

12b-1 payments are made annually. We have included a variety of time horizons in the table, and investors must make their own assumptions here.

Remember, too, that the bottom line is total expenses. The 12b-1 charge is included in the "ratio of expenses to net assets" figure; a fund with a 12b-1 charge may have a lower expense ratio than a fund without a 12b-1 charge.

The decision as to what constitutes a load is difficult, but we took a very hard-line approach in this guide:

- All funds with front-end loads were excluded, regardless of the size of the load,
- Funds that had redemption fees were excluded if they extended after six months, since that cuts into investor flexibility,
- Funds with 12b-1 plans were not excluded from the guide; it is noted, however, that the fund has a 12b-1 plan and what the maximum annual charge is. Investors should assess these plans individually. Many 12b-1 plans that charge high rates for broker compensation, however, are accompanied by redemption fees, and thus would be excluded from the guide.

Investing in No-Load Funds

Selecting a mutual fund, while less time-consuming than investing in individual securities, does require some homework. No individual should put money into an investment that he does not understand. This does not require a detailed investigation of the fund's investments, but it does require some understanding of the possible risks involved along with the possible returns.

This guide is designed to provide you with that understanding. We have kept the chapters brief and to-the-point, so that individuals new to mutual fund investing will not be overwhelmed with unnecessary details. Those who are familiar with mutual funds may want to skip directly to Chapters 4 and 5, which describe how to use this guide most effectively.

In **Chapter 1,** we provide you with an overview of the kinds of mutual funds that are available. We have divided them into categories based on shared characteristics, primarily investment objective. The category will provide a generalized guide to the kinds of investments the fund will make, and the riskiness of the fund.

In **Chapter 2,** we have described the information that is provided by the mutual fund. Much of this information is 'must reading' for the mutual fund investor, and you need to have an idea of what to look for, where to look for it and what it means.

Chapter 3 gives recordkeeping hints, as well as some things to keep in mind regarding the tax treatment of mutual funds.

Chapter 4 provides a systematic approach to selecting a mutual fund. It is really the heart of this book, and describes an approach that will allow you to pick an individual mutual fund or a group of funds that will fit in with your investment needs. It is an approach that takes into consideration your risk tolerance, and it is what we have structured the statistical section around.

Finally, **Chapter 5** presents an explanation of the performance data and the information on the individual fund data pages, and it provides a key to the statistical section on the data pages, including a guide to the abbreviations used.

Once you are familiar with mutual funds and the systematic approach to analyzing and forming a mutual fund portfolio that we have suggested, you will want to take a look at the summaries of historical performance in **Chapter 6.** While past performance is no indication of the future, it may indicate quality and consistency of fund management. From this section, you should pick out several mutual funds that meet your investment objectives and risk tolerance. You should then examine these funds more closely in the full-page fund data pages in **Chapter 7.** Call or write the funds to get a copy of the prospectus and annual report, and make sure you read the prospectus carefully before investing in any mutual fund. Information on tax-exempt bond funds can be found in the half-page data pages in **Chapter 8.**

No-load mutual funds that started up in 1986 are listed in the New Funds section at the back of this guide. Also at the back is a list of funds that are reported as 'no-loads' by the financial press but that did not meet our criteria and are thus not included in this book. And, we have provided a list at the back of the guide of no-load fund families that have two or more funds. We have listed all of the funds in a family in this section, including load funds.

1

Mutual Fund Categories

Mutual funds come in all shapes and sizes; there are over 300 funds covered in this book alone, each with its own characteristics. Many mutual funds have similar investment objectives, however. These shared investment objectives generally lead to other characteristics that are similar, particularly as measured by long-term returns and risk in terms of volatility of return.

These shared characteristics allow us to divide mutual funds into several broad categories. This chapter defines the mutual fund categories we used for this book. Figure 1-1 indicates the financial characteristics of the different fund categories. In this book, the individual fund data pages appear alphabetically; however, the fund's category is indicated beneath the fund's name.

Aggressive Growth Funds

The investment objective of aggressive growth funds is maximum capital gains. They invest aggressively in common stocks and tend

---

Figure 1-1
Characteristics of Mutual Funds by Investment Objective*

Fund Objective	1986 Return (%)	5-Year Return (%)	Bear Market Return (%)	Bull Market Return (%)	Risk (Beta)
Aggressive Growth	10.7	80.6	(21.5)	103.6	1.12
Growth	11.7	102.9	(13.1)	123.9	0.91
Growth & Income	13.9	116.0	(8.8)	131.4	0.82
Balanced	17.5	146.1	(0.3)	150.2	0.56
Bond	14.4	116.6	17.5	99.8	0.18
Tax Exempt	16.6	122.9	8.3	89.2	–
International	51.1	150.7	(19.6)	196.6	0.58
Precious Metals	39.3	16.9	(29.4)	59.0	−0.02
S&P 500	18.6	146.1	(13.5)	176.5	1.00

*For all funds covered in this guide for time period ending December 31, 1986. Returns include reinvestment of dividends.

---

to stay fully invested over the market cycle. Sometimes, these funds will use leverage (borrowed funds), and some may engage in trading listed stock options.

Aggressive growth funds typically provide low income distributions. This is because they tend to be fully invested in common stocks and do not earn a significant amount of interest income. In addition, the common stocks they invest in are generally growth-oriented stocks that do not pay significant cash dividends.

Many aggressive growth funds concentrate their assets in particular industries or segments of the market, and their degree of diversification may not be as great as other types of funds. These investment strategies result in increased risk. Thus, they tend to perform better than the overall market during bull markets, but fare worse during bear markets.

In general, long-term investors who need not be concerned with monthly or yearly variation in investment return will find investment in this class of funds the most rewarding. Because of the extreme volatility of return, however, risk-averse investors with a short-term investment horizon may find that these funds lie well outside their comfort zones. The riskiness of these funds can be offset by a greater commitment to a relatively risk-free investment, such as a money market fund (this portfolio strategy is further described in Chapter 4 in the section on risk.) It should be remembered that during prolonged market declines, these funds can sustain severe declines in net asset value.

Market timing is not a strategy we recommend, particularly over the short term. Switching in and out of no-load mutual funds has near zero transactions costs, but redemption fees may be significant and it may create significant tax liabilities. The ability to consistently time the market correctly in the short term, after adjusting for risk, costs and taxes, has not been demonstrated. However, aggressive growth funds, with their high volatility and fully invested position, do make ideal vehicles for those who believe they possess the insight or tools to guess the next market move. The investment strategy would be to invest in aggressive growth funds during up markets, and to switch to money market funds during down markets.

Growth Funds

The investment objective of growth funds is to obtain long-term growth of invested capital. They generally do not engage in speculative tactics such as using financial leverage or short selling. On occasion these funds will use stock or index options to reduce risk by hedging their portfolio positions.

Growth funds typically are more stable than aggressive growth funds. Generally, they invest in growth-oriented firms that are older, larger, and pay larger cash dividends. You are likely to find companies such as IBM, Pepsico and McDonald's in the portfolios of growth funds. The degree of concentration of assets is not as severe as with aggressive growth funds. Additionally, these funds tend to move from fully invested to partially invested positions over the market cycle. They build up cash positions during uncertain market environments.

In general, growth fund performance tends to mirror the market during bull and bear markets. The overall result is that over the longer term, the average growth fund can be expected to do about as well as the market. Some growth funds have been able to perform relatively well during recent bear markets because their managers were able to change portfolio composition by a much greater degree or to maintain much higher cash positions than aggressive growth fund managers.

Aggressive investors should consider holding both growth fund shares and aggressive growth fund shares in their overall portfolios. This is an especially appealing strategy for investors who hold aggressive growth mutual funds that invest in small stock growth firms. The portfolios of these funds complement the portfolios of growth funds, leading to greater overall diversification. The combination produces overall returns that will tend to be less volatile than an investment in only aggressive growth funds.

As with the aggressive growth funds, these funds can sustain severe declines in net asset value during prolonged bear markets. Since some portfolio managers of growth funds attempt to time the market over the longer market cycle, using these funds for market timing may be counterproductive.

Growth & Income Funds

Growth & income funds generally invest in the common stocks and convertible securities of seasoned, well-established, cash-dividend-paying companies. The funds attempt to provide shareholders with significant income along with long-term growth. They generally attempt to avoid excessive fluctuations in net asset value. One tends to find a high concentration of public utility common stocks and corporate convertible bonds in the portfolios of growth & income funds. The funds also provide higher income distributions, less variability in return, and greater diversification than growth and aggressive growth funds.

Because of the high current income offered by these kinds of funds, potential investors should keep the tax consequences in mind. Remember that, although capital gains are now taxed at the same rate as income, it is a better tax strategy to defer paying taxes whenever possible. The distributions from these funds are frequent and are fully taxed in the year paid. High tax bracket individuals should consider investing in these kinds of funds by using IRAs, Keoghs and 401(k)s.

Balanced Funds

The balanced fund category has become less distinct in recent years, and significant overlap in fund objectives exists between growth & income funds and balanced funds. In general, the portfolios of balanced funds consist of investments in common stocks and substantial investments in bonds and convertible bonds. The proportion of stocks and bonds that will be held is usually stated in the investment objective. Various names, such as equity-income, income, and total return, have been attached to funds that have all the characteristics of traditional balanced funds.

As with growth & income funds, balanced funds provide a high dividend yield. Similarly, high tax bracket investors that want to invest in these funds should consider using tax-sheltered money.

Bond Funds and Tax-Exempt Bond Funds

Bond mutual funds, not surprisingly, invest in bonds. They are attractive to bond investors because they provide diversification and liquidity that is not as readily available in direct bond investments.

Bond funds hold various kinds of fixed-income securities in their portfolios. Some specialize in municipal bond issues; others invest in only U.S. government bonds or agency issues, such as Ginnie Maes. Still others invest in corporate bonds. 'High yield' bond funds invest in lower-rated corporate and municipal bonds with a higher default risk that must therefore offer higher yields. These bond funds are commonly referred to as 'junk' bond funds.

Bond funds have portfolios with a wide range of average maturities. Many funds use their names to characterize their maturity structure. Generally, short-term means that the portfolio has a weighted average maturity of less than three years. Intermediate implies an average maturity of three to 10 years, and long-term is over 10 years. The longer the maturity, the greater the change in fund value when interest rates change. Longer-term bond funds are riskier than shorter-term funds and tend to offer higher yields.

Since bond funds can (and do) provide investors with diversification, investors should invest in funds that have a large amount of money. Large bond funds hold many more bond issues than do smaller funds, and as a result of sliding scale management fees, they tend to charge a lower percentage fee.

Bond funds that hold principally corporate or U.S. government debt obligations appear among the regular fund data listings in this book. Tax-exempt bond funds, which invest in municipal bonds, follow the regular fund listings in a separate section. Tax-exempt bond funds are similar in structure to other bond funds, but are sometimes very specialized tax shelter vehicles—state-specific tax-exempt funds are an example.

Precious Metals Funds

Precious metals mutual funds specialize in investments in both foreign and domestic companies that mine gold and other precious metals. Some funds also hold gold directly through investments in gold coins or bullion. Gold options are another method used to invest in the industry. Mutual fund investments in precious metals range from the conservative to the highly speculative.

Gold and precious metals mutual funds offer advantages similar to bond funds: They allow investors interested in this area to invest in a more liquid and diversified vehicle than would be available through a direct purchase.

The appeal of gold and precious metals is that they have performed well during extreme inflationary periods. Over the short term, the price of gold moves in response to a variety of political, economic and psychological forces. As world tension and anxiety rise, so does the price of gold. In periods of peace and stability, the price of gold declines. Because gold tends to perform in an inverse relationship to stocks, bonds, and cash, it can be used as a stabilizing component in one's portfolio. Silver and platinum react in a fashion similar to gold. Precious metals funds, like the metal itself, are very volatile, shooting from the bottom to the top and back to the bottom in fund rankings.

International Funds

International funds invest in securities of firms located in different countries. Some funds specialize in regions, such as the Pacific or Europe, and others invest worldwide.

International funds provide investors with added diversification. The most important factor when diversifying a portfolio is selecting assets that do not behave similarly to each other under similar economic scenarios. Within the U.S., investors can diversify by selecting securities of firms in different industries. In the international realm, investors take the diversification process one step further by holding securities of firms in different countries. Theoretically, the more independently these foreign markets move in relation to the U.S. market, the greater will be the diversification potential for the U.S. investor, and ultimately, the lower his risk.

In addition, international funds overcome some of the difficulties investors would face in making foreign investments directly. For instance, individuals would have to thoroughly understand the foreign brokerage process, be familiar with the various foreign marketplaces and their economies, be aware of currency fluctuation trends, and have access to reliable financial information. Obviously this can be a monumental task for the individual investor.

There are some risks to investing internationally. In addition to the risk inherent in investing in any security, there is an additional exchange rate risk. The return to a U.S. investor from a foreign security depends on both the security's return in its own currency plus the rate at which that currency can be exchanged for U.S. dollars. Another uncertainty is political risk, which includes government restriction, taxation, or even total prohibition of the exchange of one currency into another. Of course, the more the mutual fund is diversified among various countries, the less the risk involved.

Other Funds

There are many specialized mutual funds that do not have their own categories. Instead, they will be found in one of the various categories mentioned above. For instance, several funds specialize in specific industries, but one industry-specific fund does not necessarily appear in the same category as another industry-specific fund. Other specialized funds that may appear in various categories include the option-income funds, the 'socially conscious' funds, funds designed solely for tax-sheltered plans, and geographically specific funds.

One other fund category deserves a special mention—the index fund. An example of an index fund is Vanguard's Index Trust, categorized as a growth & income fund. This fund was designed to match the Standard & Poor's 500 Index, and does so by investing in all 500 stocks in the S&P 500; the amounts invested in each stock are proportional to the firm's market value representation in the S&P 500. Statistics on this fund are quite useful for comparison with other funds, since it is a representation of the market.

2

Understanding
Mutual Fund Statements

One of the advantages of mutual fund investing is the wealth of information that must be provided to fund investors and prospective investors. Taken together, the various reports provide investors with vital information concerning financial matters and how the fund is managed, both key elements in the selection process. In fact, mutual fund statements, along with performance statistics, are the only outside sources of information most investors will need in the selection process.

To new mutual fund investors, the information may seem overwhelming. However, regulations covering the industry have standardized the reports: Once you know where to look for information, the location will hold true for almost all funds.

There are basically five types of statements produced by the mutual fund: the prospectus; the Statement of Additional Information; annual, semiannual and quarterly reports; marketing brochures; and account statements. Actually, the second report—the Statement of Additional Information—is part of the prospectus. However, the Securities and Exchange Commission has allowed mutual funds to simplify and streamline the prospectus by dividing it into two parts: Part A, which all prospective investors must receive, and Part B—the Statement of Additional Information—which the fund must send investors if they specifically request it. In practice, when most people (including the funds) refer to the prospectus, they are referring to Part A. For simplicity, that is what we will do here, as well.

The Prospectus

The prospectus is the single most important document produced by the mutual fund, and it is must reading for investors before investing. By law, prospective investors must receive a prospectus before the fund can accept initial share purchases. In addition, current shareholders must receive new prospectuses when they are updated.

The prospectus is generally organized into sections, and although it must cover specific topics, the overall structure may differ somewhat among funds. The cover usually gives a quick synopsis of the fund: investment objective, sales or redemption charges, minimum investment, retirement plans available, address, and telephone number. More detailed descriptions are in the body of the prospectus.

Condensed Financial Information: One of the most important sections of the prospectus contains the condensed financial information, which provides statistics on income and capital changes per share of the fund (an example is shown in Figure 2-1). The per-share figures are given for the life of the fund or 10 years, whichever is less. Also included are important statistical summaries of investment activities throughout each period.

The per-share section summarizes the financial activity over the year to arrive at the end-of-year net asset value for the fund. The financial activity summarized includes increases in net asset value due to dividends and interest payments received and capital gains

---

Figure 2-1
The Condensed Financial Information Statement: An Example

Selected data for a share of common stock outstanding throughout each year is as follows:

	Year Ended March 31,							
	1986	1985	1984	1983	1982	1981	1980	1979*
Investment income	$ 1.22	$ 1.05	$ 1.06	$ .98	$ .90	$ .83	$ .77	$ .41
Expenses**	(.19)	(.18)	(.16)	(.15)	(.16)	(.15)	(.17)	(.09)
Net investment income	1.03	.87	.90	.83	.74	.68	.60	.32
Dividends from net investment income	(1.22)	(.96)	(.86)	(.79)	(.76)	(.62)	(.60)	(.15)
Net realized and unrealized gains (loss) on investments	4.26	(2.83)	1.12	3.99	(.83)	3.56	(.20)	.45
Distributions from realized capital gains	(.98)	(1.32)	(.73)	(.81)	(.99)	(.51)	(.13)	—
Net increase (decrease) in net asset value	3.09	1.42	.43	3.22	(1.84)	3.11	(.33)	.62
Net asset value								
Beginning of fiscal year	16.63	15.21	14.78	11.56	13.40	10.29	10.62	10.00
End of fiscal year	$19.72	$16.63	$15.21	$14.78	$11.56	$13.40	$10.29	$10.62
Selected financial ratios:								
Ratio of operating expenses to average net assets**	1.11%	1.31%	1.09%	1.29%	1.37%	1.26%	1.62%	.99%
Ratio of net investment income to average net assets**	6.06%	6.18%	6.21%	6.94%	6.20%	5.75%	5.64	3.42%
Portfolio turnover rate	65%	82%	67%	113%	100%	92%	88%	65%
Number of shares outstanding at end of year (000 omitted)	20,711	5,032	3,114	2,228	1,475	1,199	942	724

* From commencement of operations on September 7, 1978.

** Net of expense limitation in 1986.

Source: Evergreen Total Return

from investment activity. Decreases in net asset value are due to capital losses from investment activity, investment expenses and payouts to fund shareholders in the form of distributions.

Potential investors may want to note the line items in this section. *Investment income* represents the dividends and interest earned by the fund during its fiscal year. *Expenses* reflect such fund costs as the management fee, legal fees, transfer agent fees and the like. These expenses are given in detail in the statement of operations section of the annual report. *Net investment income* is investment income less expenses. This line is important for investors to note, because it reflects the level and stability of net income over the time period. A high net investment income would most likely be for funds that have income rather than growth as their investment objective. Since net investment income must be distributed to shareholders to maintain the conduit status of the fund and avoid taxation of the fund, a high net investment income has the potential of translating into a high tax liability for the investor.

Net realized and unrealized gain (loss) on investments is the change in the value of investments that have been sold or that continue to be held by the fund.

Distributions to fund shareholders are also detailed. These distributions will include dividends from net investment income from the current and sometimes previous fiscal periods. The new tax law requires that all income earned must be distributed in the year earned. Also included in distributions will be any realized capital gains.

The last line in the per-share section will be the *net asset value* at the end of the year, which reflects the value of one share of the fund. It is calculated by determining the total assets of the fund and dividing by the number of mutual fund shares outstanding. The figure will change for a variety of reasons, including changes in investment income, expenses, gains, losses and distributions. Depending upon the source of change, a decline in net asset value may or may not be due to poor performance. For instance, a decline in net asset value may be due to a significant distribution of realized gains on securities.

The selected financial ratios at the bottom of the per-share financial data are important indicators of fund performance and strategy. The *expense ratio* relates expenses incurred by the fund to average net assets. A high expense ratio detracts from your investment return. In general, common stock funds have higher expense ratios than bond funds, and smaller funds have higher expense ratios than larger funds. The average for all funds is about 1.25%. Funds with expense ratios above 1.5% are high, and those above 2.0% probably should be avoided.

The *ratio of net investment income to average net assets* is very similar to a dividend yield. This, too, should reflect the investment objective of the fund. Common stock funds with income as part of their investment objective would be expected to have a ratio higher than 3% under current market conditions, and aggressive growth funds would have a ratio closer to zero.

The *portfolio turnover rate* is the lower of purchases or sales divided by average net assets. It reflects how frequently securities are bought and sold by the fund. Fixed-income securities with a maturity of less than a year are excluded from turnover, as are all government securities, short- and long-term. For bond funds however, long-term U.S. government bonds now are included in portfolio turnover.

Investors should note the portfolio turnover rate, because the higher the turnover, the greater the brokerage costs incurred by the fund. Brokerage costs are not in the expense ratio but instead are directly reflected in a decrease in net asset value. In addition, funds with high turnover rates generally have higher capital gains distributions, which are taxed in the year paid. Aggressive growth mutual funds are most likely to have high turnover rates. Bond funds tend to have lower portfolio turnover rates, although some bond funds have very high rates. A 100% portfolio turnover rate indicates that securities in the portfolio are on average held for one year; a 200% portfolio turnover indicates that securities on average have been traded every six months. The portfolio turnover rate for the average mutual fund falls between 80% and 100%.

Investment Objective/Policy: The investment objective section of the prospectus elaborates on the brief sentence or two on the cover. In this section, the fund describes the types of investments it will make—whether it is bonds, stocks, convertible securities, options, etc.—along with some general guidelines as to the proportions these securities will represent in the fund's portfolio. In common stock funds, a statement usually indicates whether it will be oriented toward capital gains or income. In this section, the management will also briefly discuss approaches to market timing, risk assumption, and the anticipated level of portfolio turnover. Some prospectuses may indicate any investment restrictions they have placed on the fund, such as purchasing securities on margin, short sales, industry or firm concentration, foreign securities, lending of securities, and allowable proportions in certain categories. This investment restrictions section is usually given in more detail in the Statement of Additional Information.

Fund Management: The fund management section names the investment adviser and gives the advisory fee schedule. Most advisers charge a management fee on a sliding scale that decreases as assets under management increase. Occasionally, fund advisers' fees are subject to their performance relative to the market.

Some prospectuses will describe the fund's officers and directors, with a short biography of affiliations and relevant experience. For most funds, however, this information is provided in more detail in the Statement of Additional Information. The board of directors are elected by fund shareholders; the fund adviser is selected by the board of directors. The adviser is usually a firm operated by or affiliated with officers of the fund. Information on fund officers and directors is not critical to fund selection. Rarely mentioned in either the prospectus or the Statement of Additional Information, however, is the portfolio manager for the fund. The portfolio manager is responsible for the day-to-day purchases of the fund, and is employed by the fund adviser.

Other Important Sections: There are several other sections in a mutual fund prospectus that investors should be aware of. They will appear under various headings, depending upon the prospectus, but they are not difficult to find.

Some prospectuses will contain a description of what they call a distribution plan; within this section will be information on 12b-1 plans, if the fund has one. The distribution plan details the marketing aspects of the fund, and how it relates to fund expenses. For instance, advertising, distribution of fund literature, and any arrangements with brokers would be included in the marketing plan; the 12b-1 plan pays for these distribution expenses. The description of the distribution plan will sometimes be a section of its own, or it may be a paragraph mentioned in one of the other sections of the prospectus. Not all prospectuses contain information on distribution plans. However, if a fund has a 12b-1 plan, it must be described somewhere in the prospectus.

The capital stock, or fund share characteristics section, provides shareholders a summary of their voting rights, participation in dividends and distributions, and the number of authorized and issued shares of the fund. Often, a separate section will discuss the tax treatment that will apply to fund distributions, which may include dividends, interest and capital gains.

The how-to-buy-shares section gives the minimum initial investment and any subsequent minimums; it will also list load charges or fees. In addition, information on mail, wire, and telephone purchases is provided, along with dividend and/or capital gains distribution reinvestment options, and any automatic withdrawal or retirement options.

The how-to-redeem-shares section discusses telephone, written, and wire redemption options, with a special section on signature guarantees and other documents that may be needed. Also detailed are any fees for reinvestment or redemption. Shareholder services are usually outlined here, with emphasis on switching among funds in a family of funds. This will include any fees for switching, and any limits on the number of switches allowed.

Statement of Additional Information

This document elaborates on the prospectus. The investment objectives section is more in-depth, with a list and description of investment restrictions. The management section gives brief biographies of directors and officers, and the number of fund shares owned beneficially by the officers and directors named. The investment adviser section, while reiterating the major points made in the prospectus, gives all the expense items and contract provisions of the agreement between the adviser and the fund. If the fund has a 12b-1 plan, further details will likely be in the Statement of Additional Information.

Many times, the Statement of Additional Information will include much more information on the tax consequences of mutual fund distributions and investment. Conditions under which withholding for federal income tax will take place are also provided. The fund's financial statements are incorporated by reference to the annual report to shareholders, and generally do not appear in the Statement of Additional Information. Finally, the independent auditors give their opinion on the representativeness of the fund's financial statements.

Annual, Semiannual and Quarterly Reports

All funds must send their shareholders an audited annual and semiannual report. Mutual funds are allowed to combine their prospectus and annual report; some do this, but most do not.

The annual report describes the fund activities over the past year, and provides a listing of all investments of the fund at market value as of the end of the fiscal year. Usually, the cost basis of the investment is given for each. Looking in-depth at individual securities held by the fund is probably a waste of time. However, it is helpful to be aware of the overall investment categories. For instance, investors should look at the percentage invested in common stocks, bonds, convertible bonds, and any other holdings. In addition, a look at the types of common stocks held gives the investor some indication of how the portfolio will fare in various market environments.

The annual report will also have a balance sheet, which lists all assets and liabilities of the fund by general category. This holds little interest for investors.

The statement of operations, similar to an income statement, is of interest only in that the fund expenses are broken down. For most funds, the management fee is by far the largest expense; the expense ratio in the prospectus conveys much more useful information. The statement of changes in net assets is very close to the financial information provided in the prospectus, but the information is not on a per-share basis. Per-share information will, however, frequently be detailed in the annual report in a separate section. Footnotes to the financial statements elaborate on the entries, but other than any pending litigation against the fund, they are most often routine.

The quarterly or semiannual reports are current accounts of the investment portfolio, and provide more timely views of the fund's investments than does the annual report.

Marketing Brochures

These will generally provide a brief description of the fund. However, the most important bit of information will be the number to call to receive the fund prospectus and annual report, if you have not received them already.

Account Statements

Mutual funds send out periodic account statements detailing reinvestment of dividend and capital gains distributions, new purchases or redemptions, and any other account activity such as service fees. The statement provides a running account balance by date with share accumulations, account value to date and a total of distributions made to date. These statements are invaluable for tax purposes and should be saved. The fund will also send out in January a Form 1099-Div for any distributions made the previous year, and a Form 1099-B if any mutual fund shares were sold.

3

Mutual Fund Recordkeeping and Taxes

Mutual funds can be advantageous in that they minimize some of the more mundane details involved in investing. Of course, these details are not eliminated entirely, and they primarily relate to recordkeeping and taxes.

Recordkeeping

Mutual fund investing, as with any other investment, demands some amount of recordkeeping. This is made easier by the statements sent out by the individual funds.

Purchases and redemptions are acknowledged by mutual funds through a confirmation statement sent to the investor. These statements should be retained both for tax purposes, and in case any dispute with the fund arises. Most mutual funds send shareholders periodic statements of their account activity, including any investments and distributions received over a certain time period. At year-end, the fund will send a summary of the yearly account activity. In addition, the fund will send separate forms (1099-Div and 1099-B) noting all the activity in the shareholder's account that will be reported to the IRS for tax purposes. These statements should be saved, both for your own information and as backup documentation that may be necessary for income tax filings.

Investors should also make it a habit to save the latest prospectus issued by the fund, so that future purchases, exchanges, and/or redemptions can be made in accordance with the fund's latest business procedures.

Taxes

It is the unfortunate fate of investors that eventually, they all must face the IRS regulations. Mutual fund investors are no different, but mutual funds do have certain tax consequences that are not readily apparent to those unfamiliar with the area.

Investors incur two distinct types of tax liabilities from mutual funds. The first results from distributions a shareholder receives from the mutual fund, and the second results from the sale of mutual fund shares. The tax implications are quite different, and are discussed below.

Distributions From Mutual Funds: The IRS treats mutual funds as conduits between their shareholders and the corporations whose securities the fund holds. This means that the mutual fund itself is not taxed. In addition, the mutual fund itself does not pay dividends; it merely passes on income from dividends, interest and capital gains to shareholders.

Mutual funds earn income over the tax year from cash dividends and interest received from the fund's investments. The fund earns capital gains resulting from price changes of the securities it holds. Capital gains and losses can be realized through the sale of the securities during the tax year, or unrealized if the securities continue to be held by the fund at the end of the tax year. All income earned by the fund, and any capital gains and losses, cause the value of the fund's assets to increase or decrease. This is reflected in the fund's per-share net asset value.

In order to receive conduit status from the IRS, mutual funds must distribute 90% of all net investment income and net realized capital gains. They do so in the form of distributions to shareholders. Mutul funds are allowed to net out any investment expenses before distributions, and are not required to make a distribution if investment expenses are greater than net investment income. However, starting in 1987, investors will be taxed on most of those expenses.

Fund distributions are simply a transferral of assets from the fund to the shareholder. This means that when a distribution is made, the net total assets of the fund drops, and so, too, does the per-share net asset value. In fact, it drops by exactly the amount of the distribution.

Once the distribution is paid to the shareholder, whether the shareholder reinvests the distribution or not, it is a taxable event. The tax depends on the source of the income to the fund. The kinds of distributions that a mutual fund shareholder may receive include ordinary dividends, capital gains, exempt-interest dividends and return of capital (non-taxable) distributions. Mutual funds notify shareholders of the underlying sources of the distribution when it is made.

In addition, mutual funds are required to send their shareholders at the end of each year a form for tax purposes, known as Form 1099-DIV (Statement for Recipients of Dividends and Distributions). This form indicates what a shareholder must report or take into consideration on his federal income tax return concerning all fund distributions for the taxable year; an example of the 1986 version is presented in Figure 3-1. This form contains the following information:

- The amount that you must report as ordinary dividends,
- The capital gains distributions that you must report,
- The non-taxable distributions (return of capital) that usually will reduce your stock basis,
- The foreign tax paid that you may claim as a deduction or credit,
- Any federal income tax withheld, such as the 20% tax on reportable payments under backup withholding.

Capital losses realized by the fund are not passed onto shareholders, but are used by the fund to offset capital gains. The fund is

Figure 3-1
Form 1099-DIV

☐ CORRECTED

PAYER'S name, street address, city, state, and ZIP code Mutual Fund A 100 Park Road Parktown, NJ 23202		1 Gross dividends and other distributions on stock $200.00 2 Dividends qualifying for exclusion $169.40	OMB No 1545-0110 1986 Statement for Recipients of	Dividends and Distributions
PAYER'S Federal identification number 10-0001001	RECIPIENT'S identification number 000-00-0000	3 Dividends not qualifying for exclusion	4 Federal income tax withheld	Copy B For Recipient This is important tax information and is being furnished to the Internal Revenue Service If you are required to file a return, a negligence penalty or other sanction will be imposed on you if this dividend income is taxable and the IRS determines that it has not been reported
RECIPIENT'S name (first, middle, last) James and Mary Jones Street address 3702 Maple Road City, state, and ZIP code Hometown, VA 22000		5 Capital gain distributions $25.00 7 Foreign tax paid Liquidation Distributions	6 Nontaxable distributions (if determinable) $5.60 8 Foreign country or U S possession	
Account number (optional)		9 Cash	10 Noncash (Fair market value)	

Form 1099-DIV | Department of the Treasury · Internal Revenue Service allowed to carry the loss forward to net against future gains for up to eight years.

There is one important tax implication of mutual fund distributions that prospective investors should consider. Since mutual fund cash distributions result in an immediate decline in per-share net asset value equal to the per-share distribution, individuals who purchase mutual fund shares before the ex-distribution date effectively have a portion of their investment capital returned to them upon distribution. Since the distribution is taxable, the investor is left worse off by the amount of the tax he must pay on the distribution. Therefore, under normal circumstances, taxpaying investors should wait and make fund purchases after the ex-distribution date. The income and capital gains distribution months are given when available in the one-page fund summaries.

Mutual Fund Sales: The other type of tax liability mutual fund investors are likely to incur are gains and losses that result from the purchase and sale, exchange or redemption of mutual fund shares themselves. The amount of the gain or loss is the difference between the adjusted basis in the shares and the amount realized from the sale, exchange or redemption.

Mutual fund investors should keep detailed records of prior purchases in order to determine and substantiate the magnitude of gain or loss once the shares are sold. It is equally important for investors to understand the various identification methods for determining which shares were sold.

For income tax purposes, the cost, or basis, of mutual fund shares that have subsequently been sold can be determined by the 'first in, first out' (FIFO) method, by the identifiable cost method, or by an averaging method.

The FIFO method assumes that the shares sold were the first ones acquired. Using the FIFO method when shares have appreciated over time may result in a substantial capital gain and tax due. The most productive strategy would be to sell those shares with the highest cost and thereby minimize the tax liability or generate a loss that can be used to offset other gains. The identifiable cost method is useful for that purpose.

The identifiable cost method requires that the shares sold be specifically identified as the ones acquired on a specific date at a specific acquisition cost. The IRS states: "If you can definitely identify within the fund the shares of stock you sold, the basis is the cost or other basis of those shares of stock. However, when a number of shares are acquired and sold at various times in different quantities and the shares you sell cannot be identified with certainty, the basis of the shares you sell is the basis of the securities acquired first." When using the identifiable cost method of accounting for share costs, the IRS places the burden of proof on the taxpayer. That is, the taxpayer must be able to trace a sale to a specific block of shares. One method for doing this is to periodically request that the fund send stock certificates that represent the investor's holdings. When a sale is made, the investor should record the certificate number(s) and the date of acquisition, along with the original cost and proceeds received. This method, however, is time-consuming and cumbersome, and requires safeguarding of the certificates.

If the shares are left on deposit with the fund, as most fund investors do, shareholders should keep detailed records of each purchase. When a sale is desired, the shareholder should write to the fund (or telephone and follow up with a letter) and instruct the fund to sell a specific block of shares acquired on a specific date. He should also request that the fund confirm the sale in writing. A copy of the original letter and the confirmation letter should both be saved.

One other method allowed by the tax code provides investors with an averaging method to compute the basis of shares sold, as long as certain requirements are met. The approach is somewhat detailed, and is explained in IRS Publication 564.

Taxpayers who are determining their basis for tax purposes should remember that, when liquidating holdings, some of the shares may have been acquired through automatic reinvestment of distributions. Thus, the cost basis for these shares is the per-share net asset value at the time of reinvestment. The taxpayer will have already partially satisfied the income tax liability on these shares, since taxes were paid on the distribution. Ignoring the cost of shares acquired this way could result in an overpayment of income taxes. For example, suppose an individual invested $2,000 in fund XYZ two years ago. Since the per-share net asset value at that time was $10, he acquired 200 shares. Recently, he liquidated his holdings in this fund and received $3,000. It might appear in this instance that he must pay taxes on $1,000 of long-term capital gains. However, suppose that the fund made two distributions during this period totaling $600, and suppose that those distributions were reinvested. Income tax on the distribution was paid; in essence, the taxpayer used the distribution to purchase new shares totaling $600. The shareholder's basis in the fund is really $2,600, and the investment gain subject to taxation at the time of liquidation is only $400 ($3,000 − $2,600). This illustrates the need to maintain good mutual fund account records.

Taxpayers should be aware that brokers, including mutual funds, underwriters of the fund or agents of the fund, are required to report to the IRS the proceeds from sales, exchanges or redemptions. They will send shareholders a written statement, Form 1099-B, detailing the transactions by January 31 of the year following the calendar year in which the transaction occurred. This is not required, though, for transactions in money market mutual funds.

Since the tax aspects of investing and mutual fund trading are among the greatest causes of investor confusion, it is a good idea for all potential mutual fund investors to familiarize themselves with federal tax reporting requirements before they invest. The fund prospectus gives some information on the taxation of distributions and the reporting of account activity. An excellent source of information is prepared by the IRS itself, Publication 564. In addition to listing the tax rules, the booklet gives numerous examples to illustrate how the rules apply in different situations.

4

A Systematic Approach to Fund Selection

Financial data and summaries of fund services are presented in Chapters 7 and 8 for over 300 no-load mutual funds. Without an efficient approach and a firm idea of your financial goals and needs, searching through these funds for appropriate investments may consume a substantial amount of your time and energy. This chapter provides a guide for establishing a systematic approach, and the information we supply in the data pages will enable you to implement that approach.

Important Considerations

Mutual fund investments should reflect a number of variables that are defined by the individual investor. These are:

- Risk tolerance,
- Anticipated holding period,
- Liquidity needs,
- Income requirements, and
- Tax exposure.

Risk tolerance refers to the potential volatility of an investment—fluctuations in return—that an investor finds acceptable. For well-diversified portfolios, a relative measure of volatility is 'beta,' a concept that we will discuss shortly.

The anticipated holding period is important for the investor to define, because it helps determine the investor's risk tolerance. Time is a form of diversification; longer holding periods provide greater diversification across different market environments. Thus, investors who anticipate longer holding periods can take on more risk.

The liquidity needs of an investor help define the types of funds investors should consider. Liquidity implies preservation of capital, so that withdrawals from a mutual fund can be made at any time with a reasonable certainty that the per-share value will not have dropped sharply. Highly volatile aggressive growth funds are the least liquid.

Income requirements are a concern if the mutual fund investment must generate some consistent level of income for the investor on a periodic basis. Bond funds produce much more reliable income flows than common stock mutual funds.

Tax exposure presents an important decision point for investors. High tax bracket investors should seek mutual funds that are unlikely to make large distributions. The tax initiative ideally should be up to the investor, who can make the decision by timing the sale of mutual fund shares. Conversely, high tax-bracket investors can advantageously relegate high distribution funds to their tax-sheltered accounts such as IRAs or Keoghs.

Life Cycles

These investment parameters can be viewed as a function of the point in your life cycle. Table 4-1 below gives some generalized investment circumstances based on different points of an individual's life.

Many individuals, of course, do not fit neatly into life cycle categories, but they may still have similar circumstances. For instance, individuals in their early career phase may be intermediate-term, medium-risk investors, rather than long-term, high-risk investors. The important considerations are the investment circumstances themselves, because they will affect the kinds of funds chosen. Polar examples of mutual fund choices that reflect the different sets of

Figure 4-1
The Life Cycle: Risk Tolerance, Holding Period and Tax Exposure

	Early Career	Mid Career	Late Career	Retirement
Risk Tolerance	High	High	Medium	Low
Holding Period	Long	Long	Intermediate	Intermediate
Tax Exposure	Low	High	High	Low

circumstances are:

- The high-risk, long-term, high-tax-exposure individual, who would tend to hold common stock mutual funds with low dividend yields, and who would tend to use shorter-term municipal bond funds to meet liquidity needs; versus
- The low-risk, shorter-term, low-tax-exposure individual, who would tend to hold common stock mutual funds (in the growth & income, and balanced fund categories) that have some growth potential but that also pay a significant dividend, and who would tend to use shorter-term, high-yield bond or money market funds to meet liquidity needs.

Of course, these circumstances are continually changing, sometimes significantly, and the mutual fund portfolio must be viewed dynamically.

Beta: A Closer Look at Risk

Of the circumstances we discussed above, risk is the most difficult concept for many investors to define, and yet much of the selection question depends on this definition. For instance, the amount of money invested in money market or bond funds is a function of your anticipated liquidity needs, and your tax bracket dictates whether mutual fund investments should generate high or low levels of ordinary income. Which funds to choose, then, and how much to invest in each, becomes a function primarily of your risk tolerance.

The measure for risk that we use in this guide is beta. It is an important concept to understand, because beta can be used as a measure of risk for a single fund and for your entire portfolio. Thus if you define your risk in terms of beta, you can select funds with betas that, taken in combination, reflect your own risk tolerance.

Beta is a measure of the relative volatility inherent in a mutual fund investment. This volatility is measured relative to the market, which is usually defined as the Standard & Poor's 500. The market's beta is always 1.0, and a money market fund's beta is always 0. If you hold a mutual fund with a beta of 1.0, it will move on average in tandem with the market: If the market is up 10%, the fund will be up on average 10%, and if the market drops 10%, the fund will drop on average 10%. A mutual fund with a beta of 1.5 is 50% more volatile: If the market is up 10%, the fund will be up on average 50% more or 15%, and conversely, if the market is down 10%, the fund on average will be down 15%. A negative beta implies that the mutual fund moves inversely in some magnitude to the market. A few of the precious metals and bond funds have negative betas that are near zero.

The higher the fund's beta, the greater the volatility of the investment in the fund and the less appropriate the fund would be for shorter holding periods. It should be remembered that beta is a relative measure: A low beta only implies that the fund's movement is not highly related to the market. Its return, however may be quite variable. For instance, sector fund moves may not be related to the market, but changes in the industry may cause their returns to fluctuate widely. For a well-diversified stock fund, beta is a very useful measure of risk, but for concentrated funds, beta only captures a portion of the variability that the fund may experience. Beta is also less useful for measuring the risk inherent in bond funds or mutual funds with large bond holdings, since bonds may move relatively independent of the stock market.

Although the betas of individual mutual funds provide an indication of the riskiness of the fund, they also can be used to determine the appropriate proportion of your overall portfolio that should be invested in the various funds. This can be done by measuring the beta of your overall mutual fund portfolio.

The beta of a mutual fund portfolio is the weighted sum of the betas of the individual mutual fund investments, based on their percentage representation (at market value) in the portfolio. For example, if a portfolio is divided among three mutual funds, with equal investments (based on the current market value of the funds) in each, the portfolio beta would be:

$(0.33 \times \text{beta Fund A}) + (0.33 \times \text{beta Fund B}) + (0.33 \times \text{beta Fund C})$

The examples below illustrate the approach. However, they only represent four of the almost infinite combinations of mutual funds and proportions invested in each. The betas used in the examples are averages for the class of mutual fund suggested (See Figure 1-1 in Chapter 1); if you were determining your own portfolio's beta, you would use the individual mutual fund betas.

The higher-risk, longer-term holding period, higher-tax-exposure individual with minimum liquidity needs: One portfolio combination might be 90% in aggressive common stock mutual funds (high capital gains potential, low dividend yield; average beta of 1.12), and 10% in tax-exempt money market funds (beta of zero). The portfolio beta is:

$$(0.90 \times 1.12) + (0.10 \times 0) = 1.00$$

The lower-risk, shorter-term holding period, lower-tax-exposure individual with higher liquidity needs: One portfolio might have 40% in growth common stock mutual funds (average beta of 0.91), 40% in growth & income common stock mutual funds (with an average beta of 0.82), and 20% in taxable money market funds (beta of zero). The portfolio beta is:

$$(0.40 \times 0.91) + (0.40 \times 0.82) + (0.20 \times 0) = 0.69$$

Alternatively, this same risk level can be achieved with a different mix: 80% in growth & income common stock mutual funds, and 20% in a bond fund (average beta of 0.18). The portfolio beta remains the same:

$$(0.80 \times 0.82) + (0.20 \times 0.18) = 0.69$$

The lower-risk, higher-tax-exposure individual: One possible portfolio would use the same funds as the first example, but would increase the investment in money market funds so that the risk is the same as the second example. Under this scenario, 62% is in aggressive growth common stocks, and 38% is in tax-exempt money market funds. The portfolio beta is:

$$(0.62 \times 1.12) + (0.38 \times 0) = 0.69$$

Defining your risk tolerance level is a crucial step in the fund selection process. Even if you do not go through the calculations described above, you should have some idea of how the riskiness of the fund you choose will affect your overall portfolio. The individual fund beta figures, provided in the data section, will help you do this. Once you have determined your own risk tolerance, you will have a better idea of which category to choose from in selecting a mutual fund. After defining your investment parameters (taxes, liquidity, holding period, income, risk) you are ready to look at the individual mutual funds themselves.

5

An Explanation of the
Mutual Fund Statistics

When choosing among mutual funds, most investors start with performance statistics: How well have the various mutual funds performed in the past? If past performance could only perfectly predict future performance, the selection would be easy. But, of course, it can't.

What past performance can tell you is how well the fund's management has handled different market environments, how consistent the fund has been, and how well the fund has done relative to its risk level, relative to other similar funds and relative to the market. We present performance statistics in Chapter 6 in several different forms. First, we provide an overall picture, with the average performance of each mutual fund category for the last five years, along with stock market, bond market and Treasury bill benchmarks. The top 20 and bottom 20 no-load mutual fund performers for 1986 are given for a recent reference. The list changes each year and reflects the cyclical nature of financial markets and the changing success of fund managers. A list of the top 50 mutual funds ranked by five-year total return is given for a long-term perspective on investment performance.

Since the performance of a fund must be judged relative to similar funds, we have also grouped the funds by category and ranked the funds according to their total return performance for 1986; funds that are closed but would otherwise meet criteria for inclusion in the guide have their performance reported in a separate category. To make the comparison easier, we have also provided other data in this chapter. The fund's five-year total return figure gives a longer-term perspective on the performance of the fund. Consistency of performance is indicated by the actual returns during bull and bear markets and the accompanying letter designates the relative bull and bear market performance ranking for the period compared to all other funds: An 'A' indicates the fund was in the top 20% of all funds during the market cycle; an 'E' indicates the fund was in the bottom 20% during the market cycle. We also include the fund's beta as a measure of risk. Betas were not determined for tax-exempt funds.

Individual Funds

After reviewing the performance rankings, you can find more in-depth information on the individual funds in the one-page financial summaries for each no-load fund in Chapter 7, and in the half-page summaries for tax-exempt funds in Chapter 8. The funds here are presented alphabetically, not by category. Their categories, however, are indicated at the top of the page, under the fund's name. These pages provide six years of per-share data, performance and risk statistics, summaries of investment objectives, portfolio composition, services, and the telephone number and address of the fund.

Some of this information is taken directly from fund reports (the prospectus, annual and quarterly reports) and other statistics, such as fund performance and risk, were calculated by us.

The following provides definitions and explanations of the terms we have used in the summaries of the individual funds. The explanations are listed in the order in which the data appear on the fund summary pages.

Years Ending: This indicates over what time period the per-share data applies, and varies with the fiscal year of the fund. Funds with fiscal years ending in June, in particular, have year-old data. Most funds have more recent data, since the fiscal year ends near or at the end of the calendar year. The fiscal year-end is when the fund's per-share data is made available to the shareholders. The performance statistics are always calculated on a calendar-year basis no matter what fiscal year the fund uses.

Net Investment Income: Dividend and interest income earned by the fund, stated in per-share amounts.

Dividends from Net Investment Income: Per-share income distributions reported in the fiscal year.

Net Gains (Losses) on Investments: Per-share realized and un-realized capital gains. The difference between the beginning value or cost incurred during the year and current market, or realized value.

Distributions from Net Realized Capital Gains: Per-share distributions from realized capital gains after netting out realized losses. These distributions vary each year with both the investment success of the fund and the amount of securities sold.

Net Asset Value End of Year: Net asset value is the sum of all securities held, based on their market value, divided by the number of mutual fund shares outstanding at the end of the fiscal year.

Ratio of Expenses to Net Assets: The sum of administrative fees plus adviser management fees and usually 12b-1 fees divided by the average net asset value of the fund, stated as a percentage. Brokerage costs incurred by the fund are not included in the expense ratio but are instead reflected directly in net asset value.

Portfolio Turnover Rate: A measure of the trading activity of the fund, which is computed by dividing the lesser of purchases or sales for the fiscal year by the monthly average value of the securities owned by the fund during the year. Securities with maturities of less than one year are excluded from the calculation. The result is expressed as a percentage, with 100% implying a complete portfolio turnover within one year.

Total Assets: Aggregate year-end fund value expressed in millions of dollars.

Annual Rate of Return on Investment: This is a total return, expressed as a percentage increase (decrease), and was computed using monthly net asset values per share and shareholder distributions during the year. Distributions were assumed to be reinvested at the end of the month in which they were paid. Return on investment is calculated on the basis of the calendar year, regardless of the fund's fiscal year.

Five-Year Total Return: Assuming investment on January 1, 1982, the total percentage increase (decrease) in investment value if held through December 31, 1986. All distributions are assumed to have been reinvested at the end of the month in which they were paid.

Degree of Diversification: Diversification is a relative concept. We have measured fund diversification relative to the S&P 500, under the assumption that the market represents a well-diversified portfolio. The diversification rankings were assigned after statistically determining how closely the returns of the fund matched the overall market during the three-year period 1984 through 1986. The more closely the returns matched the market during that period, the higher the diversification ranking. Common stock funds that did not track the market well, and therefore had lower diversification rankings, many times had industry or special concentrations, such as sector, gold, and international funds. Some funds, however, had lower diversification rankings due to high cash positions, even though they were not sector or specialty funds. Diversification should be thought of as market tracking ability rather than number or type of investments held by the fund. We ranked all of the funds based on market tracking ability and divided them into five equal groups. An 'A' represents the group that most closely tracked the market; 'E' represents the group that tracked the market the least. The others fall evenly into the remaining groups. The lower the degree of diversification ranking, the greater the chance that the fund's return will not follow the market. This figure was not calculated for bond and tax-exempt bond funds, due to their investments solely in fixed-income securities.

Beta: A risk measure that relates the volatility in returns of the fund to the market. The higher the beta of a fund, the higher the risk of the fund. The figure is based on monthly returns for the 36 months from the beginning of 1984 through the end of 1986. A beta of 1.0 indicates that the fund's returns will on average be as volatile as the market and move in the same direction; a beta higher than 1.0 indicates that if the market rises or falls, the fund will rise or fall respectively but to a greater degree; a beta of less than 1.0 indicates that if the market rises or falls, the fund will rise or fall to a lesser degree. The S&P 500 index always has a beta of 1.0; money market funds will always have a beta of 0. Occasionally, a fund will have a negative beta. This means that on average the fund's return moves inversely to the market. Negative beta funds usually have beta values near zero and are concentrated in the precious metals and bond fund categories. Beta was not calculated for tax-exempt bond funds.

Bull: The rating reflects the fund's performance in the most recent bull (up) market, starting in August, 1982 and continuing through December 1986. The funds were ranked relative to all other funds according to their total return for the period. They were then divided into five equal groups. Group A reflects the top 20%, Group

B the next 20%, and Group E reflects the bottom 20%. Funds ranked A and B performed better than average during the bull market, funds ranked C performed average, and funds ranked D and E performed worse than average during the bull market.

Bear: The rating reflects the fund's performance in the most recent bear (down) market, starting in June 1981, and ending in July 1982. The funds were ranked relative to all other funds during the period according to their total return for the period. They were then divided into five equal groups. Group A reflects the top 20%, Group B the next 20%, and Group E reflects the bottom 20%. Funds ranked A and B performed better than average during the bear market, funds ranked C performed average, and funds ranked D and E performed worse than average during the bear market.

NA: Indicates that the statistic is not available. For the five-year total return figure, the statistic would not be available for funds that have been operating for less than five years. For the beta and degree of diversification figures, funds operating for less than 36 months would not have the statistics available. Tax-exempt bond funds do not have beta statistics; bond funds and tax-exempt bond funds do not have diversification statistics. For the bull and bear ratings, funds not operating during those entire market periods would not have these statistics available.

Information on portfolio composition was obtained directly from the fund's annual and quarterly reports, and we have indicated the date on which the information is based. Please note that some funds employ leverage, borrowing to buy securities, and this may result in the portfolio composition exceeding 100%.

The months in which income and capital gains distributions to shareholders are made is indicated when available. If a fund has a 12b-1 plan, the maximum amount that can be charged is given; remember, though, that while no fund can be charged more than the maximum, some funds are charged less than the maximum, and some are not charged at all. If the fund's advisor pays the charge, it is so noted. The minimum initial and subsequent investments in the fund are also detailed. Often, funds will have lower minimums for IRAs; this is also indicated.

Investor services provided by the fund are detailed. These include the availability for IRA, Keogh, corporate pension and profit-sharing plans, simplified employee pension plans and non-profit group retirement plans (indicated by **IRA, Keogh, Corp., SEP,** and **403(b),** respectively); whether the fund allows the automatic and systematic withdrawal of monies from the fund (indicated by **Withdraw**) and if the fund allows for automatic investments through an investor's checking account (**Deduct**). Since all funds have automatic reinvestment of dividend options, this service was not specifically noted.

Telephone exchanges with other funds in the family are also listed. If exchange privileges are allowed, we have indicated whether the family includes either a money market fund or a tax-exempt money market fund.

Finally, we list the states in which the fund is registered.

Other Lists

We have also included a list of new funds at the end of the mutual fund summaries. These funds were less than one year old as of December 31, 1986, and therefore financial data or analysis was either not useful or not possible.

Mutual funds that are shown to be no-load in the financial press but that do not appear in this book are listed after the new fund section. Examples would be funds closed to new investors, funds for institutional or corporate customers only, funds limited to employees or members of a particular organization, and 'no-load' funds with redemption fees that continue after six months.

Our last list is of fund families that contain primarily no-load funds. All of the funds within a family, including load funds, are listed.

6

Mutual Fund Performance Rankings

On the following pages, we have ranked all of the no-load mutual funds listed in this guide by their investment performance. The funds were ranked according to several different criteria. These are:

	Page
Top 20 and Bottom 20 Performers in 1986	36
Top 50 Funds Ranked by 5-Year Total Return (1982 through 1986)	37
Aggressive Growth Fund Rankings	38
Growth Fund Rankings	40
Growth & Income Fund Rankings	42
Balanced Fund Rankings	43
Bond Fund Rankings	44
Tax-Exempt Bond Fund Rankings	46
International Fund Rankings	48
Precious Metals Fund Rankings	48
Closed Funds	49

The performance statistics also include information on bull and bear market performance, and risk as measured by beta. Chapter 5 presents a detailed explanation of the performance statistics.

A summary of mutual fund total return performance by category is presented below, along with stock, bond and money market indexes for comparison.

Mutual Fund Categories: A Total Return Performance Summary

Category	1986	1985	1984	1983	1982	1981
Aggressive Growth	10.7%	26.9%	(11.5)%	19.0%	22.7%	(5.4)%
Growth	11.7	25.9	(2.3)	19.7	21.6	(2.7)
Growth & Income	13.9	25.8	4.1	21.1	20.6	(0.8)
Balanced	17.5	25.3	9.1	20.9	24.6	4.7
Bond	14.4	20.5	11.5	9.6	27.8	5.6
Tax Exempt	16.6	17.5	8.5	9.5	33.5	(7.1)
International	51.1	33.4	(5.0)	30.4	0.1	(1.5)
Precious Metals	39.3	(7.3)	(26.2)	(1.5)	39.0	(22.8)
S&P 500	18.6	31.6	6.1	22.4	21.4	(5.0)
Salomon Bond Index.	19.9	30.1	16.9	6.3	42.5	(1.2)
T-Bills	6.2	7.7	9.9	8.8	10.5	14.7

The Top 20 Performers: 1986

Type	Fund	Return (%)
Intl	Nomura Pacific Basin Fund	74.4
Intl	FSP Pacific Basin	71.8
Intl	G.T. Pacific Growth	70.0
Intl	T. Rowe Price International	60.5
Intl	G.T. Japan Growth	60.5
Intl	Vanguard World—International Growth	56.6
Bd	Benham Target Maturities Trust Series 2010	54.7
Intl	G.T. International	53.8
M	USAA Gold	53.3
Intl	Transatlantic	51.7
Intl	Scudder International	50.5
Intl	Vanguard/Trustees' Commingled Int'l.	49.9
Intl	International Equity Trust	49.6
Intl	G.T. Europe Growth	40.9
Bal	USAA Cornerstone	40.1
M	FSP Gold	38.7
M	US New Prospector	38.5
M	US Gold Shares	37.5
M	Golconda Investors	35.0
M	Lexington Goldfund	32.7

The Bottom 20 Performers: 1986

Type	Fund	Return (%)
G	Bowser Growth	(23.7)
G	Steadman American Industry	(19.7)
A	44 Wall Street	(16.3)
A	Steadman Oceanographic	(11.3)
A	Vanguard Explorer II	(7.3)
A	US LoCap	(6.6)
G	Afuture	(5.9)
A	SteinRoe Discovery	(5.3)
A	Sherman, Dean	(4.7)
A	American Investors Growth	(1.7)
A	Leverage Fund of Boston	(0.7)
A	Fiduciary Capital Growth	(0.4)
A	T. Rowe Price New Horizons	(0.2)
A	Naess & Thomas Special	0.0
Bal	Legg Mason Total Return	1.4
G	Safeco Growth	1.8
G	North Star Apollo	2.0
GI	Steadman Associated	2.8
A	Bull & Bear Capital Growth	3.6
GI	Dreyfus Third Century	4.6

Key to Fund Types

A	— Aggressive Growth	GI	— Growth & Income
Bal	— Balanced	Intl	— International
Bd	— Bond	M	— Precious Metals
G	— Growth	TE	— Tax-Exempt

Top 50 Funds: Five-Year Total Return
(1982 through 1986)

Type	Fund	Return (%)
A	Fairmont	206.1
Intl	T. Rowe Price International	199.9
A	Quest for Value	196.8
Bal	Evergreen Total Return	195.8
Intl	Scudder International	191.1
GI	Ivy Growth	181.9
Bal	Lehman Opportunity	181.3
G	Manhattan	180.5
Bal	Fidelity Puritan	177.4
Bal	Loomis-Sayles Mutual	176.7
A	20th Century Select	176.2
Bal	Safeco Income	172.9
GI	American Leaders (Liberty)	172.2
GI	Selected American Shares	170.3
A	SteinRoe Special	169.8
TE	SteinRoe Managed Municipals	168.9
G	Nicholas	167.2
G	North Star Regional	166.0
Bal	Financial Industrial Income	166.0
GI	Dodge & Cox Stock	165.7
Bd	Fidelity High Income	163.2
Bal	Mutual Shares	162.8
G	Lehman Capital	162.4
Bd	Northeast Investors Trust	162.0
Bal	Mutual Qualified Income	161.8
Bal	Vanguard/Wellington	157.4
Bal	Vanguard/Wellesley	157.0
A	Tudor	155.2
Bd	Stratton Monthly Dividend Shares	154.3
TE	Safeco Municipal	151.3
G	Scudder Capital Growth	150.2
TE	Fidelity High-Yield Municipals	150.2
G	Boston Co. Capital Appreciation	148.9
GI	Partners	148.3
GI	Fidelity Fund	144.6
Bal	Axe-Houghton Fund B	143.8
Bal	Dodge & Cox Balanced	143.6
TE	Federated Tax-Free Income (Liberty)	143.5
G	Copley Tax-Managed	143.3
GI	Guardian Mutual	143.1
G	Century Shares Trust	142.3
GI	Founders Mutual	142.2
TE	Vanguard High-Yield Municipal Bond	139.7
TE	Fidelity Municipal	138.9
Bd	Axe-Houghton Income	138.5
GI	Vanguard Index Trust	138.5
TE	Financial Tax-Free Income Shares	138.1
TE	Vanguard Long-Term Municipal Bond	137.5
A	Evergreen	137.3
TE	Dreyfus Tax-Exempt	137.1

Aggressive Growth Funds
Ranked By 1986 Total Return

Fund	Total Return (%) 1986	5-Year	Market Cycle Performance (%) Bear	Bull	Beta
Bruce	29.6	NA	NA	NA	0.90
FSP Health Sciences	29.5	NA	NA	NA	NA
Hartwell Growth	23.7	81.4	(30.1)[E]	139.4[B]	1.26
FSP Technology	22.0	NA	NA	NA	NA
20th Century Select	20.7	176.2	(13.0)[C]	189.8[A]	1.19
Lexington Growth	20.6	57.6	(30.1)[E]	101.2[D]	1.00
Janus Venture	20.2	NA	NA	NA	NA
Pacific Horizon Agg. Growth	20.1	NA	NA	NA	NA
100 Fund	20.0	59.3	(23.2)[E]	83.1[E]	0.98
20th Century Growth	19.4	95.3	(28.3)[E]	149.2[B]	1.21
Hartwell Leverage	19.3	47.3	(31.9)[E]	83.7[E]	1.59
Gintel Capital Apprec.	19.1	NA	NA	NA	NA
Founders Special	18.9	93.4	(21.5)[E]	110.4[C]	1.08
FSP Leisure	18.8	NA	NA	NA	NA
SteinRoe Stock	17.3	103.7	(16.3)[D]	112.1[C]	1.13
SteinRoe Cap. Opp.	16.8	69.2	(23.4)[E]	105.8[D]	1.22
Columbia Special	15.8	NA	NA	NA	NA
Dreyfus Capital Value	15.6	NA	NA	NA	NA
Medical Technology	15.3	92.2	(14.8)[D]	99.3[D]	1.38
GIT Equity Special Growth	15.1	NA	NA	NA	1.05
SteinRoe Special	14.8	169.8	(23.2)[E]	202.5[A]	1.08
Reich & Tang Equity	14.7	NA	NA	NA	NA
Quest for Value	14.3	196.8	10.7[A]	186.3[A]	0.66
Fairmont	14.0	206.1	NA	214.1[A]	0.91
Fidelity Freedom	13.7	NA	NA	NA	1.10
Gradison Opp. Growth	13.0	NA	NA	NA	1.00
Evergreen	12.9	137.3	(14.5)[D]	169.9[A]	0.87
Dreyfus New Leaders	12.6	NA	NA	NA	NA
Tudor	12.3	155.2	(2.2)[B]	157.1[B]	1.15
Omega	12.2	67.9	(33.7)[E]	120.1[C]	1.07
US Growth	11.5	NA	NA	NA	1.09
Axe-Houghton Stock	10.9	91.7	(23.7)[E]	132.8[C]	1.24
New Beginning Growth	10.4	NA	NA	NA	1.03
Babson Enterprise	9.0	NA	NA	NA	1.03
Neuwirth	8.7	104.8	(20.5)[D]	131.1[C]	1.24
Nova	7.7	85.7	(13.2)[C]	105.1[D]	1.00
Scudder Development	7.6	58.0	(13.9)[C]	78.8[E]	1.13
Legg Mason Special	7.5	NA	NA	NA	NA
FSP Energy	7.2	NA	NA	NA	NA
Financial Dynamics	6.4	83.4	(1.6)[B]	77.6[E]	1.23
USAA Sunbelt Era	5.5	64.0	NA	94.1[D]	1.24
Value Line Special Sit.	5.1	39.4	(14.3)[D]	52.0[E]	1.37
Bull & Bear Capital Growth	3.6	64.6	(25.4)[E]	97.2[D]	1.12
Naess & Thomas Special	0.0	58.2	(16.1)[D]	63.4[E]	1.22
T. Rowe Price New Horizons	(0.2)	60.1	(26.1)[E]	90.3[D]	1.08

Continued on opposite page

Aggressive Growth Funds
Ranked By 1986 Total Return

Fund	Total Return (%) 1986	5-Year	Market Cycle Performance (%) Bear	Bull	Beta
Continued from opposite page					
Fiduciary Capital Growth	(0.4)	131.8	NA	122.2[C]	1.00
Leverage Fund of Boston	(0.7)	NA	NA	NA	1.39
American Investors Growth	(1.7)	(24.4)	(43.6)[E]	21.9[E]	1.23
Sherman, Dean	(4.7)	(32.3)	(39.1)[E]	(6.4)[E]	0.59
SteinRoe Discovery	(5.3)	NA	NA	NA	1.44
US LoCap	(6.6)	NA	NA	NA	NA
Vanguard Explorer II	(7.3)	NA	NA	NA	NA
Steadman Oceanographic	(11.3)	(26.5)	(22.9)[E]	(16.4)[E]	1.26
44 Wall Street	(16.3)	(67.3)	(46.0)[E]	(55.8)[E]	2.13
Average	**10.7**	**80.6**	**(21.4)**	**103.6**	**1.12**

Growth Funds
Ranked By 1986 Total Return

Fund	Total Return (%) 1986	Total Return (%) 5-Year	Market Cycle Performance (%) Bear	Market Cycle Performance (%) Bull	Beta
Northeast Investors Growth	24.3	123.0	(12.7)^C	150.9^B	0.94
Value Line Leveraged	23.3	98.5	8.7^A	91.2^D	1.22
North Star Regional	22.8	166.0	(6.8)^C	173.2^A	0.90
Boston Co. Capital Apprec.	22.5	148.9	(21.0)^E	192.1^A	0.90
Gradison Established Growth ..	22.0	NA	NA	NA	0.95
T. Rowe Price Growth Stock ...	21.7	113.1	(22.8)^E	144.9^B	0.89
Lexington Research	20.2	109.5	(15.1)^D	145.4^B	0.93
Founders Growth	19.3	97.4	(6.0)^B	117.9^C	1.07
Babson Growth	19.0	105.4	(18.4)^D	142.2^B	0.99
Copley Tax-Managed	17.7	143.3	4.9^B	146.5^B	0.51
Manhattan	17.0	180.5	(11.0)^C	199.5^A	1.08
Value Line Fund	16.7	69.8	(0.5)^B	64.8^E	1.27
Acorn	16.7	135.6	(19.4)^D	159.1^B	0.80
Salem Growth	16.6	NA	NA	NA	NA
Scudder Capital Growth	16.5	150.2	(6.9)^C	140.1^B	1.01
T. Rowe Price New Era	16.2	90.2	(30.5)^E	143.1^B	0.88
AARP Capital Growth	15.9	NA	NA	NA	NA
Rainbow	15.8	57.3	(25.2)^E	91.8^D	0.76
Fidelity Value	15.1	128.8	(8.3)^C	141.1^B	0.95
Dreyfus Growth Opp.	15.0	79.7	(33.1)^E	123.4^C	0.81
101 Fund	15.0	127.6	(15.8)^D	166.9^A	0.62
Lehman Investors	14.6	133.9	(7.0)^C	143.5^B	1.01
T. Rowe Price New Am.	14.3	NA	NA	NA	NA
Lehman Capital	13.9	162.4	(1.8)^B	164.2^A	1.12
Vanguard Star	13.8	NA	NA	NA	NA
Permanent Portfolio	13.6	NA	NA	NA	0.30
Fidelity Trend	13.5	112.0	(18.1)^D	142.7^B	1.14
Unified Growth	13.5	119.3	(17.5)^D	138.0^B	0.97
SteinRoe Universe	13.2	87.1	(15.1)^D	97.2^D	1.08
Mathers	12.9	91.4	(27.1)^E	125.6^C	0.99
North Star Stock	12.9	130.7	(6.5)^B	139.1^B	0.91
Fidelity Contrafund	12.8	88.7	(19.7)^D	117.3^C	1.06
Calvert-Equity Portfolio	12.1	NA	NA	NA	1.02
Cumberland Growth	11.8	87.0	NA	92.5^D	0.59
Nicholas	11.7	167.2	(6.8)^C	176.9^A	0.70
Janus Value	11.5	NA	NA	NA	NA
US Good and Bad Times	11.3	94.0	(6.9)^C	94.3^D	0.90
Armstrong Associates	11.3	52.7	(15.0)^D	71.7^E	0.86
WPG	11.2	121.0	(7.3)^C	126.5^C	0.99
Rightime	11.0	NA	NA	NA	NA
Stratton Growth	10.7	125.0	(10.6)^C	140.8^B	1.08
Steadman Investment	10.3	20.1	(14.3)^D	28.1^E	0.85
Nicholas II	10.3	NA	NA	NA	0.67
Flex Fund Retirement	10.2	NA	NA	NA	0.63
USAA Growth	10.1	71.0	(17.9)^D	95.6^D	1.07

Continued on opposite page

Growth Funds
Ranked By 1986 Total Return

Fund	Total Return (%) 1986	Total Return (%) 5-Year	Market Cycle Performance (%) Bear	Market Cycle Performance (%) Bull	Beta
Continued from opposite page					
National Industries Fund	9.8	38.2	(17.6)ᴰ	57.7ᴱ	0.92
Farm Bureau Growth	9.5	66.2	(9.2)ᶜ	84.7ᴱ	1.06
Legg Mason Value Trust	9.4	NA	NA	215.4ᴬ	0.90
Century Shares Trust	9.4	142.3	(13.2)ᶜ	193.8ᴬ	1.01
Growth Industry Shares	9.2	87.1	(11.5)ᶜ	109.7ᶜ	1.07
Newton Growth	9.1	116.4	(12.8)ᶜ	128.8ᶜ	0.87
Financial Industrial	8.4	115.7	(0.7)ᴮ	106.9ᶜ	0.98
deVegh Mutual	8.2	65.3	(14.5)ᴰ	77.0ᴱ	1.03
SBSF Fund	8.1	NA	NA	NA	0.63
Vanguard/W.L. Morgan	7.8	116.0	(15.6)ᴰ	135.9ᶜ	1.03
Boston Co. Special	7.7	NA	NA	147.4ᴮ	1.10
Vanguard World—U.S.	7.6	NA	NA	NA	NA
Selected Special Shares	7.2	89.6	(24.6)ᴱ	129.8ᶜ	0.84
Columbia Growth	6.8	135.5	(11.7)ᶜ	148.0ᴮ	1.18
Beacon Hill Mutual	6.0	93.0	(6.1)ᴮ	107.5ᶜ	0.91
North Star Apollo	2.0	NA	NA	NA	NA
Safeco Growth	1.8	77.5	(22.6)ᴱ	111.8ᶜ	0.98
Afuture	(5.9)	32.5	(2.1)ᴮ	25.0ᴱ	1.05
Steadman American Industry ..	(19.7)	(25.7)	(20.4)ᴰ	(13.0)ᴱ	0.99
Bowser Growth	(23.7)	NA	NA	NA	NA
Average	**11.7**	**102.9**	**(13.0)**	**123.8**	**0.91**

Growth & Income Funds
Ranked By 1986 Total Return

Fund	Total Return (%) 1986	Total Return (%) 5-Year	Market Cycle Performance (%) Bear	Market Cycle Performance (%) Bull	Beta
T. Rowe Price Equity Inc.	26.6	NA	NA	NA	NA
Gintel ERISA	21.8	NA	NA	144.6[B]	0.74
Vanguard Windsor II	21.4	NA	NA	NA	NA
Babson Value	20.7	NA	NA	NA	NA
AARP Growth & Income	19.2	NA	NA	NA	NA
Dodge & Cox Stock	18.8	165.7	(11.8)[C]	189.5[A]	1.04
Vanguard Index Trust	18.3	138.5	(13.5)[C]	163.8[A]	1.00
Scudder Growth & Income	17.8	111.9	(11.9)[C]	127.2[C]	0.95
Partners	17.3	148.3	4.9[B]	141.9[B]	0.79
Selected American Shares	17.0	170.3	(1.6)[B]	175.1[A]	0.68
Founders Mutual	16.8	142.2	(17.0)[D]	165.6[A]	1.04
Ivy Growth	16.8	181.9	(2.4)[B]	192.1[A]	0.67
Viking Equity Index	16.7	NA	NA	NA	NA
Nodding Calamos Conv.	16.1	NA	NA	NA	NA
Vanguard/Trustees' U.S.	15.6	117.9	(10.2)[C]	135.9[C]	1.01
Fidelity Fund	15.4	144.6	(6.0)[B]	149.5[B]	0.95
American Leaders	14.5	172.2	(2.2)[B]	174.4[A]	0.59
Pine Street	14.3	125.1	(12.3)[C]	146.5[B]	0.92
LMH	14.1	NA	NA	NA	0.63
Wayne Hummer Growth	13.8	NA	NA	NA	0.98
Bartlett Basic Value	13.7	NA	NA	NA	NA
Penn Square Mutual	12.9	124.4	(14.6)[D]	146.2[B]	0.95
Safeco Equity	12.6	107.2	(21.7)[E]	138.8[B]	0.96
Gateway Option Income	12.6	70.8	(4.1)[B]	80.1[E]	0.44
UMB Stock	12.3	NA	NA	NA	0.84
Guardian Mutual	11.9	143.1	(9.4)[C]	158.8[B]	0.86
Unified Mutual Shares	11.6	126.6	(15.7)[D]	147.3[B]	0.81
Janus	11.2	127.9	0.4[B]	131.8[C]	0.73
AMA Growth	11.0	88.3	(20.9)[D]	109.1[C]	0.96
Analytic Optioned Equity	10.2	80.4	(5.3)[B]	95.6[D]	0.58
Energy	10.1	74.5	(20.5)[D]	111.3[C]	0.72
General Securities	9.0	108.9	(13.4)[C]	132.5[C]	0.97
Dividend/Growth—Dividend ...	8.7	80.1	13.7[A]	67.4[E]	0.85
Istel (Lepercq)	8.2	49.4	(20.7)[D]	80.4[E]	1.00
T. Rowe Price Growth & Inc. ..	7.9	NA	NA	NA	0.87
Valley Forge	5.5	88.6	10.6[A]	86.1[E]	0.14
Dreyfus Third Century	4.6	73.3	(24.8)[E]	106.1[C]	0.83
Steadman Associated	2.8	54.0	0.5[B]	50.1[E]	1.01
Average	**13.9**	**116.0**	**(8.8)**	**131.3**	**0.82**

Balanced Funds
Ranked By 1986 Total Return

Fund	Total Return (%) 1986	Total Return (%) 5-Year	Market Cycle Performance (%) Bear	Market Cycle Performance (%) Bull	Beta
USAA Cornerstone	40.1	NA	NA	NA	NA
Strong Income	29.9	NA	NA	NA	NA
Loomis-Sayles Mutual	24.8	176.7	3.3[B]	163.7[A]	0.84
Dreyfus Convertible	23.7	132.9	(4.7)[B]	144.4[B]	0.45
Axe-Houghton Fund B	23.1	143.8	(2.1)[B]	142.9[B]	0.71
Fidelity Puritan	20.8	177.4	3.0[B]	179.1[A]	0.53
Evergreen Total Return	20.3	195.8	(1.3)[B]	206.4[A]	0.59
Safeco Income	19.9	172.9	(8.4)[C]	195.8[A]	0.74
Dodge & Cox Balanced	19.2	143.6	(1.8)[B]	143.3[B]	0.74
Bull & Bear Equity-Income	18.7	112.9	(7.3)[C]	118.1[C]	0.59
Vanguard/Wellesley	18.4	157.0	8.2[A]	155.0[B]	0.46
Vanguard/Wellington	18.2	157.4	(0.9)[B]	165.6[A]	0.70
Mutual Shares	16.9	162.8	(7.4)[C]	183.4[A]	0.42
Mutual Qualified Income	16.9	161.8	1.0[B]	168.4[A]	0.40
SteinRoe Total Return	16.9	117.9	(12.0)[C]	126.4[C]	0.64
Value Line Income	16.3	104.9	14.5[A]	91.1[D]	0.71
ADTEK	16.0	NA	NA	NA	NA
Financial Industrial Income	14.6	166.0	2.8[B]	157.8[B]	0.79
Founders Income	14.5	87.7	0.5[B]	98.5[D]	0.44
USAA Income	12.6	117.8	17.4[A]	101.8[D]	0.19
Claremont Fund	12.0	NA	NA	NA	NA
Unified Income	9.8	105.4	7.2[B]	101.2[D]	0.51
Lehman Opportunity	6.4	181.3	(18.0)[D]	210.9[A]	0.84
US Income	5.5	NA	NA	NA	0.50
Legg Mason Total Return	1.4	NA	NA	NA	NA
Average	**17.5**	**146.1**	**(0.3)**	**150.2**	**0.56**

Bond Funds
Ranked By 1986 Total Return

Fund	Total Return (%) 1986	5-Year	Market Cycle Performance (%) Bear	Bull	Beta
Benham Target—2010	54.7	NA	NA	NA	NA
Benham Target—2000	32.6	NA	NA	NA	NA
Benham Target—1995	26.9	NA	NA	NA	NA
Stratton Monthly Dividend	20.4	154.3	NA	160.2ᴬ	0.49
Northeast Investors Trust	20.4	162.0	15.9ᴬ	136.0ᶜ	0.20
Financial Bond Select	18.8	110.5	22.0ᴬ	89.3ᴰ	0.25
Liberty	18.2	114.2	6.5ᴮ	107.3ᶜ	0.29
Fidelity High Income	18.0	163.2	16.0ᴬ	141.7ᴮ	0.29
Vanguard High Yield	16.9	125.5	19.2ᴬ	107.2ᶜ	0.22
SteinRoe Managed Bonds	16.3	117.6	20.5ᴬ	94.3ᴰ	0.20
Value Line Convertible	16.1	NA	NA	NA	NA
Benham Target—1990	15.9	NA	NA	NA	NA
Axe-Houghton Income	15.8	138.5	19.0ᴬ	116.7ᶜ	0.32
T. Rowe Price High Yield	15.1	NA	NA	NA	NA
Pacific Horizon High-Yield	15.0	NA	NA	NA	NA
Boston Co. Managed Income	14.9	NA	NA	NA	NA
Fidelity Government	14.7	100.9	20.3ᴬ	82.6ᴱ	0.19
Scudder Income	14.6	125.6	15.9ᴬ	111.1ᶜ	0.25
Financial Bond-High Yield	14.5	NA	NA	NA	NA
Vanguard Investment Grade	14.3	118.3	21.8ᴬ	98.6ᴰ	0.20
T. Rowe Price New Income	14.0	104.2	18.9ᴬ	87.2ᴱ	−0.06
Babson Bond Trust	13.9	118.1	19.0ᴬ	99.6ᴰ	0.14
Dreyfus A Bond Plus	13.9	113.7	20.0ᴬ	96.8ᴰ	0.23
Fidelity Flexible Bond	13.5	113.1	20.3ᴬ	91.4ᴰ	0.20
Cap. Preservation T-Note	13.4	87.9	18.0ᴬ	77.9ᴱ	0.20
Fidelity Thrift	13.1	110.8	21.7ᴬ	90.6ᴰ	0.19
Fidelity Ginnie Mae	13.0	NA	NA	NA	NA
AMA Income	12.7	107.8	16.6ᴬ	93.0ᴰ	0.23
Flex Bond	12.5	NA	NA	NA	NA
Columbia Fixed Income	12.4	NA	NA	NA	0.14
UMB Bond	12.3	NA	NA	NA	0.09
North Star Bond	12.1	121.8	18.5ᴬ	100.9ᴰ	0.19
Scudder Target Gen'l 1990	12.0	NA	NA	NA	0.14
Lexington GNMA	11.7	100.6	20.5ᴬ	82.5ᴱ	0.10
Vanguard GNMA	11.5	121.3	24.8ᴬ	96.8ᴰ	0.13
Fidelity Mortgage	11.5	NA	NA	NA	NA
Benham GNMA Income	11.4	NA	NA	NA	NA
Nicholas Income	11.4	130.5	19.2ᴬ	104.1ᴰ	0.15
AARP GNMA & U.S. Treas.	11.4	NA	NA	NA	NA
Vanguard Short-Term	11.3	NA	NA	NA	0.08
Scudder Gov't. Mortgage	11.3	NA	NA	NA	NA
Mutual of Omaha Amer.	11.1	78.3	22.0ᴬ	63.1ᴱ	0.17
T. Rowe Price GNMA	11.0	NA	NA	NA	NA
Value Line U.S. Govt.	10.7	115.0	NA	97.7ᴰ	0.15
AARP General Bond	10.7	NA	NA	NA	NA

Continued on opposite page

Bond Funds
Ranked By 1986 Total Return

Fund	Total Return (%) 1986	5-Year	Market Cycle Performance (%) Bear	Bull	Beta
Continued from opposite page					
GIT Income Maximum	10.6	NA	NA	NA	0.21
20th Century U.S. Govt.	9.9	NA	NA	NA	0.08
Dreyfus GNMA	9.5	NA	NA	NA	NA
Newton Income	9.0	100.6	11.6[A]	87.0[E]	0.06
T. Rowe Price Short-Term	9.0	NA	NA	NA	NA
Fund for U.S. Govt. (Liberty) ..	8.6	122.2	19.7[A]	95.6[D]	0.07
Delaware Treas. Reserves	7.7	NA	NA	NA	NA
American Investors Income	7.0	71.8	(11.1)[C]	85.7[E]	0.37
Bull & Bear High Yield	6.0	NA	NA	NA	0.21
Average	14.4	116.6	17.5	99.8	0.18

Tax-Exempt Bond Funds
Ranked By 1986 Total Return

Fund	Total Return (%) 1986	5-Year	Market Cycle Performance (%) Bear	Bull
California Tax Free Income Fund	22.7	NA	NA	NA
Financial Tax-Free Income Shares	22.1	138.1	NA	105.5ᴬ
SteinRoe Managed Municipals	21.7	168.9	12.3ᴬ	120.3ᶜ
Federated Tax-Free Inc. (Liberty)	20.4	143.5	7.4ᴮ	105.1ᴰ
T. Rowe Price Tax-Free High Yield	20.4	NA	NA	NA
T. Rowe Price Tax-Free Income	19.8	111.5	8.7ᴬ	95.1ᴰ
Safeco Municipal	19.8	151.3	NA	108.9ᶜ
Vanguard High-Yield Municipal	19.7	139.7	6.4ᴮ	106.3ᶜ
Safeco California Tax Free	19.7	NA	NA	NA
Bull & Bear Tax Free Income	19.6	NA	NA	NA
Fidelity Municipal	19.5	138.9	10.0ᴬ	99.3ᴰ
Vanguard Long-Term Municipal	19.4	137.5	7.3ᴮ	102.3ᴰ
GIT Tax-Free High Yield	19.4	NA	NA	NA
SteinRoe High-Yield Municipals	19.0	NA	NA	NA
Unified Municipal Indiana	19.0	NA	NA	NA
Fidelity High-Yield Municipals	18.9	150.2	11.9ᴬ	112.1ᶜ
Fidelity Michigan Tax-Free	18.7	NA	NA	NA
Benham Nat'l. Tax-Free Long-Term	18.7	NA	NA	NA
Benham Calif. Tax-Free Long-Term	18.7	NA	NA	NA
Vanguard Muni—Insured Long Term	18.7	NA	NA	NA
Pacific Horizon Calif. Tax-Exempt	18.3	NA	NA	NA
Unified Municipal General	18.3	NA	NA	NA
Babson Tax-Free Inc. Portfolio L	18.2	136.0	6.0ᴮ	100.8ᴰ
Fidelity Insured Tax-Free	18.1	NA	NA	NA
Dreyfus Mass. Tax-Exempt	17.9	NA	NA	NA
New York Muni	17.7	NA	NA	NA
Fidelity Calif. Tax-Free High Yield	17.7	NA	NA	NA
Dreyfus California Tax Exempt	17.7	NA	NA	NA
Fidelity Aggressive Tax-Free	17.6	NA	NA	NA
Calvert Tax-Free Long Term	17.4	NA	NA	NA
Dreyfus Tax-Exempt	17.4	137.1	7.9ᴮ	102.0ᴰ
Fidelity New York Tax-Free Insured	17.3	NA	NA	NA
USAA Tax Exempt High-Yield	17.2	NA	NA	87.0ᴱ
Dreyfus Insured Tax-Exempt Bond	17.1	NA	NA	NA
Dreyfus N.Y. Tax Exempt Bond	17.1	NA	NA	NA
Fidelity Minnesota Tax-Free	17.0	NA	NA	NA
Kentucky Tax-Free Income	16.9	92.7	(4.8)ᴮ	85.3ᴱ
Fidelity Massfree-Muni Bond	16.9	NA	NA	NA
AARP Tax Free Bond	16.9	NA	NA	NA
Scudder Managed Municipal	16.8	136.6	11.8ᴬ	96.5ᴰ
Scudder California Tax Free	16.8	NA	NA	NA
Fidelity N.Y. Tax-Free High Yield	16.8	NA	NA	NA
Fidelity Ohio Tax-Free	16.4	NA	NA	NA
Vanguard Intermediate-Term Muni.	16.2	108.5	6.9ᴮ	82.9ᴱ
Dreyfus Intermediate Tax Exempt	15.4	NA	NA	NA

Continued on opposite page

Tax-Exempt Bond Funds
Ranked By 1986 Total Return

	Total Return (%)		Market Cycle Performance (%)	
Fund	1986	5-Year	Bear	Bull
Continued from opposite page				
Fidelity Limited Term Muni.	15.2	105.5	9.9ᴬ	81.1ᴱ
Park Avenue N.Y. Intermediate	14.2	NA	NA	NA
Scudder New York Tax-Free	14.1	NA	NA	NA
Value Line Tax Exempt High Yield	13.4	NA	NA	NA
Scudder Tax-Free Target 93	13.2	NA	NA	NA
USAA Tax Exempt Intermediate	13.2	NA	NA	75.5ᴱ
Benham Calif. Tax-Free Int.-Term	12.7	NA	NA	NA
SteinRoe Intermediate Municipal	12.1	NA	NA	NA
Scudder Tax-Free Target 90	10.5	NA	NA	NA
T. Rowe Price Tax-Free Short-Int.	9.7	NA	NA	NA
USAA Tax Exempt Short-Term	8.7	NA	NA	41.6ᴱ
Calvert Tax-Free Limited Term	8.6	52.1	12.5ᴬ	42.2ᴱ
AARP Tax Free Short Term	8.3	NA	NA	NA
Vanguard Short-Term Municipal	7.4	42.0	11.0ᴬ	34.5ᴱ
Scudder Tax-Free Target 87	6.6	NA	NA	NA
Average	**16.6**	**122.9**	**8.3**	**89.2**

International Funds
Ranked By 1986 Total Return

Fund	Total Return (%) 1986	Total Return (%) 5-Year	Market Cycle Performance (%) Bear	Market Cycle Performance (%) Bull	Beta
Nomura Pacific Basin	74.4	NA	NA	NA	NA
FSP Pacific Basin	71.8	NA	NA	NA	NA
G.T. Pacific Growth	70.0	122.1	(17.2)[D]	166.4[A]	0.32
T. Rowe Price Internat'l.	60.5	199.9	(18.4)[D]	241.5[A]	0.51
G.T. Japan Growth	60.5	NA	NA	NA	NA
Vanguard World—Int'l.	56.6	NA	NA	NA	NA
G.T. International	53.8	NA	NA	NA	NA
Transatlantic	51.7	125.5	(34.1)[E]	191.3[A]	0.53
Scudder International	50.5	191.1	(19.2)[D]	246.0[A]	0.50
Vanguard/Trustees' Int'l.	49.9	NA	NA	NA	0.39
International Equity Trust	49.6	NA	NA	NA	NA
G.T. Europe Growth	40.9	NA	NA	NA	NA
World of Technology	16.5	NA	NA	NA	1.06
Pax World	8.4	114.9	(9.0)[C]	137.7[C]	0.71
Average	**51.1**	**150.7**	**(19.6)**	**196.6**	**0.58**

Precious Metal Funds
Ranked By 1986 Total Return

Fund	Total Return (%) 1986	Total Return (%) 5-Year	Market Cycle Performance (%) Bear	Market Cycle Performance (%) Bull	Beta
USAA Gold	53.3	NA	NA	NA	NA
FSP Gold	38.7	NA	NA	NA	NA
US New Prospector	38.5	NA	NA	NA	NA
US Gold Shares	37.5	22.7	(30.7)[E]	51.2[E]	−0.03
Golconda Investors	35.0	11.0	(28.1)[E]	34.6[E]	0.04
Lexington Goldfund	32.7	NA	NA	91.3[D]	−0.08
Average	**39.3**	**16.9**	**(29.4)**	**59.0**	**−0.02**

Statistics for Closed Funds

Type	Fund	Total Return (%) 1986	Total Return (%) 5-Year	Market Cycle Performance (%) Bear	Market Cycle Performance (%) Bull	Beta
TE	California Muni	9.5	NA	NA	NA	NA
G	Lindner	13.8	142.8	15.6[A]	135.2[C]	0.33
GI	Lindner Dividend	20.8	205.0	19.3[A]	186.0[A]	0.29
A	Loomis-Sayles Cap. Dev. .	27.5	254.0	(0.8)[B]	222.2[A]	1.26
G	Pennsylvania Mutual	10.9	170.1	(16.9)[D]	192.7[A]	0.64
A	Quasar Associates	11.4	152.3	(25.5)[E]	190.5[A]	1.28
G	Sequoia	12.6	183.6	14.7[A]	167.0[A]	0.51
A	Vanguard Explorer	(8.5)	53.1	(14.8)[D]	63.8[E]	0.89
Bal	Vanguard Qual. Div. I	21.6	255.7	13.0[A]	246.5[A]	0.57
GI	Vanguard Windsor	20.2	191.3	(4.2)[B]	216.1[A]	0.77

Mutual Fund Data Summaries

On the following pages, we present indepth information on 316 no-load mutual funds. The funds are listed alphabetically; their category is indicated at the top of the page under the fund's name. Below are brief definitions and explanations of some of the terms used on the data pages. For more complete descriptions, see Chapter 5.

Years Ending: The fiscal year-end for the per-share data information, which varies among funds. All performance information, however, is calculated on a calendar-year basis.

Annual & Five-year Total Return: Assumes reinvestment of distributions monthly.

Degree of Diversification: Measured relative to the S&P 500. Funds were ranked according to how closely their returns tracked the S&P 500. An "A" indicates the fund was in the group that most closely tracked the market; an "E" indicates the fund was in the group that tracked the market the least.

Beta: A measure of risk relative to the market. The market's beta is always 1.0; a beta higher than 1.0 indicates fund returns are more volatile than the market and a beta lower than 1.0 indicates fund returns are less volatile than the market.

Bull: Fund performance ranking (A through E) over the most recent bull market, from August 1982 through December 1986.

Bear: Fund performance ranking (A through E) over the most recent bear market, from June 1981 through July 1982.

Distributions: Months in which distributions are paid were provided when available.

12b-1: Indicates whether the fund has a 12b-1 plan. If the fund has a 12b-1 plan, either the maximum charge is indicated or it is stated that the advisor pays any distribution charges.

Investor Services: IRA, Keogh, Corp, 403(b) and **SEP** indicate the availability of IRA, Keogh, corporate pension and profit-sharing plans, simplified employee pension plans and non-profit group retirement plans. **Withdraw** indicates if the fund allows for the automatic and systematic withdrawal of monies, and **Deduct** indicates if the fund allows for automatic investments through an investor's checking account. All funds offer automatic reinvestment of distributions.

AARP CAPITAL GROWTH
Growth

Scudder Fund Distributors
175 Federal Street
Boston, MA 02110-2267
(800) 253-2277

	Years Ending 9/30					
	1981	1982	1983	1984	1985 (10 mos.)	1986
Net Investment Income ($)	–	–	–	–	.12	.18
Dividends from Net Investment Income ($)	–	–	–	–	–	.09
Net Gains (Losses) on Investments ($)	–	–	–	–	1.83	4.28
Distributions from Net Realized Capital Gains ($)	–	–	–	–	–	.19
Net Asset Value End of Year ($)	–	–	–	–	16.95	21.13
Ratio of Expenses to Net Assets (%)	–	–	–	–	1.50	1.44
Portfolio Turnover Rate (%)	–	–	–	–	42	46
Total Assets: End of Year (Millions $)	–	–	–	–	20.6	55.7

Annual Rate of Return (%) Years Ending 12/31	–	–	–	–	–	15.9

Five-Year Total Return	NA	Degree of Diversification	NA	Beta	NA	Bull NA	Bear NA

Objective: Seeks long-term capital appreciation through investment in common stocks and convertible securities. Looks for undervalued stocks with above average long-term earnings growth potential. Can invest in debt securities and put and call options.

Portfolio: (9/30/86) Common stocks 85%, short-term securities 15%, preferred stocks 1%. Largest stock holdings: media and service 29%, utilities 11%.

Distributions: **Income:** Annually   **Capital Gains:** Annually

12b-1: No

Minimum: **Initial:** $250   **Subsequent:** None

Min IRA: **Initial:** $250   **Subsequent:** None

Services: IRA, Keogh, Withdraw

Tel Exchange: Yes   **With MMF:** Yes

Registered: All states

AARP GENERAL BOND
Bond

Scudder Fund Distributors
175 Federal Street
Boston, MA 02110-2267
(800) 253-2277

	Years Ending 9/30					
	1981	**1982**	**1983**	**1984**	**1985** (10 mos.)	**1986**
Net Investment Income ($)	–	–	–	–	1.06	1.41
Dividends from Net Investment Income ($)	–	–	–	–	1.06	1.41
Net Gains (Losses) on Investments ($)	–	–	–	–	.31	.61
Distributions from Net Realized Capital Gains ($)	–	–	–	–	–	.05
Net Asset Value End of Year ($)	–	–	–	–	15.31	15.87
Ratio of Expenses to Net Assets (%)	–	–	–	–	1.50	1.30
Portfolio Turnover Rate (%)	–	–	–	–	54	63
Total Assets: End of Year (Millions $)	–	–	–	–	45.3	88.4

Annual Rate of Return (%) Years Ending 12/31	–	–	–	–	–	10.7

Five-Year Total Return	NA	Degree of Diversification	NA	Beta NA	Bull NA	Bear NA

Objective: Seeks high level of current income consistent with preservation of capital. Invests in short-, intermediate- and long-term government securities and in high quality corporate bonds. Normally has 65% of assets invested in government and corporate bonds.

Portfolio: (9/30/86) Long-term bonds 69%, intermediate-term bonds 27%, short-term securities 2%, repurchase agreements 2%.

Distributions: **Income:** Monthly **Capital Gains:** Annually

12b-1: No

Minimum: **Initial:** $250 **Subsequent:** None

Min IRA: **Initial:** $250 **Subsequent:** None

Services: IRA, Keogh, Withdraw

Tel Exchange: Yes **With MMF:** Yes

Registered: All states

AARP GNMA & U.S. TREASURY

Bond

Scudder Fund Distributors
175 Federal Street
Boston, MA 02110-2267
(800) 253-2277

	Years Ending 9/30					
	1981	1982	1983	1984	1985 (10 mos.)	1986
Net Investment Income ($)	–	–	–	–	1.17	1.54
Dividends from Net Investment Income ($)	–	–	–	–	1.17	1.54
Net Gains (Losses) on Investments ($)	–	–	–	–	.52	.50
Distributions from Net Realized Capital Gains ($)	–	–	–	–	–	.03
Net Asset Value End of Year ($)	–	–	–	–	15.52	15.99
Ratio of Expenses to Net Assets (%)	–	–	–	–	1.03	.90
Portfolio Turnover Rate (%)	–	–	–	–	67	62
Total Assets: End of Year (Millions $)	–	–	–	–	322.1	1,963
Annual Rate of Return (%) Years Ending 12/31	–	–	–	–	–	11.4

Five-Year Total Return	NA	Degree of Diversification	NA	Beta	NA	Bull NA	Bear NA

Objective:	Seeks high level of current income consistent with preservation of capital. Invests primarily in GNMA securities and other debt instruments backed by the U.S. Government.
Portfolio:	(9/30/86) GNMAs 78%, U.S. Treasury obligations 19%, repurchase agreements 2%.
Distributions:	Income: Monthly **Capital Gains:** Annually
12b-1:	No
Minimum:	Initial: $250 **Subsequent:** None
Min IRA:	Initial: $250 **Subsequent:** None
Services:	IRA, Keogh, Withdraw
Tel Exchange:	Yes **With MMF:** Yes
Registered:	All states

AARP GROWTH & INCOME

Growth & Income

Scudder Fund Distributors
175 Federal Street
Boston, MA 02110-2267
(800) 253-2277

				Years Ending 9/30		
	1981	1982	1983	1984	1985 (10 mos.)	1986
Net Investment Income ($)	–	–	–	–	.39	.73
Dividends from Net Investment Income ($)	–	–	–	–	.19	.70
Net Gains (Losses) on Investments ($)	–	–	–	–	1.64	4.10
Distributions from Net Realized Capital Gains ($)	–	–	–	–	–	.09
Net Asset Value End of Year ($)	–	–	–	–	16.84	20.88
Ratio of Expenses to Net Assets (%)	–	–	–	–	1.50	1.21
Portfolio Turnover Rate (%)	–	–	–	–	13	37
Total Assets: End of Year (Millions $)	–	–	–	–	26.7	99.3

Annual Rate of Return (%) Years Ending 12/31	–	–	–	–	–	19.2

Five-Year Total Return	NA	Degree of Diversification	NA	Beta NA	Bull NA	Bear NA

Objective: Seeks long-term growth of capital, current income and growth of income. Invests primarily in common stocks and convertible securities. Looks for companies with good earnings growth potential which pay dividends.

Portfolio: (9/30/86) Common stocks 72%, convertible securities 18%, short-term securities 12%. Largest stock holdings: utilities 17%, financial 11%.

Distributions: Income: Quarterly   **Capital Gains:** Annually

12b-1: No

Minimum: Initial: $250   **Subsequent:** None

Min IRA: Initial: $250   **Subsequent:** None

Services: IRA, Keogh, Withdraw

Tel Exchange: Yes   **With MMF:** Yes

Registered: All states

ACORN
Growth

Harris Associates, Inc.
120 S. LaSalle St.
Chicago, IL 60603-3596
(312) 621-0630

	Years Ending 12/31					
	1981	1982	1983	1984	1985	1986
Net Investment Income ($)	.99	1.14	.60	.67	.58	.67
Dividends from Net Investment Income ($)	.88	1.03	1.04	.55	.51	.50
Net Gains (Losses) on Investments ($)	(2.98)	2.87	5.95	.58	8.72	5.35
Distributions from Net Realized Capital Gains ($)	2.44	.04	1.04	1.63	1.86	6.07
Net Asset Value End of Year ($)	24.41	27.35	31.82	30.89	37.82	37.27
Ratio of Expenses to Net Assets (%)	.95	.92	.85	.85	.78	.79
Portfolio Turnover Rate (%)	16	32	22	33	32	34
Total Assets: End of Year (Millions $)	105.9	132.4	173.8	210.2	317.5	414.6
Annual Rate of Return (%) Years Ending 12/31	(7.3)	17.5	25.1	4.5	31.4	16.7

Five-Year Total Return 135.6%	Degree of Diversification C	Beta .80	Bull B	Bear D

Objective: Seeks capital growth through investment in common stocks and convertibles of smaller companies which are not yet widely recognized as growth companies. May invest in foreign securities.

Portfolio: (12/31/86) Common stocks 87%, money markets 9%, fixed income 3%, cash and other 2%. Largest stock holdings: information group 26%, foreign securities 15%.

Distributions: Income: Jan, July   **Capital Gains:** Feb

12b-1: No

Minimum: Initial: $1,000   Subsequent: $200

Min IRA: Initial: $200   Subsequent: $50

Services: IRA, Keogh, SEP, Withdraw, Deduct

Tel Exchange: Yes   **With MMF:** Yes

Registered: All states except MS, NH

ADTEK
Balanced

Heath, Schneider, Mueller & Toll Co.
4920 W. Vliet St.
Milwaukee, WI 53208
(414) 257-1842

	Years Ending 5/31					
	1981	1982	1983	1984	1985	1986
Net Investment Income ($)	—	—	—	—	.30	.37
Dividends from Net Investment Income ($)	—	—	—	—	—	.29
Net Gains (Losses) on Investments ($)	—	—	—	—	.80	1.70
Distributions from Net Realized Capital Gains ($)	—	—	—	—	—	.18
Net Asset Value End of Year ($)	—	—	—	—	11.10	12.70
Ratio of Expenses to Net Assets (%)	—	—	—	—	1.95	1.87
Portfolio Turnover Rate (%)	—	—	—	—	179	232
Total Assets: End of Year (Millions $)	—	—	—	—	23.9	29.6

Annual Rate of Return (%) Years Ending 12/31	—	—	—	—	13.5	16.0

Five-Year Total Return	NA	Degree of Diversification	NA	Beta	NA	Bull	NA	Bear	NA

Objective: Seeks long-term capital appreciation and protection of capital through a balance of common stocks of established companies, corporate bonds and money market instruments. The particular balance is determined by economic and market conditions indicated by various technical and fundamental analysis techniques. May enter into repos.

Portfolio: (11/30/86) Common stocks 77%, cash equivalents 28%. Largest stock holdings: consumer non-durables 28%, capital goods 17%.

Distributions: **Income:** Annually   **Capital Gains:** Annually

12b-1: No

Minimum: **Initial:** $1,000   **Subsequent:** $50

Min IRA: **Initial:** $250   **Subsequent:** None

Services: IRA, Keogh, Corp, 403(b), Withdraw, Deduct

Tel Exchange: No

Registered: WI

AFUTURE
Growth

Carlisle-Asher Management
Legal Arts Building
Front & Lemon Sts.
Media, PA 19063
(800) 523-7594/(215) 565-3131

	Years Ending 12/31					
	1981	1982	1983	1984	1985	1986
Net Investment Income ($)	.50	.86	.09	.07	.10	(.02)
Dividends from Net Investment Income ($)	.41	.50	.82	.09	.08	.11
Net Gains (Losses) on Investments ($)	(.84)	2.58	1.77	(2.78)	2.28	(.76)
Distributions from Net Realized Capital Gains ($)	3.09	1.23	.96	2.01	—	—
Net Asset Value End of Year ($)	14.10	15.81	15.89	11.08	13.38	12.49
Ratio of Expenses to Net Assets (%)	1.60	1.60	1.60	1.60	1.60	1.40
Portfolio Turnover Rate (%)	98	160	152	121	193	200
Total Assets: End of Year (Millions $)	27.6	33.1	34.6	24.9	24.6	16.2
Annual Rate of Return (%) Years Ending 12/31	(1.8)	27.7	12.2	(19.2)	21.5	(5.9)

Five-Year Total Return	32.5%	Degree of Diversification	C	Beta 1.05	Bull E	Bear B

Objective: Capital appreciation through long-term holdings of common stock of large, well-established companies. Current dividend income is not a substantial factor in selecting investments. May take defensive posture in debt securities.

Portfolio: (12/31/86) Common stocks 81%, short-term notes 6%, other assets 13%. Largest stock holdings: manufacturing 25%, banks/financial 14%.

Distributions: Income: Jan   **Capital Gains:** Jan

12b-1: No

Minimum: Initial: $500   Subsequent: $30

Min IRA: Initial: $500   Subsequent: $30

Services: IRA, Keogh, Withdraw

Tel Exchange: No

Registered: All states except AK, AR, CT, ID, KS, KY, LA, ME, MS, ND, NH, NM, NV, SC, SD, UT, VA, VT, WY

AMA GROWTH FUND
Growth & Income

AMA Advisers, Inc.
5 Sentry Pkwy. W. Suite 120
P O Box 1111
Blue Bell, PA 19422
(800) 523-0864/(215) 825-0400

	Years Ending 9/30					
	1981	1982	1983	1984	1985	1986
Net Investment Income ($)	.25	.27	.22	.33	.32	.14
Dividends from Net Investment Income ($)	.31	.23	.26	.26	.38	.16
Net Gains (Losses) on Investments ($)	(.92)	.28	2.45	(.62)	.73	2.12
Distributions from Net Realized Capital Gains ($)	—	—	—	—	—	.41
Net Asset Value End of Year ($)	7.38	7.70	10.11	9.56	10.23	11.92
Ratio of Expenses to Net Assets (%)	1.21	1.26	1.26	1.30	1.32	1.34
Portfolio Turnover Rate (%)	71	77	114	129	158	127
Total Assets: End of Year (Millions $)	34.8	35.6	35.1	29.6	26.9	26.8
Annual Rate of Return (%) Years Ending 12/31	(8.8)	21.2	7.5	5.4	23.5	11.0

Five-Year Total Return	88.3%	Degree of Diversification	A	Beta	.96	Bull	C	Bear	D

Objective: Seeks capital appreciation. Fund favors equity investments in companies which have potential for above-average, long-term growth in sales and earnings on a sustained and predictable basis.

Portfolio: (9/30/86) Common stocks 82%, convertible bonds 10%, commercial paper 19%. Largest stock holdings: financial 26%, consumer non-durables 10%.

Distributions: Income: Jan, April, July, Oct   **Capital Gains:** Oct
12b-1: Yes   **Amount:** .50%
Minimum: Initial: $1,000   **Subsequent:** None
Min IRA: Initial: $500   **Subsequent:** $50
Services: IRA, Keogh, SEP, Corp, 403(b), Withdraw, Deduct
Tel Exchange: Yes   **With MMF:** Yes
Registered: All states

AMA INCOME
Bond

AMA Advisers
5 Sentry Pkwy. W.
Suite 120, PO 1111
Blue Bell, PA 19422
(800) 523-0864/(215) 825-0400

	Years Ending 3/31					
	1981	1982	1983	1984	1985	1986
Net Investment Income ($)	.92	.97	.85	.81	.86	.77
Dividends from Net Investment Income ($)	.88	.97	.89	.79	.87	.80
Net Gains (Losses) on Investments ($)	(.03)	(.49)	1.64	(.60)	.02	1.13
Distributions from Net Realized Capital Gains ($)	—	—	—	—	—	—
Net Asset Value End of Year ($)	7.80	7.31	8.91	8.33	8.34	9.44
Ratio of Expenses to Net Assets (%)	1.15	1.16	1.16	1.25	1.50	1.39
Portfolio Turnover Rate (%)	121	122	256	105	62	147
Total Assets: End of Year (Millions $)	20.3	20.1	23.7	21.2	19.7	19.2
Annual Rate of Return (%) Years Ending 12/31	4.3	31.7	9.1	8.4	18.3	12.7

Five-Year Total Return	107.8%	Degree of Diversification	NA	Beta	.23	Bull	D	Bear	A

Objective: Seeks the highest investment income available consistent with preservation of capital. At least 80% of assets are in short-term money market instruments or marketable debt securities of only the three highest investment ratings. May enter into repurchase agreements comprising no more than 10% of fund's assets.

Portfolio: (9/30/86) U.S. Treasury securities 38%, non-convertible bonds 30%, convertible bonds 15%, temporary investments 15%, other assets 2%.

Distributions: Income: Jan, Apr, July, Oct   Capital Gains: Apr
12b-1: Yes   Amount: .50%
Minimum: Initial: $300   Subsequent: None
Min IRA: Initial: $300   Subsequent: $50
Services: IRA, Keogh, Corp, 403(b), SEP, Withdraw, Deduct
Tel Exchange: Yes   With MMF: Yes
Registered: All states

AMERICAN INVESTORS GROWTH
Aggressive Growth

American Investors Corp.
777 W. Putnam Ave.
PO Box 2500
Greenwich, CT 06836
(800) 243-5353/(203) 531-5000

	Years Ending 12/31					
	1981	1982	1983	1984	1985	1986
Net Investment Income ($)	—	.22	.08	.12	.17	.02
Dividends from Net Investment Income ($)	—	—	.23	.14	.19	—
Net Gains (Losses) on Investments ($)	(.80)	(2.30)	.26	(1.95)	.80	(.14)
Distributions from Net Realized Capital Gains ($)	.30	—	.76	—	.44	.60
Net Asset Value End of Year ($)	11.53	9.45	8.80	6.83	7.17	6.45
Ratio of Expenses to Net Assets (%)	.88	1.20	1.14	1.41	1.33	1.40
Portfolio Turnover Rate (%)	50	53	59	127	204	161
Total Assets: End of Year (Millions $)	180.5	138.1	116.7	85.0	80.1	64.2
Annual Rate of Return (%) Years Ending 12/31	(6.3)	(18.0)	3.6	(20.8)	14.3	(1.7)

Five-Year Total Return (24.4)%	Degree of Diversification A	Beta 1.23	Bull E	Bear E

Objective: Growth of investment capital through investment in common stocks. Securities are almost exclusively chosen on the basis of market action determined through statistics, charts of industry, company and market. Uses technical analysis of banking and money. May take defensive posture in debt investments.

Portfolio: (12/31/86) Common stocks 95%, bonds 2%, preferred stock 2%, notes 1%. Largest stock holdings: oil 14%, forest products 14%.

Distributions: Income: Dec   **Capital Gains:** Dec

12b-1: No

Minimum: Initial: $400   Subsequent: $20

Min IRA: Initial: $400   Subsequent: $20

Services: IRA, Keogh, SEP, Corp, Withdraw, Deduct

Tel Exchange: Yes   **With MMF:** Yes

Registered: All states

AMERICAN INVESTORS INCOME
Bond

American Investors Corp.
777 W. Putnam Ave.
PO Box 2500
Greenwich, CT 06836
(800) 243-5353/(203) 531-5000

| | Years Ending 6/30 | | | | | |
	1981	1982	1983	1984	1985	1986
Net Investment Income ($)	1.36	1.27	1.21	1.26	1.12	1.12
Dividends from Net Investment Income ($)	1.36	1.27	1.21	1.25	1.12	1.12
Net Gains (Losses) on Investments ($)	(.22)	(2.78)	3.01	(2.46)	.27	.16
Distributions from Net Realized Capital Gains ($)	.31	—	—	—	—	—
Net Asset Value End of Year ($)	11.03	8.25	11.26	8.81	9.08	9.24
Ratio of Expenses to Net Assets (%)	1.41	1.47	1.56	1.55	1.51	1.41
Portfolio Turnover Rate (%)	93	71	132	77	117	97
Total Assets: End of Year (Millions $)	16.1	12.7	18.2	16.4	20.2	23.4
Annual Rate of Return (%) Years Ending 12/31	(4.6)	12.6	26.9	(8.5)	22.7	7.0

Five-Year Total Return	71.8%	Degree of Diversification	NA	Beta	.37	Bull	E	Bear	C

Objective: High current income. Invests in high yielding, lower rated bonds and preferred stocks, most of which will reflect speculative characteristics being of medium or lower grade (Ba or BB or lower). May buy convertible fixed-income and convertible preferred stocks.

Portfolio: (9/30/86) Bonds 94%, preferred stock 3%, commercial paper 3%.

Distributions: Income: Jan, April, July, Oct   **Capital Gains:** July

12b-1: Yes   **Amount:** .50%

Minimum: Initial: $400   **Subsequent:** $20

Min IRA: Initial: $400   **Subsequent:** $20

Services: IRA, Keogh, Corp, SEP, Withdraw, Deduct

Tel Exchange: Yes   **With MMF:** Yes

Registered: All states

AMERICAN LEADERS* (Liberty)
Growth & Income

Federated Securities Corp.
421 Seventh Ave.
Pittsburgh, PA 15219
(800) 245-4770

	Years Ending 2/28					
	1981	1982	1983	1984	1985	1986
Net Investment Income ($)	.62	.60	.59	.58	.54	.53
Dividends from Net Investment Income ($)	.60	.70	.63	.57	.52	.52
Net Gains (Losses) on Investments ($)	1.08	(.76)	2.52	1.23	1.91	2.88
Distributions from Net Realized Capital Gains ($)	.07	—	.14	.86	1.35	.84
Net Asset Value End of Year ($)	9.12	8.26	10.59	10.97	11.55	13.64
Ratio of Expenses to Net Assets (%)	1.37	1.41	1.45	1.37	1.29	1.09
Portfolio Turnover Rate (%)	19	34	58	42	32	31
Total Assets: End of Year (Millions $)	49.2	40.7	47.9	47.9	71.5	112.5
Annual Rate of Return (%) Years Ending 12/31	2.3	29.0	26.1	14.0	28.1	14.5

Five-Year Total Return 172.2%	Degree of Diversification E	Beta .59	Bull A	Bear B

Objective: Seeks capital growth and income growth through investment in common stocks of high quality companies from the "Leaders List" of 100 blue chip companies chosen on the basis of traditional fundamental research techniques. May enter into repos and buy restricted securities.

Portfolio: (9/30/86) Common stocks 73%, repos 28%. Largest stock holdings: office equipment & supplies 12%, oil & gas 11%.

Distributions: Income: Feb, May, Aug, Nov   **Capital Gains:** May
12b-1: Yes   **Amount:** Pd. by Advisor
Minimum: Initial: $500   Subsequent: $100
Min IRA: Initial: $50   Subsequent: $50
Services: IRA, Keogh, Corp, Withdraw
Tel Exchange: Yes   **With MMF:** Yes
Registered: All states

Instituted a 4% front-end load starting 3/1/87.

ANALYTIC OPTIONED EQUITY

Growth & Income

Analytic Investment Management
2222 Martin St. #230
Irvine, CA 92715
(714) 833-0294

	Years Ending 6/30			Years Ending 12/31		
	1981	1982	1983*	1984	1985	1986
Net Investment Income ($)	.52	.52	.46	.47	.56	.45
Dividends from Net Investment Income ($)	.52	.52	.60	.44	.48	.45
Net Gains (Losses) on Investments ($)	1.38	(1.03)	1.86	.44	1.65	1.06
Distributions from Net Realized Capital Gains ($)	.49	.52	.24	.02	1.20	2.20
Net Asset Value End of Year ($)	12.25	10.70	13.86	14.31	14.84	13.70
Ratio of Expenses to Net Assets (%)	1.50	1.50	1.23	1.30	1.23	1.18
Portfolio Turnover Rate (%)	42	36	49	45	54	64
Total Assets: End of Year (Millions $)	6.5	16.7	54.2	76.7	85.5	76.4

Year-end changed from 6/30 to 12/31; 6 months' data 6/30/82 to 12/31/82 not included.
All per share data is adjusted for a 10 for 1 stock split on 6/30/86.

Annual Rate of Return (%) Years Ending 12/31	7.0	10.3	19.3	6.7	16.5	10.2

Five-Year Total Return 80.4%	Degree of Diversification A	Beta .58	Bull D	Bear B

Objective: Obtain a greater long-term total return and smaller fluctuations in quarterly total return from a diversified, optioned common stock portfolio than would be realized from the same portfolio unoptioned.

Portfolio: (12/31/86) Common stocks 98%, other assets 5%. Largest stock holdings: computer equipment 9%, telephone utilities 9%.

Distributions: Income: Quarterly   **Capital Gains:** Annually

12b-1: No

Minimum: Initial: $5,000   Subsequent: $500

Min IRA: Initial: None   Subsequent: None

Services: IRA, Keogh, Corp, 403(b), SEP, Withdraw

Tel Exchange: No

Registered: All states except AR, MT, ND, NM, OK, RI, SC, VT

ARMSTRONG ASSOCIATES
Growth

Armstrong Associates, Inc.
311 N. Market St., #205
Dallas, TX 75202
(214) 744-5558

	Years Ending 6/30					
	1981	**1982**	**1983**	**1984**	**1985**	**1986**
Net Investment Income ($)	.24	.41	.21	.16	.24	.14
Dividends from Net Investment Income ($)	.23	.19	.43	.20	.14	.24
Net Gains (Losses) on Investments ($)	2.62	(1.28)	3.72	(2.51)	1.02	1.17
Distributions from Net Realized Capital Gains ($)	1.00	1.21	.38	.38	.76	—
Net Asset Value End of Year ($)	9.37	7.10	10.22	7.29	7.65	8.72
Ratio of Expenses to Net Assets (%)	1.50	1.70	1.60	1.60	1.70	1.6
Portfolio Turnover Rate (%)	60	34	59	96	53	54
Total Assets: End of Year (Millions $)	8.3	7.7	12.9	9.8	11.0	11.7
Annual Rate of Return (%) Years Ending 12/31	(0.4)	15.5	11.0	(11.5)	21.0	11.3

Five-Year Total Return	52.7%	Degree of Diversification	B	Beta	.86	Bull	E	Bear	D

Objective: Seeks growth of capital through investment in common stock of large, established companies expected to have growth in earnings over a one- to three-year period. May invest in short-term debt securities as a defensive measure.

Portfolio: (9/30/86) Common stocks 95%, short-term debt and cash 5%. Largest stock holdings: air transportation 15%, petroleum products 12%.

Distributions: Income: Oct   **Capital Gains:** Oct

12b-1: No

Minimum: Initial: $250   **Subsequent:** None

Min IRA: Initial: $250   **Subsequent:** None

Services: IRA, Keogh, Corp, Withdraw, Deduct

Tel Exchange: No

Registered: AK, LA, NM, TX

AXE-HOUGHTON FUND B
Balanced

Axe-Houghton Management, Inc.
400 Benedict Avenue
Tarrytown, NY 10591
(800) 431-1030/(914) 631-8131

	Years Ending 10/31					
	1981	1982	1983	1984	1985	1986
Net Investment Income ($)	.55	.59	.68	.62	.71	.72
Dividends from Net Investment Income ($)	.48	.51	.59	.59	.66	.66
Net Gains (Losses) on Investments ($)	(.55)	1.24	.73	(.09)	1.23	2.90
Distributions from Net Realized Capital Gains ($)	.10	.13	.13	.13	—	.70
Net Asset Value End of Year ($)	7.80	8.99	9.68	9.49	10.77	13.03
Ratio of Expenses to Net Assets (%)	.67	.76	.73	.76	.74	.98
Portfolio Turnover Rate (%)	10	19	64	88	97	239
Total Assets: End of Year (Millions $)	139.9	147.5	147.7	141.2	152.6	190.0

Annual Rate of Return (%) Years Ending 12/31	(1.4)	26.1	11.1	6.3	32.9	23.1

Five-Year Total Return	143.8%	Degree of Diversification	C	Beta	.71	Bull	B	Bear	B

Objective: Seeks conservation of capital, reasonable income, and long-term capital growth. May not invest more than 75% of its assets in common stocks at one time. Also invests in bonds and preferred stocks.

Portfolio: (10/31/86) Common stocks 51%, bonds and other notes 38%, short-term notes 12%. Largest stock holdings: materials and processing 15%, consumer staples 10%.

Distributions: Income: Quarterly   **Capital Gains:** Annually

12b-1: Yes   **Amount:** .45%

Minimum: Initial: $1,000   **Subsequent:** None

Min IRA: Initial: $25   **Subsequent:** $25

Services: IRA, Keogh, Corp, 403(b), Withdraw, Deduct

Tel Exchange: Yes   **With MMF:** Yes

Registered: All states

AXE-HOUGHTON INCOME
Bond

Axe-Houghton Management, Inc.
400 Benedict Avenue
Tarrytown, NY 10591
(800) 431-1030/(914) 631-8131

	Years Ending 11/30					
	1981	1982	1983	1984	1985	1986
Net Investment Income ($)	.50	.52	.47	.49	.51	.50
Dividends from Net Investment Income ($)	.45	.50	.50	.50	.50	.50
Net Gains (Losses) on Investments ($)	(.05)	.47	(.10)	.08	.45	.51
Distributions from Net Realized Capital Gains ($)	—	—	—	—	—	—
Net Asset Value End of Year ($)	4.16	4.65	4.52	4.59	5.05	5.56
Ratio of Expenses to Net Assets (%)	.99	1.02	1.01	1.09	1.04	1.37
Portfolio Turnover Rate (%)	47	55	30	13	90	90
Total Assets: End of Year (Millions $)	32.3	35.2	33.9	35.3	40.2	48.5
Annual Rate of Return (%) Years Ending 12/31	5.8	31	7.5	15.5	26.6	15.8

Five-Year Total Return	138.5%	Degree of Diversification	NA	Beta	.32	Bull	C	Bear	A

Objective: Seeks high current income consistent with prudent investment risk. Invests in bonds and debentures, dividend-paying common stocks, convertible preferred stocks and bonds, government notes and short-term money market instruments.

Portfolio: (11/30/86) Bonds and other notes 96%, short-term notes 4%.

Distributions: **Income:** Quarterly   **Capital Gains:** Annually
12b-1: Yes   **Amount:** .45%
Minimum: Initial: $1,000   Subsequent: None
Min IRA: Initial: $25   Subsequent: $25
Services: IRA, Keogh, Corp, 403(b), Withdraw, Deduct
Tel Exchange: Yes   **With MMF:** Yes
Registered: All states

AXE-HOUGHTON STOCK

Aggressive Growth

Axe-Houghton Management, Inc.
400 Benedict Avenue
Tarrytown, NY 10591
(800) 431-1030/(914) 631-8131

	Years Ending 12/31					
	1981	1982	1983	1984	1985	1986
Net Investment Income ($)	.06	.05	.07	.05	.06	.01
Dividends from Net Investment Income ($)	.06	.05	.02	.05	–	.04
Net Gains (Losses) on Investments ($)	(.49)	2.33	2.66	(2.16)	2.07	.96
Distributions from Net Realized Capital Gains ($)	–	–	.20	5.01	–	1.80
Net Asset Value End of Year ($)	9.18	11.51	14.02	6.85	8.98	8.11
Ratio of Expenses to Net Assets (%)	.86	.88	.84	.95	.95	1.28
Portfolio Turnover Rate (%)	76	89	119	134	191	218
Total Assets: End of Year (Millions $)	123.5	160.5	150.8	87	107.3	96.2

Annual Rate of Return (%) Years Ending 12/31	(4.5)	26.1	23.7	(15.5)	31.1	10.9

Five-Year Total Return 91.7%	Degree of Diversification B	Beta 1.24	Bull C	Bear E

Objective: Primary objective is long-term capital growth. Looks to invest in companies with above-average growth prospects. Also invests in convertible preferred and foreign stocks. For defensive purposes the fund can invest in bonds.

Portfolio: (12/31/86) Common stocks 100%. Largest stock holdings: technology 20%, materials and processing 18%.

Distributions: Income: Annually   **Capital Gains:** Annually

12b-1: Yes   **Amount:** .45%

Minimum: Initial: $1,000   **Subsequent:** None

Min IRA: Initial: $25   **Subsequent:** $25

Services: IRA, Keogh, Corp, 403(b), Withdraw, Deduct

Tel Exchange: Yes   **With MMF:** Yes

Registered: All states

BABSON BOND TRUST

Bond

Jones and Babson, Inc.
3 Crown Ctr.,
2440 Pershing Rd.
Kansas City, MO 64108
(800) 821-5591/(816) 471-5200

	Years Ending 11/30					
	1981	1982	1983	1984	1985	1986
Net Investment Income ($)	.17	.17	.17	.17	.16	.16
Dividends from Net Investment Income ($)	.17	.17	.17	.12	.21	.16
Net Gains (Losses) on Investments ($)	(.04)	.10	Nil	(.01)	.11	.10
Distributions from Net Realized Capital Gains ($)	—	—	—	—	—	—
Net Asset Value End of Year ($)	1.38	1.48	1.48	1.52	1.58	1.68
Ratio of Expenses to Net Assets (%)	.75	.75	.75	.92	.98	.97
Portfolio Turnover Rate (%)	59	91	49	42	39	41
Total Assets: End of Year (Millions $)	28.5	32.8	37.1	42.1	54.7	69.7
Annual Rate of Return (%) Years Ending 12/31	5.9	28.1	9.6	12.9	20.7	13.9

Five-Year Total Return 118.1%	Degree of Diversification NA	Beta .14	Bull D	Bear A

Objective: Seeks current regular income and stability of principal. Long-term capital growth is a secondary aim. Maturity structure is conservative, with all issues rated A or higher. Most agency securities are mortgages.

Portfolio: (11/30/86) Corporate bonds 80%, U.S. government bonds 16%, repos 2%, other 2%.

Distributions: Income: Feb, May, Aug, Nov   **Capital Gains:** Nov

12b-1: No

Minimum: Initial: $500   Subsequent: $50

Min IRA: Initial: $250   Subsequent: None

Services: IRA, Keogh, Corp, SEP, Withdraw

Tel Exchange: Yes   **With MMF:** Yes

Registered: All states

BABSON ENTERPRISE

Aggressive Growth

Jones & Babson
3 Crown Center
2440 Pershing Road
Kansas City, MO 64108
(800) 821-5591/(816) 471-5200

	Years Ending 11/30					
	1981	1982	1983	1984 (11 mos.)	1985	1986
Net Investment Income ($)	–	–	–	.07	.07	.04
Dividends from Net Investment Income ($)	–	–	–	–	.07	.05
Net Gains (Losses) on Investments ($)	–	–	–	(.77)	3.35	1.51
Distributions from Net Realized Capital Gains ($)	–	–	–	–	.13	.47
Net Asset Value End of Year ($)	–	–	–	9.30	12.52	13.56
Ratio of Expenses to Net Assets (%)	–	–	–	1.67	1.58	1.37
Portfolio Turnover Rate (%)	–	–	–	14	38	32
Total Assets: End of Year (Millions $)	–	–	–	7.3	34.5	47.9
Annual Rate of Return (%) Years Ending 12/31	–	–	–	(5.0)	38.6	9.0

Five-Year Total Return	NA	Degree of Diversification	D	Beta 1.03	Bull NA	Bear NA

Objective: Seeks long-term capital growth through investment in smaller, faster-growing companies whose capitalization is between $15 million and $300 million.

Portfolio: (11/30/86) Common stocks 94%, repos 3%, short-term corporate notes 2%. Largest stock holdings: leisure 14%, building & construction 11%.

Distributions: **Income:** Jan   **Capital Gains:** Jan

12b-1: No

Minimum: **Initial:** $1,000   **Subsequent:** $100

Min IRA: **Initial:** $250   **Subsequent:** None

Services: IRA, Keogh, Corp, SEP, Withdraw

Tel Exchange: Yes   **With MMF:** Yes

Registered: All states

BABSON GROWTH
Growth

Jones & Babson
3 Crown Ctr.,
2440 Pershing Rd.
Kansas City, MO 64108
(800) 821-5591/(816) 471-5200

	Years Ending 6/30					
	1981	**1982**	**1983**	**1984**	**1985**	**1986**
Net Investment Income ($)	.41	.45	.38	.35	.39	.34
Dividends from Net Investment Income ($)	.41	.44	.38	.38	.21	.55
Net Gains (Losses) on Investments ($)	1.49	(2.29)	4.96	(1.90)	2.38	3.64
Distributions from Net Realized Capital Gains ($)	—	.79	.23	1.62	.01	3.21
Net Asset Value End of Year ($)	12.74	9.67	14.40	10.85	13.40	13.62
Ratio of Expenses to Net Assets (%)	.59	.60	.61	.76	.76	.75
Portfolio Turnover Rate (%)	15	22	26	52	35	20
Total Assets: End of Year (Millions $)	281.9	205.8	249.2	208.2	215.4	253.8
Annual Rate of Return (%) Years Ending 12/31	(6.0)	14.5	15.9	0.2	29.7	19.0

Five-Year Total Return	105.4%	Degree of Diversification	A	Beta	.99	Bull	B	Bear	D

Objective: Invests in common stocks which are selected for their long-term possibilities of both capital and income growth. Invests in common stocks of established, well-managed companies in growing industries deemed to have potential for maintaining earnings and dividend growth.

Portfolio: (9/30/86) Common stocks 98%, other 1%. Largest stock holdings: energy 15%, consumer cyclical 15%.

Distributions: Income: Jan, July   **Capital Gains:** July

12b-1: No

Minimum: Initial: $500   Subsequent: $50

Min IRA: Initial: $250   Subsequent: None

Services: IRA, Keogh, Corp, SEP, Withdraw

Tel Exchange: Yes   **With MMF:** Yes

Registered: All states

BABSON VALUE
Growth & Income

Jones & Babson
2440 Pershing Rd.
Kansas City, MO 64108
(800) 821-5591/(816) 471-5200

	\multicolumn{6}{c}{Years Ending 11/30}
	1981	1982	1983	1984	1985	1986
Net Investment Income ($)	–	–	–	–	.56	.49
Dividends from Net Investment Income ($)	–	–	–	–	.09	.87
Net Gains (Losses) on Investments ($)	–	–	–	–	1.90	3.01
Distributions from Net Realized Capital Gains ($)	–	–	–	–	–	.18
Net Asset Value End of Year ($)	–	–	–	–	12.59	15.04
Ratio of Expenses to Net Assets (%)	–	–	–	–	.93	1.20
Portfolio Turnover Rate (%)	–	–	–	–	13	28
Total Assets: End of Year (Millions $)	–	–	–	–	2.8	6.9
Annual Rate of Return (%) Years Ending 12/31	–	–	–	–	26.5	20.7

Five-Year Total Return	NA	Degree of Diversification	NA	Beta	NA	Bull	NA	Bear	NA

Objective: Seeks long-term growth of capital and income through investment in common stocks of companies rated B– or better (by S&P or Value Line) in terms of growth and stability of earnings and dividends. Holds contrarian attitude seeking undervalued stocks.

Portfolio: (11/30/86) Common stocks 90%, convertible bonds 3%, repos 13%. Largest stock holdings: financial services 13%, petroleum 12%.

Distributions: Income: Dec   **Capital Gains:** Dec

12b-1: No

Minimum: Initial: $1,000   Subsequent: $100

Min IRA: Initial: $250   Subsequent: None

Services: IRA, Keogh, Corp, SEP, Withdraw

Tel Exchange: Yes   **With MMF:** Yes

Registered: All states except WI

BARTLETT BASIC VALUE
Growth & Income

Bartlett & Company
36 E. Fourth St.
Cincinnati, OH 45202
(800) 543-0863/(513) 621-0066

	Years Ending 3/31					
	1981	1982	1983	1984 (11 mos.)	1985	1986
Net Investment Income ($)	–	–	–	.58	.63	.48
Dividends from Net Investment Income ($)	–	–	–	.46	.57	.49
Net Gains (Losses) on Investments ($)	–	–	–	.08	.80	3.28
Distributions from Net Realized Capital Gains ($)	–	–	–	–	.18	1.02
Net Asset Value End of Year ($)	–	–	–	10.20	10.88	13.13
Ratio of Expenses to Net Assets (%)	–	–	–	1.99	1.78	1.56
Portfolio Turnover Rate (%)	–	–	–	8	36	82
Total Assets: End of Year (Millions $)	–	–	–	12.4	22.8	52.7
Annual Rate of Return (%) Years Ending 12/31	–	–	–	–	25.6	13.7

Five-Year Total Return	NA	Degree of Diversification	NA	Beta	NA	Bull NA	Bear NA

Objective: Seeks capital appreciation and secondarily current income through investment in common stocks and convertible securities considered to be undervalued and having at least three years history. May temporarily invest in investment grade debt securities and cash as defensive move. May enter into repos, invest in foreign securities, lend its securities, and hedge its portfolio with options, futures contracts and options on futures contracts.

Portfolio: (9/30/86) Common stocks 79%, corporate bonds 12%, repos 4%, commercial paper 4%, U.S. government notes 3%. Largest stock holdings: natural gas transmission 12%, oil services 10%.

Distributions: Income: Mar, June, Sep, Dec   **Capital Gains:** Mar
12b-1: Yes   **Amount:** Pd. by Advisor
Minimum: Initial: $5,000   Subsequent: $100
Min IRA: Initial: $250   Subsequent: $50
Services: IRA, Keogh, Corp, 403(b), Withdraw, Deduct
Tel Exchange: Yes   With MMF: Yes
Registered: AZ, CA, CO, DC, IL, IN, HI, KY, MA, MI, MN, MO, NY, OH, PA

BEACON HILL MUTUAL
Growth

Beacon Hill Management
75 Federal St.
Boston, MA 02110
(617) 482-0795

	Years Ending 6/30					
	1981	1982	1983	1984	1985	1986
Net Investment Income ($)	.04	.05	.03	(.02)	(.03)	(.22)
Dividends from Net Investment Income ($)	.07	.05	.03	—	—	—
Net Gains (Losses) on Investments ($)	2.50	(.67)	4.69	(1.00)	4.60	7.35
Distributions from Net Realized Capital Gains ($)	—	—	—	—	—	—
Net Asset Value End of Year ($)	12.74	12.07	16.76	15.74	20.31	27.44
Ratio of Expenses to Net Assets (%)	3.60	4.00	3.70	3.40	3.30	3.5
Portfolio Turnover Rate (%)	4	1	20	0	2	8
Total Assets: End of Year (Millions $)	2.2	2.0	2.6	2.3	2.9	3.9
Annual Rate of Return (%) Years Ending 12/31	1.9	12.7	16.6	3.8	33.5	6.0

Five-Year Total Return	93.0%	Degree of Diversification	C	Beta	.91	Bull	C	Bear	B

Objective:	Seeks long-term capital growth through investment in common stocks of well-established companies. As defensive measure, may hold debt securities.
Portfolio:	(12/31/86) Common stocks 94%, other 6%. Largest stock holdings: drugs & cosmetics 21%, food products 14%.
Distributions:	**Income:** July **Capital Gains:** July
12b-1:	No
Minimum:	**Initial:** None **Subsequent:** None
Min IRA:	**Initial:** None **Subsequent:** None
Services:	IRA, Keogh, Corp, Withdraw
Tel Exchange:	No
Registered:	Call for information—many pending

BENHAM GNMA INCOME
Bond

Benham Management Corp.
755 Page Mill Road
Palo Alto, CA 94304
(800) 227-8380/(415) 858-3600

	Years Ending 3/31					
	1981	**1982**	**1983**	**1984**	**1985**	**1986** (6 mos.)
Net Investment Income ($)	–	–	–	–	–	.56
Dividends from Net Investment Income ($)	–	–	–	–	–	.58
Net Gains (Losses) on Investments ($)	–	–	–	–	–	.45
Distributions from Net Realized Capital Gains ($)	–	–	–	–	–	–
Net Asset Value End of Year ($)	–	–	–	–	–	10.42
Ratio of Expenses to Net Assets (%)	–	–	–	–	–	.29
Portfolio Turnover Rate (%)	–	–	–	–	–	264
Total Assets: End of Year (Millions $)	–	–	–	–	–	169.7

Annual Rate of Return (%) Years Ending 12/31	–	–	–	–	–	11.4

Five-Year Total Return	NA	Degree of Diversification	NA	Beta	NA	Bull NA	Bear NA

Objective: Seeks high level of current income through investment in GNMAs and other U.S. government backed debt securities. At least 65% of the portfolio must be invested in GNMAs.

Portfolio: (9/30/86) GNMAs 85%, repos 14%, U.S. Treasury notes 1%.

Distributions: Income: Monthly   **Capital Gains:** Annually

12b-1: No

Minimum: Initial: $1,000   **Subsequent:** $100

Min IRA: Initial: $100   **Subsequent:** $100

Services: IRA, Keogh, Withdraw, Deduct

Tel Exchange: Yes   **With MMF:** Yes

Registered: All states

BENHAM TARGET MATURITIES TRUST SERIES 1990
Bond

Benham Management Corp.
755 Page Mill Road
Palo Alto, CA 94304
(800) 227-8380/(415) 858-2400

	Years Ending 12/31					
	1981	**1982**	**1983**	**1984**	**1985**	**1986**
Net Investment Income ($)	–	–	–	–	4.00	5.39
Dividends from Net Investment Income ($)	–	–	–	–	–	–
Net Gains (Losses) on Investments ($)	–	–	–	–	7.41	5.57
Distributions from Net Realized Capital Gains ($)	–	–	–	–	–	–
Net Asset Value End of Year ($)	–	–	–	–	68.16	79.12
Ratio of Expenses to Net Assets (%)	–	–	–	–	.53	.70
Portfolio Turnover Rate (%)	–	–	–	–	46	113
Total Assets: End of Year (Millions $)	–	–	–	–	4.1	5.9

Annual Rate of Return (%) Years Ending 12/31	–	–	–	–	–	15.9

Five-Year Total Return	NA	Degree of Diversification	NA	Beta	NA	Bull	NA	Bear	NA

Objective: Seeks highest attainable return through investment in zero coupon U.S. Treasury securities and other full-coupon Treasury securities. The trust will terminate on December 31 of its target maturity year of 1990, and will be liquidated during the January following the termination.

Portfolio: (12/31/86) Separate trading of registered interest and principal of securities (STRIPS) 59%, certificates of accrual on Treasury securities (CATS) 11%, Treasury receipts (TR) 27%, Treasury notes 2%.

Distributions: **Income:** Annually   **Capital Gains:** Annually

12b-1: No

Minimum: **Initial:** $1,000   **Subsequent:** $100

Min IRA: **Initial:** $100   **Subsequent:** None

Services: IRA, Keogh

Tel Exchange: Yes   **With MMF:** Yes

Registered: All states

BENHAM TARGET MATURITIES TRUST SERIES 1995
Bond

Benham Management Corp.
755 Page Mill Road
Palo Alto, CA 94304
(800) 227-8380/(415) 858-2400

	Years Ending 12/31					
	1981	**1982**	**1983**	**1984**	**1985**	**1986**
Net Investment Income ($)	—	—	—	—	2.51	3.69
Dividends from Net Investment Income ($)	—	—	—	—	—	—
Net Gains (Losses) on Investments ($)	—	—	—	—	7.37	7.65
Distributions from Net Realized Capital Gains ($)	—	—	—	—	—	—
Net Asset Value End of Year ($)	—	—	—	—	42.99	54.33
Ratio of Expenses to Net Assets (%)	—	—	—	—	.53	.70
Portfolio Turnover Rate (%)	—	—	—	—	—	89
Total Assets: End of Year (Millions $)	—	—	—	—	2.2	5.1

Annual Rate of Return (%) Years Ending 12/31	—	—	—	—	—	26.9

Five-Year Total Return	NA	Degree of Diversification	NA	Beta	NA	Bull NA	Bear NA

Objective: Seeks highest attainable return through investment in zero coupon U.S. Treasury securities and other full-coupon Treasury securities. The trust will terminate on December 31 of its target maturity year of 1995, and will be liquidated the following January.

Portfolio: (12/31/86) Separate trading of interest and principal of securities (STRIPS) 60%, Treasury receipts (TR) 33%, certificates of accrual on Treasury securities (CATS) 4%, Treasury bond receipts (TBR) 3%.

Distributions: **Income:** Annually   **Capital Gains:** Annually
12b-1: No
Minimum: **Initial:** $1,000   **Subsequent:** $100
Min IRA: **Initial:** $100   **Subsequent:** None
Services: IRA, Keogh
Tel Exchange: Yes   **With MMF:** Yes
Registered: All states

BENHAM TARGET MATURITIES TRUST SERIES 2000
Bond

Benham Management Corp.
755 Page Mill Road
Palo Alto, CA 94304
(800) 277-8380/(415) 858-2400

	Years Ending 12/31					
	1981	**1982**	**1983**	**1984**	**1985**	**1986**
Net Investment Income ($)	–	–	–	–	1.53	2.40
Dividends from Net Investment Income ($)	–	–	–	–	–	–
Net Gains (Losses) on Investments ($)	–	–	–	–	5.73	6.27
Distributions from Net Realized Capital Gains ($)	–	–	–	–	–	–
Net Asset Value End of Year ($)	–	–	–	–	26.77	35.44
Ratio of Expenses to Net Assets (%)	–	–	–	–	.52	.70
Portfolio Turnover Rate (%)	–	–	–	–	34	39
Total Assets: End of Year (Millions $)	–	–	–	–	2.2	5.1
Annual Rate of Return (%) Years Ending 12/31	–	–	–	–	–	32.6

Five-Year Total Return	NA	Degree of Diversification	NA	Beta	NA	Bull NA	Bear NA

Objective: Seeks highest attainable return through investment in zero coupon U.S. Treasury securities and other full-coupon Treasury securities. The trust will terminate on December 31, 2000, and will be liquidated the following January.

Portfolio: (12/31/86) Separate trading of interest and principal of securities (STRIPS) 66%, certificates of accrual on Treasury securities (CATS) 16%, Treasury bond receipts (TBR) 14%, Treasury receipts (TR) 3%.

Distributions: **Income:** Annually   **Capital Gains:** Annually

12b-1: No

Minimum: **Initial:** $1,000   **Subsequent:** $100

Min IRA: **Initial:** $100   **Subsequent:** None

Services: IRA, Keogh

Tel Exchange: Yes   **With MMF:** Yes

Registered: All states

BENHAM TARGET MATURITIES TRUST SERIES 2010
Bond

Benham Management Corp.
755 Page Mill Road
Palo Alto, CA 94304
(800) 227-8380/(415) 858-2400

	Years Ending 12/31					
	1981	1982	1983	1984	1985	1986
Net Investment Income ($)	–	–	–	–	.76	1.09
Dividends from Net Investment Income ($)	–	–	–	–	–	–
Net Gains (Losses) on Investments ($)	–	–	–	–	2.83	5.13
Distributions from Net Realized Capital Gains ($)	–	–	–	–	–	–
Net Asset Value End of Year ($)	–	–	–	–	11.43	17.65
Ratio of Expenses to Net Assets (%)	–	–	–	–	.49	.70
Portfolio Turnover Rate (%)	–	–	–	–	18	91
Total Assets: End of Year (Millions $)	–	–	–	–	1.2	4.9

Annual Rate of Return (%) Years Ending 12/31	–	–	–	–	–	54.7

Five-Year Total Return	NA	Degree of Diversification	NA	Beta	NA	Bull NA	Bear NA

Objective: Seeks highest attainable return through investment in zero coupon U.S. Treasury securities and other full-coupon Treasury securities. The trust will terminate on December 31, 2010, and will be liquidated the following January.

Portfolio: (12/31/86) Separate trading of interest and principal of securities (STRIPS) 100%.

Distributions: Income: Annually   **Capital Gains:** Annually

12b-1: No

Minimum: Initial: $1,000   Subsequent: $100

Min IRA: Initial: $100   Subsequent: None

Services: IRA, Keogh

Tel Exchange: Yes   **With MMF:** Yes

Registered: All states

BOSTON CO. CAPITAL APPRECIATION
Growth

The Boston Company Advisors
One Boston Place
Boston, MA 02108
(800) 225-5267/(617) 956-9740

	Years Ending 12/31					
	1981	**1982**	**1983**	**1984**	**1985**	**1986**
Net Investment Income ($)	.95	.73	.71	.86	1.00	.90
Dividends from Net Investment Income ($)	1.11	.81	.64	.69	.74	.50
Net Gains (Losses) on Investments ($)	(1.97)	1.95	4.80	.73	7.50	5.69
Distributions from Net Realized Capital Gains ($)	1.07	3.37	.82	2.91	1.56	5.80
Net Asset Value End of Year ($)	25.37	23.87	27.92	25.91	32.11	32.40
Ratio of Expenses to Net Assets (%)	.77	1.07	.98	1.00	.96	.95
Portfolio Turnover Rate (%)	49	86	47	26	59	37
Total Assets: End of Year (Millions $)	196.2	212.9	238.1	259.7	369.7	452.9

Annual Rate of Return (%) Years Ending 12/31	(3.7)	13.6	24.0	6.9	35.0	22.5

Five-Year Total Return	148.9%	Degree of Diversification	A	Beta	.90	Bull	A	Bear	E

Objective: Seeks long-term growth of capital through investment in companies with strong growth features and which meet other investment criteria based on studies of trends in industries and companies. May engage in repos, invest in foreign securities and employ leverage.

Portfolio: (12/31/86) Common stocks 87%, U.S. Treasury obligations 4%, repos 4%, municipal bonds 3%, convertible bonds 2%. Largest stock holdings: financial services 25%, technology 10%.

Distributions: Income: Jan, April, July, Oct　　　**Capital Gains:** Jan

12b-1: Yes　　　**Amount:** .45%

Minimum: Initial: $1,000　　　**Subsequent:** None

Min IRA: Initial: $500　　　**Subsequent:** None

Services: IRA, Keogh, Corp, Withdraw

Tel Exchange: Yes　　　**With MMF:** Yes

Registered: All states

BOSTON CO. MANAGED INCOME

Bond

The Boston Company Advisors
One Boston Place
Boston, MA 02108
(800) 225-5267/(617) 956-9740

	Years Ending 12/31					
	1981	1982	1983	1984	1985*	1986
Net Investment Income ($)	–	–	–	–	1.20	.86
Dividends from Net Investment Income ($)	–	–	–	–	.99	.96
Net Gains (Losses) on Investments ($)	–	–	–	–	.99	.28
Distributions from Net Realized Capital Gains ($)	–	–	–	–	–	.07
Net Asset Value End of Year ($)	–	–	–	–	11.80	11.91
Ratio of Expenses to Net Assets (%)	–	–	–	–	1.48	.88
Portfolio Turnover Rate (%)	–	–	–	–	173	71
Total Assets: End of Year (Millions $)	–	–	–	–	16.7	49.3

Objectives changed Nov. 1984; prior history not meaningful.

	1981	1982	1983	1984	1985	1986
Annual Rate of Return (%) Years Ending 12/31	–	–	–	–	21.8	14.9

Five-Year Total Return	NA	Degree of Diversification	NA	Beta	NA	Bull	NA	Bear	NA

Objective: Seeks high current income through investment in debt securities such as corporate bonds, debentures, convertibles, preferred stocks, U.S. government obligations and money market instruments. May engage in repos and in foreign securities.

Portfolio: (12/31/86) Corporate bonds 70%, U.S. government notes 24%, repos 4%, other assets 2%, preferred stock 1%.

Distributions: **Income:** Monthly　　　　　　**Capital Gains:** Jan

12b-1: Yes　　　　　　**Amount:** .45%

Minimum: **Initial:** $1,000　　**Subsequent:** None

Min IRA: **Initial:** $500　　**Subsequent:** None

Services: IRA, Keogh, Corp, Withdraw

Tel Exchange: Yes　　　　　　**With MMF:** Yes

Registered: All states

BOSTON CO. SPECIAL GROWTH
Growth

The Boston Company Advisors
One Boston Place
Boston, MA 02108
(800) 225-5267/(617) 956-9740

		Years Ending 12/31				
	1981	1982 (8 mos.)	1983	1984	1985	1986
Net Investment Income ($)	–	.22	.50	.38	.36	.13
Dividends from Net Investment Income ($)	–	–	–	.09	.35	.31
Net Gains (Losses) on Investments ($)	–	3.27	4.67	(2.36)	5.07	1.40
Distributions from Net Realized Capital Gains ($)	–	–	.61	.11	–	4.96
Net Asset Value End of Year ($)	–	13.49	18.05	15.87	20.95	17.21
Ratio of Expenses to Net Assets (%)	–	1.43	1.49	1.50	1.35	1.32
Portfolio Turnover Rate (%)	–	102	247	261	258	192
Total Assets: End of Year (Millions $)	–	1.4	25.5	27.6	53.6	35.9

Annual Rate of Return (%) Years Ending 12/31	–	–	38.3	(10.9)	34.7	7.7

Five-Year Total Return	NA	Degree of Diversification	C	Beta 1.10	Bull B	Bear NA

Objective: Seeks above-average growth of capital through investment in securities thought to have significant growth potential—primarily common stocks and convertible securities of smaller companies, and larger, more established companies with above-average growth potential. May engage in repos, invest in foreign securities, and employ leverage.

Portfolio: (12/31/86) Common stocks 85%, repos 6%, convertible bonds 5%, other assets 3%, convertible preferred stock 1%. Largest stock holdings: financial services 17%, transportation 13%.

Distributions: Income: Jan   **Capital Gains:** Jan

12b-1: Yes   Amount: .45%

Minimum: Initial: $1,000   Subsequent: None

Min IRA: Initial: $500   Subsequent: None

Services: IRA, Keogh, Corp, Withdraw

Tel Exchange: Yes   **With MMF:** Yes

Registered: All states

BOWSER GROWTH
Growth

Commonwealth Capital Mgmt.
1500 Forest Ave., Suite 223
Richmond, VA 23228
(800) 527-9500/(804) 285-8211

	Years Ending 12/31					
	1981	**1982**	**1983**	**1984** (10 mos.)	**1985**	**1986**
Net Investment Income ($)	–	–	–	.02	–	.06
Dividends from Net Investment Income ($)	–	–	–	–	.03	.01
Net Gains (Losses) on Investments ($)	–	–	–	(.49)	(.13)	.49
Distributions from Net Realized Capital Gains ($)	–	–	–	–	–	–
Net Asset Value End of Year ($)	–	–	–	2.53	2.37	1.81
Ratio of Expenses to Net Assets (%)	–	–	–	4.94	3.93	4.77
Portfolio Turnover Rate (%)	–	–	–	–	9	47
Total Assets: End of Year (Millions $)	–	–	–	3.1	3.8	2.5

Annual Rate of Return (%) Years Ending 12/31	–	–	–	–	(5.7)	(23.7)

Five-Year Total Return	NA	Degree of Diversification	NA	Beta	NA	Bull	NA	Bear	NA

Objective: Seeks capital appreciation through investment in common stocks that are undervalued, based on the underlying financial strength of the company and its future prospects. May take defensive posture in debt securities. May invest in repos, and lend its portfolio securities.

Portfolio: (12/31/86) Common stocks 91%, repos 10%, bonds 2%. Largest stock holdings: manufacturing 22%, computer and electronics 19%.

Distributions: Income: Annually   **Capital Gains:** Annually

12b-1: Yes   **Amount:** .50%

Minimum: Initial: $300   **Subsequent:** $50

Min IRA: Initial: $300   **Subsequent:** $50

Services: IRA, Deduct

Tel Exchange: No

Registered: All states except ME, NH

BRUCE FUND

Aggressive Growth

Bruce and Co.
20 North Wacker Dr.
Chicago, IL 60606
(312) 236-9160

	Years Ending 6/30					
	1981	1982	1983	1984	1985	1986
Net Investment Income ($)	–	–	–	7.17	5.63	2.21
Dividends from Net Investment Income ($)	–	–	–	3.74	8.25	10.20
Net Gains (Losses) on Investments ($)	–	–	–	(36.82)	36.65	42.16
Distributions from Net Realized Capital Gains ($)	–	–	–	29.56	99.23	36.94
Net Asset Value End of Year ($)	–	–	–	185.44	120.24	117.47
Ratio of Expenses to Net Assets (%)	–	–	–	2.92	4.89	2.68
Portfolio Turnover Rate (%)	–	–	–	99	85	0
Total Assets: End of Year (Millions $)	–	–	–	1.1	1.0	2.9

Annual Rate of Return (%) Years Ending 12/31	–	–	–	6.2	37	29.6

Five-Year Total Return	NA	Degree of Diversification	D	Beta	.90	Bull NA	Bear NA

Objective: Seeks long-term capital appreciation; dividend income is a secondary consideration. Can invest in stocks, bonds and convertible securities. May also invest in unseasoned companies where the risks are greater than for established companies.

Portfolio: (9/30/86) Common stocks 46%, bonds 48%, cash 6%. Largest holdings: zero coupon bonds 48%.

Distributions: **Income:** Annually   **Capital Gains:** Annually

12b-1: No

Minimum: **Initial:** $1,000   **Subsequent:** $500

Min IRA: **Initial:** $1,000   **Subsequent:** $500

Services: IRA

Tel Exchange: No

Registered: CA, CO, CT, FL, GA, IL, IN, KY, MA, MD, MI, MN, MO, MS, NJ, NV, NY, OH, OR, PA, SC, TN, TX, VA, WA, WI

BULL & BEAR
CAPITAL GROWTH
Aggressive Growth

Bull & Bear Advisers
11 Hanover Sq.
New York, NY 10005
(800) 847-4200/(212) 363-1100

	Years Ending 12/31					
	1981	**1982**	**1983**	**1984**	**1985**	**1986**
Net Investment Income ($)	.26	.26	.33	.09	.14	(.02)
Dividends from Net Investment Income ($)	.15	.27	.23	.30	.13	.20
Net Gains (Losses) on Investments ($)	(1.99)	1.24	1.80	(.89)	3.34	.69
Distributions from Net Realized Capital Gains ($)	–	–	–	1.96	.35	5.91
Net Asset Value End of Year ($)	12.74	13.97	15.87	12.81	15.81	10.37
Ratio of Expenses to Net Assets (%)	1.46	1.42	1.23	1.33	1.41	2.25
Portfolio Turnover Rate (%)	22	34	67	94	78	78
Total Assets: End of Year (Millions $)	45.2	72.7	76.1	63.6	91.8	61.7
Annual Rate of Return (%) Years Ending 12/31	(12.1)	12.6	15.5	(4.3)	27.8	3.6

Five-Year Total Return 64.6%	Degree of Diversification A	Beta 1.12	Bull D	Bear E

Objective: Seeks long-term capital appreciation through a diversified portfolio consisting primarily of common stocks of emerging growth companies and in special situations. May invest in foreign securities, may employ leverage and may engage in repos.

Portfolio: (12/31/86) Common stocks 96%, U.S. government obligations 5%, short-term securities 4%, convertibles 1%. Largest stock holdings: financial 18%, technology 10%.

Distributions: **Income:** Annually   **Capital Gains:** Annually

12b-1: Yes   **Amount:** .50%

Minimum: **Initial:** $1,000   **Subsequent:** $100

Min IRA: **Initial:** $100   **Subsequent:** None

Services: IRA, Keogh, 403(b), SEP, Withdraw, Deduct

Tel Exchange: Yes   **With MMF:** Yes

Registered: All states except ME, MO

BULL & BEAR
EQUITY-INCOME
Balanced

Bull & Bear Advisers
11 Hanover Sq.
New York, NY 10005
(800) 847-4200/(212) 363-1100

	Years Ending 12/31					
	1981	**1982**	**1983**	**1984**	**1985**	**1986**
Net Investment Income ($)	.51	.75	.65	.71	.67	.38
Dividends from Net Investment Income ($)	.50	.75	.65	.70	.70	.38
Net Gains (Losses) on Investments ($)	(1.33)	.88	.64	.04	1.82	1.63
Distributions from Net Realized Capital Gains ($)	—	.65	—	.25	1.31	2.01
Net Asset Value End of Year ($)	10.26	10.49	11.13	10.93	11.41	11.03
Ratio of Expenses to Net Assets (%)	2.07	2.02	2.03	1.98	2.17	3.00
Portfolio Turnover Rate (%)	81	21	36	155	103	93
Total Assets: End of Year (Millions $)	3.2	4.4	5.3	4.5	6.3	11.3
Annual Rate of Return (%) Years Ending 12/31	(7.1)	18.3	12.4	7.2	25.8	18.7

Five-Year Total Return	112.9%	Degree of Diversification	C	Beta	.59	Bull	C	Bear	C

Objective: Intends to provide current income and long-term growth through investment in large, major corporations' common stock and senior convertibles. May also invest in corporate bonds and money market instruments.

Portfolio: (12/31/86) Convertible bonds 47%, common stocks 30%, U.S. government obligations 9%. Largest stock holdings: utilities 6%, consumer products 5%.

Distributions: Income: Quarterly   Capital Gains: Annually

12b-1: Yes   Amount: .50%

Minimum: Initial: $1,000   Subsequent: $100

Min IRA: Initial: $100   Subsequent: None

Services: IRA, Keogh, Corp, 403(b), SEP, Withdraw, Deduct

Tel Exchange: Yes   With MMF: Yes

Registered: All states except LA, ME, OH

BULL & BEAR
HIGH YIELD
Bond

Bull & Bear Management Corp.
11 Hanover Square
New York, NY 10005
(800) 847-4200/(212) 363-1100

	1981	1982	1983	1984 (10 mos.)	1985	1986
Years Ending 6/30						
Net Investment Income ($)	—	—	—	1.62	1.94	1.89
Dividends from Net Investment Income ($)	—	—	—	1.62	1.94	1.89
Net Gains (Losses) on Investments ($)	—	—	—	(1.75)	1.17	.54
Distributions from Net Realized Capital Gains ($)	—	—	—	—	—	—
Net Asset Value End of Year ($)	—	—	—	13.25	14.42	14.96
Ratio of Expenses to Net Assets (%)	—	—	—	.99	1.16	1.37
Portfolio Turnover Rate (%)	—	—	—	95	127	77
Total Assets: End of Year (Millions $)	—	—	—	8.7	33.5	113.1

Annual Rate of Return (%) Years Ending 12/31	—	—	—	7.8	20.9	6.0

Five-Year Total Return	NA	Degree of Diversification	NA	Beta	.21	Bull NA	Bear NA

Objective: Seeks the highest income over the long term through investment in high-yield fixed-income debt securities of short-, intermediate-, or long-term maturities graded in the lower categories. Value of shares subject to influence by changes in interest rates. May invest up to 15% of assets in foreign securities and may enter into repos.

Portfolio: (6/30/86) Corporate bonds 100%.

Distributions: **Income:** Monthly   **Capital Gains:** August

12b-1: Yes   **Amount:** .50%

Minimum: **Initial:** $1,000   **Subsequent:** $100

Min IRA: **Initial:** $100   **Subsequent:** $100

Services: IRA, Keogh, SEP, 403(b), Withdraw, Deduct

Tel Exchange: Yes   **With MMF:** Yes

Registered: All states except ME

CALVERT
Equity Portfolio
Growth

Calvert Asset Management Co.
1700 Pennsylvania Ave., NW
Washington, DC 20006
(800) 368-2748/(301) 951-4820

	Years Ending 9/30					
	1981	1982	1983	1984	1985	1986
Net Investment Income ($)	–	–	.38	.44	.34	.17
Dividends from Net Investment Income ($)	–	–	–	.37	.44	.34
Net Gains (Losses) on Investments ($)	–	–	3.51	(1.98)	.14	5.35
Distributions from Net Realized Capital Gains ($)	–	–	–	.04	–	–
Net Asset Value End of Year ($)	–	–	18.89	16.94	16.98	22.16
Ratio of Expenses to Net Assets (%)	–	–	2.25	2.06	1.98	1.83
Portfolio Turnover Rate (%)	–	–	12	148	38	56
Total Assets: End of Year (Millions $)	–	–	8.6	6.8	5.9	7.6
Annual Rate of Return (%) Years Ending 12/31	–	–	9.0	(6.7)	23.6	12.1

Five-Year Total Return	NA	Degree of Diversification	A	Beta 1.02	Bull NA	Bear NA

Objective: Seeks growth of capital through investment in equity securities considered neither speculative nor conservative. Chosen through analysis of cash flow, book value, dividend growth potential, management quality and current and future earnings.

Portfolio: (9/30/86) Common stocks 93%, convertible bonds 1%. Largest stock holdings: energy 13%, industrials 18%.

Distributions: Income: Oct — **Capital Gains:** Oct

12b-1: Yes — **Amount:** .75%

Minimum: Initial: $2,000 — Subsequent: $250

Min IRA: Initial: $1,000 — Subsequent: $250

Services: IRA, Keogh, Corp, 403(b), Withdraw

Tel Exchange: Yes — **With MMF:** Yes

Registered: All states

CAPITAL PRESERVATION TREASURY NOTE TRUST

Bond

Benham Management Corp.
755 Page Mill Rd.
Palo Alto, CA 94304
(800) 227-8380/(415) 858-3600

	Years Ending 3/31					
	1981 (10 mos.)	1982	1983	1984	1985	1986
Net Investment Income ($)	.77	.91	1.01	.96	.99	.90
Dividends from Net Investment Income ($)	.47	.86	.91	1.03	.93	.83
Net Gains (Losses) on Investments ($)	(.58)	.06	.42	(.15)	.16	1.55
Distributions from Net Realized Capital Gains ($)	—	—	—	—	—	—
Net Asset Value End of Year ($)	9.72	9.83	10.35	10.13	10.35	11.97
Ratio of Expenses to Net Assets (%)	—	.88	1.00	1.00	1.00	1.00
Portfolio Turnover Rate (%)	—	—	—	—	53	294
Total Assets: End of Year (Millions $)	6.6	7.1	11.1	9.2	12.5	28.5
Annual Rate of Return (%) Years Ending 12/31	10.4	17.1	7.4	12.0	17.6	13.4

Five-Year Total Return	87.9%	Degree of Diversification	NA	Beta	.20	Bull	E	Bear	A

Objective: Seeks high current income consistent with safety of principal; at least 90% of the trust's portfolio invested in U.S. Treasury notes, and up to 10% in U.S. Treasury bills and U.S. Treasury securities repurchase agreements.

Portfolio: (12/31/86) U.S. Treasury notes 99%, cash 1%.

Distributions: **Income:** Monthly   **Capital Gains:** Mar

12b-1: No

Minimum: **Initial:** $1,000   **Subsequent:** $100

Min IRA: **Initial:** $100   **Subsequent:** None

Services: IRA, Keogh, Withdraw

Tel Exchange: Yes   **With MMF:** Yes

Registered: All states

CENTURY SHARES TRUST
Growth

Century Shares Trust
One Liberty Square
Boston, MA 02109
(800) 321-1928/(617) 482-3060

	Years Ending 12/31					
	1981	1982	1983	1984	1985	1986
Net Investment Income ($)	.60	.60	.60	.55	.50	.50
Dividends from Net Investment Income ($)	.60	.64	.64	.60	.54	.51
Net Gains (Losses) on Investments ($)	1.55	.61	1.86	1.36	5.15	1.20
Distributions from Net Realized Capital Gains ($)	.70	.49	.45	.91	.91	1.11
Net Asset Value End of Year ($)	12.17	12.25	13.62	14.02	18.22	18.30
Ratio of Expenses to Net Assets (%)	.97	1.13	.94	.95	.84	.77
Portfolio Turnover Rate (%)	1	5	4	4	6	6
Total Assets: End of Year (Millions $)	69.0	68.0	74.4	76.8	123.2	141
Annual Rate of Return (%) Years Ending 12/31	20.5	11.0	21.2	15.6	42.6	9.4

Five-Year Total Return	142.3%	Degree of Diversification	D	Beta	1.01	Bull	A	Bear	C

Objective:	Seeks long-term growth of capital and current income through investments exclusively in insurance and banking stock and in bonds and obligations which are legal investments for savings banks in Massachusetts.
Portfolio:	(12/31/86) Common stocks 96%, other 4%. Largest stock holdings: insurance 92%, banking 4%.
Distributions:	**Income:** June, Dec **Capital Gains:** Jan
12b-1:	No
Minimum:	**Initial:** $500 **Subsequent:** $25
Min IRA:	**Initial:** $500 **Subsequent:** $25
Services:	IRA
Tel Exchange:	No
Registered:	All states

CLAREMONT COMBINED PORTFOLIO
Balanced

Claremont Company
250 West First Street
Claremont, CA 91711
(800) 826-8896

	Years Ending 12/31					
	1981	1982	1983	1984	1985 (7 mos.)	1986
Net Investment Income ($)	–	–	–	–	.25	.24
Dividends from Net Investment Income ($)	–	–	–	–	.03	.09
Net Gains (Losses) on Investments ($)	–	–	–	–	.84	1.10
Distributions from Net Realized Capital Gains ($)	–	–	–	–	–	.22
Net Asset Value End of Year ($)	–	–	–	–	11.06	12.09
Ratio of Expenses to Net Assets (%)	–	–	–	–	1.99	2.10
Portfolio Turnover Rate (%)	–	–	–	–	48	111
Total Assets: End of Year (Millions $)	–	–	–	–	1.8	7.7

Annual Rate of Return (%) Years Ending 12/31	–	–	–	–	–	12.0

Five-Year Total Return	NA	Degree of Diversification	NA	Beta	NA	Bull	NA	Bear	NA

Objective: Seeks maximum long-term return composed of capital appreciation and income from stocks and debt instruments, while preserving capital. There are no restrictions on the proportion of fund assets that can be invested in equity or debt.

Portfolio: (12/31/86) Common stocks 61%, short-term securities 21%, government bonds/notes 14%. Largest stock holdings: consumer goods and services—nondurable 23%, consumer goods and services—durable 16%.

Distributions: Income: Quarterly   **Capital Gains:** Annually
12b-1: Yes   Amount: .25%
Minimum: Initial: $500   Subsequent: $50
Min IRA: Initial: $500   Subsequent: $50
Services: IRA, Keogh
Tel Exchange: Yes   **With MMF:** No
Registered: CA, CO, CT, DC, FL, GA, HI, IL, IN NV, NY, OH, SC, TX, WA

COLUMBIA FIXED INCOME SECURITIES
Bond

Columbia Financial Center
1301 S.W. Fifth Ave.
PO Box 1350
Portland, OR 97207-1350
(800) 547-1037/(503) 222-3600

	Years Ending 12/31					
	1981	1982	1983	1984	1985	1986
Net Investment Income ($)	–	–	1.35	1.44	1.40	1.21
Dividends from Net Investment Income ($)	–	–	1.35	1.44	1.40	1.21
Net Gains (Losses) on Investments ($)	–	–	(.30)	(.07)	.91	.32
Distributions from Net Realized Capital Gains ($)	–	–	–	–	–	–
Net Asset Value End of Year ($)	–	–	12.21	12.14	13.05	13.37
Ratio of Expenses to Net Assets (%)	–	–	1.22	1.05	.88	.79
Portfolio Turnover Rate (%)	–	–	46	98	94	97
Total Assets: End of Year (Millions $)	–	–	29.4	38.1	83.2	124.4

Annual Rate of Return (%) Years Ending 12/31	–	–	–	12.3	20.1	12.4

Five-Year Total Return	NA	Degree of Diversification	NA	Beta .14	Bull NA	Bear NA

Objective: Seeks high level of current income, consistent with conservation of capital, through investment in a broad range of investment-grade fixed-income securities, amounting to 80% of its assets. Other 20% may be in lower-grade debt securities as well as those of the U.S. government.

Portfolio: (12/31/86) U.S. government and agency obligations 78%, corporate bonds 20%, repos 1%, cash 1%.

Distributions: Income: Monthly   **Capital Gains:** Jan

12b-1: Yes   **Amount:** .15%

Minimum: Initial: $1,000   **Subsequent:** $100

Min IRA: Initial: $1,000   **Subsequent:** $100

Services: IRA, Keogh, Withdraw

Tel Exchange: Yes   **With MMF:** Yes

Registered: AK, AZ, CA, CO, CT, DC, FL, GA, HI, IA, ID, IL, MA, MD, MI, MN, MO, MT, NC, NJ, NV, NY, OH, OR, PA, TX, VA, WA, WY

COLUMBIA GROWTH
Growth

Columbia Financial Center
1301 S.W. Fifth Ave.
PO Box 1350
Portland, OR 97207-1350
(800) 547-1037/(503) 222-3600

	Years Ending 12/31					
	1981	1982	1983	1984	1985	1986
Net Investment Income ($)	.43	.39	.37	.20	.29	.25
Dividends from Net Investment Income ($)	.51	.40	.12	.19	.33	.40
Net Gains (Losses) on Investments ($)	(1.31)	6.82	4.20	(1.52)	6.53	1.49
Distributions from Net Realized Capital Gains ($)	3.84	4.14	2.42	2.41	—	6.48
Net Asset Value End of Year ($)	20.75	23.42	25.45	21.53	28.02	22.88
Ratio of Expenses to Net Assets (%)	1.22	1.15	1.10	1.18	1.06	1.00
Portfolio Turnover Rate (%)	100	160	95	90	93	131
Total Assets: End of Year (Millions $)	34.9	74.1	145.5	155.1	250.6	200.9
Annual Rate of Return (%) Years Ending 12/31	(2.9)	44.9	21.5	(5.1)	32.0	6.8

Five-Year Total Return	135.5%	Degree of Diversification	A	Beta 1.18	Bull B	Bear C

Objective: Seeks capital growth and preservation through selection of common stocks of large, established, dividend-paying companies on the basis of sales trends, earnings and profit margins, new products, industry environment, management and future orientation, all in the framework of the economy and market conditions. May adopt defensive posture in bonds or commercial paper.

Portfolio: (12/31/86) Common stocks 86%, repos 14%. Largest stock holdings: technology 16%, entertainment and media 11%.

Distributions: Income: Jan   Capital Gains: Jan
12b-1: Yes   Amount: .15%
Minimum: Initial: $1,000   Subsequent: $100
Min IRA: Initial: $1,000   Subsequent: $100
Services: IRA, Keogh, Withdraw
Tel Exchange: Yes   With MMF: Yes
Registered: All states except NH

COLUMBIA SPECIAL
Aggressive Growth

Columbia Financial Center
1301 S.W. Fifth Avenue
PO Box 1350
Portland, OR 97207
(800) 547-1037/(503) 222-3600

	Years Ending 12/31					
	1981	1982	1983	1984	1985 (5 mos.)	1986
Net Investment Income ($)	—	—	—	—	.03	.13
Dividends from Net Investment Income ($)	—	—	—	—	—	.70
Net Gains (Losses) on Investments ($)	—	—	—	—	5.43	3.88
Distributions from Net Realized Capital Gains ($)	—	—	—	—	—	.04
Net Asset Value End of Year ($)	—	—	—	—	23.96	26.97
Ratio of Expenses to Net Assets (%)	—	—	—	—	1.24	1.54
Portfolio Turnover Rate (%)	—	—	—	—	112	203
Total Assets: End of Year (Millions $)	—	—	—	—	3.1	20.4

Annual Rate of Return (%) Years Ending 12/31	—	—	—	—	—	15.8

Five-Year Total Return	NA	Degree of Diversification	NA	Beta NA	Bull NA	Bear NA

Objective: Seeks significant capital appreciation by investing in securities which are more aggressive and carry more risk than the market as a whole. Invests in small companies with capitalizations less than the average of those companies in the S&P 500.

Portfolio: (12/31/86) Common stocks 98%, warrants 3%, repos 1%. Largest stock holdings: consumer non-durables 26%, entertainment and media 26%.

Distributions: **Income:** Annually   **Capital Gains:** Annually

12b-1: Yes   **Amount:** .15%

Minimum: **Initial:** $10,000   **Subsequent:** $100

Min IRA: **Initial:** $2,000   **Subsequent:** $100

Services: IRA, Keogh

Tel Exchange: Yes   **With MMF:** Yes

Registered: AK, AZ, CO, CT, DC, FL, GA, HI, IA, ID, IL, MA, MD, MI, MN, MT, NC, NJ, NV, NY, OH, OR, PA, TX, VA, WA, WY

COPLEY
TAX-MANAGED
Growth

Copley Financial Services Corp.
109 Howe St.
Fall River, MA 02724
(617) 674-8459

	Years Ending 2/28					
	1981	1982	1983	1984	1985	1986
Net Investment Income ($)	.25	.30	.40	.52	.53	.59
Dividends from Net Investment Income ($)	–	–	–	–	–	–
Net Gains (Losses) on Investments ($)	.06	(.11)	.92	(.06)	1.01	1.77
Distributions from Net Realized Capital Gains ($)	–	–	–	–	–	–
Net Asset Value End of Year ($)	4.17	4.36	5.68	6.14	7.68	10.04
Ratio of Expenses to Net Assets (%)	2.99	2.75	2.23	1.40	1.50	1.47
Portfolio Turnover Rate (%)	36	9	56	39	29	19
Total Assets: End of Year (Millions $)	1.7	1.6	2.7	5.6	8.4	21.6
Annual Rate of Return (%) Years Ending 12/31	4.1	19.9	11.6	23.9	24.6	17.7

Five-Year Total Return 143.3%	Degree of Diversification D	Beta .51	Bull B	Bear B

Objective: Seeks high income without concern for level of dividend income as it is tax-free. Set up as corporation which is entitled to 85% exemption from federal income taxes on dividends received, and the 15% balance can be used as expenses to run the fund. Invests in highly visible companies with strong balance sheets that pay high dividends that have been increasing.

Portfolio: (8/31/86) Common and preferred stocks 87%, short-term securities 13%. Largest stock holdings: electric and gas 25%, electric power 21%, telephone 13%.

Distributions: Income: NA **Capital Gains:** NA
12b-1: No
Minimum: Initial: $1,000 Subsequent: $100
Min IRA: Initial: $100 Subsequent: None
Services: IRA, Keogh, Withdraw
Tel Exchange: None
Registered: All states

CUMBERLAND GROWTH
Growth

Cumberland Advisors
614 Landis Avenue
Vineland, NJ 08360
(800) 257-7013/(609) 692-6690

| | Years Ending 12/31 | | | | | |
	1981	1982	1983	1984	1985	1986
Net Investment Income ($)	.94	.57	.95	.64	.77	.44
Dividends from Net Investment Income ($)	–	.91	.47	.73	.51	.52
Net Gains (Losses) on Investments ($)	(1.08)	4.75	2.34	(2.36)	4.53	.99
Distributions from Net Realized Capital Gains ($)	–	–	–	.94	–	–
Net Asset Value End of Year ($)	21.28	25.65	29.22	25.83	30.65	33.63
Ratio of Expenses to Net Assets (%)	4.8	5.3	4.1	4.1	3.8	3.4
Portfolio Turnover Rate (%)	102	172	219	71	194	187
Total Assets: End of Year (Millions $)	.43	.51	.91	.77	1.6	2.4

Annual Rate of Return (%) Years Ending 12/31	–	25.9	16.4	(6.0)	21.5	11.8

Five-Year Total Return	87.0%	Degree of Diversification	D	Beta	.59	Bull	D	Bear	NA

Objective: Primary objective is capital appreciation; current income is a secondary consideration. Invests primarily in common stocks, but may invest in bonds rated BBB or lower by S&P. Can leverage the fund through bank borrowings, and may also sell stock short.

Portfolio: (12/31/86) Common stocks 55%, cash 25%, bonds 15%, convertible bonds 5%. Largest stock holdings: electrical 5%, communications 4%.

Distributions: **Income:** Annually   **Capital Gains:** Annually

12b-1: Yes   **Amount:** .50%

Minimum: **Initial:** $1,000   **Subsequent:** $100

Min IRA: **Initial:** $100   **Subsequent:** $100

Services: IRA, Keogh

Tel Exchange: No

Registered: DE, NJ, NY, PA

DE VEGH MUTUAL
Growth

Wood, Struthers & Winthrop
Mgmt. Corp.
140 Broadway
New York, NY 10005
(800) 221-5672/(212) 902-4135

	Years Ending 3/31					
	1981	**1982**	**1983**	**1984**	**1985**	**1986**
Net Investment Income ($)	1.41	1.36	2.19	.50	.89	.30
Dividends from Net Investment Income ($)	1.15	1.37	1.90	1.44	.74	.27
Net Gains (Losses) on Investments ($)	15.58	(11.55)	11.66	(3.56)	5.08	3.92
Distributions from Net Realized Capital Gains ($)	—	1.32	2.74	6.96	2.32	.64
Net Asset Value End of Year ($)	52.90	40.02	49.23	37.77	40.68	16.87
Ratio of Expenses to Net Assets (%)	.98	1.09	1.12	1.11	1.13	1.22
Portfolio Turnover Rate (%)	17	78	330	77	55	61
Total Assets: End of Year (Millions $)	70.5	55.0	65.0	53.8	53.8	60.9
Annual Rate of Return (%) Years Ending 12/31	(12.1)	10.1	16.1	(6.9)	28.5	8.2

Five-Year Total Return	65.3%	Degree of Diversification	D	Beta	1.03	Bull	E	Bear	D

Objective: Long-term capital appreciation primarily through investment in common stocks of both well-seasoned and new companies. Current income is incidental to objective.

Portfolio: (9/30/86) Common stocks 91%, commercial paper 7%. Largest stock holdings: consumer products & services 38%, basic industries 23%.

Distributions: Income: Jan, May   Capital Gains: May

12b-1: Yes   Amount: .30%

Minimum: Initial: $1,000   Subsequent: $100

Min IRA: Initial: $250   Subsequent: $50

Services: IRA, Keogh, Corp, Withdraw

Tel Exchange: No

Registered: All states except HI

DELAWARE TREASURY RESERVES INVESTORS SERIES
Bond

Delaware Management Company
Ten Penn Center Plaza
Philadelphia, PA 19103
(800) 523-4640/(215) 988-1200

	\multicolumn{6}{c}{Years Ending 12/31}					
	1981	1982	1983	1984	1985 (1 mo.)	1986
Net Investment Income ($)	–	–	–	–	.06	.84
Dividends from Net Investment Income ($)	–	–	–	–	.06	.84
Net Gains (Losses) on Investments ($)	–	–	–	–	.04	.06
Distributions from Net Realized Capital Gains ($)	–	–	–	–	–	–
Net Asset Value End of Year ($)	–	–	–	–	10.04	9.98
Ratio of Expenses to Net Assets (%)	–	–	–	–	–	1.02
Portfolio Turnover Rate (%)	–	–	–	–	–	39
Total Assets: End of Year (Millions $)	–	–	–	–	8.1	182.8
Annual Rate of Return (%) Years Ending 12/31	–	–	–	–	–	7.7

Five-Year Total Return	NA	Degree of Diversification	NA	Beta	NA	Bull NA	Bear NA

Objective: Seeks high stable level of current income while attempting to minimize fluctuations in principal and provide maximum liquidity. Invests in short- and intermediate-term securities guaranteed by the U.S. government. Average maturity of the portfolio is no more than 5 years.

Portfolio: (12/25/86) U.S. Treasury obligations 43%, repos 34%, U.S. government agency obligations 18%, cash, 3%, GNMA 2%.

Distributions: Income: Monthly   **Capital Gains:** Annually

12b-1: Yes   **Amount:** .30%

Minimum: Initial: $1,000   Subsequent: $25

Min IRA: Initial: $50   Subsequent: $25

Services: IRA, Keogh, Corp, SEP, 403(b), Withdraw, Deduct

Tel Exchange: Yes   **With MMF:** Yes

Registered: All states

DIVIDEND/ GROWTH—
Dividend Series
Growth & Income

A.I.M. Management
107 N. Adams St.
Rockville, MD 20850
(800) 638-2042/(301) 251-1002

	Years Ending 12/31					
	1981	1982*	1983	1984	1985	1986
Net Investment Income ($)	1.36	1.54	.88	.88	.86	.66
Dividends from Net Investment Income ($)	–	–	1.15	.87	.85	1.50
Net Gains (Losses) on Investments ($)	.95	.95	2.25	1.64	2.46	1.53
Distributions from Net Realized Capital Gains ($)	–	–	–	–	1.70	1.68
Net Asset Value End of Year ($)	18.91	21.40	23.38	25.03	25.80	24.81
Ratio of Expenses to Net Assets (%)	3.54	3.10	2.43	2.00	2.00	2.00
Portfolio Turnover Rate (%)	43	150	67	56	34	43
Total Assets: End of Year (Millions $)	1.7	2.8	3.7	4.0	4.3	4.4

Fund reorganized in 1982 and name changed.

Annual Rate of Return (%) Years Ending 12/31	13.9	13.2	15.2	11.4	14.1	8.7

Five-Year Total Return	80.1%	Degree of Diversification	C	Beta	.85	Bull	E	Bear	A

Objective: Seeks income growth with secondary emphasis on growth of capital through investment in income-producing, large, well-established companies that are fundamentally sound. May take short positions, may use leverage and may write covered call options. May invest minor portion in new companies or in special situations.

Portfolio: (12/31/86) Common stocks 97%, short-term securities 3%. Largest stock holdings: computers & electronics 97%, electric utilities 11%.

Distributions: Income: Feb   **Capital Gains:** Feb

12b-1: Yes   **Amount:** .25%

Minimum: Initial: $300   Subsequent: $50

Min IRA: Initial: $300   Subsequent: $50

Services: IRA, Keogh, SEP, Withdraw, Deduct

Tel Exchange: Yes   **With MMF:** Yes

Registered: AZ, CA, CO, CT, DC, DE, FL, GA, HI, IL, MA, MD, MI, NJ, NV, NY, PA, TX, VA, WA

DODGE & COX BALANCED
Balanced

Dodge & Cox
One Post St. 35th Flr.
San Francisco, CA 94104
(415) 981-1710

	Years Ending 12/31					
	1981	1982	1983	1984	1985	1986
Net Investment Income ($)	1.60	1.68	1.71	1.72	1.71	1.62
Dividends from Net Investment Income ($)	1.59	1.67	1.72	1.73	1.70	1.62
Net Gains (Losses) on Investments ($)	(2.19)	3.65	2.45	(.57)	6.37	4.24
Distributions from Net Realized Capital Gains ($)	1.01	.50	.31	.83	.37	3.55
Net Asset Value End of Year ($)	22.04	25.20	27.33	25.92	31.93	32.62
Ratio of Expenses to Net Assets (%)	.79	.80	.76	.76	.75	.73
Portfolio Turnover Rate (%)	7	7	10	7	26	14
Total Assets: End of Year (Millions $)	15.2	18.1	19.6	19.1	24.5	27.5

Annual Rate of Return (%) Years Ending 12/31	(2.5)	26.0	17.0	4.7	32.5	19.2

Five-Year Total Return	143.6%	Degree of Diversification	B	Beta .74	Bull B	Bear B

Objective: To provide shareholders with regular income, conservation of principal and an opportunity for long-term growth of principal and income through investment in no more than 75% common stocks of dividend-paying, financially strong companies with sound economic backgrounds. Remaining 25% shall be invested in high-grade bonds and preferred stocks.

Portfolio: (12/31/86) Common stocks 68%, bonds 28%, short-term securities 5%. Largest stock holdings: public utilities 8%, oil 8%.

Distributions: Income: Mar, June, Sept, Dec   **Capital Gains:** Mar

12b-1: No

Minimum: Initial: $250   Subsequent: $50

Min IRA: Initial: $250   Subsequent: $50

Services: IRA, Keogh, Withdraw

Tel Exchange: No

Registered: CA, DC, HI, NV, OR, UT, WY

DODGE & COX STOCK

Growth & Income

Dodge & Cox
One Post St. 35th Flr.
San Francisco, CA 94104
(415) 981-1710

	Years Ending 12/31					
	1981	1982	1983	1984	1985	1986
Net Investment Income ($)	.97	.99	1.02	1.01	1.02	.94
Dividends from Net Investment Income ($)	.98	.99	1.00	1.02	1.01	.94
Net Gains (Losses) on Investments ($)	(1.48)	3.03	4.71	.15	7.72	4.61
Distributions from Net Realized Capital Gains ($)	1.58	.30	.77	1.88	1.23	3.90
Net Asset Value End of Year ($)	19.50	22.23	26.19	24.45	30.95	31.66
Ratio of Expenses to Net Assets (%)	.75	.75	.70	.69	.68	.66
Portfolio Turnover Rate (%)	26	17	17	14	22	10
Total Assets: End of Year (Millions $)	19.0	22.4	27.3	27.8	38.5	45.1
Annual Rate of Return (%) Years Ending 12/31	(2.5)	22.0	26.7	5.1	37.7	18.8

Five-Year Total Return	165.7%	Degree of Diversification	C	Beta	1.04	Bull	A	Bear	C

Objective: Seeks long-term growth of principal and income through investment in dividend-paying, financially strong companies with sound economic background. Must be from variety of industries and be traded readily. A secondary objective is to achieve some current income.

Portfolio: (12/31/86) Common stocks 97%, short-term securities 3%. Largest stock holdings: electronics 12%, office equipment 11%.

Distributions: Income: Mar, June, Sept, Dec   **Capital Gains:** Mar

12b-1: No

Minimum: Initial: $250   Subsequent: $50

Min IRA: Initial: $250   Subsequent: $50

Services: IRA, Keogh, Withdraw

Tel Exchange: No

Registered: CA, DC, HI, NV, OR, UT, WY

DREYFUS A BONDS PLUS
Bond

The Dreyfus Corp.
600 Madison Ave.
New York, NY 10022
(800) 645-6561/(718) 895-1206

	Years Ending 3/31					
	1981	1982	1983	1984	1985	1986
Net Investment Income ($)	1.52	1.62	1.57	1.50	1.50	1.45
Dividends from Net Investment Income ($)	1.54	1.61	1.57	1.52	1.48	1.42
Net Gains (Losses) on Investments ($)	(.54)	(.48)	1.64	(1.03)	.27	2.19
Distributions from Net Realized Capital Gains ($)	—	—	—	—	—	—
Net Asset Value End of Year ($)	12.69	12.22	13.86	12.81	13.10	15.32
Ratio of Expenses to Net Assets (%)	1.03	1.04	.95	.93	.94	.87
Portfolio Turnover Rate (%)	110	—	10	5	21	61
Total Assets: End of Year (Millions $)	13.8	27.2	97.6	105.5	123.3	222.9
Annual Rate of Return (%) Years Ending 12/31	9.0	26.0	7.6	12.4	23.1	13.9

Five-Year Total Return	113.7%	Degree of Diversification	NA	Beta	.23	Bull	D	Bear	A

Objective: Seeks maximization of current income with preservation of liquidity and capital. Invests 80% of assets in debt obligations rated A or better. The other components must be of high quality as well.

Portfolio: (9/30/86) Corporate bonds 97%, cash 2%, short-term securities 1%.

Distributions: Income: Monthly   **Capital Gains:** April

12b-1: No

Minimum: Initial: $2,500   Subsequent: $100

Min IRA: Initial: $750   Subsequent: None

Services: IRA, Keogh, Corp, SEP, 403(b), Withdraw, Deduct

Tel Exchange: Yes   **With MMF:** Yes

Registered: All states

DREYFUS CAPITAL VALUE
Aggressive Growth

The Dreyfus Corp.
600 Madison Avenue
New York, NY 10022
(800) 645-6561/(718) 895-1206

	Years Ending 9/30					
	1981	1982	1983	1984	1985	1986
Net Investment Income ($)	–	–	–	–	–	.08
Dividends from Net Investment Income ($)	–	–	–	–	–	–
Net Gains (Losses) on Investments ($)	–	–	–	–	–	4.50
Distributions from Net Realized Capital Gains ($)	–	–	–	–	–	–
Net Asset Value End of Year ($)	–	–	–	–	–	19.08
Ratio of Expenses to Net Assets (%)	–	–	–	–	–	1.47
Portfolio Turnover Rate (%)	–	–	–	–	–	141
Total Assets: End of Year (Millions $)	–	–	–	–	–	9.4

Annual Rate of Return (%) Years Ending 12/31	–	–	–	–	–	15.6

Five-Year Total Return	NA	Degree of Diversification	NA	Beta	NA	Bull NA	Bear NA

Objective: To maximize capital appreciation. Invests in the common stock of small and medium sized companies, both foreign and domestic. May also invest in the debt securities of foreign governments.

Portfolio: (9/30/86) Common stocks 75%, short-term securities 21%. Largest stock holdings: Consumer disposables 10.5%, conglomerates 9.5%.

Distributions: Income: Annually   Capital Gains: Annually
12b-1: No
Minimum: Initial: $2,500   Subsequent: $100
Min IRA: Initial: $750   Subsequent: None
Services: IRA, Keogh, Corp, SEP, 403(b), Withdraw, Deduct
Tel Exchange: Yes   With MMF: Yes
Registered: All states

DREYFUS CONVERTIBLE SECURITIES
Balanced

The Dreyfus Corp.
600 Madison Ave.
New York, NY 10022
(800) 645-6561/(718) 895-1206

	Years Ending 4/30					
	1981	1982	1983	1984	1985	1986
Net Investment Income ($)	.63	.69	.65	.62	.57	.63
Dividends from Net Investment Income ($)	.62	.70	.67	.63	.60	.56
Net Gains (Losses) on Investments ($)	.54	(.85)	1.44	.13	.26	1.78
Distributions from Net Realized Capital Gains ($)	.15	.29	.08	.04	.28	.24
Net Asset Value End of Year ($)	7.50	6.35	7.69	7.77	7.72	9.33
Ratio of Expenses to Net Assets (%)	.93	.87	.85	.85	.85	.85
Portfolio Turnover Rate (%)	70	6	27	25	32	62
Total Assets: End of Year (Millions $)	74.8	61.3	83.2	92.2	101.1	143.4
Annual Rate of Return (%) Years Ending 12/31	1.0	17.1	21.0	7.6	23.5	23.7

Five-Year Total Return	132.9%	Degree of Diversification	E	Beta	.45	Bull	B	Bear	B

Objective: Seeks to maximize current income. Invests primarily in bonds, debentures and preferred stocks and secondarily in common stocks with high current dividend and appreciation potential. May lend securities from its portfolio and write (sell) covered call options and invest in foreign securities.

Portfolio: (10/31/86) Equity-related securities 48%, short-term securities 28%, bonds 25%. Largest stock holdings: forest products 10%, utilities 6%.

Distributions: **Income:** Monthly   **Capital Gains:** May

12b-1: No

Minimum: **Initial:** $2,500 **Subsequent:** $100

Min IRA: **Initial:** $750 **Subsequent:** None

Services: IRA, Keogh, Corp, 403(b), SEP, Withdraw, Deduct

Tel Exchange: Yes **With MMF:** Yes

Registered: All states

DREYFUS GNMA
Bond

The Dreyfus Corp.
600 Madison Ave.
New York, NY 10022
(800) 645-6561/(718) 895-1206

	Years Ending 4/30					
	1981	1982	1983	1984	1985	1986 (11 mos.)
Net Investment Income ($)	−	−	−	−	−	1.44
Dividends from Net Investment Income ($)	−	−	−	−	−	1.32
Net Gains (Losses) on Investments ($)	−	−	−	−	−	1.19
Distributions from Net Realized Capital Gains ($)	−	−	−	−	−	−
Net Asset Value End of Year ($)	−	−	−	−	−	15.81
Ratio of Expenses to Net Assets (%)	−	−	−	−	−	.96
Portfolio Turnover Rate (%)	−	−	−	−	−	245
Total Assets: End of Year (Millions $)	−	−	−	−	−	1,739.5

Annual Rate of Return (%) Years Ending 12/31	−	−	−	−	−	9.5

Five-Year Total Return	NA	Degree of Diversification	NA	Beta	NA	Bull NA	Bear NA

Objective: Seeks high current income consistent with capital preservation through investing at least 65% of its net assets in GNMAs. May also invest in other U.S. Government-backed debt securities.

Portfolio: (10/31/86) GNMAs 104%, U.S. Treasury bonds 3%, U.S. Treasury notes 8%.

Distributions: **Income:** Monthly   **Capital Gains:** Annually

12b-1: Yes   **Amount:** .20%

Minimum: **Initial:** $2,500   **Subsequent:** $100

Min IRA: **Initial:** $750   **Subsequent:** None

Services: IRA, Keogh, SEP, Corp, 403(b), Withdraw, Deduct

Tel Exchange: Yes   **With MMF:** Yes

Registered: All states

DREYFUS GROWTH OPPORTUNITY
Growth

The Dreyfus Corp.
600 Madison Ave.
New York, NY 10022
(800) 645-6561/(718) 895-1206

	Years Ending 2/28					
	1981	1982	1983	1984	1985	1986
Net Investment Income ($)	.15	.33	.22	.17	.16	.23
Dividends from Net Investment Income ($)	.18	.14	.29	.25	.18	.21
Net Gains (Losses) on Investments ($)	2.23	(2.98)	2.47	1.07	(.45)	2.64
Distributions from Net Realized Capital Gains ($)	.59	.60	.81	.34	.88	.34
Net Asset Value End of Year ($)	12.39	9.00	10.59	11.24	9.89	12.21
Ratio of Expenses to Net Assets (%)	1.09	1.08	1.06	.99	1.02	.98
Portfolio Turnover Rate (%)	29	35	68	60	44	56
Total Assets: End of Year (Millions $)	114.1	110.4	251.5	369.7	441.9	478.0

Annual Rate of Return (%) Years Ending 12/31	(15.1)	3.6	31.5	(12.1)	30.7	15.0

Five-Year Total Return	79.7%	Degree of Diversification	E	Beta .81	Bull C	Bear E

Objective: Primarily aims to promote growth of capital through investment in established companies up to 25% of which may be foreign. Income is secondary but in periods of market weakness the fund will emphasize investment in money market and other high-yielding securities.

Portfolio: (8/31/86) Common stocks 94%, short-term securities 5%, cash 1%. Largest stock holdings: drugs and health care 10%, forest and paper products 10%.

Distributions: Income: April   **Capital Gains:** April

12b-1: No

Minimum: Initial: $2,500   Subsequent: $100

Min IRA: Initial: $750   Subsequent: none

Services: IRA, Keogh, Corp, 403(b), Withdraw, Deduct, SEP

Tel Exchange: Yes   **With MMF:** Yes

Registered: All states

DREYFUS NEW LEADERS

Aggressive Growth

The Dreyfus Corp.
600 Madison Avenue
New York, NY 10153
(800) 645-6561/(516) 794-5210

	Years Ending 12/31					
	1981	1982	1983	1984	1985 (11 mos.)	1986
Net Investment Income ($)	—	—	—	—	.20	.15
Dividends from Net Investment Income ($)	—	—	—	—	—	.01
Net Gains (Losses) on Investments ($)	—	—	—	—	4.41	2.12
Distributions from Net Realized Capital Gains ($)	—	—	—	—	—	.01
Net Asset Value End of Year ($)	—	—	—	—	18.11	20.36
Ratio of Expenses to Net Assets (%)	—	—	—	—	1.46	1.30
Portfolio Turnover Rate (%)	—	—	—	—	81	195
Total Assets: End of Year (Millions $)	—	—	—	—	5.1	65.1

Annual Rate of Return (%) Years Ending 12/31	—	—	—	—	—	12.6

Five-Year Total Return	NA	Degree of Diversification	NA	Beta	NA	Bull NA	Bear NA

Objective: The fund's goal is to maximize capital appreciation. Invests in small emerging growth stocks of both foreign and domestic issues. May invest up to 25% of assets in foreign stocks. May also buy and sell put and call options.

Portfolio: (12/31/86) Common stocks 79%, short-term securities 22%. Largest stock holdings: consumer goods and services 17%, technology 11%.

Distributions: **Income:** Annually   **Capital Gains:** Annually

12b-1: No

Minimum: Initial: $2,500   Subsequent: $100

Min IRA: Initial: $750   Subsequent: None

Services: IRA, Keogh, Corp, SEP, 403(b), Withdraw, Deduct

Tel Exchange: Yes   **With MMF:** Yes

Registered: All states

DREYFUS THIRD CENTURY
Growth & Income

The Dreyfus Corp.
600 Madison Ave.
New York, NY 10022
(800) 645-6561/(718) 895-1206

	Years Ending 5/31					
	1981	1982	1983	1984	1985	1986
Net Investment Income ($)	.22	.33	.25	.20	.19	.30
Dividends from Net Investment Income ($)	.16	.21	.32	.26	.20	.21
Net Gains (Losses) on Investments ($)	2.25	(2.24)	2.05	(.83)	1.54	1.13
Distributions from Net Realized Capital Gains ($)	.68	.48	.45	.55	.53	.51
Net Asset Value End of Year ($)	8.93	6.33	7.86	6.42	7.42	8.13
Ratio of Expenses to Net Assets (%)	1.06	1.10	1.01	1.03	1.01	.97
Portfolio Turnover Rate (%)	16	19	63	26	45	63
Total Assets: End of Year (Millions $)	119.3	91.8	151.5	114.4	174.3	176.7
Annual Rate of Return (%) Years Ending 12/31	(10.8)	4.8	20.2	1.6	29.5	4.6

Five-Year Total Return	73.3%	Degree of Diversification	C	Beta	.83	Bull	C	Bear	E

Objective: Seeks capital growth through investment in the common stocks of companies which meet traditional investment standards and show evidence of contributing to the enhancement of the quality of life in the U.S. in four areas: protection and proper use of natural resources, occupational health and safety, consumer protection and equal employment opportunity.

Portfolio: (5/31/86) Common stocks 73%, short-term securities 25%, cash 1%. Largest stock holdings: paper/forest products 13%, petroleum producers and marketers 9%.

Distributions: Income: July   **Capital Gains:** July

12b-1: No

Minimum: Initial: $2,500   Subsequent: $100

Min IRA: Initial: $750   Subsequent: None

Services: IRA, Keogh, Corp, 403(b), SEP, Withdraw, Deduct

Tel Exchange: Yes   **With MMF:** Yes

Registered: All states

ENERGY
Growth & Income

Neuberger & Berman Mgmt.
342 Madison Ave.
New York, NY 10173
(800) 367-0770/(212) 850-8300

	Years Ending 9/30					
	1981	1982	1983	1984	1985	1986
Net Investment Income ($)	1.13	1.08	.97	.87	.89	.83
Dividends from Net Investment Income ($)	1.12	1.00	1.01	.86	.92	.88
Net Gains (Losses) on Investments ($)	(2.26)	(1.62)	4.31	.08	.95	2.21
Distributions from Net Realized Capital Gains ($)	2.11	.51	.79	.66	.93	1.66
Net Asset Value End of Year ($)	16.61	14.56	18.04	17.47	17.46	17.96
Ratio of Expenses to Net Assets (%)	.82	.88	.83	.88	.89	.88
Portfolio Turnover Rate (%)	37	18	32	22	18	28
Total Assets: End of Year (Millions $)	276.5	300.2	334.6	337.9	333.9	376.5
Annual Rate of Return (%) Years Ending 12/31	(10.2)	1.0	22.1	4.8	22.6	10.1

Five-Year Total Return	74.5%	Degree of Diversification	D	Beta	.72	Bull	C	Bear	D

Objective: Seeks long-term capital growth by investing in companies whose activities are related to the field of energy—two-thirds directly related and remainder indirectly related. Familiar energy sources as well as newer sources and transformed energy are all possibilities. Up to 20% of portfolio may be unrelated to energy. May invest in foreign securities, write covered call options and loan its securities.

Portfolio: (9/30/86) Common stocks 77%, U.S. government obligations 15%, short-term corporate notes 4%, repos 4%. Largest stock holdings: oil 28%, gas 7%.

Distributions: Income: Sept   **Capital Gains:** Sept

12b-1: No

Minimum: Initial: $500   Subsequent: $50

Min IRA: Initial: $250   Subsequent: $50

Services: IRA, Keogh, Withdraw, Deduct

Tel Exchange: Yes   **With MMF:** Yes

Registered: All states except NH

EVERGREEN
Aggressive Growth

Saxon Woods Asset Management
550 Mamaroneck Ave.
Harrison, NY 10528
(800) 235-0064/(914) 698-5711/
(800) 262-4471

	Years Ending 9/30					
	1981	1982	1983	1984	1985	1986
Net Investment Income ($)	.14	.20	.17	.15	.16	.14
Dividends from Net Investment Income ($)	.08	.15	.19	.17	.16	.14
Net Gains (Losses) on Investments ($)	(.01)	.49	4.23	(.51)	1.66	3.18
Distributions from Net Realized Capital Gains ($)	.69	1.08	.05	1.20	.41	.66
Net Asset Value End of Year ($)	7.89	7.35	11.51	9.78	11.03	13.55
Ratio of Expenses to Net Assets (%)	1.25	1.13	1.11	1.10	1.08	1.04
Portfolio Turnover Rate (%)	123	86	78	53	59	48
Total Assets: End of Year (Millions $)	87.0	112.6	210.4	240.0	334.2	638.6
Annual Rate of Return (%) Years Ending 12/31	(1.0)	20.3	29.1	0.6	34.6	12.9

Five-Year Total Return	137.3%	Degree of Diversification	B	Beta	.87	Bull	A	Bear	D

Objective:	Achieve capital appreciation by investing principally in securities of little-known companies, relatively small companies and companies undergoing changes that are believed favorable.
Portfolio:	(9/30/86) Common stocks 97%, short-term corporate notes 2%, other assets 2%. Largest stock holdings: banks 23%, thrift institutions 14%.
Distributions:	**Income:** Annually **Capital Gains:** Annually
12b-1:	No
Minimum:	**Initial:** $2,000 **Subsequent:** None
Min IRA:	**Initial:** None **Subsequent:** None
Services:	IRA, Keogh, SEP, Withdraw
Tel Exchange:	Yes **With MMF:** No
Registered:	All states

EVERGREEN TOTAL RETURN
Balanced

Saxon Woods Asset Mgmt.
550 Mamaroneck Ave.
Harrison, NY 10528
(800) 235-0064/(914) 698-5711

	Years Ending 3/31					
	1981	**1982**	**1983**	**1984**	**1985**	**1986**
Net Investment Income ($)	.68	.74	.83	.90	.87	1.03
Dividends from Net Investment Income ($)	.62	.76	.79	.86	.96	1.22
Net Gains (Losses) on Investments ($)	3.56	(.83)	3.99	1.12	2.83	4.26
Distributions from Net Realized Capital Gains ($)	.51	.99	.81	.73	1.32	.98
Net Asset Value End of Year ($)	13.40	11.56	14.78	15.21	16.63	19.72
Ratio of Expenses to Net Assets (%)	1.26	1.37	1.29	1.09	1.31	1.11
Portfolio Turnover Rate (%)	92	100	113	67	82	65
Total Assets: End of Year (Millions $)	16.1	17.1	32.9	47.4	83.7	408.4
Annual Rate of Return (%) Years Ending 12/31	8.9	25.5	30.3	14.4	31.5	20.3

Five-Year Total Return **195.8%**	Degree of Diversification **C**	Beta **.59**	Bull **A**	Bear **B**

Objective: The fund invests primarily in common and preferred stocks and fixed-income securities that are established and income-producing, with the objective of obtaining current income and capital appreciation. May write covered call options. Portfolio usually 75% in equity securities and 25% in debt securities.

Portfolio: (9/30/86) Common stocks 66%, convertible debentures 16%, short-term notes 10%, convertible preferred stocks 8%. Largest stock holdings: electric utilities 24%, telephone utilities 13%.

Distributions: Income: Jan, April, July, Oct   **Capital Gains:** April
12b-1: No
Minimum: Initial: $2,000   Subsequent: $250
Min IRA: Initial: $2,000   Subsequent: $250
Services: IRA, Keogh, SEP
Tel Exchange: No
Registered: All states except NH

THE FAIRMONT
Aggressive Growth

Morton H. Sachs & Co.
1346 S. Third St.
Louisville, KY 40208
(502) 636-5633

	1981	1982 (6 mos.)	1983	1984	1985	1986
			Years Ending 2/28			
Net Investment Income ($)	–	.90	1.13	.94	.60	.62
Dividends from Net Investment Income ($)	–	–	1.13	.94	.60	.62
Net Gains (Losses) on Investments ($)	–	.67	13.64	6.90	8.78	16.00
Distributions from Net Realized Capital Gains ($)	–	–	3.82	1.93	3.28	7.43
Net Asset Value End of Year ($)	–	24.77	34.59	39.56	45.06	53.64
Ratio of Expenses to Net Assets (%)	–	1.88	1.99	2.15	2.05	1.48
Portfolio Turnover Rate (%)	–	0	1	1	1	1
Total Assets: End of Year (Millions $)	–	1.5	5.7	14.7	24.5	60.7
Annual Rate of Return (%) Years Ending 12/31	–	35.0	35.9	10.8	32.1	14.0

Five-Year Total Return 206.1%	Degree of Diversification C	Beta .91	Bull A	Bear NA

Objective: Seeks capital appreciation through investment in common stocks chosen on the basis of economic projections, technical analysis and earnings projections. Market timing is also used. May invest in foreign securities and enter into repos. May convert to cash or U.S. government securities for defensive purposes.

Portfolio: (8/31/86) Common stocks 97%, repos 3%. Largest stock holdings: electronic 17%, retail 13%.

Distributions: Income: Feb, Aug   Capital Gains: Feb

12b-1: No

Minimum: Initial: $5,000   Subsequent: $1,000

Min IRA: Initial: $5,000   Subsequent: $1,000

Services: IRA, Keogh, Corp, 403(b)

Tel Exchange: No

Registered: AL, CA, CO, DC, FL, GA, HI, IL, IN, KY, MA, MD, MI, MN, MO, MS, NC, NJ, NM, NY, OH, OR, PA, SC, TX, UT, VA, WA, WI, WV, WY

FARM BUREAU GROWTH

Growth

PFS Mgmt. Services, Inc.
5400 University Ave.
West Des Moines, IA 50265
(800) 247-4170/(515) 225-5524

	Years Ending 7/31					
	1981	1982	1983	1984	1985	1986
Net Investment Income ($)	.87	.90	.66	.42	.36	.35
Dividends from Net Investment Income ($)	.76	.90	.91	.65	.43	.40
Net Gains (Losses) on Investments ($)	1.29	(2.22)	3.71	(2.00)	3.05	1.36
Distributions from Net Realized Capital Gains ($)	.08	.34	.02	1.23	.15	.85
Net Asset Value End of Year ($)	14.85	12.29	15.73	12.27	15.10	15.56
Ratio of Expenses to Net Assets (%)	.84	.81	.77	.94	1.01	.99
Portfolio Turnover Rate (%)	15	1	29	18	22	30
Total Assets: End of Year (Millions $)	38.8	34.3	46.6	40.5	43.9	42.9
Annual Rate of Return (%) Years Ending 12/31	3.1	11.3	13.4	(4.2)	25.5	9.5

Five-Year Total Return	66.2%	Degree of Diversification	A	Beta	1.06	Bull	E	Bear	C

Objective: Seeks capital appreciation with current income as a secondary objective. The fund invests in common stocks which appear to possess above-average growth potential because of established records or promising new products or processes. Cyclical industry companies' stock may be bought. May take defensive posture in debt securities. May engage in repos.

Portfolio: (7/31/86) Common stocks 93%, short-term securities 7%. Largest stock holdings: automotive and related 13%, drugs and hospital supplies 10%.

Distributions: Income: Aug — Capital Gains: Aug
12b-1: Yes — Amount: .25%
Minimum: Initial: $100 — Subsequent: None
Min IRA: Initial: None — Subsequent: None
Services: IRA, Keogh, Corp, 403(b) Withdraw
Tel Exchange: Yes — With MMF: Yes
Registered: All states

FIDELITY
CONTRAFUND
Growth

Fidelity Investments Co.
82 Devonshire St.
Boston, MA 02109
(800) 544-6666/(617) 523-1919

	Years Ending 12/31					
	1981	**1982**	**1983**	**1984**	**1985**	**1986**
Net Investment Income ($)	.63	.55	.45	.27	.43	.05
Dividends from Net Investment Income ($)	.63	.50	.45	.29	.25	.25
Net Gains (Losses) on Investments ($)	(.27)	1.07	2.05	(1.25)	2.21	1.48
Distributions from Net Realized Capital Gains ($)	2.29	1.23	.38	1.69	–	2.15
Net Asset Value End of Year ($)	11.17	11.06	12.73	9.77	12.16	11.29
Ratio of Expenses to Net Assets (%)	.92	1.01	.96	.99	.95	.88
Portfolio Turnover Rate (%)	253	220	452	234	135	190
Total Assets: End of Year (Millions $)	62.7	72.7	86.2	80.8	86.7	84.0
Annual Rate of Return (%) Years Ending 12/31	3.1	16.6	23.2	(8.3)	27.0	12.8

Five-Year Total Return	88.7%	Degree of Diversification	B	Beta 1.06	Bull C	Bear D

Objective: Seeks capital growth through investment in securities believed to be undervalued due to an overly pessimistic appraisal by the public. Income received from investments is incidental to the objective.

Portfolio: (12/31/86) Common stock 97%, convertible preferred stocks 1%, corporate bonds 1%. Largest stock holdings: electric and utilities 15%, transportation 8%.

Distributions: Income: Dec   **Capital Gains:** Feb

12b-1: Yes   **Amount:** Pd. by Advisor

Minimum: Initial: $1,000   **Subsequent:** $250

Min IRA: Initial: $500   **Subsequent:** $250

Services: IRA, Keogh, Corp, 403(b), Withdraw, Deduct

Tel Exchange: Yes   **With MMF:** Yes

Registered: All states

FIDELITY FLEXIBLE BOND
Bond

Fidelity Investments Co.
82 Devonshire St.
Boston, MA 02109
(800) 544-6666/(617) 523-1919

	Years Ending 4/30					
	1981	1982	1983	1984	1985	1986
Net Investment Income ($)	.83	.86	.80	.76	.79	.74
Dividends from Net Investment Income ($)	.83	.86	.80	.76	.79	.74
Net Gains (Losses) on Investments ($)	(1.08)	.05	1.07	(.95)	.26	.86
Distributions from Net Realized Capital Gains ($)	—	—	—	—	—	—
Net Asset Value End of Year ($)	6.17	6.22	7.29	6.34	6.60	7.46
Ratio of Expenses to Net Assets (%)	.75	.81	.81	.77	.79	.67
Portfolio Turnover Rate (%)	141	204	378	164	164	243
Total Assets: End of Year (Millions $)	86.7	112.7	169.2	134.6	166.5	250.5
Annual Rate of Return (%) Years Ending 12/31	3.9	30.1	6.6	11.8	21.1	13.5

Five-Year Total Return 113.1%	Degree of Diversification NA	Beta .20	Bull D	Bear A

Objective: Seeks current income and security of shareholders' capital. At least 80% of assets are in investment grade (BBB or higher) debt securities.

Portfolio: (10/31/86) Corporate obligations 52%, U.S. government obligations 34%, foreign obligations 9%, repos 5%.

Distributions: **Income:** Monthly   **Capital Gains:** April

12b-1: Yes   **Amount:** Pd. by Advisor

Minimum: **Initial:** $2,500   **Subsequent:** $250

Min IRA: **Initial:** $500   **Subsequent:** $250

Services: IRA, Keogh, 403(b), Corp, Withdraw, Deduct

Tel Exchange: Yes   **With MMF:** Yes

Registered: All states

FIDELITY FREEDOM
Aggressive Growth

Fidelity Investments Co.
82 Devonshire St.
Boston, MA 02109
(800) 544-6666/(617) 523-1919

	Years Ending 11/30					
	1981	1982	1983 (8 mos.)	1984	1985	1986
Net Investment Income ($)	–	–	.07	.24	.37	.16
Dividends from Net Investment Income ($)	–	–	–	.04	.24	.35
Net Gains (Losses) on Investments ($)	–	–	2.61	(.31)	2.75	3.22
Distributions from Net Realized Capital Gains ($)	–	–	–	.42	.15	.98
Net Asset Value End of Year ($)	–	–	12.68	12.15	14.88	16.93
Ratio of Expenses to Net Assets (%)	–	–	1.26	1.13	1.14	1.07
Portfolio Turnover Rate (%)	–	–	116	97	100	161
Total Assets: End of Year (Millions $)	–	–	141.3	388.3	600.5	916.0
Annual Rate of Return (%) Years Ending 12/31	–	–	–	3.4	28.5	13.7

Five-Year Total Return	NA	Degree of Diversification	A	Beta 1.10	Bull NA	Bear NA

Objective: Seeks long- and short-term capital gains by investing in common stocks of well-known and established companies as well as small companies. Best suited to retirement plans where the tax status of distributions is immaterial.

Portfolio: (11/30/86) Common stocks 93%, short-term obligations 6%, corporate bonds 1%. Largest stock holdings: insurance 9%, petroleum and gas 8%.

Distributions: Income: Jan   **Capital Gains:** Jan
12b-1: Yes   **Amount:** Pd. by Advisor
Minimum: Initial: $500   **Subsequent:** $250
Min IRA: Initial: $500   **Subsequent:** $250
Services: IRA, Keogh, Corp, 403(b), Deduct, Withdraw
Tel Exchange: Yes   **With MMF:** Yes
Registered: All states

FIDELITY FUND
Growth & Income

Fidelity Investments Co.
82 Devonshire St.
Boston, MA 02109
(800) 544-6666/(617) 523-1919

	Years Ending 12/31					
	1981	1982	1983	1984	1985	1986
Net Investment Income ($)	.93	.89	.84	.74	.70	.63
Dividends from Net Investment Income ($)	.85	.89	.84	.71	.72	.66
Net Gains (Losses) on Investments ($)	(1.65)	3.89	2.96	(.70)	3.33	2.08
Distributions from Net Realized Capital Gains ($)	1.39	3.00	1.97	4.40	.05	4.08
Net Asset Value End of Year ($)	18.01	18.90	19.89	14.82	18.08	16.05
Ratio of Expenses to Net Assets (%)	.74	.73	.71	.66	.66	.60
Portfolio Turnover Rate (%)	103	165	210	200	215	214
Total Assets: End of Year (Millions $)	490.2	588.2	668.9	617.6	761.5	780.7
Annual Rate of Return (%) Years Ending 12/31	(3.3)	33.3	22.4	1.4	28.0	15.4

Five-Year Total Return	144.6%	Degree of Diversification	A	Beta	.95	Bull	B	Bear	B

Objective: Seeks long-term capital growth. In order to provide a reasonable current return, invests in securities selected for their current income characteristics. Companies are well-established and dividend-paying from variety of industries that show potential for stability and reliability of earnings.

Portfolio: (12/31/86) Common stocks 75%, corporate bonds 10%, short-term obligations 7%, convertible preferred stocks 6%, U.S. government obligations 3%. Largest stock holdings: electric and utilities 9%, chemicals and plastics 7%.

Distributions: Income: Mar, June, Sept, Dec   **Capital Gains:** Jan
12b-1: Yes   **Amount:** Pd. by Advisor
Minimum: Initial: $1,000   Subsequent: $250
Min IRA: Initial: $500   Subsequent: $250
Services: IRA, Keogh, Corp, 403(b), Withdraw, Deduct
Tel Exchange: Yes   **With MMF:** Yes
Registered: All states

FIDELITY GINNIE MAE
Bond

Fidelity Investments
82 Devonshire St.
Boston, MA 02109
(800) 544-6666/(617) 523-1919

	Years Ending 7/31					
	1981	**1982**	**1983**	**1984**	**1985**	**1986** (9 mos.)
Net Investment Income ($)	–	–	–	–	–	.72
Dividends from Net Investment Income ($)	–	–	–	–	–	.72
Net Gains (Losses) on Investments ($)	–	–	–	–	–	.58
Distributions from Net Realized Capital Gains ($)	–	–	–	–	–	–
Net Asset Value End of Year ($)	–	–	–	–	–	10.58
Ratio of Expenses to Net Assets (%)	–	–	–	–	–	.75
Portfolio Turnover Rate (%)	–	–	–	–	–	106
Total Assets: End of Year (Millions $)	–	–	–	–	–	652.9

Annual Rate of Return (%) Years Ending 12/31	–	–	–	–	–	13.0

Five-Year Total Return	NA	Degree of Diversification	NA	Beta	NA	Bull NA	Bear NA

Objective: Seeks high level of current income through investment primarily in GNMAs and other debt securities guaranteed by the U.S. government. May hedge the portfolio with futures contracts and put options.

Portfolio: (7/31/86) GNMAs 63%, U.S. Treasury notes 37%, short-term securities 16%.

Distributions: **Income:** Monthly   **Capital Gains:** Annually

12b-1: Yes   **Amount:** Pd. by Advisor

Minimum: **Initial:** $1,000   **Subsequent:** $250

Min IRA: **Initial:** $500   **Subsequent:** $250

Services: IRA, Keogh, 403(b), Withdraw, Deduct

Tel Exchange: Yes   **With MMF:** Yes

Registered: All states

FIDELITY GOVERNMENT SECURITIES
Bond

Fidelity Investments Co.
82 Devonshire St.
Boston, MA 02109
(800) 544-6666/(617) 523-1919

	Years Ending 12/31					
	1981	**1982**	**1983**	**1984**	**1985**	**1986**
Net Investment Income ($)	1.17	1.14	.94	1.01	.98	.90
Dividends from Net Investment Income ($)	1.17	1.14	.94	1.01	.98	.90
Net Gains (Losses) on Investments ($)	(.29)	1.03	(.38)	(.04)	.56	.48
Distributions from Net Realized Capital Gains ($)	–	–	.28	–	–	–
Net Asset Value End of Year ($)	8.91	9.94	9.28	9.24	9.80	10.28
Ratio of Expenses to Net Assets (%)	1.05	.91	.88	.85	.81	.84
Portfolio Turnover Rate (%)	NA	NA	NA	NA	137	138
Total Assets: End of Year (Millions $)	65.0	89.2	85.6	89.2	269.6	751.7

Annual Rate of Return (%) Years Ending 12/31	10.2	26.2	6.0	11.3	17.6	14.7

Five-Year Total Return 100.9%	Degree of Diversification NA	Beta .19	Bull E	Bear A

Objective: Seeks income from investment in U.S. government obligations. Income is exempt from state and local income taxes in all states.

Portfolio: (12/31/86) U.S. government and agency obligations 100%.

Distributions: **Income:** Monthly   **Capital Gains:** Dec
12b-1: Yes   **Amount:** Pd. by Advisor
Minimum: **Initial:** $1,000   **Subsequent:** $250
Min IRA: **Initial:** $500   **Subsequent:** $250
Services: IRA, Keogh, Corp, Withdraw, Deduct
Tel Exchange: Yes   **With MMF:** Yes
Registered: All states

FIDELITY HIGH INCOME
Bond

Fidelity Investments Co.
82 Devonshire St.
Boston, MA 02109
(800) 544-6666/(617) 523-1919

	Years Ending 11/30					
	1981	1982	1983	1984	1985	1986
Net Investment Income ($)	1.16	1.15	1.10	1.16	1.15	1.10
Dividends from Net Investment Income ($)	1.16	1.15	1.10	1.16	1.15	1.10
Net Gains (Losses) on Investments ($)	(.58)	.78	.59	(.33)	.56	.83
Distributions from Net Realized Capital Gains ($)	—	—	—	—	—	.13
Net Asset Value End of Year ($)	7.64	8.42	9.01	8.68	9.24	9.94
Ratio of Expenses to Net Assets (%)	.89	.83	.87	.85	.83	.80
Portfolio Turnover Rate (%)	87	90	129	71	157	104
Total Assets: End of Year (Millions $)	123.0	177.2	261.1	395.9	782.9	1,645.7
Annual Rate of Return (%) Years Ending 12/31	6.9	35.7	18.5	10.5	25.5	18.0

Five-Year Total Return	163.2%	Degree of Diversification	NA	Beta	.29	Bull	B	Bear	A

Objective: High current income through investments in high-yielding, fixed-income corporate securities that are rated Baa (BBB) or lower and securities unrated by rating services and further screened for future potential financial strength of the issuing company.

Portfolio: (11/30/86) Corporate bonds 92%, U.S. government obligations 7%, short-term obligations 2%.

Distributions: Income: Monthly   **Capital Gains:** Annually

12b-1: Yes   **Amount:** Pd. by Advisor

Minimum: Initial: $2,500   **Subsequent:** $250

Min IRA: Initial: $500   **Subsequent:** $250

Services: IRA, Keogh, Corp, 403(b), Withdraw, Deduct

Tel Exchange: Yes   **With MMF:** Yes

Registered: All states

FIDELITY MORTGAGE SECURITIES
Bond

Fidelity Investments
82 Devonshire St.
Boston, MA 02109
(800) 544-6666/(617) 523-1919

	Years Ending 7/31					
	1981	**1982**	**1983**	**1984**	**1985** (7 mos.)	**1986**
Net Investment Income ($)	–	–	–	–	.70	1.06
Dividends from Net Investment Income ($)	–	–	–	–	.70	1.06
Net Gains (Losses) on Investments ($)	–	–	–	–	.29	.39
Distributions from Net Realized Capital Gains ($)	–	–	–	–	–	–
Net Asset Value End of Year ($)	–	–	–	–	10.10	10.49
Ratio of Expenses to Net Assets (%)	–	–	–	–	.75	.75
Portfolio Turnover Rate (%)	–	–	–	–	72	59
Total Assets: End of Year (Millions $)	–	–	–	–	140.6	642.3

Annual Rate of Return (%) Years Ending 12/31	–	–	–	–	19.6	11.5

Five-Year Total Return	NA	Degree of Diversification	NA	Beta	NA	Bull NA	Bear NA

Objective: Seeks high current income through investment in mortgage-related securities such as GNMAs, FNMAs, FHLMCs and CMOs comprising 65% of the portfolio. Other 35% can be long- or short-term debt.

Portfolio: (7/31/86) Mortgage-related securities 65%, Federal Farm Credit Bank 13%, U.S. Treasury notes 11%, short-term securities 11%.

Distributions: **Income:** Monthly   **Capital Gains:** Annually

12b-1: Yes   **Amount:** Pd. by Advisor

Minimum: **Initial:** $1,000   **Subsequent:** $250

Min IRA: **Initial:** $500   **Subsequent:** $250

Services: IRA, Keogh, 403(b), Withdraw, Deduct

Tel Exchange: Yes   **With MMF:** Yes

Registered: All states

FIDELITY PURITAN
Balanced

Fidelity Investments Co.
82 Devonshire St.
Boston, MA 02109
(800) 544-6666/(617) 523-1919

	Years Ending 7/31					
	1981	1982	1983	1984	1985	1986
Net Investment Income ($)	.94	.99	.98	.96	.99	.97
Dividends from Net Investment Income ($)	.89	.97	1.00	.97	.97	.92
Net Gains (Losses) on Investments ($)	.60	(.83)	3.68	(.59)	2.82	1.46
Distributions from Net Realized Capital Gains ($)	.44	1.07	.31	1.37	.82	1.16
Net Asset Value End of Year ($)	11.43	9.55	12.90	10.93	12.95	13.30
Ratio of Expenses to Net Assets (%)	.67	.65	.63	.60	.61	.63
Portfolio Turnover Rate (%)	66	70	90	74	133	85
Total Assets: End of Year (Millions $)	663.9	577.6	801.4	772.3	1,082.8	2,205.8
Annual Rate of Return (%) Years Ending 12/31	11.2	28.6	25.7	10.5	28.5	20.8

Five-Year Total Return 177.4%	Degree of Diversification C	Beta .53	Bull A	Bear B

Objective: Seeks to maximize income by investing in a broadly diversified portfolio of high-yielding securities, including common stocks, preferred stocks and bonds. Up to one-third of the value of its assets is the basis on which its securities may be loaned. May engage in repurchase agreements.

Portfolio: (7/31/86) Corporate bonds 35%, common stocks 33%, short-term obligations 12%, preferred stocks 7%, foreign government obligations 6%, municipal bonds 3%, foreign bonds 2%, units 2%, U.S. government obligations 1%. Largest stock holdings: intermediate goods/services 9%, utilities 8%.

Distributions: Income: Jan, April, Aug, Oct   **Capital Gains:** Sept

12b-1: Yes   **Amount:** Pd. by Advisor

Minimum: Initial: $1,000   **Subsequent:** $250

Min IRA: Initial: $500   **Subsequent:** $250

Services: IRA, Keogh, Corp, 403(b), SEP, Withdraw, Deduct

Tel Exchange: Yes   **With MMF:** Yes

Registered: All states

FIDELITY THRIFT
Bond

Fidelity Investments Co.
82 Devonshire St.
Boston, MA 02109
(800) 544-6666/(617) 523-1919

	Years Ending 12/31					
	1981	1982	1983	1984	1985	1986
Net Investment Income ($)	1.27	1.21	1.03	1.10	1.08	.92
Dividends from Net Investment Income ($)	1.27	1.21	1.03	1.10	.74	.66
Net Gains (Losses) on Investments ($)	(.22)	.82	(.14)	.11	.84	.50
Distributions from Net Realized Capital Gains ($)	—	—	—	—	—	.22
Net Asset Value End of Year ($)	9.04	9.86	9.72	9.83	11.01	11.55
Ratio of Expenses to Net Assets (%)	.78	.70	.69	.73	.79	.75
Portfolio Turnover Rate (%)	148	180	238	80	68	101
Total Assets: End of Year (Millions $)	57.5	88.0	114.2	151.7	244.1	367.9

Annual Rate of Return (%) Years Ending 12/31	12.4	24.1	9.4	13.5	20.9	13.1

Five-Year Total Return	110.8%	Degree of Diversification	NA	Beta	.19	Bull	D	Bear	A

Objective: Seeks current income through investment in corporate bonds rated A or better, government securities and money market instruments. Average maturity less than 10 years.

Portfolio: (12/31/86) U.S. government agency and government obligations 49%, corporate bonds 34%, repos 9%, dollar-denominated foreign obligations 8%.

Distributions: Income: Jan   **Capital Gains:** Jan
12b-1: No
Minimum: Initial: $1,000   Subsequent: $250
Min IRA: Initial: $500   Subsequent: $250
Services: IRA, Keogh, Corp, 403(b), Withdraw, Deduct
Tel Exchange: Yes   **With MMF:** Yes
Registered: All states

FIDELITY TREND
Growth

Fidelity Investments Co.
82 Devonshire St.
Boston, MA 02109
(800) 544-6666/(617) 523-1919

	Years Ending 12/31					
	1981	**1982**	**1983**	**1984**	**1985**	**1986**
Net Investment Income ($)	.99	1.19	.96	1.04	.98	.96
Dividends from Net Investment Income ($)	.77	.79	.78	.83	.79	.61
Net Gains (Losses) on Investments ($)	(2.70)	2.76	7.31	(1.91)	9.22	5.10
Distributions from Net Realized Capital Gains ($)	—	1.49	—	—	1.25	10.64
Net Asset Value End of Year ($)	29.40	31.07	38.56	36.86	45.02	39.83
Ratio of Expenses to Net Assets (%)	.87	.78	.66	.56	.52	.52
Portfolio Turnover Rate (%)	110	129	71	57	62	71
Total Assets: End of Year (Millions $)	537.1	553.6	637.6	602.4	712.7	669.1

Annual Rate of Return (%) Years Ending 12/31	(5.2)	19.0	25.2	(2.2)	28.2	13.5

Five-Year Total Return	112.0%	Degree of Diversification	A	Beta 1.14	Bull B	Bear D

Objective: Seeks growth of capital through investment in securities of both well-established companies and smaller firms. Decisions based on studies of momentum in trends of earnings and security prices of individual companies, industries and the market. May loan its portfolio securities, use leverage and engage in repos. Income return is incidental to the objective of capital growth.

Portfolio: (12/31/86) Common stocks 97%, short-term obligations 3%. Largest stock holdings: industrial machinery & equipment 14%, chemicals & plastics 9%.

Distributions:	**Income:** Jan	**Capital Gains:** Feb
12b-1:	Yes	**Amount:** Pd. by Advisor
Minimum:	**Initial:** $1,000	**Subsequent:** $250
Min IRA:	**Initial:** $500	**Subsequent:** $250
Services:	IRA, Keogh, Corp, 403(b), Withdraw, Deduct	
Tel Exchange:	Yes	**With MMF:** Yes
Registered:	All states	

FIDELITY VALUE
Growth

Fidelity Investments Co.
82 Devonshire St.
Boston, MA 02109
(800) 544-6666/(617) 523-1919

	Years Ending 10/31					
	1981	**1982**	**1983**	**1984**	**1985**	**1986**
Net Investment Income ($)	1.06	.72	.75	.94	.69	.59
Dividends from Net Investment Income ($)	.09	.19	—	.27	.49	.42
Net Gains (Losses) on Investments ($)	.20	2.85	5.28	(1.55)	1.56	6.03
Distributions from Net Realized Capital Gains ($)	.56	1.31	—	3.63	—	—
Net Asset Value End of Year ($)	14.94	17.01	23.04	18.53	20.29	26.49
Ratio of Expenses to Net Assets (%)	1.14	1.10	.88	1.26	1.13	1.07
Portfolio Turnover Rate (%)	52	105	353	389	246	281
Total Assets: End of Year (Millions $)	23.2	41.5	96.9	114.0	100.8	142.8
Annual Rate of Return (%) Years Ending 12/31	6.8	35.2	31.9	(8.7)	22.1	15.1

Five-Year Total Return	128.8%	Degree of Diversification	C	Beta	.95	Bull	B	Bear	C

Objective: Seeks capital growth through investment in securities of companies that possess valuable fixed assets or which fund management believes to be undervalued in the marketplace because of changes in the company, the economy, or the industry. May loan its portfolio securities and engage in repos.

Portfolio: (10/31/86) Common stocks 84%, short-term obligations 14%, preferred stock 2%. Largest stock holdings: real estate investment trusts 13%, lodging and resorts 10%.

Distributions: Income: Dec   **Capital Gains:** Dec
12b-1: Yes   Amount: Pd. by Advisor
Minimum: Initial: $1,000   Subsequent: $250
Min IRA: Initial: $500   Subsequent: $250
Services: IRA, Keogh, Corp, 403(b), Withdraw, Deduct
Tel Exchange: Yes   **With MMF:** Yes
Registered: All states

FIDUCIARY CAPITAL GROWTH
Aggressive Growth

Fiduciary Management, Inc.
222 E. Mason St.
Milwaukee, WI 53202
(414) 271-6666

		Years Ending 9/30				
	1981	1982 (9 mos)	1983	1984	1985	1986
Net Investment Income ($)	–	.25	.18	.29	.20	.09
Dividends from Net Investment Income ($)	–	–	.25	.16	.31	.19
Net Gains (Losses) on Investments ($)	–	1.61	7.61	(1.29)	1.47	3.54
Distributions from Net Realized Capital Gains ($)	–	–	–	.30	.20	.03
Net Asset Value End of Year ($)	–	11.86	19.40	17.94	19.10	22.51
Ratio of Expenses to Net Assets (%)	–	2.00	1.80	1.50	1.30	1.2
Portfolio Turnover Rate (%)	–	36	30	26	38	57
Total Assets: End of Year (Millions $)	–	2.5	20.8	28.5	41.5	51.9
Annual Rate of Return (%) Years Ending 12/31	–	45.1	29.0	(4.2)	29.8	(.4)

Five-Year Total Return 131.8%	Degree of Diversification D	Beta 1.00	Bull C	Bear NA

Objective: Seeks long-term capital appreciation principally through investing in common stocks underpriced relative to growth prospects, of unseasoned companies and those in special situations such as mergers. May invest in foreign securities.

Portfolio: (9/30/86) Common stocks 92%, short-term investments 7%, preferred stocks 1%. Largest stock holdings: retail trade 9%, health 9%.

Distributions: Income: Oct   **Capital Gains:** Oct

12b-1: No

Minimum: Initial: $1,000   Subsequent: $100

Min IRA: Initial: $1,000   Subsequent: $100

Services: IRA, Keogh, Withdraw

Tel Exchange: No

Registered: All states except AK, AR, ID, ME, MS, MT, NC, ND, NE, NH, SD, VT, WV, WY

FINANCIAL BOND SHARES—High Yield Portfolio
Bond

Financial Programs, Inc.
PO Box 2040
Denver, CO 80201
(800) 525-8085/(303) 779-1233

	Years Ending 12/31					
	1981	1982	1983	1984 (10 mos.)	1985	1986
Net Investment Income ($)	—	—	—	.81	1.03	1.00
Dividends from Net Investment Income ($)	—	—	—	.81	1.03	1.01
Net Gains (Losses) on Investments ($)	—	—	—	—	.86	.19
Distributions from Net Realized Capital Gains ($)	—	—	—	—	—	.17
Net Asset Value End of Year ($)	—	—	—	7.51	8.37	8.38
Ratio of Expenses to Net Assets (%)	—	—	—	.43	.93	.76
Portfolio Turnover Rate (%)	—	—	—	35	96	134
Total Assets: End of Year (Millions $)	—	—	—	3.8	18.3	46.6
Annual Rate of Return (%) Years Ending 12/31	—	—	—	—	26.6	14.5

Five-Year Total Return	NA	Degree of Diversification	NA	Beta	NA	Bull NA	Bear NA

Objective: Seeks high current income through investment in bonds and other debt securities and preferred stock rated low and medium (BBB/Baa or lower). More than 25% of its assets may be concentrated in the public utility industry.

Portfolio: (12/31/86) Corporate bonds 87%, corporate short-term notes 7%, U.S. government obligations 6%, preferred stocks 1%.

Distributions: Income: Mar, June, Sept, Dec   **Capital Gains:** Jan

12b-1: No

Minimum: Initial: $250   Subsequent: $50

Min IRA: Initial: $250   Subsequent: $50

Services: IRA, Keogh, SEP, Corp, 403(b), Withdraw, Deduct

Tel Exchange: Yes   **With MMF:** Yes

Registered: All states

FINANCIAL BOND SHARES—Select Income Portfolio

Bond

Financial Programs, Inc.
PO Box 2040
Denver, CO 80201
(800) 525-8085/(303) 779-1233

	Years Ending 12/31					
	1981	1982	1983	1984	1985	1986
Net Investment Income ($)	.85	.82	.78	.74	.72	.67
Dividends from Net Investment Income ($)	.86	.81	.78	.73	.72	.68
Net Gains (Losses) on Investments ($)	(.55)	.95	(.42)	(.44)	.62	.60
Distributions from Net Realized Capital Gains ($)	—	—	.05	—	—	.32
Net Asset Value End of Year ($)	6.16	7.12	6.65	6.22	6.84	7.10
Ratio of Expenses to Net Assets (%)	0	0	0	.23	.97	.85
Portfolio Turnover Rate (%)	43	36	33	188	146	153
Total Assets: End of Year (Millions $)	4.4	7.3	8.5	8.1	15.1	24.7
Annual Rate of Return (%) Years Ending 12/31	5.1	30.5	5.1	5.2	22.7	18.8

Five-Year Total Return	110.5%	Degree of Diversification	NA	Beta	.25	Bull	D	Bear	A

Objective: Seeks a high level of current income through investment in bonds and other debt securities of established companies and of government and municipal issues. 50% of assets invested in investment-grade securities (Baa/BBB or higher). Remaining 50% invested in lower-grade or unrated securities.

Portfolio: (12/31/86) Corporate bonds 85%, municipal bonds 6%, U.S. government obligations 6%, corporate short-term notes 3%.

Distributions: Income: Mar, June, Sept, Dec   **Capital Gains:** Jan

12b-1: No

Minimum: Initial: $250   Subsequent: $50

Min IRA: Initial: $250   Subsequent: $50

Services: IRA, Keogh, Corp, 403(b), SEP, Withdraw, Deduct

Tel Exchange: Yes   **With MMF:** Yes

Registered: All states

FINANCIAL DYNAMICS

Aggressive Growth

Financial Programs, Inc.
PO Box 2040
Denver, CO 80201
(800) 525-8085/(303) 779-1233

	Years Ending 4/30					
	1981	1982	1983	1984	1985	1986
Net Investment Income ($)	.48	.28	.17	.15	.09	.06
Dividends from Net Investment Income ($)	.47	.28	.18	.15	.09	.06
Net Gains (Losses) on Investments ($)	1.50	(.42)	3.95	(1.77)	.41	2.56
Distributions from Net Realized Capital Gains ($)	.37	—	.99	1.38	—	1.24
Net Asset Value End of Year ($)	7.49	7.07	10.02	6.87	7.28	8.59
Ratio of Expenses to Net Assets (%)	.70	.69	.66	.66	.78	.90
Portfolio Turnover Rate (%)	203	101	114	56	152	246
Total Assets: End of Year (Millions $)	58.4	62.5	94.5	66.6	73.8	87.7
Annual Rate of Return (%) Years Ending 12/31	(0.5)	36.9	13.1	(13.8)	29.1	6.4

Five-Year Total Return 83.4%	Degree of Diversification C	Beta 1.23	Bull E	Bear B

Objective: Seeks capital growth through aggressive investment policies. Invests primarily in common stocks appearing to be in an early stage of growth, and gives no consideration to immediate income return. Stocks chosen by fundamental analysis techniques. May use leverage.

Portfolio: (10/31/86) Common stocks 88%, corporate short-term notes 8%, fixed-income securities 3%. Largest stock holdings: computer related 9%, savings & loan 9%.

Distributions: Income: April   **Capital Gains:** April

12b-1: No

Minimum: Initial: $250   Subsequent: $50

Min IRA: Initial: $250   Subsequent: $50

Services: IRA, Keogh, Corp, 403(b), SEP, Withdraw, Deduct

Tel Exchange: Yes   **With MMF:** Yes

Registered: All states

FINANCIAL INDUSTRIAL
Growth

Financial Programs, Inc.
PO Box 2040
Denver, CO 80201
(800) 525-8085/(303) 779-1233

	Years Ending 8/31					
	1981	**1982**	**1983**	**1984**	**1985**	**1986**
Net Investment Income ($)	.23	.30	.17	.16	.14	.10
Dividends from Net Investment Income ($)	.22	.29	.20	.16	.14	.12
Net Gains (Losses) on Investments ($)	(.39)	.31	1.37	(.36)	.46	1.09
Distributions from Net Realized Capital Gains ($)	.22	—	.89	.04	.46	1.02
Net Asset Value End of Year ($)	3.73	4.04	4.49	4.09	4.09	4.14
Ratio of Expenses to Net Assets (%)	.64	.64	.63	.64	.72	.74
Portfolio Turnover Rate (%)	131	122	88	80	133	227
Total Assets: End of Year (Millions $)	272.4	297.2	363.8	336.2	342.3	397.1

Annual Rate of Return (%) Years Ending 12/31	(14.0)	36.3	15.3	(1.2)	28.2	8.4

Five-Year Total Return	115.7%	Degree of Diversification	B	Beta .98	Bull C	Bear B

Objective: Seeks long-term capital growth and a reasonable degree of current income through investment in well-established, dividend-paying companies from major fields of business and industrial activity.

Portfolio: (8/31/86) Common stocks 88%, corporate short-term notes 8%, fixed-income securities 4%. Largest stock holdings: computer related 11%, retail 9%.

Distributions: Income: Feb, May, Aug, Nov   **Capital Gains:** Aug

12b-1: No

Minimum: Initial: $250   Subsequent: $50

Min IRA: Initial: $250   Subsequent: $50

Services: IRA, Keogh, Corp, 403(b), SEP, Withdraw, Deduct

Tel Exchange: Yes   **With MMF:** Yes

Registered: All states

FINANCIAL INDUSTRIAL INCOME
Balanced

Financial Programs, Inc.
PO Box 2040
Denver, CO 80201
(800) 525-8085/(303) 779-1233

	Years Ending 6/30					
	1981	1982	1983	1984	1985	1986
Net Investment Income ($)	.59	.61	.44	.53	.46	.45
Dividends from Net Investment Income ($)	.56	.58	.48	.54	.48	.48
Net Gains (Losses) on Investments ($)	.04	(.50)	2.99	(.69)	1.81	2.61
Distributions from Net Realized Capital Gains ($)	.93	—	.56	.96	.66	1.89
Net Asset Value End of Year ($)	7.05	6.58	8.97	7.30	8.42	9.10
Ratio of Expenses to Net Assets (%)	.66	.65	.63	.64	.68	.71
Portfolio Turnover Rate (%)	110	72	57	54	54	160
Total Assets: End of Year (Millions $)	164.6	148.4	222.7	182.7	249.3	341.7
Annual Rate of Return (%) Years Ending 12/31	(5.7)	30.9	23.5	9.7	30.8	14.6

Five-Year Total Return	166.0%	Degree of Diversification	A	Beta	.79	Bull	B	Bear	B

Objective: Seeks current income through investment in common and preferred stocks and convertible bonds of well-established, dividend-paying companies as well as debt securities with high payments.

Portfolio: (12/31/86) Common stocks 68%, fixed-income securities 24%, preferred stocks 4%, short-term corporate notes 3%. Largest stock holdings: utilities 9%, pharmaceuticals 8%.

Distributions: Income: Mar, June, Sept, Dec   **Capital Gains:** June

12b-1: No

Minimum: Initial: $250   Subsequent: $50

Min IRA: Initial: $250   Subsequent: $250

Services: IRA, Keogh, SEP, Corp, 403(b), Withdraw, Deduct

Tel Exchange: Yes   **With MMF:** Yes

Registered: All states

FINANCIAL STRATEGIC PORTFOLIO— ENERGY

Aggressive Growth

Financial Programs, Inc.
PO Box 2040
Denver, CO 80201
(800) 525-8085/(303) 779-1233

	Years Ending 10/31					
	1981	1982	1983	1984 (9 mos.)	1985	1986
Net Investment Income ($)	–	–	–	.14	.15	.14
Dividends from Net Investment Income ($)	–	–	–	.13	.16	.14
Net Gains (Losses) on Investments ($)	–	–	–	(.52)	.81	.21
Distributions from Net Realized Capital Gains ($)	–	–	–	–	–	.17
Net Asset Value End of Year ($)	–	–	–	7.49	8.29	8.33
Ratio of Expenses to Net Assets (%)	–	–	–	1.17	1.50	1.50
Portfolio Turnover Rate (%)	–	–	–	28	235	629
Total Assets: End of Year (Millions $)	–	–	–	.3	.5	1.7
Annual Rate of Return (%) Years Ending 12/31	–	–	–	–	13.6	7.2

Five-Year Total Return	NA	Degree of Diversification	NA	Beta	NA	Bull NA	Bear NA

Objective: Seeks capital appreciation through investment in energy-related stocks. These include companies which explore, develop, produce or distribute known sources of energy such as oil, gas, coal, uranium, geothermal or solar.

Portfolio: (10/31/86) Common stocks 96%, preferred stocks 3%. Largest stock holdings: oil & gas—domestic 60%, oil & gas—international 19%.

Distributions: Income: Annually   **Capital Gains:** Annually

12b-1: No

Minimum: Initial: $250   **Subsequent:** $50

Min IRA: Initial: $250   **Subsequent:** $50

Services: IRA, Keogh, Corp, SEP, 403(b), Withdraw, Deduct

Tel Exchange: Yes   **With MMF:** Yes

Registered: All states

FINANCIAL STRATEGIC PORTFOLIO—GOLD
Aggressive Growth

Financial Programs, Inc.
PO Box 2040
Denver, CO 80201
(800) 525-8085/(303) 779-1233

	Years Ending 10/31					
	1981	**1982**	**1983**	**1984** (9 mos.)	**1985**	**1986**
Net Investment Income ($)	–	–	–	.07	.10	.08
Dividends from Net Investment Income ($)	–	–	–	.06	.11	.08
Net Gains (Losses) on Investments ($)	–	–	–	(3.10)	(.91)	1.13
Distributions from Net Realized Capital Gains ($)	–	–	–	–	–	.05
Net Asset Value End of Year ($)	–	–	–	4.91	3.99	5.08
Ratio of Expenses to Net Assets (%)	–	–	–	1.17	1.50	1.50
Portfolio Turnover Rate (%)	–	–	–	110	46	232
Total Assets: End of Year (Millions $)	–	–	–	1.2	2.4	5.2
Annual Rate of Return (%) Years Ending 12/31	–	–	–	–	(4.4)	38.7

Five-Year Total Return	NA	Degree of Diversification	NA	Beta	NA	Bull	NA	Bear	NA

Objective: Seeks capital appreciation through investment in companies involved in the gold industry. These include companies engaged in mining, exploration, processing, dealing or investing in gold.

Portfolio: (10/31/86) Common stocks 100%. Largest stock holdings: mining 100%.

Distributions: **Income:** Annually   **Capital Gains:** Annually

12b-1: No

Minimum: **Initial:** $250   **Subsequent:** $50

Min IRA: **Initial:** $250   **Subsequent:** $50

Services: IRA, Keogh, Corp, SEP, 403(b), Withdraw, Deduct

Tel Exchange: Yes   **With MMF:** Yes

Registered: All states

FINANCIAL STRATEGIC PORTFOLIO— HEALTH SCIENCES
Aggressive Growth

Financial Programs, Inc.
PO Box 2040
Denver, CO 80201
(800) 525-8085/(303) 779-1233

	Years Ending 10/31					
	1981	1982	1983	1984 (9 mos.)	1985	1986
Net Investment Income ($)	–	–	–	.03	.01	(.03)
Dividends from Net Investment Income ($)	–	–	–	.03	.01	–
Net Gains (Losses) on Investments ($)	–	–	–	.13	1.62	4.42
Distributions from Net Realized Capital Gains ($)	–	–	–	–	–	1.37
Net Asset Value End of Year ($)	–	–	–	8.13	9.75	12.78
Ratio of Expenses to Net Assets (%)	–	–	–	1.17	1.50	1.50
Portfolio Turnover Rate (%)	–	–	–	101	203	479
Total Assets: End of Year (Millions $)	–	–	–	.3	1.4	4.1
Annual Rate of Return (%) Years Ending 12/31	–	–	–	–	31.5	29.5

Five-Year Total Return	NA	Degree of Diversification	NA	Beta	NA	Bull NA	Bear NA

Objective: Primary objective is capital appreciation through investment in companies engaged in the development, production or distribution of products or services related to the health sciences industry, including pharmaceutical companies, R&D companies and hospital chains.

Portfolio: (10/31/86) Common stocks 87%, corporate short-term notes 13%. Largest stock holdings: pharmaceuticals 36%, medical equipment & supplies 16%.

Distributions: **Income:** Annually   **Capital Gains:** Annually

12b-1: No

Minimum: **Initial:** $250   **Subsequent:** $50

Min IRA: **Initial:** $250   **Subsequent:** $50

Services: IRA, Keogh, Corp, SEP, 403(b), Withdraw, Deduct

Tel Exchange: Yes   **With MMF:** Yes

Registered: All states

FINANCIAL STRATEGIC PORTFOLIO— LEISURE

Aggressive Growth

Financial Programs, Inc.
PO Box 2040
Denver, CO 80201
(800) 525-8085/(303) 779-1233

	Years Ending 10/31					
	1981	1982	1983	1984 (9 mos.)	1985	1986
Net Investment Income ($)	–	–	–	.07	.04	(.01)
Dividends from Net Investment Income ($)	–	–	–	.06	.04	–
Net Gains (Losses) on Investments ($)	–	–	–	.46	1.56	4.13
Distributions from Net Realized Capital Gains ($)	–	–	–	–	–	2.76
Net Asset Value End of Year ($)	–	–	–	8.47	10.03	11.38
Ratio of Expenses to Net Assets (%)	–	–	–	1.17	1.50	1.50
Portfolio Turnover Rate (%)	–	–	–	23	160	458
Total Assets: End of Year (Millions $)	–	–	–	.3	1.2	2.8
Annual Rate of Return (%) Years Ending 12/31	–	–	–	–	32.3	18.8

Five-Year Total Return	NA	Degree of Diversification	NA	Beta	NA	Bull NA	Bear NA

Objective: Seeks capital appreciation through investment in companies engaged in the design, production or distribution of products or services related to the leisure-time activities of individuals, including companies in the motion picture, casino, and recreation industries.

Portfolio: (10/31/86) Common stocks 88%, corporate short-term notes 10%, other securities 2%. Largest stock holdings: retail 32%, motion pictures 11%.

Distributions: **Income:** Annually   **Capital Gains:** Annually
12b-1: No
Minimum: **Initial:** $250   **Subsequent:** $50
Min IRA: **Initial:** $250   **Subsequent:** $50
Services: IRA, Keogh, Corp, SEP, 403(b), Withdraw, Deduct
Tel Exchange: Yes   **With MMF:** Yes
Registered: All states

FINANCIAL STRATEGIC PORTFOLIO— PACIFIC BASIN
International

Financial Programs, Inc.
PO Box 2040
Denver, CO 80201
(800) 525-8085/(303) 779-1233

			Years Ending 10/31			
	1981	1982	1983	1984 (9 mos.)	1985	1986
Net Investment Income ($)	–	–	–	.09	.04	.03
Dividends from Net Investment Income ($)	–	–	–	.09	.04	.04
Net Gains (Losses) on Investments ($)	–	–	–	(.95)	1.34	4.85
Distributions from Net Realized Capital Gains ($)	–	–	–	–	–	1.73
Net Asset Value End of Year ($)	–	–	–	7.05	8.39	11.52
Ratio of Expenses to Net Assets (%)	–	–	–	1.17	1.50	1.47
Portfolio Turnover Rate (%)	–	–	–	99	161	199
Total Assets: End of Year (Millions $)	–	–	–	.8	2.9	8.5
Annual Rate of Return (%) Years Ending 12/31	–	–	–	–	27.3	71.8

Five-Year Total Return	NA	Degree of Diversification	NA	Beta	NA	Bull	NA	Bear	NA

Objective: Seeks capital appreciation through investment in companies domiciled in Far Eastern or Western Pacific countries, including Japan, Australia, Hong Kong, Singapore and the Philippines. May use currency futures to hedge the portfolio.

Portfolio: (10/31/86) Common stocks 100%. Largest stock holdings: electrical equipment 13%, commercial development 11%.

Distributions: Income: Annually   **Capital Gains:** Annually

12b-1: No

Minimum: Initial: $250   Subsequent: $50

Min IRA: Initial: $250   Subsequent: $50

Services: IRA, Keogh, Corp, SEP, 403(b), Withdraw, Deduct

Tel Exchange: Yes   **With MMF:** Yes

Registered: All states

FINANCIAL STRATEGIC PORTFOLIO— TECHNOLOGY

Aggressive Growth

Financial Programs, Inc.
PO Box 2040
Denver, CO 80201
(800) 525-8085/(303) 779-1233

	Years Ending 10/31					
	1981	1982	1983	1984 (9 mos.)	1985	1986
Net Investment Income ($)	–	–	–	.02	–	(.04)
Dividends from Net Investment Income ($)	–	–	–	.02	–	–
Net Gains (Losses) on Investments ($)	–	–	–	(.89)	.48	2.82
Distributions from Net Realized Capital Gains ($)	–	–	–	–	–	1.07
Net Asset Value End of Year ($)	–	–	–	7.11	7.59	9.29
Ratio of Expenses to Net Assets (%)	–	–	–	1.17	1.50	1.50
Portfolio Turnover Rate (%)	–	–	–	91	175	368
Total Assets: End of Year (Millions $)	–	–	–	1.0	2.5	4.7
Annual Rate of Return (%) Years Ending 12/31	–	–	–	–	27.3	22.0

Five-Year Total Return	NA	Degree of Diversification	NA	Beta	NA	Bull NA	Bear NA

Objective: Primary objective is capital appreciation through investment in companies in the technology industries. These companies derive at least 25% of their sales from technology-related areas such as computers, communications, video, electronics and robotics.

Portfolio: (10/31/86) Common stocks 80%, short-term securities 16%, fixed-income securities 3%. Largest stock holdings: computer services & software 18%, computer supplies & peripherals 11%.

Distributions: **Income:** Annually   **Capital Gains:** Annually

12b-1: No

Minimum: **Initial:** $250   **Subsequent:** $50

Min IRA: **Initial:** $250   **Subsequent:** $50

Services: IRA, Keogh, Corp, SEP, 403(b), Withdraw, Deduct

Tel Exchange: Yes   **With MMF:** Yes

Registered: All states

FLEX-FUND
Retirement Growth
Growth

R. Meeder & Associates
6000 Memorial Drive
PO Box 7177
Dublin, OH 43017
(800) 325-3539/(614) 766-7000

	Years Ending 12/31					
	1981	1982	1983	1984	1985	1986
Net Investment Income ($)	–	–	.54	.62	.43	.26
Dividends from Net Investment Income ($)	–	–	.05	.41	.52	.42
Net Gains (Losses) on Investments ($)	–	–	1.37	(.81)	1.06	.89
Distributions from Net Realized Capital Gains ($)	–	–	–	1.06	–	1.27
Net Asset Value End of Year ($)	–	–	12.14	10.48	11.45	10.91
Ratio of Expenses to Net Assets (%)	–	–	1.51	1.48	1.50	1.44
Portfolio Turnover Rate (%)	–	–	201	143	244	141
Total Assets: End of Year (Millions $)	–	–	39.6	52.7	48.4	59.0
Annual Rate of Return (%) Years Ending 12/31	–	–	18.6	(1.2)	14.1	10.2

Five-Year Total Return	NA	Degree of Diversification	D	Beta	.63	Bull	NA	Bear	NA

Objective: Seeks capital appreciation through investment in common stocks of companies with market value above $100 million and records of financial strength and strong earnings. Intended for retirement accounts, so will not avoid ordinary income or short-term capital gains. May convert entire portfolio to cash during down markets.

Portfolio: (12/31/86) Short-term investments: commercial paper 63%, repos 26%, time deposits 10%, U.S. Treasury bills 1%.

Distributions: Income: Feb   **Capital Gains:** Feb

12b-1: Yes   **Amount:** .20%

Minimum: Initial: $2,500   **Subsequent:** $100

Min IRA: Initial: $500   **Subsequent:** $100

Services: IRA, Keogh, 403(b), Withdraw

Tel Exchange: Yes   **With MMF:** Yes

Registered: AL, AZ, CA, CO, DC, FL, GA, HI, IL, IN, MA, MD, MI, MN, MO, NC, NJ, NV, NY, OH, PA, SC, TN, TX, VA, WA

FLEX BOND
Bond

R. Meeder & Associates
PO Box 21100
Columbus, OH 43221
(800) 325-3539/(614) 766-7000

	Years Ending 12/31					
	1981	**1982**	**1983**	**1984**	**1985** (8 mos.)	**1986**
Net Investment Income ($)	–	–	–	–	1.21	1.83
Dividends from Net Investment Income ($)	–	–	–	–	1.21	1.83
Net Gains (Losses) on Investments ($)	–	–	–	–	.84	.47
Distributions from Net Realized Capital Gains ($)	–	–	–	–	–	.17
Net Asset Value End of Year ($)	–	–	–	–	20.84	21.31
Ratio of Expenses to Net Assets (%)	–	–	–	–	1.05	.78
Portfolio Turnover Rate (%)	–	–	–	–	239	150
Total Assets: End of Year (Millions $)	–	–	–	–	4.2	13.6

Annual Rate of Return (%) Years Ending 12/31	–	–	–	–	–	12.5

Five-Year Total Return	NA	Degree of Diversification	NA	Beta	NA	Bull NA	Bear NA

Objective: Seeks to maximize current income through investment in fixed-income securities. Investments will be limited to debt obligations of the U.S. government and its agencies and high-grade corporate bonds rated A or better by S&P. For defensive purposes the fund can invest in money market securities.

Portfolio: (12/31/86) U.S. government and agency obligations 63%, short-term securities 27%, U.S. Treasury obligations 9%.

Distributions: Income: Monthly   Capital Gains: Annually

12b-1: Yes   Amount: .20%

Minimum: Initial: $2,500   Subsequent: $100

Min IRA: Initial: $500   Subsequent: $100

Services: IRA, Keogh, 403(b), Withdraw

Tel Exchange: Yes   With MMF: Yes

Registered: AL, AZ, CA, CO, DC, FL, GA, HI, IL IN, MA, MD, MI, MN, MO, NJ, NV, NY, OH, PA, SC, TN, TX, VA, WA

44 WALL STREET
Aggressive

Forty-Four Management Ltd.
1 State St. Plaza
New York, NY 10004
(800) 221-7836/(212) 344-4224

	Years Ending 6/30					
	1981	1982	1983	1984	1985	1986
Net Investment Income ($)	(.80)	(.28)	(.06)	(.52)	(.23)	(.22)
Dividends from Net Investment Income ($)	–	–	–	–	–	–
Net Gains (Losses) on Investments ($)	8.07	(8.43)	11.28	(10.01)	(2.82)	.50
Distributions from Net Realized Capital Gains ($)	.26	3.18	1.09	4.02	.58	–
Net Asset Value End of Year ($)	23.87	11.98	22.11	7.56	3.93	4.21
Ratio of Expenses to Net Assets (%)	.96	1.19	.93	1.16	1.38	3.26
Portfolio Turnover Rate (%)	37	40	113	95	163	104
Total Assets: End of Year (Millions $)	135.2	98.7	248.5	82.0	55.4	34.3

Annual Rate of Return (%) Years Ending 12/31	(22.6)	7.7	9.7	(58.6)	(20.1)	(16.3)

Five-Year Total Return (67.3)%	Degree of Diversification D	Beta 2.13	Bull E	Bear E

Objective: Seeks long-term capital growth through selection of a limited number of investments, principally common stocks of established companies in technology and computer industries. The fund may invest up to 35% of its assets in warrants, obtain leverage by borrowing from banks and invest in foreign securities.

Portfolio: (6/30/86) Common stocks 100%. Largest stock holdings: computer systems 20%, medical 18%.

Distributions: Income: Annually   **Capital Gains:** Oct

12b-1: No

Minimum: Initial: $1,000   Subsequent: $100

Min IRA: Initial: $1,000   Subsequent: $100

Services: IRA, 403(b), SEP, Withdraw, Deduct

Tel Exchange: Yes   **With MMF:** Yes

Registered: All states except AK, AL, AR, CA, IA, ID, IL, IN, KS, KY, LA, ME, MI, MS, MT, NC, ND, NH, OH, RI, SC, SD, TN, TX, VT, WV, WI, WY

FOUNDERS EQUITY INCOME
Balanced

Founders Mutual Depositor Corp.
3033 E. First Ave., #810
Denver, CO 80206
(800) 525-2440/(303) 394-4404

	Years Ending 9/30					
	1981	**1982**	**1983**	**1984**	**1985**	**1986**
Net Investment Income ($)	1.11	.92	.84	.93	.75	.65
Dividends from Net Investment Income ($)	.94	.92	.59	1.01	.92	.74
Net Gains (Losses) on Investments ($)	.53	.49	2.33	0	.95	1.65
Distributions from Net Realized Capital Gains ($)	2.73	–	–	.50	.64	.31
Net Asset Value End of Year ($)	11.89	12.38	14.96	14.38	14.52	15.77
Ratio of Expenses to Net Assets (%)	1.50	1.50	1.50	1.50	1.50	1.59
Portfolio Turnover Rate (%)	196	180	159	145	126	178
Total Assets: End of Year (Millions $)	5.2	6.0	7.3	7.3	10.0	12.1
Annual Rate of Return (%) Years Ending 12/31	14.9	13.0	15.4	11.5	12.7	14.5

Five-Year Total Return	87.7%	Degree of Diversification	D	Beta	.44	Bull	D	Bear	B

Objective: Intends to provide as high income as is consistent with investment quality of companies that are well established and pay dividends. Debt investments will yield interest income. May invest in foreign securities.

Portfolio: (9/30/86) Common stocks 64%, U.S. Treasury securities 21%, corporate short-term notes 12%. Largest stock holdings: telephone utilities 8%, consumer products 8%.

Distributions: Income: Jan, April, July, Oct   **Capital Gains:** Oct

12b-1: Yes   **Amount:** .25%

Minimum: Initial: $1,000   **Subsequent:** $100

Min IRA: Initial: $25   **Subsequent:** $25

Services: IRA, Keogh, 403(b), Corp, Withdraw, Deduct

Tel Exchange: Yes   **With MMF:** Yes

Registered: All states except NH

FOUNDERS GROWTH
Growth

Founders Mutual Depositor Corp.
3033 E. First Ave., #810
Denver, CO 80206
(800) 525-2440/(303) 394-4404

	Years Ending 10/31					
	1981	1982	1983	1984	1985	1986
Net Investment Income ($)	.26	.29	.17	.17	.20	.10
Dividends from Net Investment Income ($)	.28	.26	.29	.16	.18	.17
Net Gains (Losses) on Investments ($)	.97	.72	2.06	(.99)	.86	2.47
Distributions from Net Realized Capital Gains ($)	.20	1.44	.34	2.51	–	–
Net Asset Value End of Year ($)	9.17	8.48	10.08	6.59	7.47	9.87
Ratio of Expenses to Net Assets (%)	1.30	1.37	1.24	1.22	1.17	1.27
Portfolio Turnover Rate (%)	116	179	150	203	186	142
Total Assets: End of Year (Millions $)	38.4	37.7	46.6	41.3	42.7	61.6
Annual Rate of Return (%) Years Ending 12/31	3.6	21.4	18.9	(11.1)	28.8	19.3

Five-Year Total Return	97.4%	Degree of Diversification	B	Beta	1.07	Bull	C	Bear	B

Objective: Seeks capital appreciation by investing in common stocks of established companies. Current dividends are considered but are not a major factor in stock selection. Engages in short-term trading so that portfolio turnover usually exceeds 100% and brokerage commission expenses are correspondingly high.

Portfolio: (10/31/86) Common stocks 84%, corporate short-term notes 13%, cash 3%. Largest stock holdings: financial services 11%, drugs 11%.

Distributions: Income: Jan   **Capital Gains:** Jan

12b-1: Yes   **Amount:** .25%

Minimum: Initial: $1,000   Subsequent: $100

Min IRA: Initial: $25   Subsequent: $25

Services: IRA, Keogh, Corp, 403(b), Withdraw, Deduct

Tel Exchange: Yes   **With MMF:** Yes

Registered: All states except NH

FOUNDERS MUTUAL*

Growth & Income

Founders Mutual Depositor Corp.
3033 E. First Ave., #810
Denver, CO 80206
(800) 525-2440/(303) 394-4404

	Years Ending 9/30					
	1981	1982	1983	1984	1985	1986
Net Investment Income ($)	.43	.43	.41	.41	.36	.28
Dividends from Net Investment Income ($)	.44	.44	.40	.31	.38	.32
Net Gains (Losses) on Investments ($)	(.76)	.19	3.41	(.30)	.72	2.56
Distributions from Net Realized Capital Gains ($)	.41	.03	.71	—	1.17	1.85
Net Asset Value End of Year ($)	7.82	7.97	10.68	10.48	10.01	10.68
Ratio of Expenses to Net Assets (%)	.40	.47	.42	.74	.70	.74
Portfolio Turnover Rate (%)	—	—	—	16	18	42
Total Assets: End of Year (Millions $)	112.7	112.0	143.6	134.9	138.8	175.0

Annual Rate of Return (%) Years Ending 12/31	(7.4)	24.4	25.0	1.6	31.3	16.8

Five-Year Total Return	142.2%	Degree of Diversification	A	Beta 1.04	Bull A	Bear D

Objective: Seeks long-term growth of income and capital through investment in common stocks of companies that have at least $500 million in revenues, have proven earnings records and are in sound financial condition. May invest in foreign securities.

Portfolio: (9/30/86) Common stocks 93%, corporate short-term notes 5%, cash 2%. Largest stock holdings: data processing equipment 16%, drugs 9%.

Distributions: Income: Jan, April, July, Oct **Capital Gains:** Oct
12b-1: Yes Amount: .25%
Minimum: Initial: $1,000 Subsequent: $100
Min IRA: Initial: $25 Subsequent: $25
Services: IRA, Keogh, Corp, 403(b), Withdraw, Deduct
Tel Exchange: Yes **With MMF:** Yes
Registered: All states except NH

Fund was a unit investment trust prior to December 1, 1983.

FOUNDERS SPECIAL
Aggressive Growth

Founders Mutual Depositor Corp.
3033 E. First Ave., #810
Denver, CO 80206
(800) 525-2440/(303) 394-4404

	Years Ending 12/31					
	1981	**1982**	**1983**	**1984**	**1985**	**1986**
Net Investment Income ($)	.32	.45	.28	.53	.22	.23
Dividends from Net Investment Income ($)	.29	.41	.23	.57	.27	.29
Net Gains (Losses) on Investments ($)	(3.23)	5.40	5.52	(3.85)	3.33	4.83
Distributions from Net Realized Capital Gains ($)	–	–	3.06	–	–	3.47
Net Asset Value End of Year ($)	19.34	24.78	27.29	23.40	26.68	27.98
Ratio of Expenses to Net Assets (%)	1.39	1.42	1.20	1.11	1.02	1.06
Portfolio Turnover Rate (%)	145	214	141	191	192	138
Total Assets: End of Year (Millions $)	30.7	45.9	94.5	81.3	95.4	70.2
Annual Rate of Return (%) Years Ending 12/31	(12.9)	30.2	23.4	(12.2)	15.2	18.9

Five-Year Total Return	93.4%	Degree of Diversification	B	Beta	1.08	Bull	C	Bear	E

Objective: Seeks above-average capital growth by investing in common stocks of smaller companies that are rapidly growing. Dividends play a minor role in the fund's strategy.

Portfolio: (12/31/86) Common stocks 91%, corporate short-term notes 8%, cash 1%. Largest stock holdings: drugs 10%, diversified 9%.

Distributions: Income: Jan **Capital Gains:** Jan

12b-1: No

Minimum: Initial: $1,000 Subsequent: $100

Min IRA: Initial: $25 Subsequent: $25

Services: IRA, Keogh, 403(b), Withdraw, Deduct

Tel Exchange: Yes **With MMF:** Yes

Registered: All states except ME, NH

FUND FOR U.S. GOVERNMENT SECURITIES (Liberty)
Bond

Federated Securities Corp.
421 Seventh Ave.
Pittsburgh, PA 15219
(800) 245-4770

	Years Ending 6/30				3/31	
	1981	1982	1983	1984	1985*	1986
Net Investment Income ($)	.73	.75	.78	.92	.74	.93
Dividends from Net Investment Income ($)	.72	.74	.76	.91	.75	.99
Net Gains (Losses) on Investments ($)	(1.70)	(.02)	1.60	(.72)	.64	.46
Distributions from Net Realized Capital Gains ($)	—	—	—	—	—	—
Net Asset Value End of Year ($)	6.85	6.84	8.45	7.74	8.37	8.77
Ratio of Expenses to Net Assets (%)	1.39	1.50	1.29	1.15	.89	.91
Portfolio Turnover Rate (%)	3	3	90	117	121	179
Total Assets: End of Year (Millions $)	52.9	50.3	54.9	47.9	156.9	761.4

For the nine months ended March 31, 1985; fiscal year changed.

Annual Rate of Return (%) Years Ending 12/31	(0.4)	40.1	11.1	12.8	16.6	8.6

Five-Year Total Return 122.2%	Degree of Diversification NA	Beta .07	Bull D	Bear A

Objective: Seeks current income through investment in direct obligations of the U.S. government or debt securities that are guaranteed as to payment of principal and interest by the U.S. government. May enter into repos.

Portfolio: (9/30/86) Long-term U.S. government securities 96%, other government securities .2%, repos .1%.

Distributions: **Income:** Monthly   **Capital Gains:** April
12b-1: Yes   **Amount:** Pd. by Advisor
Minimum: **Initial:** $500   **Subsequent:** $100
Min IRA: **Initial:** $50   **Subsequent:** $50
Services: IRA, Keogh, Withdraw
Tel Exchange: Yes   **With MMF:** Yes
Registered: All states

G.T. EUROPE GROWTH
International

G.T. Capital Management, Inc.
601 Montgomery Street,
Suite 1400
San Francisco, CA 94111
(800) 824-1580/(415) 392-6181

	Years Ending 12/31					
	1981	**1982**	**1983**	**1984**	**1985** (5 mos.)	**1986**
Net Investment Income ($)	—	—	—	—	(.05)	(.06)
Dividends from Net Investment Income ($)	—	—	—	—	—	—
Net Gains (Losses) on Investments ($)	—	—	—	—	3.69	5.65
Distributions from Net Realized Capital Gains ($)	—	—	—	—	—	—
Net Asset Value End of Year ($)	—	—	—	—	13.64	19.23
Ratio of Expenses to Net Assets (%)	—	—	—	—	2.8	2.0
Portfolio Turnover Rate (%)	—	—	—	—	0	102
Total Assets: End of Year (Millions $)	—	—	—	—	1.3	9.9

Annual Rate of Return (%) Years Ending 12/31	—	—	—	—	—	40.9

Five-Year Total Return	NA	Degree of Diversification	NA	Beta	NA	Bull NA	Bear NA

Objective: Seeks long-term capital appreciation through investment in common stocks of growth companies in growth economies of Europe. May invest in other kinds of securities including Eurobonds and depository receipts.
Portfolio: (12/31/86) France 24%, Germany 18%, England 14%.
Distributions: Income: Annually   **Capital Gains:** Annually
12b-1: No
Minimum: Initial: $500   Subsequent: $100
Min IRA: Initial: $500   Subsequent: $100
Services: IRA, Withdraw, Deduct
Tel Exchange: Yes   **With MMF:** No
Registered: All states except NE, NH

G.T. INTERNATIONAL GROWTH

International

G.T. Capital Management, Inc.
601 Montgomery Street,
Suite 1400
San Francisco, CA 94111
(800) 824-1580/(415) 392-6181

	Years Ending 12/31					
	1981	**1982**	**1983**	**1984**	**1985** (5 mos.)	**1986**
Net Investment Income ($)	–	–	–	–	(.05)	(.14)
Dividends from Net Investment Income ($)	–	–	–	–	–	–
Net Gains (Losses) on Investments ($)	–	–	–	–	2.52	6.66
Distributions from Net Realized Capital Gains ($)	–	–	–	–	–	.61
Net Asset Value End of Year ($)	–	–	–	–	12.47	18.38
Ratio of Expenses to Net Assets (%)	–	–	–	–	2.4	1.9
Portfolio Turnover Rate (%)	–	–	–	–	37	122
Total Assets: End of Year (Millions $)	–	–	–	–	1.8	12.0

Annual Rate of Return (%) Years Ending 12/31	–	–	–	–	–	53.8

Five-Year Total Return	NA	Degree of Diversification	NA	Beta	NA	Bull	NA	Bear	NA

Objective: Primary objective is capital appreciation through investment in equity securities of non-U.S. issuers. Normally will have 80% of the fund's assets invested in growth companies located throughout Europe and the Pacific Basin.

Portfolio: (12/31/86) Japan 31%, Germany 13%, France 12%, England 10%.

Distributions: Income: Annually　　　　**Capital Gains:** Annually

12b-1: No

Minimum: Initial: $500　　Subsequent: $100

Min IRA: Initial: $500　　Subsequent: $100

Services: IRA, Withdraw, Deduct

Tel Exchange: Yes　　　　**With MMF:** No

Registered: All states except NE, NH

G.T. JAPAN GROWTH
International

G.T. Capital Management, Inc.
601 Montgomery Street,
Suite 1400
San Francisco, CA 94111
(800) 824-1580/(415) 392-6181

	1981	1982	1983	1984	1985 (5 mos.)	1986
Net Investment Income ($)	–	–	–	–	(.02)	(.28)
Dividends from Net Investment Income ($)	–	–	–	–	–	.02
Net Gains (Losses) on Investments ($)	–	–	–	–	2.42	7.82
Distributions from Net Realized Capital Gains ($)	–	–	–	–	–	.16
Net Asset Value End of Year ($)	–	–	–	–	12.40	19.76
Ratio of Expenses to Net Assets (%)	–	–	–	–	3.8	2.2
Portfolio Turnover Rate (%)	–	–	–	–	93	207
Total Assets: End of Year (Millions $)	–	–	–	–	.5	7.3

Annual Rate of Return (%) Years Ending 12/31	–	–	–	–	–	60.5

Five-Year Total Return	NA	Degree of Diversification	NA	Beta	NA	Bull NA	Bear NA

Objective: Primary objective is capital appreciation through investment in equity securities of non-U.S. issuers. Normally will have 80% of the fund's assets invested in growth companies located in Japan. Can use currency futures to hedge the portfolio.

Portfolio: (12/31/86) Japan 100%. Largest stock holdings: construction/real estate 22%, computers/electronics 21%.

Distributions: Income: Annually   **Capital Gains:** Annually

12b-1: No

Minimum: Initial: $500   Subsequent: $100

Min IRA: Initial: $500   Subsequent: $100

Services: IRA, Withdraw, Deduct

Tel Exchange: Yes   **With MMF:** No

Registered: All states except NE, NH

G.T. PACIFIC GROWTH

International

G. T. Capital Management
601 Montgomery St., #1400
San Francisco, CA 94111
(800) 824-1580/(415) 392-6181

	Years Ending 12/31					
	1981	1982	1983	1984	1985	1986
Net Investment Income ($)	.12	.43	.08	.11	.07	(.10)
Dividends from Net Investment Income ($)	.04	.14	.36	.06	.06	.01
Net Gains (Losses) on Investments ($)	1.46	(2.25)	4.80	(.60)	1.44	12.43
Distributions from Net Realized Capital Gains ($)	—	1.10	.47	.36	.79	—
Net Asset Value End of Year ($)	16.90	13.84	17.89	16.98	17.64	29.96
Ratio of Expenses to Net Assets (%)	1.50	1.50	1.50	1.40	1.40	1.40
Portfolio Turnover Rate (%)	64	71	130	68	81	229
Total Assets: End of Year (Millions $)	13.1	13.9	22.6	46.1	41.6	50.6

Annual Rate of Return (%) Years Ending 12/31	10.3	(10.1)	37.5	(3.3)	9.3	70.0

Five-Year Total Return	122.1%	Degree of Diversification	E	Beta	.32	Bull A	Bear D

Objective: Seeks long-term capital growth through investment in common stocks of Far Eastern issuers. Normally 80% of its assets will be invested in equity securities of growth companies in Japan, Hong Kong, Singapore, Malaysia, and Australia. Current income is not a major factor in stock selection.

Portfolio: (12/31/86) Japanese securities 47%, Hong Kong securities 24%, Singapore/Malaysian securities 18%, Australian securities 2%.

Distributions: **Income:** Annually   **Capital Gains:** Annually

12b-1: No

Minimum: **Initial:** $500   **Subsequent:** $100

Min IRA: **Initial:** $500   **Subsequent:** $100

Services: IRA, Withdraw, Deduct

Tel Exchange: Yes   **With MMF:** No

Registered: All states except NE, NH

GATEWAY OPTION INCOME

Growth & Income

Gateway Investment Advisors
PO Box 458167
Cincinnati, OH 45245
(800) 354-6339/(513) 248-2700

	Years Ending 12/31					
	1981	**1982**	**1983**	**1984**	**1985***	**1986**
Net Investment Income ($)	.67	.61	.52	.53	.40	.33
Dividends from Net Investment Income ($)	.64	.64	.55	.57	.46	.34
Net Gains (Losses) on Investments ($)	.01	.64	1.57	.01	1.74	1.41
Distributions from Net Realized Capital Gains ($)	1.46	.62	1.31	.65	.20	1.46
Net Asset Value End of Year ($)	14.69	14.68	14.91	14.23	14.69	14.63
Ratio of Expenses to Net Assets (%)	1.50	1.45	1.41	1.45	1.50	1.49
Portfolio Turnover Rate (%)	68	115	170	103	96	85
Total Assets: End of Year (Millions $)	19.3	20.7	26.9	21.6	28.4	45.3

Changed objective March 1985.

Annual Rate of Return (%) Years Ending 12/31	4.2	9.5	14.9	4.0	16.0	12.6

Five-Year Total Return	70.8%	Degree of Diversification	B	Beta	.44	Bull	E	Bear	B

Objective: Seeks a high current return at a reduced level of risk, primarily by investing in the common stocks listed in the S&P 100 index and selling call options on that index. May engage in repos as well.

Portfolio: (12/31/86) Common stocks 100%. Largest stock holdings: capital goods—information processing 16%, energy 15%.

Distributions: Income: Jan, April, July, Oct   **Capital Gains:** Jan

12b-1: No

Minimum: Initial: $500   **Subsequent:** $100

Min IRA: Initial: $500   **Subsequent:** $100

Services: IRA, Keogh, SEP, Withdraw

Tel Exchange: Yes   **With MMF:** No

Registered: All states except AK, AL, AR, ID, KS, ME, MS, MT, ND, NE, NH, NM, SD, UT, WV, WY—some states pending

GENERAL SECURITIES
Growth & Income

Craig-Hallum, Inc.
133 S. Seventh St.
Minneapolis, MN 55402
(612) 332-1212

	Years Ending 11/30					
	1981	1982	1983	1984	1985	1986
Net Investment Income ($)	.79	.46	.63	.44	.31	.66
Dividends from Net Investment Income ($)	.83	.48	.58	.51	.30	.38
Net Gains (Losses) on Investments ($)	(.66)	1.77	1.26	(.98)	2.91	1.72
Distributions from Net Realized Capital Gains ($)	.58	.52	1.50	.87	1.25	2.13
Net Asset Value End of Year ($)	11.05	12.28	12.09	10.17	11.84	11.71
Ratio of Expenses to Net Assets (%)	1.50	1.50	1.50	1.50	1.50	1.45
Portfolio Turnover Rate (%)	61	46	13	70	76	68
Total Assets: End of Year (Millions $)	9.8	11.8	11.6	10.9	13.6	14.2

Annual Rate of Return (%) Years Ending 12/31	1.9	28.1	8.9	(0.9)	38.6	9.0

Five-Year Total Return	108.9%	Degree of Diversification	D	Beta	.97	Bull	C	Bear	C

Objective: Seeks long-term capital appreciation and security of principal by investing primarily in common stocks of large, seasoned companies. May write covered call options. May adopt defensive posture in debt securities.

Portfolio: (11/30/86) U.S. Treasury notes & bills 67%, common stocks 43%, preferred stocks 2%. Largest stock holdings: financial 12%, leasing 7%.

Distributions: Income: Feb, May, Aug, Nov   Capital Gains: Nov

12b-1: No

Minimum: Initial: $100   Subsequent: $10

Min IRA: Initial: $100   Subsequent: $10

Services: IRA, Keogh, SEP, Corp, Withdraw

Tel Exchange: No

Registered: All states except AR, FL, HI, KY, LA, MA, MO, MS, ND, SC, TN, TX, WI

GINTEL CAPITAL APPRECIATION

Aggressive Growth

Gintel Equity Management, Inc.
Greenwich Office Park OP-6
Greenwich, CT 06830
(800) 243-5808/(203) 622-6400

	Years Ending 12/31					
	1981	1982	1983	1984	1985	1986 (12 mos.)
Net Investment Income ($)	–	–	–	–	–	.16
Dividends from Net Investment Income ($)	–	–	–	–	–	–
Net Gains (Losses) on Investments ($)	–	–	–	–	–	1.82
Distributions from Net Realized Capital Gains ($)	–	–	–	–	–	.91
Net Asset Value End of Year ($)	–	–	–	–	–	11.07
Ratio of Expenses to Net Assets (%)	–	–	–	–	–	1.9
Portfolio Turnover Rate (%)	–	–	–	–	–	119
Total Assets: End of Year (Millions $)	–	–	–	–	–	21.8
Annual Rate of Return (%) Years Ending 12/31	–	–	–	–	–	19.1

Five-Year Total Return	NA	Degree of Diversification	NA	Beta	NA	Bull	NA	Bear	NA

Objective: Seeks capital appreciation through investment in common stocks of major companies listed on the NYSE or AMEX and up to 25% of total assets in the OTC. May concentrate investments in 12 issues or 4 industry groups and invest in foreign securities, employ leverage, lend its securities and make short sales of securities it holds.

Portfolio: (12/31/86) Common stocks 89%, cash equivalents 17%. Largest stock holdings: telecommunications 16%, savings and loan 16%.

Distributions: Income: Annually   **Capital Gains:** Annually

12b-1: Yes   **Amount:** .50%

Minimum: Initial: $5,000   **Subsequent:** None

Min IRA: Initial: $2,000   **Subsequent:** None

Services: IRA, Keogh, Corp, SEP 403(b), Withdraw

Tel Exchange: Yes   **With MMF:** Yes

Registered: All states except IA, NH, TN

GINTEL ERISA
Growth & Income

Gintel Equity Management
Greenwich Office Park OP-6
Greenwich, CT 06830
(800) 243-5808/(203) 622-6400

	Years Ending 12/31					
	1981	1982	1983	1984	1985	1986
Net Investment Income ($)	–	2.02	1.38	1.43	1.11	.66
Dividends from Net Investment Income ($)	–	–	1.43	.85	1.10	1.08
Net Gains (Losses) on Investments ($)	–	4.95	6.84	(.70)	6.65	7.70
Distributions from Net Realized Capital Gains ($)	–	–	1.19	2.75	1.88	1.47
Net Asset Value End of Year ($)	–	31.97	37.57	34.70	39.48	45.29
Ratio of Expenses to Net Assets (%)	–	1.50	1.40	1.40	1.30	1.30
Portfolio Turnover Rate (%)	–	1	59	109	100	69
Total Assets: End of Year (Millions $)	–	27.7	54.3	71.9	85.4	88.6
Annual Rate of Return (%) Years Ending 12/31	–	–	27.5	2.6	23.9	21.8

Five-Year Total Return	NA	Degree of Diversification	D	Beta	.74	Bull	B	Bear	NA

Objective: Exclusively an investment vehicle for tax-exempt investors or retirement plans. The fund seeks long-term capital growth, investment income, and short-term capital gains by investing in common stocks of major corporations listed on NYSE or AMEX and up to 25% traded OTC and having at least three years' continuous operation.

Portfolio: (12/31/86) Common and preferred stocks 86%, cash equivalents 18%. Largest stock holdings: financial services 18%, telecommunications 14%.

Distributions: Income: Jan   **Capital Gains:** Jan
12b-1: Yes   **Amount:** .40%
Minimum: Initial: $10,000   **Subsequent:** None
Min IRA: Initial: $2,000   **Subsequent:** None
Services: IRA, Keogh, Corp, SEP, 403(b), Withdraw
Tel Exchange: No
Registered: AZ, CA, CO, CT, DC, DE, FL, GA, HI, IN, LA, MA, MD, MO, NJ, NY, OR, PA, SD, TX, UT, WA

GIT EQUITY SPECIAL GROWTH

Aggressive Growth

Bankers Finance Investment
Mgmt. Corp.
1655 North Ft. Myer Drive
Arlington, VA 22209
(800) 336-3063/(703) 528-3600

	Years Ending 3/31					
	1981	1982	1983	1984 (10 mos.)	1985	1986
Net Investment Income ($)	–	–	–	.20	.09	.12
Dividends from Net Investment Income ($)	–	–	–	.20	.09	.12
Net Gains (Losses) on Investments ($)	–	–	–	(.79)	2.27	5.22
Distributions from Net Realized Capital Gains ($)	–	–	–	–	–	.25
Net Asset Value End of Year ($)	–	–	–	9.21	11.47	16.44
Ratio of Expenses to Net Assets (%)	–	–	–	.36	1.09	1.35
Portfolio Turnover Rate (%)	–	–	–	18	30	35
Total Assets: End of Year (Millions $)	–	–	–	.64	2.5	10.7
Annual Rate of Return (%) Years Ending 12/31	–	–	–	(1.2)	47.2	15.1

Five-Year Total Return	NA	Degree of Diversification	D	Beta 1.05	Bull NA	Bear NA

Objective: Seeks maximum capital appreciation through investment in small growth companies. Current income is not a consideration. Designed for investors who can assume an above-average level of risk from investment in common stock.

Portfolio: (9/30/86) Common stocks 88%, repurchase agreements 10%, convertible bonds 2%. Largest stock holdings: automotive 11%, electronic instruments 8%.

Distributions: **Income:** Annually   **Capital Gains:** Annually

12b-1: Yes   **Amount:** 1.00%

Minimum: **Initial:** $1,000   **Subsequent:** None

Min IRA: **Initial:** $500   **Subsequent:** None

Services: IRA, Keogh, Withdraw

Tel Exchange: Yes   **With MMF:** Yes

Registered: All states except: AK, MT, ND, NH, OK, SD, UT

GIT INCOME
Maximum

Bond

Bankers Finance Investment
Mgmt. Corp.
1655 N. Fort Myer Dr.
Arlington, VA 22209
(800) 336-3063/(703) 528-6500

	Years Ending 3/31					
	1981	1982	1983	1984	1985	1986
Net Investment Income ($)	–	–	–	.91	1.23	1.16
Dividends from Net Investment Income ($)	–	–	–	.91	1.23	1.16
Net Gains (Losses) on Investments ($)	–	–	–	(.91)	(.11)	.98
Distributions from Net Realized Capital Gains ($)	–	–	–	–	–	–
Net Asset Value End of Year ($)	–	–	–	9.09	8.99	9.97
Ratio of Expenses to Net Assets (%)	–	–	–	–	.93	1.10
Portfolio Turnover Rate (%)	–	–	–	21	70	47
Total Assets: End of Year (Millions $)	–	–	–	3.3	7.3	12.9
Annual Rate of Return (%) Years Ending 12/31	–	–	–	9.6	22.0	10.6

Five-Year Total Return	NA	Degree of Diversification	NA	Beta	.21	Bull NA	Bear NA

Objective:	Seeks high current income through investment in long-term lower medium grade (BB) and low grade (Caa/CCC) debt securities of U.S. government, corporations and foreign governments. May enter into repos and may temporarily hold short-term debt securities and cash for defensive purposes.
Portfolio:	(9/30/86) Corporate bonds 93%, repos 7%.
Distributions:	**Income:** Monthly **Capital Gains:** Annually
12b-1:	Yes **Amount:** 1.00%
Minimum:	**Initial:** $1,000 **Subsequent:** None
Min IRA:	**Initial:** $500 **Subsequent:** None
Services:	IRA, Keogh, Withdraw
Tel Exchange:	Yes **With MMF:** Yes
Registered:	All states except NE, UT

GOLCONDA INVESTORS LTD.
Precious Metals

Golconda Management Corp.
11 Hanover Square
New York, NY 10005
(800) 847-4200/(212) 363-1100

	Years Ending 6/30					
	1981	1982	1983	1984	1985	1986
Net Investment Income ($)	.51	.68	.40	.16	.11	.02
Dividends from Net Investment Income ($)	–	.75	.50	.20	.12	.04
Net Gains (Losses) on Investments ($)	(.65)	(4.46)	4.72	(2.03)	(1.82)	(.21)
Distributions from Net Realized Capital Gains ($)	–	–	–	–	–	–
Net Asset Value End of Year ($)	14.02	9.49	14.11	12.04	10.21	9.98
Ratio of Expenses to Net Assets (%)	2.02	2.02	1.71	1.71	1.74	2.39
Portfolio Turnover Rate (%)	38	107	12	31	30	32
Total Assets: End of Year (Millions $)	7.6	6.2	23.4	23.0	21.6	20.6

Annual Rate of Return (%) Years Ending 12/31	(17.8)	6.4	0.6	(25.2)	2.6	35.0

Five-Year Total Return 11.0%	Degree of Diversification E	Beta .04	Bull E	Bear E

Objective: Seeks capital appreciation by concentrating its investments in gold bullion, stocks of companies mining, processing or dealing in gold and other foreign securities. May hold any or all of its cash in foreign currencies including gold coins.

Portfolio: (6/30/86) Common stocks 56%, gold bullion 38%, convertible bonds 5%, convertible preferred stocks 1%. Largest stock holdings: North American mining companies 28%, South African mining companies 15%.

Distributions:	**Income:** Aug	**Capital Gains:** Aug
12b-1:	Yes	**Amount:** 1.00%
Minimum:	**Initial:** $1,000	**Subsequent:** $100
Min IRA:	**Initial:** $100	**Subsequent:** $100
Services:	IRA, Keogh, SEP, 403(b), Withdraw, Deduct	
Tel Exchange:	Yes	**With MMF:** Yes
Registered:	All states except IA, ME, MN, MO, TX, WI	

GRADISON ESTABLISHED GROWTH
Growth

Gradison & Co.
The 580 Building, 6th & Walnut
Cincinnati, OH 45202
(800) 543-1818/(513) 579-5700

	Years Ending 4/30					
	1981	1982	1983	1984 (8 mos.)	1985	1986
Net Investment Income ($)	—	—	—	.19	.25	.31
Dividends from Net Investment Income ($)	—	—	—	.10	.26	.30
Net Gains (Losses) on Investments ($)	—	—	—	.09	1.49	3.38
Distributions from Net Realized Capital Gains ($)	—	—	—	—	—	—
Net Asset Value End of Year ($)	—	—	—	10.17	11.66	15.04
Ratio of Expenses to Net Assets (%)	—	—	—	2.00	2.00	1.72
Portfolio Turnover Rate (%)	—	—	—	20	71	80
Total Assets: End of Year (Millions $)	—	—	—	6.7	12.6	30.7
Annual Rate of Return (%) Years Ending 12/31	—	—	—	4.5	28.8	22.0

Five-Year Total Return	NA	Degree of Diversification	A	Beta	.95	Bull NA	Bear NA

Objective: Seeks long-term growth of capital by investing in common stocks of established companies in the S&P 500 Stock Index. Employs computer model to screen companies on basis of earnings, P/E ratios, rate of return, etc.

Portfolio: (10/31/86) Common stocks 88%, commercial paper 10%, other assets 2%. Largest stock holdings: financial services 12%, building materials 10%.

Distributions: Income: Nov, Feb, May, Aug   **Capital Gains:** May

12b-1: Yes   **Amount:** .25%

Minimum: Initial: $1,000   **Subsequent:** $50

Min IRA: Initial: $1,000   **Subsequent:** $50

Services: IRA, Withdraw

Tel Exchange: Yes   **With MMF:** Yes

Registered: AZ, CA, FL, GA, IL, IN, KY, MA, MI, NJ, OH, SC, WA

GRADISON OPPORTUNITY GROWTH

Aggressive Growth

Gradison & Co.
The 580 Building, 6th & Walnut
Cincinnati, OH 45202
(800) 543-1818/(513) 579-5700

	Years Ending Years 4/30					
	1981	1982	1983	1984 (8 mos.)	1985	1986
Net Investment Income ($)	–	–	–	.01	.02	.02
Dividends from Net Investment Income ($)	–	–	–	.01	Nil	.03
Net Gains (Losses) on Investments ($)	–	–	–	(1.97)	1.24	3.87
Distributions from Net Realized Capital Gains ($)	–	–	–	–	–	–
Net Asset Value End of Year ($)	–	–	–	8.04	9.30	13.16
Ratio of Expenses to Net Assets (%)	–	–	–	2.00	2.00	2.00
Portfolio Turnover Rate (%)	–	–	–	108	99	83
Total Assets: End of Year (Millions $)	–	–	–	3.9	4.8	14.4
Annual Rate of Return (%) Years Ending 12/31	–	–	–	(3.2)	28.1	13.0

Five-Year Total Return	NA	Degree of Diversification	D	Beta 1.00	Bull NA	Bear NA

Objective: Seeks long-term capital growth through investment in common stocks of smaller companies (under $350 million) that show dynamic growth potential.

Portfolio: (10/31/86) Common stocks 82%, commercial paper 17%, other assets 1%. Largest stock holdings: consumer nondurables 15%, consumer durables 14%.

Distributions: Income: May   **Capital Gains:** May

12b-1: Yes   Amount: .25%

Minimum: Initial: $1,000   Subsequent: $50

Min IRA: Initial: $1,000   Subsequent: $50

Services: IRA, Withdraw

Tel Exchange: Yes   **With MMF:** Yes

Registered: AZ, CA, FL, GA, IL, IN, KY, MA, MI, NJ, OH, SC, WA

GROWTH INDUSTRY SHARES
Growth

William Blair and Co.
135 S. LaSalle St.
Chicago, IL 60603
(312) 346-4830

	Years Ending 12/31					
	1981	**1982**	**1983**	**1984**	**1985**	**1986**
Net Investment Income ($)	.16	.17	.21	.21	.21	.18
Dividends from Net Investment Income ($)	.15	.17	.19	.19	.23	.22
Net Gains (Losses) on Investments ($)	.32	2.16	1.21	(.73)	2.11	.84
Distributions from Net Realized Capital Gains ($)	.29	.33	.34	.70	.57	3.52
Net Asset Value End of Year ($)	8.97	10.81	11.69	10.29	11.82	9.10
Ratio of Expenses to Net Assets (%)	.90	.94	.87	.92	.95	.90
Portfolio Turnover Rate (%)	6	10	10	13	43	26
Total Assets: End of Year (Millions $)	43.0	54.1	63.5	58.4	72.2	68.6
Annual Rate of Return (%) Years Ending 12/31	5.6	27.7	13.5	(4.1)	23.3	9.2

Five-Year Total Return	87.1%	Degree of Diversification	C	Beta 1.07	Bull C	Bear C

Objective: Seeks long-term capital growth by investing in well-managed companies in growth industries. Secondary objective is growth of income. Companies chosen on eight criteria: leader in field, unique or specialty company, quality products, outstanding marketing, value-based pricing, competitive internationally, above-average return on equity, sound financial practices.

Portfolio: (12/31/86) Common stocks 90%, temporary investments 9%, U.S. government obligations 2%. Largest stock holdings: consumer retail 18%, consumer services and products 16%.

Distributions: Income: Feb, May, Aug, Nov   **Capital Gains:** Feb

12b-1: No

Minimum: Initial: $200   Subsequent: $25

Min IRA: Initial: $200   Subsequent: $25

Services: IRA, Keogh, Corp, SEP, Withdraw, Deduct

Tel Exchange: No

Registered: All states except NH

GUARDIAN MUTUAL
Growth & Income

Neuberger and Berman
Management Inc.
342 Madison Ave.
New York, NY 10173
(800) 367-0770/(212) 850-8300

	Years Ending 10/31					
	1981	1982	1983	1984	1985	1986
Net Investment Income ($)	1.71	1.61	1.51	1.40	1.90	1.49
Dividends from Net Investment Income ($)	1.70	1.58	1.45	1.43	1.76	1.51
Net Gains (Losses) on Investments ($)	(1.19)	5.25	7.22	1.82	5.25	7.50
Distributions from Net Realized Capital Gains ($)	1.81	.82	2.38	1.12	6.44	4.50
Net Asset Value End of Year ($)	27.56	32.02	36.92	37.59	36.54	39.52
Ratio of Expenses to Net Assets (%)	.81	.76	.67	.77	.76	.73
Portfolio Turnover Rate (%)	154	68	50	32	57	70
Total Assets: End of Year (Millions $)	152.7	209.5	276.1	344.9	388.5	531.8
Annual Rate of Return (%) Years Ending 12/31	(4.7)	28.7	25.3	7.5	25.3	11.9

Five-Year Total Return	143.1%	Degree of Diversification	B	Beta	.86	Bull	B	Bear	C

Objective: Seeks capital appreciation through investment in common stocks of dividend-paying, seasoned companies. Current income is a secondary objective. May invest in foreign securities, lend its securities, engage in repos, and write covered call options.

Portfolio: (10/31/86) Common stocks 88%, U.S. government obligations 9%, repos 5%. Largest stock holdings: retail 13%, utilities/telephone 13%.

Distributions: Income: Jan, April, July, Oct   **Capital Gains:** Oct

12b-1: No

Minimum: Initial: $500   Subsequent: $50

Min IRA: Initial: $250   Subsequent: $50

Services: IRA, Keogh, Withdraw, Deduct

Tel Exchange: Yes   **With MMF:** Yes

Registered: All states except NH

HARTWELL GROWTH

Aggressive Growth

Hartwell Management Co.
515 Madison Ave. 31st Flr.
New York, NY 10022
(800) 645-6405/(212) 308-3355

	Years Ending 12/31					
	1981	**1982**	**1983**	**1984**	**1985**	**1986**
Net Investment Income ($)	(.09)	(.03)	(.11)	(.02)	(.14)	(.21)
Dividends from Net Investment Income ($)	–	–	–	–	–	–
Net Gains (Losses) on Investments ($)	(.81)	1.47	3.10	(2.37)	2.31	2.77
Distributions from Net Realized Capital Gains ($)	–	1.51	.35	2.12	.70	1.95
Net Asset Value End of Year ($)	11.87	11.80	14.44	9.93	11.40	12.01
Ratio of Expenses to Net Assets (%)	2.60	2.30	2.60	2.40	2.70	2.90
Portfolio Turnover Rate (%)	73	94	70	108	93	102
Total Assets: End of Year (Millions $)	8.7	9.9	13.6	10.4	10.3	12.0
Annual Rate of Return (%) Years Ending 12/31	(7.0)	16.1	25.5	(17.8)	22.4	23.7

Five-Year Total Return	81.4%	Degree of Diversification	D	Beta	1.26	Bull	B	Bear	E

Objective: Seeks capital appreciation through investment in securities of companies that show potential for growth based on fundamental analysis selected generally for the longer term. May borrow up to 10% of total assets.

Portfolio: (12/31/86) Common stocks 100%. Largest stock holdings: broadcasting & publishing 23%, health care products 21%.

Distributions: Income: Annually   **Capital Gains:** Feb

12b-1: No

Minimum: Initial: $1,000   Subsequent: $50

Min IRA: Initial: $500   Subsequent: $50

Services: IRA, Withdraw, Deduct

Tel Exchange: Yes   **With MMF:** Yes

Registered: AL, AZ, CO, CT, DC, DE, FL, GA, HI, ID, IN, MA, MD, MI, MN, NC, NJ, NV, NY, OH, PA, RI, SC, VA, VT, WA, WV, WY

HARTWELL LEVERAGE
Aggressive Growth

Hartwell Management Co.
515 Madison Ave., 31st Flr.
New York, NY 10022
(800) 645-6405/(212) 308-3355

	Years Ending 9/30					
	1981	**1982**	**1983**	**1984**	**1985**	**1986**
Net Investment Income ($)	(.04)	(.02)	(.05)	(.04)	(.11)	(.26)
Dividends from Net Investment Income ($)	—	—	—	—	—	—
Net Gains (Losses) on Investments ($)	.08	.14	8.67	(7.29)	.53	4.03
Distributions from Net Realized Capital Gains ($)	—	.99	—	1.39	—	—
Net Asset Value End of Year ($)	11.72	10.85	19.47	10.75	11.17	14.94
Ratio of Expenses to Net Assets (%)	1.70	1.40	1.40	1.20	1.40	2.0
Portfolio Turnover Rate (%)	82	83	80	118	107	123
Total Assets: End of Year (Millions $)	16.5	19.1	67.2	40.1	29.8	24.9
Annual Rate of Return (%) Years Ending 12/31	(13.5)	28.9	10.3	(31.6)	27.0	19.3

Five-Year Total Return	47.3%	Degree of Diversification	D	Beta	1.59	Bull	E	Bear	E

Objective: Seeks capital appreciation through investment in securities of seasoned companies selected primarily for the longer term. The fund may utilize the investment techniques of leveraging, short selling, hedging, and purchasing option contracts, encountering above average risk. May invest up to 7.5% of assets in unseasoned companies.

Portfolio: (9/30/86) Common stock 100%. Largest stock holdings: broadcasting & publishing 19%, casualty insurance 19%.

Distributions: **Income:** Annually   **Capital Gains:** Annually

12b-1: No

Minimum: **Initial:** $2,000   **Subsequent:** $50

Min IRA: **Initial:** $500   **Subsequent:** $50

Services: IRA, Withdraw, Deduct

Tel Exchange: Yes   **With MMF:** Yes

Registered: AL, AZ, CA, CO, CT, DC, DE, FL, GA, HI, IL, IN, MA, MD, MI, MN, NC, NJ, NV, NY, OH, PA, RI, SC, TX, VA, VT, WA, WY

INTERNATIONAL EQUITY TRUST
International

Furman Selz
230 Park Ave.
New York, NY 10169
(800) 845-8406/(212) 309-8400

	\multicolumn{6}{c}{Years Ending 9/30}
	1981	**1982**	**1983**	**1984**	**1985**	**1986** (9 mos.)
Net Investment Income ($)	–	–	–	–	–	.02
Dividends from Net Investment Income ($)	–	–	–	–	–	–
Net Gains (Losses) on Investments ($)	–	–	–	–	–	4.05
Distributions from Net Realized Capital Gains ($)	–	–	–	–	–	–
Net Asset Value End of Year ($)	–	–	–	–	–	14.07
Ratio of Expenses to Net Assets (%)	–	–	–	–	–	2.47
Portfolio Turnover Rate (%)	–	–	–	–	–	78
Total Assets: End of Year (Millions $)	–	–	–	–	–	9.2

Annual Rate of Return (%) Years Ending 12/31	–	–	–	–	–	49.6

Five-Year Total Return	NA	Degree of Diversification	NA	Beta	NA	Bull NA	Bear NA

Objective: Seeks long-term capital appreciation through investment in securities markets outside the United States. The fund will normally have 65% of its assets invested in foreign equity securities. May also invest in foreign debt obligations and use currency futures to hedge the portfolio.

Portfolio: (9/30/86) Common stocks 96%, cash 3%. Largest country holdings: Japan 39%, Germany 13%.

Distributions: Income: Semi-Annually   **Capital Gains:** Annually

12b-1: Yes   **Amount:** .50%

Minimum: Initial: $2,500   Subsequent: $100

Min IRA: Initial: $250   Subsequent: $100

Services: IRA, Keogh, Corp, 403(b), Withdraw

Tel Exchange: No

Registered: All states except NM

ISTEL (LEPERCQ)
Growth & Income

Lepercq, de Neuflize & Co.
345 Park Ave.
New York, NY 10154
(212) 702-0174

	Years Ending 12/31					
	1981	1982	1983	1984	1985	1986
Net Investment Income ($)	.97	.85	.61	.53	.63	.40
Dividends from Net Investment Income ($)	.75	.93	.95	.60	.74	.64
Net Gains (Losses) on Investments ($)	(2.74)	(.52)	1.71	(1.31)	1.89	.72
Distributions from Net Realized Capital Gains ($)	1.50	.41	—	.73	1.47	1.08
Net Asset Value End of Year ($)	15.33	14.32	15.69	13.58	13.89	13.29
Ratio of Expenses to Net Assets (%)	.96	1.06	1.02	1.04	1.12	1.67
Portfolio Turnover Rate (%)	10	6	27	26	28	45
Total Assets: End of Year (Millions $)	121.1	111.9	111.1	91.9	28.7	23.6

Annual Rate of Return (%) Years Ending 12/31	(9.9)	3.6	17.1	(5.1)	20.0	8.2

Five-Year Total Return	49.4%	Degree of Diversification	C	Beta 1.00	Bull E	Bear D

Objective: Seeks long-term growth of capital and reasonable current income from investment in securities of companies that through fundamental analysis show potential for growth and value. Fund chooses a few from each industry group that show promise in prevailing industrial and economic environment. Looks for promising geographical regions. May invest in international securities. May write covered call options.

Portfolio: (12/31/86) Common stocks 88%, U.S. gov't. securities 11%. Largest stock holdings: consumer/cyclical 31%, interest rate sensitive 23%.

Distributions: Income: Feb, July　　　　　**Capital Gains:** Feb

12b-1: Yes　　　　　**Amount:** 1.00%

Minimum: Initial: $500　　　　　**Subsequent:** 1 Full Share

Min IRA: Initial: $500　　　　　**Subsequent:** 1 Full Share

Services: IRA, Keogh, Withdraw

Tel Exchange: No

Registered: All states

IVY GROWTH
Growth & Income

Hingham Management Inc.
40 Industrial Park Rd.
Hingham, MA 02043
(800) 235-3322/(617) 749-1416

	Years Ending 12/31					
	1981	**1982**	**1983**	**1984**	**1985**	**1986**
Net Investment Income ($)	.58	.75	.77	.89	.51	.61
Dividends from Net Investment Income ($)	.36	.59	.74	.78	.96	.46
Net Gains (Losses) on Investments ($)	—	2.45	2.85	.06	3.23	1.87
Distributions from Net Realized Capital Gains ($)	—	—	.38	1.78	.76	4.48
Net Asset Value End of Year ($)	10.38	12.99	15.49	13.88	15.90	13.44
Ratio of Expenses to Net Assets (%)	1.27	1.28	1.22	1.29	1.27	1.29
Portfolio Turnover Rate (%)	74	86	59	97	132	95
Total Assets: End of Year (Millions $)	54.3	76.7	114.4	63.5*	136.7	158.1

Change in size reflects halving of total assets in the forming of the other fund in this series, Ivy Institutional Investors Fund.

Annual Rate of Return (%) Years Ending 12/31	5.9	32.9	30.1	7.9	29.4	16.8

Five-Year Total Return	181.9%	Degree of Diversification	B	Beta	.67	Bull	A	Bear	B

Objective: Seeks long-term growth of capital primarily through investment in equity securities of large, well-established companies. May write covered call options and may convert portfolio to debt investments as a defensive posture.

Portfolio: (12/31/86) Common stocks 67%, U.S. government securities 33%, short-term notes 5%. Largest stock holdings: petroleum 12%, food and beverage 5%.

Distributions: Income: Annually   **Capital Gains:** Annually

12b-1: No

Minimum: Initial: $1,000   **Subsequent:** $100

Min IRA: Initial: None   **Subsequent:** None

Services: IRA, Keogh, Withdraw

Tel Exchange: No

Registered: All states except CA

JANUS
Growth & Income

Janus Management Corp.
100 Filmore St. #300
Denver, CO 80206
(800) 525-3713/(303) 333-3863

	Years Ending 10/31					
	1981	**1982**	**1983**	**1984**	**1985**	**1986**
Net Investment Income ($)	.17	.31	.15	.45	.48	.42
Dividends from Net Investment Income ($)	.10	.16	.25	.14	.48	.47
Net Gains (Losses) on Investments ($)	1.79	1.41	3.42	(.20)	1.23	2.20
Distributions from Net Realized Capital Gains ($)	1.67	1.91	.14	1.03	–	.80
Net Asset Value End of Year ($)	10.28	9.93	13.11	12.19	13.42	14.77
Ratio of Expenses to Net Assets (%)	1.43	1.31	1.11	1.06	1.03	1.00
Portfolio Turnover Rate (%)	154	106	94	162	163	254
Total Assets: End of Year (Millions $)	39.1	76.5	264.7	319.1	410.7	474.4

Annual Rate of Return (%) Years Ending 12/31	7.1	30.6	26.1	(0.1)	24.5	11.2

Five-Year Total Return 127.9%	Degree of Diversification B	Beta .73	Bull C	Bear B

Objective: Seeks long-term capital growth by investing in securities selected solely for their capital appreciation. Emphasizes companies, their divisions, or new products in early growth stage. Companies may be quite new or small. May convert portfolio to debt securities as a defensive posture.

Portfolio: (10/31/86) Common and preferred stocks 72%, corporate short-term notes 30%. Largest stock holdings: communications 10%, airlines 9%.

Distributions: Income: Dec   **Capital Gains:** Dec
12b-1: Yes   **Amount:** Pd. by Advisor
Minimum: Initial: $1,000   **Subsequent:** $50
Min IRA: Initial: $500   **Subsequent:** $50
Services: IRA, Keogh, Corp, Withdraw, Deduct
Tel Exchange: Yes   **With MMF:** Yes
Registered: All states

JANUS VALUE
Growth

Janus Capital Corp
100 Fillmore Street, Suite 300
Denver, CO 80206
(800) 525-3713/(303) 333-3863

	Years Ending 5/31					
	1981	**1982**	**1983**	**1984**	**1985** (7 mos.)	**1986**
Net Investment Income ($)	—	—	—	—	.36	.19
Dividends from Net Investment Income ($)	—	—	—	—	—	.23
Net Gains (Losses) on Investments ($)	—	—	—	—	1.21	3.05
Distributions from Net Realized Capital Gains ($)	—	—	—	—	—	.31
Net Asset Value End of Year ($)	—	—	—	—	11.57	14.27
Ratio of Expenses to Net Assets (%)	—	—	—	—	1.99	2.00
Portfolio Turnover Rate (%)	—	—	—	—	68	152
Total Assets: End of Year (Millions $)	—	—	—	—	2.5	10.1

Annual Rate of Return (%) Years Ending 12/31	—	—	—	—	—	11.5

Five-Year Total Return	NA	Degree of Diversification	NA	Beta	NA	Bull NA	Bear NA

Objective: Seeks capital appreciation through investment in common stocks chosen primarily from a "contrarian" viewpoint, including a strong financial position and low P/E. May invest 25% of assets in ADRs of foreign issues.

Portfolio: (11/30/86) Common stocks 69%, U.S. government obligations 12%, cash 12%, short-term corporate notes 7%. Largest stock holdings: money center banks 21%, utilities 15%.

Distributions: Income: Annually   **Capital Gains:** Annually

12b-1: Yes   **Amount:** Pd. by Advisor

Minimum: Initial: $1,000   Subsequent: $50

Min IRA: Initial: $500   Subsequent: $50

Services: IRA, Keogh, Corp, Withdraw, Deduct

Tel Exchange: Yes   **With MMF:** Yes

Registered: All states except NH

JANUS VENTURE
Aggressive Growth

Janus Capital Corp.
100 Fillmore Street, Suite 300
Denver, CO 80206
(800) 525-3713/(303) 333-3863

	Years Ending 7/31					
	1981	1982	1983	1984	1985 (3 mos.)	1986
Net Investment Income ($)	–	–	–	–	.26	.11
Dividends from Net Investment Income ($)	–	–	–	–	–	.18
Net Gains (Losses) on Investments ($)	–	–	–	–	3.91	7.88
Distributions from Net Realized Capital Gains ($)	–	–	–	–	–	1.20
Net Asset Value End of Year ($)	–	–	–	–	24.17	30.78
Ratio of Expenses to Net Assets (%)	–	–	–	–	2.00	1.90
Portfolio Turnover Rate (%)	–	–	–	–	293	248
Total Assets: End of Year (Millions $)	–	–	–	–	4.1	30.9
Annual Rate of Return (%) Years Ending 12/31	–	–	–	–	–	20.2

Five-Year Total Return	NA	Degree of Diversification	NA	Beta	NA	Bull NA	Bear NA

Objective: Seeks capital appreciation through investment primarily in common stocks of small companies with less than $250 million in annual revenues. May also invest in larger companies with strong growth potential and in foreign companies through ADRs.

Portfolio: (7/31/86) Short-term corporate notes 50%, common stocks 46%, cash and other 4%. Largest stock holdings: retail 8%, consumer goods 7%.

Distributions: Income: Annually   **Capital Gains:** Annually

12b-1: Yes   **Amount:** Pd. by Advisor

Minimum: Initial: $1,000   **Subsequent:** $50

Min IRA: Initial: $500   **Subsequent:** $50

Services: IRA, Keogh, Corp, Withdraw, Deduct

Tel Exchange: Yes   **With MMF:** No

Registered: All states except NH

LEGG MASON SPECIAL INVESTMENT TRUST
Aggressive Growth

Legg Mason Wood Walker
7 E. Redwood Street
Baltimore, MD 21202
(800) 822-5544/(301) 539-3400

	Years Ending 3/31					
	1981	**1982**	**1983**	**1984**	**1985**	**1986** (3 mos.)
Net Investment Income ($)	–	–	–	–	–	.04
Dividends from Net Investment Income ($)	–	–	–	–	–	–
Net Gains (Losses) on Investments ($)	–	–	–	–	–	1.49
Distributions from Net Realized Capital Gains ($)	–	–	–	–	–	–
Net Asset Value End of Year ($)	–	–	–	–	–	11.53
Ratio of Expenses to Net Assets (%)	–	–	–	–	–	2.5
Portfolio Turnover Rate (%)	–	–	–	–	–	41
Total Assets: End of Year (Millions $)	–	–	–	–	–	34.3
Annual Rate of Return (%) Years Ending 12/31	–	–	–	–	–	7.5

Five-Year Total Return	NA	Degree of Diversification	NA	Beta	NA	Bull	NA	Bear	NA

Objective: Seeks capital appreciation through investment in equity securities of out-of-favor companies, not closely followed by analysts. Current income is not a consideration. Also invests in companies involved in reorganization or restructuring.

Portfolio: (9/30/86) Common stocks 82%, corporate bonds 9%, repos 5%, preferred stock 3%. Largest stock holdings: savings & loan 15%, multi-industry 14%.

Distributions: **Income:** Annually   **Capital Gains:** Annually

12b-1: Yes   **Amount:** 1.00%

Minimum: **Initial:** $1,000   **Subsequent:** $500

Min IRA: **Initial:** $1,000   **Subsequent:** $500

Services: IRA, Keogh, Corp, SEP, 403(b), Withdraw, Deduct

Tel Exchange: Yes   **With MMF:** Yes

Registered: All states except AK, CA, MO

LEGG MASON TOTAL RETURN TRUST
Balanced

Legg Mason Wood Walker
7 E. Redwood St.
Baltimore, MD 21202
(800) 822-5544/(301) 539-3400

	Years Ending 3/31					
	1981	**1982**	**1983**	**1984**	**1985**	**1986** (4 mos.)
Net Investment Income ($)	–	–	–	–	–	.13
Dividends from Net Investment Income ($)	–	–	–	–	–	–
Net Gains (Losses) on Investments ($)	–	–	–	–	–	.65
Distributions from Net Realized Capital Gains ($)	–	–	–	–	–	–
Net Asset Value End of Year ($)	–	–	–	–	–	10.78
Ratio of Expenses to Net Assets (%)	–	–	–	–	–	2.2
Portfolio Turnover Rate (%)	–	–	–	–	–	40
Total Assets: End of Year (Millions $)	–	–	–	–	–	44.3
Annual Rate of Return (%) Years Ending 12/31	–	–	–	–	–	1.4

Five-Year Total Return	NA	Degree of Diversification	NA	Beta	NA	Bull NA	Bear NA

Objective: To obtain capital appreciation and current income in order to achieve an attractive total return consistent with reasonable risk. Invests primarily in dividend-paying common stocks, convertible securities and bonds. Will invest no more than 25% of assets in bonds rated BBB or less.

Portfolio: (9/30/86) Common stocks 88%, repos 9%, corporate bonds 4%, preferred stock 1%. Largest stock holdings: banking 22%, multi-industry 15%.

Distributions: Income: Quarterly   **Capital Gains:** Annually

12b-1: Yes   **Amount:** 1.00%

Minimum: Initial: $1,000   Subsequent: $500

Min IRA: Initial: $1,000   Subsequent: $500

Services: IRA, Keogh, Corp, SEP, 403(b), Withdraw, Deduct

Tel Exchange: Yes   **With MMF:** Yes

Registered: All states except AK, MO

LEGG MASON VALUE TRUST
Growth

Legg Mason Wood Walker
7 E. Redwood St.
Baltimore, MD 21203
(800) 822-5544/(301) 539-3400

			Years Ending 3/31			
	1981	**1982**	**1983** (13 mos.)	**1984**	**1985**	**1986**
Net Investment Income ($)	–	–	.54	.46	.46	.50
Dividends from Net Investment Income ($)	–	–	.20	.27	.34	.36
Net Gains (Losses) on Investments ($)	–	–	5.82	2.52	4.49	8.31
Distributions from Net Realized Capital Gains ($)	–	–	–	.05	.34	.86
Net Asset Value End of Year ($)	–	–	16.16	18.82	23.09	30.68
Ratio of Expenses to Net Assets (%)	–	–	2.50	2.50	2.40	2.10
Portfolio Turnover Rate (%)	–	–	6	18	38	33
Total Assets: End of Year (Millions $)	–	–	15.1	61.1	163.4	599.1
Annual Rate of Return (%) Years Ending 12/31	–	–	42.8	12.0	31.7	9.4

Five-Year Total Return	NA	Degree of Diversification	B	Beta	.90	Bull	A	Bear	NA

Objective: Seeks long-term capital growth through investment in undervalued companies, temporarily depressed due to any of a variety of factors, but deemed to have potential for superior performance.

Portfolio: (9/30/86) Common stocks 89%, repos 9%, corporate bonds 1%, preferred stock 1%. Largest stock holdings: banks 19%, oil and gas 10%.

Distributions: Income: Jan, May, July, Oct   **Capital Gains:** May

12b-1: Yes   **Amount:** 1.00%

Minimum: Initial: $1,000   **Subsequent:** $500

Min IRA: Initial: $1,000   **Subsequent:** $500

Services: IRA, Keogh, SEP, 403(b), Corp, Withdraw, Deduct

Tel Exchange: Yes   **With MMF:** Yes

Registered: All states except AK, MO

LEHMAN CAPITAL*
Growth

Lehman Management Co.
55 Water St.
New York, NY 10041
(800) 221-5350/(212) 668-8578

	Years ending 6/30			12/31		
	1982	1983	1984	1984† (6 mos.)	1985	1986
Net Investment Income ($)	.57	.38	.60	.19	.23	.13
Dividends from Net Investment Income ($)	.49	.63	.39	.62	.19	.25
Net Gains (Losses) on Investments ($)	(1.17)	12.23	(2.33)	.30	3.57	2.28
Distributions from Net Realized Capital Gains ($)	4.10	1.09	4.17	2.57	.39	4.04
Net Asset Value End of Year ($)	14.62	25.51	19.22	16.52	19.75	17.87
Ratio of Expenses to Net Assets (%)	1.30	1.22	1.13	1.15	1.13	1.13
Portfolio Turnover Rate (%)	80	114	137	122	162	279
Total Assets: End of Year (Millions $)	38.1	113.4	105.3	95.3	116.8	105.2

†Changed fiscal year to end Dec. 31 from June 30.

Annual Rate of Return (%) Years Ending 12/31	40.6	38.2	(4.0)	–	23.4	13.9

Five-Year Total Return 162.4%	Degree of Diversification A	Beta 1.12	Bull A	Bear B

Objective: Seeks capital growth through investment in common stocks and convertibles which are believed to have above-average market appreciation potential and may also involve above-average risk. The fund may borrow, write covered options, and invest in restricted and foreign securities.

Portfolio: (12/31/86) Common stocks 88%, short-term corporate notes 11%, cash 2%. Largest stock holdings: services 20%, technology 13%.

Distributions: Income: Annually   **Capital Gains:** Annually

12b-1: No

Minimum: Initial: $1,000   Subsequent: $100

Min IRA: Initial: $250   Subsequent: $100

Services: IRA, Keogh, Withdraw

Tel Exchange: Yes   **With MMF:** Yes

Registered: All states

Subject to sales charge beginning March 15, 1987.

LEHMAN INVESTORS*
Growth

Lehman Management Co.
55 Water St.
New York, NY 10041
(800) 221-5350/(212) 668-8578

	Years Ending 12/31					
	1981	1982	1983	1984	1985	1986
Net Investment Income ($)	.82	.68	.66	.60	.59	.51
Dividends from Net Investment Income ($)	.79	.80	.65	.62	.55	.54
Net Gains (Losses) on Investments ($)	(.91)	3.78	3.69	(.73)	3.71	2.09
Distributions from Net Realized Capital Gains ($)	2.13	1.73	1.44	3.19	1.51	4.55
Net Asset Value End of Year ($)	17.35	19.28	21.54	17.61	19.86	17.37
Ratio of Expenses to Net Assets (%)	.58	.63	.61	.60	.62	.45
Portfolio Turnover Rate (%)	31	33	42	40	46	62
Total Assets: End of Year (Millions $)	282.5	332.7	389.2	351.9	403.4	398.7
Annual Rate of Return (%) Years Ending 12/31	(0.1)	30.2	24.3	(0.2)	26.3	14.6

Five-Year Total Return 133.9%	Degree of Diversification A	Beta 1.01	Bull B	Bear C

Objective: Long-term growth of capital through investment in common stock of leading, well-established companies from broad cross-section of the economy. Fund's policy is to retain flexibility in the management of its portfolio, without restrictions as to the proportion of assets which may be invested in any class of securities. May invest up to 7.5% of its assets in foreign domiciled companies.

Portfolio: (12/31/86) Common stocks 90%, corporate short-term notes 9%, convertible bond 1%. Largest stock holdings: office equipment 13%, financial services 12%.

Distributions: Income: Quarterly   **Capital Gains:** Annually
12b-1: No
Minimum: Initial: $500   Subsequent: $50
Min IRA: Initial: $250   Subsequent: $50
Services: IRA, Keogh, Withdraw
Tel Exchange: Yes   **With MMF:** Yes
Registered: All states

Subject to sales charge beginning March 15, 1987.

LEHMAN OPPORTUNITY
Balanced

Lehman Management Co.
55 Water St.
New York, NY 10041
(800) 221-5350/(212) 668-8578

	Years Ending 8/31					
	1981	**1982**	**1983**	**1984**	**1985**	**1986**
Net Investment Income ($)	.49	.48	.42	.41	.52	.53
Dividends from Net Investment Income ($)	.41	.47	.48	.43	.41	.48
Net Gains (Losses) on Investments ($)	.50	(.74)	7.56	1.92	4.69	5.48
Distributions from Net Realized Capital Gains ($)	.31	.79	—	1.39	1.37	1.40
Net Asset Value End of Year ($)	13.79	12.28	19.78	20.30	23.73	27.87
Ratio of Expenses to Net Assets (%)	1.34	1.33	1.30	1.23	1.23	1.16
Portfolio Turnover Rate (%)	30	27	46	32	24	28
Total Assets: End of Year (Millions $)	21.3	20.3	38.7	48.5	71.2	110.1
Annual Rate of Return (%) Years Ending 12/31	0.1	29.0	38.9	11.1	32.8	6.4

Five-Year Total Return	181.3%	Degree of Diversification	B	Beta	.84	Bull	A	Bear	D

Objective: Seeks above-average long-term capital appreciation by investing principally in common stocks and convertible securities of both seasoned, established companies and small new companies. May invest up to 5% of its assets in foreign securities, foreign bank acceptances and may use leverage.

Portfolio: (8/31/86) Common stocks 89%, short-term notes 10%, preferred stocks 1%. Largest stock holdings: finance 17%, insurance 17%.

Distributions: Income: Annually   **Capital Gains:** Annually

12b-1: No

Minimum: Initial: $1,000   Subsequent: $100

Min IRA: Initial: $250   Subsequent: $50

Services: IRA, Keogh, Withdraw, SEP

Tel Exchange: Yes   **With MMF:** Yes

Registered: All states

LEVERAGE FUND OF BOSTON

Aggressive Growth

Eaton Vance Management
24 Federal St.
Boston, MA 02110
(800) 225-6265/(617) 482-8260

		Years Ending 12/31				
	1981	1982*	1983	1984	1985	1986
Net Investment Income ($)	–	.36	(.06)	(.18)	–	(.15)
Dividends from Net Investment Income ($)	–	.36	–	–	–	–
Net Gains (Losses) on Investments ($)	–	2.92	1.63	(.91)	2.14	.10
Distributions from Net Realized Capital Gains ($)	–	2.30	3.04	.50	–	1.53
Net Asset Value End of Year ($)	–	9.76	8.29	6.70	8.84	7.26
Ratio of Expenses to Net Assets (%)	–	1.26	3.47	4.30	2.73	2.76
Portfolio Turnover Rate (%)	–	82	75	48	78	53
Total Assets: End of Year (Millions $)	–	39.9	41.5	28.9	33.2	23.4

Was closed-end fund prior to 1/4/82.

Annual Rate of Return (%) Years Ending 12/31	–	–	16.1	(13.1)	32.1	(0.7)

Five-Year Total Return	NA	Degree of Diversification	D	Beta 1.39	Bull NA	Bear NA

Objective: Seeks growth of capital primarily through investment in equity securities of large and small companies that show growth promise because of new products, other changes or special situations. May employ leverage by borrowing money to purchase securities but must have assets representing three times borrowings. May invest in foreign securities and engage in repos.

Portfolio: (12/31/86) Common stocks 97%, convertible bonds 3%. Largest stock holdings: drugs and medical 18%, office equipment 13%.

Distributions: Income: Jan, July   Capital Gains: Jan

12b-1: No

Minimum: Initial: $1,000   Subsequent: $50

Min IRA: Initial: $1,000   Subsequent: $20

Services: IRA, Keogh, Corp, 403(b), Withdraw, Deduct

Tel Exchange: Yes   With MMF: Yes

Registered: All states

LEXINGTON GNMA
Bond

Lexington Management Corp.
PO Box 1515
Park 80 W. Plaza 2
Saddle Brook, NJ 07662
(800) 526-0056

	Years Ending 12/31					
	1981*	1982	1983	1984	1985	1986
Net Investment Income ($)	.99	.83	.74	.87	.76	.74
Dividends from Net Investment Income ($)	.98	.88	.80	.82	.93	.75
Net Gains (Losses) on Investments ($)	(.87)	.90	(.17)	(.03)	.49	.17
Distributions from Net Realized Capital Gains ($)	—	—	—	—	—	—
Net Asset Value End of Year ($)	7.10	7.95	7.72	7.74	8.06	8.22
Ratio of Expenses to Net Assets (%)	1.56	1.59	1.47	1.22	1.01	.86
Portfolio Turnover Rate (%)	72	95	207	133	168	300
Total Assets: End of Year (Millions $)	5.2	9.2	22.4	25.4	87.4	141.4

Changed to a GNMA fund.

Annual Rate of Return (%) Years Ending 12/31	1.6	26.1	7.6	11.9	18.3	11.7

Five-Year Total Return **100.6%**	Degree of Diversification NA	Beta .10	Bull E	Bear A

Objective: Seeks high level of current income, retaining liquidity and safety of principal. At least 80% of assets invested in GNMA certificates and balance in other U.S. government securities. May buy repos.

Portfolio: (12/31/86) GNMA 79%, U.S. government obligations 21%.

Distributions: Income: Monthly   **Capital Gains:** Jan

12b-1: Yes   Amount: .25%

Minimum: Initial: $1,000   Subsequent: $50

Min IRA: Initial: $250   Subsequent: $50

Services: IRA, Keogh, SEP, Corp, 403(b), Withdraw, Deduct

Tel Exchange: Yes   **With MMF:** Yes

Registered: All states

LEXINGTON GOLDFUND
Precious Metals

Lexington Management Corp.
PO Box 1515
Park 80 W. Plaza 2
Saddle Brook, NJ 07662
(800) 526-0056

	Years Ending 3/31		Years Ending 12/31				
	1981	1982	1982* (9 mos.)	1983	1984	1985	1986
Net Investment Income ($)	.21	.09	.02	.07	.03	.02	.04
Dividends from Net Investment Income ($)	—	.22	.11	.06	.04	.04	.02
Net Gains (Losses) on Investments ($)	1.11	(1.75)	1.91	(.36)	(.98)	.37	1.07
Distributions from Net Realized Capital Gains ($)	—	.62	.04	.05	.10	—	—
Net Asset Value End of Year ($)	5.26	2.76	4.54	4.14	3.05	3.40	4.49
Ratio of Expenses to Net Assets (%)	2.50	2.12	1.50	1.50	1.50	1.50	1.50
Portfolio Turnover Rate (%)	60	5	43	16	17	30	15
Total Assets: End of Year (Millions $)	1.3	0.9	3.8	7.0	7.5	12.4	24.6

Changed fiscal year-end from 3/31 to 12/31 and changed management company.

Annual Rate of Return (%) Years Ending 12/31	—	—	—	(6.4)	(23.7)	13.0	32.7

Five-Year Total Return	NA	Degree of Diversification	E	Beta −.08	Bull D	Bear NA

Objective: Seeks capital appreciation and a hedge against inflation through investment in gold bullion, and debt and equity securities of domestic and foreign firms engaged in mining or processing gold. May buy repos and CDs.

Portfolio: (12/31/86) Common stocks 68%, gold bullion 28%, short-term securities 4%. Largest stock holdings: North American gold mining 40%, South African gold mining 19%.

Distributions: Income: Feb, Aug   **Capital Gains:** Feb

12b-1: Yes   Amount: .25%

Minimum: Initial: $1,000   Subsequent: $50

Min IRA: Initial: $250   Subsequent: $50

Services: IRA, Keogh, SEP, Corp, 403(b), Withdraw, Deduct

Tel Exchange: Yes   **With MMF:** Yes

Registered: All states except AZ, MO, NH, TX, WI

LEXINGTON GROWTH
Aggressive Growth

Lexington Management Corp.
PO Box 1515
Park 80 W. Plaza 2
Saddle Brook, NJ 07662
(800) 526-0056

	Years Ending 12/31					
	1981	1982	1983	1984	1985	1986
Net Investment Income ($)	.21	.11	.20	.25	.18	.16
Dividends from Net Investment Income ($)	.33	.22	.11	.30	.12	.20
Net Gains (Losses) on Investments ($)	(.92)	.34	.74	(1.48)	1.92	1.88
Distributions from Net Realized Capital Gains ($)	2.93	.94	.06	.73	–	–
Net Asset Value End of Year ($)	10.18	9.47	10.24	7.98	9.96	11.80
Ratio of Expenses to Net Assets (%)	1.43	1.56	1.21	1.50	1.43	1.32
Portfolio Turnover Rate (%)	24	24	57	141	151	54
Total Assets: End of Year (Millions $)	16.7	27.6	35.0	22.7	28.0	29.9
Annual Rate of Return (%) Years Ending 12/31	(5.9)	6.7	9.9	(12.0)	26.7	20.6

Five-Year Total Return	57.6%	Degree of Diversification	B	Beta	1.00	Bull	D	Bear	E

Objective: Seeks capital growth. May invest in securities of newer, less-seasoned companies, companies whose earnings are cyclically depressed but which have good potential for recovery, or established companies experiencing important changes such as product innovation. May also buy repos.

Portfolio: (12/31/86) Common stocks 90%, short-term securities 7%, bonds 4%. Largest stock holdings: consumer products 14%, drugs & healthcare 12%.

Distributions: Income: Feb   **Capital Gains:** Feb

12b-1: Yes   **Amount:** .25%

Minimum: Initial: $1,000   Subsequent: $50

Min IRA: Initial: $250   Subsequent: $50

Services: IRA, Keogh, SEP, 403(b), Corp, Withdraw

Tel Exchange: Yes   **With MMF:** Yes

Registered: All states except NH

LEXINGTON RESEARCH
Growth

Lexington Management Corp.
PO Box 1515
Park 80 W. Plaza 2
Saddle Brook, NJ 07662
(800) 526-0056

	Years Ending 12/31					
	1981	1982	1983	1984	1985	1986
Net Investment Income ($)	.65	.75	.80	.63	.60	.47
Dividends from Net Investment Income ($)	.51	.65	.72	.80	.60	.66
Net Gains (Losses) on Investments ($)	.32	.99	3.87	(1.75)	3.36	3.06
Distributions from Net Realized Capital Gains ($)	3.30	.68	1.11	2.73	.11	2.33
Net Asset Value End of Year ($)	16.77	17.18	20.02	15.37	18.62	19.16
Ratio of Expenses to Net Assets (%)	1.04	1.07	.95	1.00	1.00	.95
Portfolio Turnover Rate (%)	18	27	64	59	86	82
Total Assets: End of Year (Millions $)	91.3	93.4	111.7	100.0	114.3	124.7
Annual Rate of Return (%) Years Ending 12/31	6.4	12.0	28.7	(4.3)	26.3	20.2

Five-Year Total Return 109.5%	Degree of Diversification B	Beta .93	Bull B	Bear D

Objective: Seeks capital growth over the long-term through investments in stocks of large, ably-managed and well-financed companies. Income is a secondary objective. May buy repos.

Portfolio: (12/31/86) Common stocks 81%, short-term securities 16%, bonds 4%. Largest stock holdings: drugs & health care 14%, electronics & electrical equipment 8%.

Distributions: Income: Feb, May, Aug, Nov   **Capital Gains:** Feb

12b-1: Yes   **Amount:** .25%

Minimum: Initial: $1,000   **Subsequent:** $50

Min IRA: Initial: $250   **Subsequent:** $50

Services: IRA, Keogh, SEP, Corp, 403(b), Withdraw

Tel Exchange: Yes   **With MMF:** Yes

Registered: All states except NH

LIBERTY

Bond

Neuberger and Berman
Management Inc.
342 Madison Avenue
New York, NY 10173
(800) 367-0770/(212) 850-8300

	Years Ending 3/31					
	1981	1982	1983	1984	1985	1986
Net Investment Income ($)	.47	.44	.34	.36	.37	.32
Dividends from Net Investment Income ($)	.46	.47	.36	.30	.40	.32
Net Gains (Losses) on Investments ($)	.09	(.44)	.58	.02	(.01)	.68
Distributions from Net Realized Capital Gains ($)	—	—	—	—	—	—
Net Asset Value End of Year ($)	3.80	3.33	3.89	3.97	3.93	4.61
Ratio of Expenses to Net Assets (%)	1.50	1.50	1.50	1.50	2.00	2.00
Portfolio Turnover Rate (%)	125	58	171	225	110	256
Total Assets: End of Year (Millions $)	8.8	7.5	8.6	8.1	8.0	9.9
Annual Rate of Return (%) Years Ending 12/31	3.3	21.1	16.7	6.1	20.9	18.2

Five-Year Total Return	114.2%	Degree of Diversification	NA	Beta	.29	Bull	C	Bear	B

Objective: Seeks a high level of current income by investing in a diversified portfolio of higher yielding, lower rated (BBB or lower) fixed-income securities. May invest in foreign securities.

Portfolio: (9/30/86) Corporate bonds 90%, common stocks 6%, cash 3%, corporate short-term notes 1%.

Distributions: **Income:** Feb, April, July, Oct   **Capital Gains:** May

12b-1: No

Minimum: **Initial:** $500   **Subsequent:** $50

Min IRA: **Initial:** $250   **Subsequent:** $50

Services: IRA, Keogh, Withdraw, Deduct

Tel Exchange: Yes   **With MMF:** Yes

Registered: All states except AZ, IA, IL, LA, ME, MS, NC, NH, TN

LMH
Growth & Income

Heine Management Group
253 Post Rd. West
PO Box 830
Westport, CT 06881
(800) 225-8558/(203) 222-1624

	Years Ending 6/30					
	1981	1982	1983	1984	1985	1986
Net Investment Income ($)	—	—	—	.20	.46	1.10
Dividends from Net Investment Income ($)	—	—	—	—	.11	.52
Net Gains (Losses) on Investments ($)	—	—	—	.35	4.51	4.12
Distributions from Net Realized Capital Gains ($)	—	—	—	—	.11	.80
Net Asset Value End of Year ($)	—	—	—	20.55	25.30	29.20
Ratio of Expenses to Net Assets (%)	—	—	—	2.60	1.42	1.25
Portfolio Turnover Rate (%)	—	—	—	13	25	50
Total Assets: End of Year (Millions $)	—	—	—	30.5	77.1	83.9
Annual Rate of Return (%) Years Ending 12/31	—	—	—	9.4	22.8	14.1

Five-Year Total Return	NA	Degree of Diversification	C	Beta	.63	Bull NA	Bear NA

Objective: Seeks capital appreciation through investment in common stocks of well-established, dividend-paying companies which are currently undervalued considering the strength of their financial position. May also invest in preferred stocks and convertible securities as well as up to 10% of total assets in U.S. traded foreign securities.

Portfolio: (9/30/86) Common stocks 49%, commercial paper 50%, other 1%. Largest stock holdings: utilities 19%, conglomerates 4%.

Distributions: Income: Annually   **Capital Gains:** Annually

12b-1: No

Minimum: Initial: $2,500   Subsequent: $1,000

Min IRA: Initial: $500   Subsequent: $500

Services: IRA, Keogh, Corp

Tel Exchange: No

Registered: All states except AL, AR, AZ, KY, ME, NC, ND, NH, NM, RI, TN, TX, UT, WV

LOOMIS-SAYLES MUTUAL
Balanced

Loomis-Sayles & Co., Inc.
PO Box 449
Back Bay Annex
Boston, MA 02117
(800) 345-4048/(617) 266-3700

	Years Ending 12/31					
	1981	1982	1983	1984	1985	1986
Net Investment Income ($)	1.10	1.09	.94	1.08	.94	.82
Dividends from Net Investment Income ($)	0.97	1.09	1.09	.95	1.08	.94
Net Gains (Losses) on Investments ($)	(1.08)	4.26	.80	(.07)	4.66	4.20
Distributions from Net Realized Capital Gains ($)	—	—	—	1.86	—	2.75
Net Asset Value End of Year ($)	13.90	18.16	18.81	17.01	21.53	22.86
Ratio of Expenses to Net Assets (%)	.81	.84	.87	.85	.86	.84
Portfolio Turnover Rate (%)	70	102	194	135	186	127
Total Assets: End of Year (Millions $)	69.2	86.9	95.5	90.6	121.1	203.4
Annual Rate of Return (%) Years Ending 12/31	(0.1)	40.9	10.0	6.4	34.4	24.8

Five-Year Total Return 176.7%	Degree of Diversification C	Beta .84	Bull A	Bear B

Objective: Seeks high total return from income and capital growth by investing in a diversified portfolio of stocks and bonds of seasoned, well-established, dividend-paying companies.

Portfolio: (12/31/86) Common stocks 69%, bonds and notes 22%, preferred stocks 8%, short-term securities 1%. Largest stock holdings: health-care 14%, insurance 13%.

Distributions: **Income:** Quarterly   **Capital Gains:** Annually
12b-1: No
Minimum: **Initial:** $250   **Subsequent:** $50
Min IRA: **Initial:** $25   **Subsequent:** $25
Services: IRA, Keogh, Corp, Withdraw, Deduct
Tel Exchange: Yes   **With MMF:** Yes
Registered: All states

MANHATTAN
Growth

Neuberger and Berman
Management Inc.
342 Madison Ave.
New York, NY 10173
(800) 367-0770/(212) 850-8300

	Years Ending 12/31					
	1981	1982	1983	1984	1985	1986
Net Investment Income ($)	.17	.18	.19	.11	.07	.10
Dividends from Net Investment Income ($)	.10	.13	.17	.18	.11	.08
Net Gains (Losses) on Investments ($)	(.49)	.96	1.16	.31	2.34	1.31
Distributions from Net Realized Capital Gains ($)	—	—	—	—	—	1.24
Net Asset Value End of Year ($)	4.13	5.14	6.32	6.56	8.86	8.95
Ratio of Expenses to Net Assets (%)	1.40	1.50	1.30	1.50	1.40	1.10
Portfolio Turnover Rate (%)	159	177	173	186	155	96
Total Assets: End of Year (Millions $)	57.2	65.8	75.5	79.4	158.9	293.6
Annual Rate of Return (%) Years Ending 12/31	(7.1)	28.7	26.8	7.1	37.1	17.0

Five-Year Total Return 180.5%	Degree of Diversification A	Beta 1.08	Bull A	Bear C

Objective: Seeks capital growth; any income received is incidental to growth objective. May invest in preferred stocks and debt securities without limitation as defensive tactic. Common stock investment is in well-established, leading companies with maximum growth potential.

Portfolio: (12/31/86) Common stocks 93%, short-term corporate notes 6%. Largest stock holdings: retailing 9%, consumer goods and services 8%.

Distributions: Income: Feb   **Capital Gains:** Feb
12b-1: Yes   **Amount:** .25%
Minimum: Initial: $500   **Subsequent:** $50
Min IRA: Initial: $250   **Subsequent:** $50
Services: IRA, Keogh, Withdraw
Tel Exchange: Yes   **With MMF:** Yes
Registered: All states except ME, NH, TN

MATHERS
Growth

Mathers & Company, Inc.
125 S. Wacker Dr.
Chicago, IL 60606
(312) 236-8215

	Years Ending 12/31					
	1981	1982	1983	1984	1985	1986
Net Investment Income ($)	.71	.68	.86	.61	.75	.34
Dividends from Net Investment Income ($)	.78	.65	.63	.86	.55	.81
Net Gains (Losses) on Investments ($)	(2.62)	2.11	2.49	(1.17)	4.30	2.16
Distributions from Net Realized Capital Gains ($)	1.64	1.00	1.49	2.68	1.82	7.38
Net Asset Value End of Year ($)	21.70	22.84	24.07	19.97	22.65	16.96
Ratio of Expenses to Net Assets (%)	.59	.63	.60	.69	.74	.77
Portfolio Turnover Rate (%)	17	35	85	71	278	174
Total Assets: End of Year (Millions $)	195.1	214.7	217.2	182.1	187.3	134.8
Annual Rate of Return (%) Years Ending 12/31	(7.7)	16.2	16.1	(1.5)	27.5	12.9

Five-Year Total Return	91.4%	Degree of Diversification	D	Beta	.99	Bull	C	Bear	E

Objective: Long-term capital appreciation principally through investment in common stocks of growth companies and a small percentage of companies in special situations (mergers, etc.) or which are unseasoned. Current income is a secondary consideration.

Portfolio: (12/31/86) Common stocks 94%, short-term notes 9%. Largest stock holdings: metals & mining 13%, electronics 9%.

Distributions: Income: Jan   **Capital Gains:** Jan

12b-1: No

Minimum: Initial: $1,000   Subsequent: $200

Min IRA: Initial: None   Subsequent: None

Services: IRA, Keogh

Tel Exchange: No

Registered: All states except AK, ID, ME, MT, ND, NH, SD, UT, VT, WY

MEDICAL TECHNOLOGY

Aggressive Growth

AMA Advisers, Inc.
5 Sentry Pkwy. West
Suite 120, PO Box 1111
Blue Bell, PA 19422
(800) 523-0864/(215) 825-0400

	Years Ending 6/30					
	1981	**1982**	**1983**	**1984**	**1985**	**1986**
Net Investment Income ($)	.03	.03	.03	(.04)	.02	(.02)
Dividends from Net Investment Income ($)	—	.03	.02	.02	—	.02
Net Gains (Losses) on Investments ($)	2.64	(1.23)	6.04	(4.45)	2.00	5.56
Distributions from Net Realized Capital Gains ($)	—	.31	.02	.04	.07	.06
Net Asset Value End of Year ($)	8.51	6.97	13.00	8.46	10.41	15.87
Ratio of Expenses to Net Assets (%)	1.88	1.56	1.40	1.56	1.49	1.44
Portfolio Turnover Rate (%)	23	18	8	23	21	15
Total Assets: End of Year (Millions $)	15.1	17.9	72.7	49.8	66.7	97.6
Annual Rate of Return (%) Years Ending 12/31	(7.8)	37.9	(0.7)	(12.5)	39.0	15.3

Five-Year Total Return	92.2%	Degree of Diversification	B	Beta	1.38	Bull	D	Bear	D

Objective: Seeks capital appreciation through concentration of investments in companies engaged in the design, manufacture or sale of products or services which are derived from technology for use in medicine or health care. May move out up to 75% of assets as defensive position. May invest in foreign securities.

Portfolio: (9/30/86) Common stocks 100%, other assets 2%. Largest holdings: therapeutic technology 34%, supportive technology 26%.

Distributions: Income: July   **Capital Gains:** July

12b-1: Yes   **Amount:** .50%

Minimum: Initial: $1,000   **Subsequent:** None

Min IRA: Initial: $500   **Subsequent:** $50

Services: IRA, Keogh, 403(b), SEP, Withdraw, Deduct

Tel Exchange: Yes   **With MMF:** Yes

Registered: All states

MUTUAL OF OMAHA AMERICA
Bond

Mutual of Omaha Fund
Management Co.
10235 Regency Cir.
Omaha, NE 68114
(800) 228-9596/(402) 397-8555

	Years Ending 12/31					
	1981	1982	1983	1984	1985	1986
Net Investment Income ($)	1.24	1.09	.97	1.01	.90	.92
Dividends from Net Investment Income ($)	1.24	1.14	.94	1.03	.91	.92
Net Gains (Losses) on Investments ($)	(.05)	.37	(.39)	.05	.68	.21
Distributions from Net Realized Capital Gains ($)	—	—	—	—	—	—
Net Asset Value End of Year ($)	9.78	10.10	9.74	9.77	10.44	10.65
Ratio of Expenses to Net Assets (%)	1.40	1.38	1.21	1.11	1.05	.98
Portfolio Turnover Rate (%)	NA	NA	NA	NA	168	76
Total Assets: End of Year (Millions $)	8.5	11.0	20.4	19.1	28.3	49.1

Annual Rate of Return (%) Years Ending 12/31	12.9	15.4	6.6	11.7	16.9	11.1

Five-Year Total Return	78.3%	Degree of Diversification	NA	Beta	.17	Bull	E	Bear	A

Objective:	Seeks current income through investing at least 80% of its total assets in the securities of the U.S. government or its instrumentalities.
Portfolio:	(12/31/86) U.S. government and agency securities 100%.
Distributions:	**Income:** Mar, June, Sept, Dec **Capital Gains:** Dec
12b-1:	No
Minimum:	**Initial:** $250 **Subsequent:** $50
Min IRA:	**Initial:** $250 **Subsequent:** $50
Services:	IRA, Keogh, Corp, 403(b), Withdraw, Deduct
Tel Exchange:	Yes **With MMF:** Yes
Registered:	All states

MUTUAL QUALIFIED INCOME
Balanced

Mutual Shares Corporation
26 Broadway
New York, NY 10004
(800) 344-4515/(212) 908-4048

	Years Ending 12/31					
	1981	**1982**	**1983**	**1984**	**1985**	**1986**
Net Investment Income ($)	.36	.31	.36	.42	.61	.90
Dividends from Net Investment Income ($)	.36	.30	.39	.35	.61	.85
Net Gains (Losses) on Investments ($)	2.07	1.52	4.19	1.90	3.57	2.42
Distributions from Net Realized Capital Gains ($)	1.19	.25	1.33	1.13	1.17	1.56
Net Asset Value End of Year ($)	11.80	13.08	15.91	16.75	19.15	20.06
Ratio of Expenses to Net Assets (%)	.85	1.48	1.11	.81	.70	.68
Portfolio Turnover Rate (%)	143	125	79	107	96	124
Total Assets: End of Year (Millions $)	6.3	28.9	56.3	178.1	432.5	561.4
Annual Rate of Return (%) Years Ending 12/31	22.3	15.4	34.9	14.7	25.5	16.9

Five-Year Total Return	161.8%	Degree of Diversification	D	Beta	.40	Bull	A	Bear	B

Objective: Primary objective is capital appreciation from either short- or long-term investment in companies involved in prospective mergers, consolidations, liquidations and reorganizations. Current income is a secondary objective.

Portfolio: (12/31/86) Common stocks 48%, corporate bonds 13%, foreign investments 12%, bonds in reorganization 10%, temporary investments 9%, preferred stock 8%. Largest stock holdings: banking and financial institutions 9%, industrials 8%.

Distributions: Income: Annually   **Capital Gains:** Annually

12b-1: No

Minimum: Initial: $1,000   Subsequent: None

Min IRA: Initial: $1,000   Subsequent: None

Services: IRA, Keogh, Deduct, 403(b)

Tel Exchange: No

Registered: All states

MUTUAL SHARES
Balanced

Mutual Shares Corporation
26 Broadway
New York, NY 10004
(800) 344-4515/(212) 908-4048

	Years Ending 12/31					
	1981	1982	1983	1984	1985	1986
Net Investment Income ($)	1.78	2.00	1.40	1.45	1.93	2.43
Dividends from Net Investment Income ($)	1.67	2.12	1.37	1.42	1.88	2.34
Net Gains (Losses) on Investments ($)	1.86	3.15	13.51	5.61	11.34	7.29
Distributions from Net Realized Capital Gains ($)	3.63	2.68	4.63	4.83	4.12	4.52
Net Asset Value End of Year ($)	40.23	40.58	49.49	50.30	57.57	60.43
Ratio of Expenses to Net Assets (%)	.75	.78	.83	.73	.67	.70
Portfolio Turnover Rate (%)	88	78	70	102	91	122
Total Assets: End of Year (Millions $)	126.5	154.1	241.1	496.0	1,076.2	1,402.6
Annual Rate of Return (%) Years Ending 12/31	8.7	13.4	37.0	14.4	26.6	16.9

Five-Year Total Return 162.8%	Degree of Diversification D	Beta .42	Bull A	Bear C

Objective: Primary objective is capital appreciation from either short- or long-term investment in the debt or equity securities of companies involved in prospective mergers, consolidations, liquidations and reorganizations. Income is secondary objective.

Portfolio: (12/31/86) Common stocks 52%, temporary investments 13%, foreign investments 10%, corporate bonds 9%, bonds in reorganization 9%, preferred stock 8%. Largest stock holdings: banking and financial institutions 9%, industrials 9%.

Distributions: Income: Annually   **Capital Gains:** Annually

12b-1: No

Minimum: Initial: $1,000   **Subsequent:** None

Min IRA: Initial: $1,000   **Subsequent:** None

Services: IRA, Keogh, Deduct, 403(b), Withdraw

Tel Exchange: No

Registered: All states

NAESS & THOMAS SPECIAL

Aggressive Growth

Vanguard Group
Vanguard Financial Ctr.
Valley Forge, PA 19482
(800) 662-7447/(215) 648-6000

	Years Ending 9/30					
	1981	1982	1983	1984	1985	1986
Net Investment Income ($)	.15	.97	(.25)	.43	(.11)	(.03)
Dividends from Net Investment Income ($)	.40	.10	.91	—	.45	—
Net Gains (Losses) on Investments ($)	(1.49)	6.70	25.72	(12.76)	(1.54)	4.70
Distributions from Net Realized Capital Gains ($)	7.63	6.32	2.76	7.53	2.31	—
Net Asset Value End of Year ($)	36.26	37.51	59.31	39.45	35.04	39.71
Ratio of Expenses to Net Assets (%)	1.52	2.19	1.41	1.05	1.00	.92
Portfolio Turnover Rate (%)	63	114	83	100	103	88
Total Assets: End of Year (Millions $)	12.1	16.0	41.2	37.1	31.6	30.8

Annual Rate of Return (%) Years Ending 12/31	(2.9)	47.2	17.9	(25.1)	21.7	0.0

Five-Year Total Return	58.2%	Degree of Diversification	D	Beta 1.22	Bull E	Bear D

Objective: Fund is intended for that portion of an investor's funds which can appropriately be invested in special risks of various kinds with the basic aim of growth of principal. Invests in securities of small companies from different sectors of the economy. May invest up to 25% of assets in foreign securities.

Portfolio: (9/30/86) Common stocks 96%, cash 4%. Largest stock holdings: technology 19%, consumer related 15%.

Distributions: Income: Nov   **Capital Gains:** Nov

12b-1: No

Minimum: Initial: $3,000   Subsequent: $100

Min IRA: Initial: $500   Subsequent: $50

Services: IRA, Keogh, 403(b), Corp, Withdraw, Deduct

Tel Exchange: No

Registered: All states

NATIONAL INDUSTRIES FUND
Growth

Stonebridge Capital Management
1880 Century Park East, Suite 717
Los Angeles, CA 90067
(303) 759-2400

	Years Ending 11/30					
	1981	1982	1983	1984	1985	1986
Net Investment Income ($)	.48	.61	.38	.33	.25	.13
Dividends from Net Investment Income ($)	.42	.48	.61	.39	.34	.25
Net Gains (Losses) on Investments ($)	(2.96)	(.78)	1.50	(1.14)	.99	1.39
Distributions from Net Realized Capital Gains ($)	1.70	1.36	.43	1.17	.18	.50
Net Asset Value End of Year ($)	15.30	13.12	13.96	11.59	12.31	13.08
Ratio of Expenses to Net Assets (%)	1.66	1.70	1.67	1.70	1.70	1.68
Portfolio Turnover Rate (%)	33	76	50	57	70	74
Total Assets: End of Year (Millions $)	30.3	29.1	31.2	27.8	27.9	28.0
Annual Rate of Return (%) Years Ending 12/31	(10.7)	4.7	11.3	(2.3)	10.5	9.8

Five-Year Total Return	38.2%	Degree of Diversification	B	Beta	.92	Bull	E	Bear	D

Objective: Seeks long-term capital appreciation and growth in income. Current income is a secondary consideration. Invests in companies which appear to have good prospects for increased earnings and dividends.

Portfolio: (11/30/86) Common stocks 94%, U.S. government obligations 4%, short-term securities 1%. Largest stock holdings: pharmaceuticals 14%, communications 11%.

Distributions: Income: Annually   **Capital Gains:** Annually
12b-1: No
Minimum: Initial: $250   **Subsequent:** $25
Min IRA: Initial: NA   **Subsequent:** NA
Services: Withdraw
Tel Exchange: No
Registered: All states

NEUWIRTH
Aggressive Growth

Wood, Struthers & Winthrop
Management Corp.
140 Broadway
New York, NY 10005
(800) 221-5672/(212) 504-4000

	Years Ending 12/31					
	1981	**1982**	**1983**	**1984**	**1985**	**1986**
Net Investment Income ($)	.06	.18	(.03)	.06	.05	(.07)
Dividends from Net Investment Income ($)	.17	.06	.16	—	.08	.04
Net Gains (Losses) on Investments ($)	(1.38)	2.20	1.62	(1.28)	4.27	1.47
Distributions from Net Realized Capital Gains ($)	—	—	—	.37	—	3.21
Net Asset Value End of Year ($)	8.80	11.13	12.56	10.98	15.21	13.35
Ratio of Expenses to Net Assets (%)	1.87	1.79	1.58	1.64	1.55	1.78
Portfolio Turnover Rate (%)	92	120	81	83	86	74
Total Assets: End of Year (Millions $)	13.4	20.1	23.0	18.2	23.9	23.3

Annual Rate of Return (%) Years Ending 12/31	(12.3)	28.1	15	(8.0)	39.1	8.7

Five-Year Total Return	104.8%	Degree of Diversification	C	Beta	1.24	Bull	C	Bear	D

Objective: Seeks capital growth through investment in securities of established companies in growth industries. May invest in lesser-known emerging growth companies and up to 20% of total assets may be invested in foreign securities. May write put and call options.

Portfolio: (12/30/86) Common stocks 94%, commercial paper 6%, convertible bonds 1%. Largest stock holdings: broadcasting 13%, specialty equipment 7%.

Distributions: Income: Jan   **Capital Gains:** Jan
12b-1: Yes   Amount: .40%
Minimum: Initial: $1,000   Subsequent: $100
Min IRA: Initial: $250   Subsequent: $100
Services: IRA, Keogh, Withdraw
Tel Exchange: No
Registered: All states except AZ, CA, ME, TN, TX

NEW BEGINNING GROWTH

Aggressive Growth

Sit Investment Associates, Inc.
1714 First Bank Place West
Minneapolis, MN 55402
(612) 332-3223

	1981	1982	1983	1984	1985	1986
			Years Ending 6/30			
Net Investment Income ($)	–	–	.07	.20	.21	.04
Dividends from Net Investment Income ($)	–	–	.08	.17	.23	–
Net Gains (Losses) on Investments ($)	–	–	13.36	(3.77)	4.87	9.75
Distributions from Net Realized Capital Gains ($)	–	–	1.01	.39	.76	–
Net Asset Value End of Year ($)	–	–	23.01	18.88	22.97	32.76
Ratio of Expenses to Net Assets (%)	–	–	1.50	1.50	1.50	1.32
Portfolio Turnover Rate (%)	–	–	67	80	130	99
Total Assets: End of Year (Millions $)	–	–	9.4	13.3	19.6	40.8
Annual Rate of Return (%) Years Ending 12/31	–	–	27.0	(3.1)	43.6	10.4

Five-Year Total Return	NA	Degree of Diversification	C	Beta 1.03	Bull NA	Bear NA

Objective: Seeks to maximize long-term capital appreciation. Invests primarily in the common stock of small emerging-growth companies. For defensive purposes, can invest 100% of assets in corporate or government fixed-income securities.

Portfolio: (12/31/86) Common stocks 88%, short-term securities 10%, convertible bonds 1%. Largest stock holdings: Consumer cyclicals 25%, technology 19%.

Distributions: **Income:** Annually   **Capital Gains:** Annually

12b-1: No

Minimum: Initial: $10,000   Subsequent: $500

Min IRA: Initial: NA   Subsequent: NA

Tel Exchange: No

Registered: CA, CO, CT, DC, DE, ID, IL, KS, MA, MI, MN, MO, MS, NV, NY, OH, PA, TX, VA, WA, WY

NEWTON GROWTH
Growth

M&I Investment Management
330 E. Kilbourn
Two Plaza East, #1150
Milwaukee, WI 53202
(800) 247-7039/(414) 347-1141

	Years Ending 12/31					
	1981	1982	1983	1984	1985	1986
Net Investment Income ($)	.48	.56	.20	.55	.69	.33
Dividends from Net Investment Income ($)	.47	.55	.19	.52	—	1.06
Net Gains (Losses) on Investments ($)	(.86)	6.09	5.30	(2.74)	6.25	1.91
Distributions from Net Realized Capital Gains ($)	1.16	.77	1.89	—	—	11.73
Net Asset Value End of Year ($)	18.31	23.64	27.06	24.35	31.29	20.74
Ratio of Expenses to Net Assets (%)	1.20	1.21	1.16	1.17	1.18	1.23
Portfolio Turnover Rate (%)	109	72	55	44	143	136
Total Assets: End of Year (Millions $)	16.4	21.6	31.5	30.0	33.9	33.9

Annual Rate of Return (%) Years Ending 12/31	(1.9)	36.1	23.5	(8.2)	28.7	9.1

Five-Year Total Return 116.4%	Degree of Diversification D	Beta .87	Bull C	Bear C

Objective: Long-term growth of capital through investment primarily in common stocks of large, established companies that are dividend-paying. Current income of lesser importance.

Portfolio: (12/31/86) Common stocks 83%, short-term investments 14%, convertible bonds 4%. Largest stock holdings: capital goods 33%, consumer goods & services 23%.

Distributions: Income: Annually   **Capital Gains:** Annually
12b-1: Yes   **Amount:** .25%
Minimum: Initial: $1,000   Subsequent: $50
Min IRA: Initial: $500   Subsequent: $50
Services: IRA, Keogh, Corp, 403(b), Withdraw, Deduct
Tel Exchange: Yes   **With MMF:** Yes
Registered: All states

NEWTON INCOME
Bond

M&I Investment Management
330 E. Kilbourn
Two Plaza East, #1150
Milwaukee, WI 53202
(800) 247-7039/(414) 347-1141

	Years Ending 7/31					
	1981	1982	1983	1984	1985	1986
Net Investment Income ($)	.84	.87	.87	.82	.76	.78
Dividends from Net Investment Income ($)	.85	.87	.87	.82	.77	.60
Net Gains (Losses) on Investments ($)	(1.17)	(.11)	1.05	.03	.31	.14
Distributions from Net Realized Capital Gains ($)	–	–	–	–	–	–
Net Asset Value End of Year ($)	6.95	6.84	7.89	7.92	8.22	8.54
Ratio of Expenses to Net Assets (%)	1.50	1.72	1.49	1.66	1.60	1.51
Portfolio Turnover Rate (%)	40	43	41	-0-	480	56
Total Assets: End of Year (Millions $)	5.0	5.1	6.3	7.1	11.7	11.5
Annual Rate of Return (%) Years Ending 12/31	1.6	30.2	11.6	12.2	12.8	9.0

Five-Year Total Return	100.6%	Degree of Diversification	NA	Beta	.06	Bull	E	Bear	A

Objective: Seeks above-average income through investment in investment-grade bonds (rated Baa or BBB or better) varying in maturity as fits in relationship with current economic conditions. May invest in income-producing common stocks.

Portfolio: (7/31/86) Federal agency securities 40%, short-term securities 24%, corporate bonds 22%, U.S. government securities 20%.

Distributions: Income: Feb, May, Aug, Nov   **Capital Gains:** Aug

12b-1: Yes   **Amount:** .25%

Minimum: Initial: $1,000   Subsequent: $50

Min IRA: Initial: $500   Subsequent: $50

Services: IRA, Keogh, 403(b), Corp, Withdraw, Deduct

Tel Exchange: Yes   **With MMF:** Yes

Registered: Call regarding registration

NICHOLAS
Growth

Nicholas Company, Inc.
700 N. Water St., #1010
Milwaukee, WI 53202
(414) 272-6133

	Years Ending 3/31					
	1981	1982	1983	1984	1985	1986
Net Investment Income ($)	.50	.63	.68	.66	.62	.89
Dividends from Net Investment Income ($)	.39	.52	.62	.64	.64	.57
Net Gains (Losses) on Investments ($)	7.28	(1.74)	8.99	.44	6.37	6.31
Distributions from Net Realized Capital Gains ($)	—	.84	1.01	1.07	1.58	.61
Net Asset Value End of Year ($)	19.51	17.04	25.08	24.47	29.24	35.26
Ratio of Expenses to Net Assets (%)	1.06	1.03	.95	.87	.82	.86
Portfolio Turnover Rate (%)	52	45	31	22	14	14
Total Assets: End of Year (Millions $)	57.1	56.6	126.1	153.4	309.0	955.5
Annual Rate of Return (%) Years Ending 12/31	8.5	35.5	23.9	9.9	29.7	11.7

Five-Year Total Return	167.2%	Degree of Diversification	C	Beta	.70	Bull	A	Bear	C

Objective: Capital appreciation through investment primarily in common stocks showing favorable long-term prospects. Investment in unseasoned companies is limited to 5%.

Portfolio: (9/30/86) Common stocks 61%, short-term securities 37%, corporate bond 1%, convertible bonds 1%, convertible preferred stock 1%. Largest stock holdings: banks and savings & loans 9%, insurance 8%.

Distributions: Income: April   **Capital Gains:** April

12b-1: No

Minimum: Initial: $500   Subsequent: $100

Min IRA: Initial: $500   Subsequent: $100

Services: IRA, Keogh, SEP, Withdraw

Tel Exchange: None

Registered: All states

NICHOLAS II
Growth

Nicholas Company, Inc.
700 N. Water St., #1010
Milwaukee, WI 53202
(414) 272-6133

	Years Ending 9/30					
	1981	1982	1983	1984	1985	1986
Net Investment Income ($)	–	–	–	.09	.18	.40
Dividends from Net Investment Income ($)	–	–	–	–	.09	.16
Net Gains (Losses) on Investments ($)	–	–	–	1.57	2.83	2.33
Distributions from Net Realized Capital Gains ($)	–	–	–	–	.19	.06
Net Asset Value End of Year ($)	–	–	–	11.66	14.39	16.90
Ratio of Expenses to Net Assets (%)	–	–	–	1.85	1.11	.79
Portfolio Turnover Rate (%)	–	–	–	29	10	15
Total Assets: End of Year (Millions $)	–	–	–	11.4	140.1	299.2
Annual Rate of Return (%) Years Ending 12/31	–	–	–	16.9	33.8	10.3

Five-Year Total Return	NA	Degree of Diversification	D	Beta	.67	Bull NA	Bear NA

Objective: Primary objective is long-term growth; current income is a secondary consideration. Invests primarily in common stocks which are believed to have favorable long-term growth prospects. May invest 5% of the fund's assets in unseasoned companies which have an operating history of less than three years.

Portfolio: (9/30/86) Common stocks 89%, short-term securities 9%, convertible bonds 2%. Largest stock holdings: banks and savings and loans 12%, insurance 11%.

Distributions: Income: Annually   **Capital Gains:** Annually
12b-1: No
Minimum: Initial: $1,000   Subsequent: $100
Min IRA: Initial: $1,000   Subsequent: None
Services: IRA, Keogh
Tel Exchange: No
Registered: All states

NICHOLAS INCOME
Bond

Nicholas Company, Inc.
700 N. Water St., #1010
Milwaukee, WI 53202
(414) 272-6133

	Years Ending 12/31					
	1981	**1982**	**1983**	**1984**	**1985**	**1986**
Net Investment Income ($)	.47	.46	.44	.45	.43	.40
Dividends from Net Investment Income ($)	.47	.46	.44	.44	.42	.38
Net Gains (Losses) on Investments ($)	(.35)	.54	(.01)	(.03)	.30	.03
Distributions from Net Realized Capital Gains ($)	—	—	—	—	—	—
Net Asset Value End of Year ($)	3.14	3.68	3.67	3.65	3.96	4.01
Ratio of Expenses to Net Assets (%)	1.00	1.00	1.00	1.00	1.00	.96
Portfolio Turnover Rate (%)	22	31	19	14	12	20
Total Assets: End of Year (Millions $)	9.9	13.2	14.6	16.9	34.8	65.0
Annual Rate of Return (%) Years Ending 12/31	3.9	34.9	12.4	12.6	21.2	11.4

Five-Year Total Return	130.5%	Degree of Diversification	NA	Beta	.15	Bull	D	Bear	A

Objective: High current income and consistent conservation of capital. Must invest at least 25% of total assets in geographically diversified and state-regulated electric utilities and systems. Balance is invested in investment-grade debt securities and may include repos and other cash investments.

Portfolio: (12/31/86) Non-convertible bonds 82%, short-term securities 8%, preferred stocks 4%, common stocks 3%, cash 3%, convertible bonds 1%.

Distributions: Income: Jan, April, July, Oct   **Capital Gains:** Jan

12b-1: No

Minimum: Initial: $500   **Subsequent:** $50

Min IRA: Initial: $500   **Subsequent:** $50

Services: IRA, Keogh, Withdraw

Tel Exchange: No

Registered: All states except ME, NH

NODDINGS-CALAMOS CONVERTIBLE INCOME

Growth & Income

Nodding-Calamos Asset
Management, Inc.
2001 Spring Road, #750
Oak Brook, IL 60521
(800) 251-2411/(312) 571-7100

	Years Ending 4/30					
	1981	**1982**	**1983**	**1984**	**1985**	**1986** (10 mos.)
Net Investment Income ($)	—	—	—	—	—	.32
Dividends from Net Investment Income ($)	—	—	—	—	—	.25
Net Gains (Losses) on Investments ($)	—	—	—	—	—	1.92
Distributions from Net Realized Capital Gains ($)	—	—	—	—	—	—
Net Asset Value End of Year ($)	—	—	—	—	—	11.99
Ratio of Expenses to Net Assets (%)	—	—	—	—	—	2.00
Portfolio Turnover Rate (%)	—	—	—	—	—	26
Total Assets: End of Year (Millions $)	—	—	—	—	—	10.2
Annual Rate of Return (%) Years Ending 12/31	—	—	—	—	—	16.1

Five-Year Total Return	NA	Degree of Diversification	NA	Beta	NA	Bull NA	Bear NA

Objective:	Seeks high current income. Capital appreciation is a secondary objective. Invests at least 65% of its assets in convertible bonds and preferred stocks. May invest 30% of fund's assets in issues rated BB or lower by S&P.
Portfolio:	(10/31/86) Convertible bonds 75.8%, convertible preferred stocks 14.2, cash 8.4%. Largest holdings: publishing 5.9%, financial services 5.1%.
Distributions:	**Income:** Quarterly **Capital Gains:** Annually
12b-1:	No
Minimum:	**Initial:** $5,000 **Subsequent:** $500
Min IRA:	**Initial:** $2,000 **Subsequent:** $500
Services:	IRA, Keogh, Deduct, Withdraw
Tel Exchange:	Yes **With MMF:** No
Registered:	All states except: AL, AK, AR, DE, ID, KS, ME, MS, ND, NE, NH, SD, UT, VT, WV, WY

NOMURA PACIFIC BASIN
International

Nomura Capital Management
180 Maiden Lane
New York, NY 10038
(212) 208-9366/(800) 833-0018

	Years Ending 3/31					
	1981	1982	1983	1984	1985	1986 (9 mos.)
Net Investment Income ($)	—	—	—	—	—	.06
Dividends from Net Investment Income ($)	—	—	—	—	—	—
Net Gains (Losses) on Investments ($)	—	—	—	—	—	5.62
Distributions from Net Realized Capital Gains ($)	—	—	—	—	—	—
Net Asset Value End of Year ($)	—	—	—	—	—	15.68
Ratio of Expenses to Net Assets (%)	—	—	—	—	—	1.50
Portfolio Turnover Rate (%)	—	—	—	—	—	3
Total Assets: End of Year (Millions $)	—	—	—	—	—	32.4

Annual Rate of Return (%) Years Ending 12/31	—	—	—	—	—	74.4

Five-Year Total Return	NA	Degree of Diversification	NA	Beta	NA	Bull NA	Bear NA

Objective: Seeks long-term capital appreciation primarily through investment of 70% of the fund's assets in equity securities of corporations located in the Pacific Basin, including Japan, Australia and the Philippines. Portfolio companies will range from large and well-established to small and unseasoned.

Portfolio: (9/30/86) Common stocks 77%, short-term securities 23%. Largest stock holdings: Japan 67%, Australia 4%.

Distributions: Income: Annually **Capital Gains:** Annually
12b-1: Yes **Amount:** Pd. by Advisor
Minimum: Initial: $20,000 **Subsequent:** $5,000
Min IRA: Initial: None **Subsequent:** None
Services: IRA
Tel Exchange: No
Registered: AK, AZ, CA, CO, CT, DE, FL, GA, HI, ID, IL, IN, MA, MD, MI, MN, MO, NY, OH, OR, PA, TN, TX, UT, VA, WA, WI, WY

NORTH STAR
APOLLO
Growth

Investment Advisors, Inc.
1100 Dain Tower
Minneapolis, MN 55440
(612) 371-7780

| | Years Ending 3/31 | | | | | |
	1981	1982	1983	1984 (10 mos.)	1985	1986
Net Investment Income ($)	–	–	–	.23	.22	.20
Dividends from Net Investment Income ($)	–	–	–	–	.22	.20
Net Gains (Losses) on Investments ($)	–	–	–	(.02)	–	1.59
Distributions from Net Realized Capital Gains ($)	–	–	–	–	.14	.20
Net Asset Value End of Year ($)	–	–	–	10.21	10.07	11.46
Ratio of Expenses to Net Assets (%)	–	–	–	1.00	1.00	1.0
Portfolio Turnover Rate (%)	–	–	–	20	36	85
Total Assets: End of Year (Millions $)	–	–	–	12.9	18.2	24.7
Annual Rate of Return (%) Years Ending 12/31	–	–	–	–	12.7	2.0

Five-Year Total Return	NA	Degree of Diversification	NA	Beta	NA	Bull NA	Bear NA

Objective: Seeks long-term capital appreciation through investment in common stocks of companies that are unpopular, undervalued or in severe financial difficulties. A minor portion of portfolio may be invested in Ba (BB) or lower-rated debt securities. May enter into repos, invest in venture capital limited partnerships, restricted securities and foreign securities.

Portfolio: (9/30/86) Common stocks 79%, short-term securities 17%. Largest stock holdings: miscellaneous capital goods 11%, office equipment 10%.

Distributions: Income: May, Nov   **Capital Gains:** May

12b-1: No

Minimum: Initial: $2,500   Subsequent: $100

Min IRA: Initial: None   Subsequent: None

Services: IRA, Keogh, Corp, 403(b), Withdraw

Tel Exchange: No

Registered: AR, CA, CO, IA, IL, MD, MI, MN, MO, MT, ND, NE, NY, PA, SD, TN, TX, WA, WI

NORTH STAR BOND
Bond

Investment Advisors, Inc.
1100 Dain Tower
Minneapolis, MN 55440
(612) 371-7780

	Years Ending 3/31					
	1981	1982	1983	1984	1985	1986
Net Investment Income ($)	.88	.95	.98	.91	1.01	.95
Dividends from Net Investment Income ($)	.87	.92	1.00	.91	1.00	.95
Net Gains (Losses) on Investments ($)	(.26)	(.42)	1.51	(.58)	.41	1.31
Distributions from Net Realized Capital Gains ($)	—	—	—	—	—	—
Net Asset Value End of Year ($)	8.47	8.08	9.57	8.99	9.41	10.72
Ratio of Expenses to Net Assets (%)	1.00	1.00	.90	.80	.70	.70
Portfolio Turnover Rate (%)	35	23	83	40	22	76
Total Assets: End of Year (Millions $)	6.1	8.0	11.2	16.8	22.8	31.5

Annual Rate of Return (%) Years Ending 12/31	3.0	32.1	8.0	15.5	20.1	12.1

Five-Year Total Return	121.8%	Degree of Diversification	NA	Beta	.19	Bull D	Bear A

Objective: Seeks high level of current income and preservation of capital through investment in a diversified portfolio of investment grade bonds and other debt securities of similar quality. May enter into repos and invest in foreign securities.

Portfolio: (9/30/86) Long-term government and corporate bonds 92%, short-term securities 6%, corporate bonds 2%.

Distributions: Income: Jan, Apr, July, Oct   **Capital Gains:** Annually

12b-1: No

Minimum: Initial: $1,000   **Subsequent:** $100

Min IRA: Initial: None   **Subsequent:** None

Services: IRA, Keogh, Corp, 403(b), Withdraw

Tel Exchange: No

Registered: AR, CA, CO, IA, IL, MD, MI, MN, MO, MT, ND, NE, NY, PA, SD, TN, TX, WA, WI

NORTH STAR REGIONAL
Growth

Investment Advisors, Inc.
1100 Dain Tower
Minneapolis, MN 55440
(612) 371-7780

| | Years Ending 3/31 | | | | | |
	1981 (11 mos.)	1982	1983	1984	1985	1986
Net Investment Income ($)	.12	.57	.39	.43	.46	.41
Dividends from Net Investment Income ($)	.04	.51	.45	.40	.48	.43
Net Gains (Losses) on Investments ($)	2.96	(1.18)	6.48	(.53)	1.81	6.57
Distributions from Net Realized Capital Gains ($)	–	.15	.03	1.19	1.11	.40
Net Asset Value End of Year ($)	13.18	11.91	18.30	16.61	17.29	23.44
Ratio of Expenses to Net Assets (%)	1.00	1.00	1.00	.90	.80	.80
Portfolio Turnover Rate (%)	4	84	116	77	80	112
Total Assets: End of Year (Millions $)	11.7	14.1	38.4	44.9	56.5	77.8
Annual Rate of Return (%) Years Ending 12/31	(3.3)	41.4	13.1	(2.1)	38.4	22.8

Five-Year Total Return	166.0%	Degree of Diversification	B	Beta	.90	Bull	A	Bear	C

Objective: Seeks capital appreciation through investment of at least 80% of its equity investments in companies headquartered in MN, WI, IA, NE, MT, ND or SD. For defensive purposes, may convert entire portfolio to debt securities. May enter into repos, invest in restricted securities, venture capital, limited partnerships and foreign securities.

Portfolio: (9/30/86) Common stocks 65%, short-term securities 27%, corporate bonds 1%. Largest stock holdings: miscellaneous consumer cyclicals 9%, health care 7%.

Distributions: Income: May, Nov   **Capital Gains:** May

12b-1: No

Minimum: Initial: $2,500   Subsequent: $100

Min IRA: Initial: None   Subsequent: None

Services: IRA, Keogh, Corp, 403(b), Withdraw

Tel Exchange: No

Registered: AR, CA, CO, IA, IL, MD, MI, MN, MO, MT, ND, NE, NY, PA, SD, TN, TX, WA, WI

NORTH STAR STOCK
Growth

Investment Advisors, Inc.
1100 Dain Tower
Minneapolis, MN 55440
(612) 371-7780

	Years Ending 3/31					
	1981	1982	1983	1984	1985	1986
Net Investment Income ($)	.51	.54	.40	.37	.45	.42
Dividends from Net Investment Income ($)	.52	.52	.48	.35	.41	.48
Net Gains (Losses) on Investments ($)	3.27	(1.30)	4.38	.27	1.07	3.36
Distributions from Net Realized Capital Gains ($)	–	1.05	.64	.62	1.39	.46
Net Asset Value End of Year ($)´	12.53	10.20	13.86	13.53	13.25	16.09
Ratio of Expenses to Net Assets (%)	.80	.80	.80	.70	.70	.70
Portfolio Turnover Rate (%)	113	76	81	69	62	50
Total Assets: End of Year (Millions $)	14.9	16.9	35.3	48.7	60.2	69.1
Annual Rate of Return (%) Years Ending 12/31	(1.3)	33.9	19.4	3.7	23.2	12.9

Five-Year Total Return	130.7%	Degree of Diversification	A	Beta	.91	Bull	B	Bear	B

Objective: Seeks capital appreciation and income secondarily through investment in common stocks of primarily widely known companies and some not so well-known. May enter into repos, invest in restricted securities, REITS and venture capital limited partnerships.

Portfolio: (9/30/86) Common stocks 77%, short-term securities 23%. Largest stock holdings: office equipment 10%, restaurant 6%.

Distributions: Income: May, Nov   Capital Gains: May

12b-1: No

Minimum: Initial: $1,000   Subsequent: $100

Min IRA: Initial: None   Subsequent: None

Services: IRA, Keogh, Corp, 403(b), Withdraw

Tel Exchange: No

Registered: AR, CA, CO, IA, IL, MD, MI, MN, MO, MT, ND, NE, NY, PA, SD, TN, TX, WA, WI

NORTHEAST INVESTORS GROWTH
Growth

Northeast Management &
Research Co., Inc.
50 Congress Street
Boston, MA 02109
(617) 523-3588/(800) 225-6704

| | Years Ending 12/31 | | | | | |
	1981	1982	1983	1984	1985	1986
Net Investment Income ($)	.26	.30	.13	.13	.11	.08
Dividends from Net Investment Income ($)	.11	.22	.21	.12	.05	.13
Net Gains (Losses) on Investments ($)	(.64)	.91	1.05	.29	3.91	3.56
Distributions from Net Realized Capital Gains ($)	.01	.12	.15	.30	.09	.52
Net Asset Value End of Year ($)	9.67	10.54	11.36	11.36	15.24	18.23
Ratio of Expenses to Net Assets (%)	2.02	2.47	2.01	2.02	2.00	1.87
Portfolio Turnover Rate (%)	40	66	63	34	37	13
Total Assets: End of Year (Millions $)	1.6	2.8	4.0	4.1	6.4	20.5
Annual Rate of Return (%) Years Ending 12/31	(3.9)	15.2	9.6	3.9	36.7	24.3

Five-Year Total Return	123.0%	Degree of Diversification	B	Beta	.94	Bull	B	Bear	C

Objective: Seeks long-term growth of both capital and future income. Invests in stocks, bonds and short-term money market instruments. Ordinarily no more than 25% of the fund's assets will be invested in fixed-income securities.

Portfolio: (12/31/86) Common stocks 96%, repurchase agreements 4%. Largest stock holdings: banking and finance 19%, food and beverages 18%.

Distributions: **Income:** Semi-Annually   **Capital Gains:** Annually

12b-1: No

Minimum: **Initial:** $100   **Subsequent:** None

Min IRA: **Initial:** $100   **Subsequent:** None

Services: IRA, Keogh, Corp, 403(b)

Tel Exchange: Yes   **With MMF:** No

Registered: All states except AL, DE, ID, IA, KS, ME, ND, NH, OR, SC, SD, UT, WV, WY

NORTHEAST INVESTORS TRUST
Bond

Trustees, Northeast
Investor's Trust
50 Congress St.
Boston, MA 02109
(800) 225-6704/(617) 523-3588

	Years Ending 9/30					
	1981	**1982**	**1983**	**1984**	**1985**	**1986**
Net Investment Income ($)	1.42	1.43	1.47	1.45	1.48	1.47
Dividends from Net Investment Income ($)	1.40	1.41	1.44	1.46	1.46	1.46
Net Gains (Losses) on Investments ($)	(1.90)	1.48	.92	(.84)	1.19	1.40
Distributions from Net Realized Capital Gains ($)	—	—	—	—	—	—
Net Asset Value End of Year ($)	9.38	10.88	11.83	10.98	12.19	13.60
Ratio of Expenses to Net Assets (%)	.66	.69	.67	.67	.72	.72
Portfolio Turnover Rate (%)	1	7	30	14	22	43
Total Assets: End of Year (Millions $)	114.9	145.4	169.4	168.2	218.1	313.3
Annual Rate of Return (%) Years Ending 12/31	5.8	36.9	11.2	13.9	25.6	20.4

Five-Year Total Return 162.0%	Degree of Diversification NA	Beta .20	Bull C	Bear A

Objective: Seeks production of income with capital growth as a secondary objective. Between 25% and 50% of the trust's assets will be invested in the electric utility industry. Common stock investments will be in established, dividend-paying companies. May use leverage.

Portfolio: (9/30/86) Corporate bonds 99%, preferred stocks 1%.

Distributions: **Income:** Feb, May, Aug, Nov   **Capital Gains:** Sept

12b-1: No

Minimum: **Initial:** $500   **Subsequent:** None

Min IRA: **Initial:** $100   **Subsequent:** None

Services: IRA, Keogh, Corp, 403(b)

Tel Exchange: Yes   **With MMF:** No

Registered: All states

NOVA
Aggressive Growth

Nova Advisers, Inc.
260 Franklin Street
Boston, MA 02110
(800) 572-0006/(617) 439-9683

	Years Ending 12/31					
	1981	1982	1983	1984	1985	1986
Net Investment Income ($)	.77	.22	.16	.18	.04	(.07)
Dividends from Net Investment Income ($)	.03	.29	.20	.19	.18	.04
Net Gains (Losses) on Investments ($)	(.41)	2.79	2.31	(1.33)	3.29	1.24
Distributions from Net Realized Capital Gains ($)	.47	.35	.85	3.23	—	2.28
Net Asset Value End of Year ($)	13.16	15.53	16.95	12.38	15.53	14.38
Ratio of Expenses to Net Assets (%)	2.00	1.70	1.50	1.50	1.50	1.70
Portfolio Turnover Rate (%)	218	184	158	129	89	99
Total Assets: End of Year (Millions $)	11.1	21.9	28.6	23.9	27.7	24.9
Annual Rate of Return (%) Years Ending 12/31	3.0	24.1	16.7	(6.2)	27.1	7.7

Five-Year Total Return	85.7%	Degree of Diversification	D	Beta	1.00	Bull	D	Bear	C

Objective: Long-term growth of capital by investing primarily in common stocks of companies expected to have growth in various fields of science and technology. Invests in a mix of established growth, emerging growth, and companies in special situations.

Portfolio: (12/31/86) Common stocks 86%, short-term securities 15%. Largest stock holdings: emerging growth companies 41%, established growth companies 26%.

Distributions: Income: Feb   **Capital Gains:** Feb

12b-1: No

Minimum: Initial: $2,000   Subsequent: None

Min IRA: Initial: None   Subsequent: None

Services: IRA, Deduct

Tel Exchange: No

Registered: AZ, CA, CO, CT, DC, DE, FL, GA, IL, IN, MA, MD, MI, MN, MO, NJ, NY, OH, PA, RI, TX, VA, VT, WA, WI

OMEGA
Aggressive Growth

Endowment Management &
Research Corp.
77 Franklin St.
Boston, MA 02110
(617) 357-8480

	Years Ending 12/31					
	1981	1982	1983	1984	1985	1986
Net Investment Income ($)	(.04)	.14	.09	.13	.28	.23
Dividends from Net Investment Income ($)	–	–	.16	.10	.12	.28
Net Gains (Losses) on Investments ($)	(1.49)	(1.51)	2.21	(.29)	3.18	1.49
Distributions from Net Realized Capital Gains ($)	2.90	2.53	–	1.66	–	2.12
Net Asset Value End of Year ($)	14.45	10.55	12.69	10.78	14.12	13.44
Ratio of Expenses to Net Assets (%)	1.39	1.39	1.50	1.53	1.65	1.47
Portfolio Turnover Rate (%)	394	286	242	164	188	178
Total Assets: End of Year (Millions $)	30.4	26.0	28.6	25.3	31.0	31.8
Annual Rate of Return (%) Years Ending 12/31	(9.2)	(7.5)	22.0	0.2	32.3	12.2

Five-Year Total Return	67.9%	Degree of Diversification	B	Beta	1.07	Bull	C	Bear	E

Objective: Maximum capital appreciation through investments in common stocks, convertibles or warrants, of growth companies, some of which may be unseasoned. Engages in short-term trading resulting in high portfolio turnover rate. Will not invest in energy source leases or exploration programs. May employ leverage up to one-third of total assets.

Portfolio: (12/31/86) Common stocks 82%, short-term commercial paper 7%, corporate bonds and notes 6%, convertible notes 6%. Largest stock holdings: consumer products/services 25%, technology 21%.

Distributions:	Income: Feb		**Capital Gains:** Feb
12b-1:	Yes	Amount: 1.00%	
Minimum:	Initial: $1,000	Subsequent: None	
Min IRA:	Initial: NA	Subsequent: NA	
Tel Exchange:	No		
Registered:	All states except AK, DE, HI, ID, KY, LA, ME, MS, MT, NC, ND, NH, NM, NV, OH, SD, TN, UT, VT, WV, WY		

100 FUND
Aggressive Growth

Berger Associates, Inc.
899 Logan St.
Denver, CO 80203
(303) 837-1020/(816) 474-8520

	Years Ending 9/30					
	1981	1982	1983	1984	1985	1986
Net Investment Income ($)	.26	.14	(.09)	.32	(.10)	.09
Dividends from Net Investment Income ($)	.17	.27	.13	–	.34	–
Net Gains (Losses) on Investments ($)	.33	.25	7.51	(6.34)	.99	5.22
Distributions from Net Realized Capital Gains ($)	–	–	–	–	–	–
Net Asset Value End of Year ($)	13.08	13.20	20.49	14.47	15.02	20.15
Ratio of Expenses to Net Assets (%)	1.63	1.75	1.70	1.90	2.00	1.71
Portfolio Turnover Rate (%)	125	137	155	272	130	122
Total Assets: End of Year (Millions $)	11.2	10.3	14.4	9.6	8.9	10.6
Annual Rate of Return (%) Years Ending 12/31	(1.5)	13.0	17.0	(20.1)	25.7	20.0

Five-Year Total Return	59.3%	Degree of Diversification	D	Beta	.98	Bull	E	Bear	E

Objective: Long-term capital appreciation through investment in common stocks of established companies on the basis of fundamental analysis, industry trends and earnings trends in relation to the current market environment.

Portfolio: (9/30/86) Common stocks 100%. Largest stock holdings: health care 15%, data services 7%.

Distributions: Income: Oct   **Capital Gains:** Annually

12b-1: Yes   **Amount:** .30%

Minimum: Initial: $250   **Subsequent:** $50

Min IRA: Initial: $250   **Subsequent:** $50

Services: IRA, Keogh, Withdraw

Tel Exchange: Yes   **With MMF:** No

Registered: AL, CA, CO, FL, IL, MA, MI, MS, NV, NY, PA, TX, WA

101 FUND
Growth

Berger Associates, Inc.
899 Logan St.
Denver, CO 80203
(303) 837-1020/(816) 474-8520

	Years Ending 9/30					
	1981	1982	1983	1984	1985	1986
Net Investment Income ($)	.51	.50	.49	.52	.33	.57
Dividends from Net Investment Income ($)	.61	.53	.48	.45	.43	.57
Net Gains (Losses) on Investments ($)	(.35)	(.47)	5.41	(.69)	1.11	3.86
Distributions from Net Realized Capital Gains ($)	—	—	—	1.00	—	.29
Net Asset Value End of Year ($)	9.98	9.48	14.90	13.28	14.29	17.86
Ratio of Expenses to Net Assets (%)	2.00	2.00	2.00	2.00	2.00	1.96
Portfolio Turnover Rate (%)	157	120	168	267	166	187
Total Assets: End of Year (Millions $)	1.0	0.9	1.3	1.4	1.6	2.7
Annual Rate of Return (%) Years Ending 12/31	3.2	13.8	35.2	(0.3)	29.1	15.0

Five-Year Total Return	127.6%	Degree of Diversification	D	Beta	.62	Bull	A	Bear	D

Objective:	Seeks capital appreciation and a moderate level of current income through investment in dividend-paying common stocks of large, established companies and senior debt securities.
Portfolio:	(9/30/86) Convertibles 47%, common stocks 44%. Largest stock holdings: utilities 22%, telecommunications 9%.
Distributions:	Income: Quarterly **Capital Gains:** Annually
12b-1:	Yes Amount: .30%
Minimum:	Initial: $250 Subsequent: $50
Min IRA:	Initial: $250 Subsequent: $50
Services:	IRA, Keogh, Withdraw
Tel Exchange:	Yes **With MMF:** No
Registered:	AL, CA, CO, FL, IL, MA, MI, MS, NV, NY, PA, TX, WA

PACIFIC HORIZON AGGRESSIVE GROWTH

Aggressive Growth

Pacific Horizon Funds
3550 Wilshire Blvd., Suite 932
Los Angeles, CA 90010
(800) 645-3515

	Years Ending 2/28					
	1981	1982	1983	1984	1985 (11 mos.)	1986
Net Investment Income ($)	–	–	–	–	.12	.02
Dividends from Net Investment Income ($)	–	–	–	–	–	.07
Net Gains (Losses) on Investments ($)	–	–	–	–	6.31	6.95
Distributions from Net Realized Capital Gains ($)	–	–	–	–	–	–
Net Asset Value End of Year ($)	–	–	–	–	17.93	24.83
Ratio of Expenses to Net Assets (%)	–	–	–	–	1.38	1.50
Portfolio Turnover Rate (%)	–	–	–	–	514	234
Total Assets: End of Year (Millions $)	–	–	–	–	4.9	34.8

Annual Rate of Return (%) Years Ending 12/31	–	–	–	–	37.5	20.1

Five-Year Total Return	NA	Degree of Diversification	NA	Beta	NA	Bull NA	Bear NA

Objective: Seeks capital appreciation through investment in common stocks of companies with capitalizations between $50 million and $1 billion, emphasizing the smaller. May invest in foreign securities through ADRs, convert portfolio to debt securities for defensive purposes, enter into repos, lend its securities and enter into stock index futures contracts.

Portfolio: (8/31/86) Common stocks 85%, short-term securities 17%. Largest stock holdings: foreign 17%, regional banks 14%.

Distributions: **Income:** Annually   **Capital Gains:** Annually

12b-1: Yes   **Amount:** .10%

Minimum: **Initial:** $1,000   **Subsequent:** $100

Min IRA: **Initial:** $750   **Subsequent:** None

Services: IRA, SEP, Withdraw, Deduct

Tel Exchange: Yes   **With MMF:** Yes

Registered: All states except AR, MO, OH, WI

PACIFIC HORIZON HIGH YIELD BOND
Bond

Pacific Horizon Funds
3550 Wilshire Blvd., Suite 932
Los Angeles, CA 90010
(800) 645-3515

| | Years Ending 2/28 | | | | | |
	1981	1982	1983	1984	1985 (11 mos.)	1986
Net Investment Income ($)	–	–	–	–	1.80	2.00
Dividends from Net Investment Income ($)	–	–	–	–	1.65	2.01
Net Gains (Losses) on Investments ($)	–	–	–	–	1.48	1.48
Distributions from Net Realized Capital Gains ($)	–	–	–	–	–	.18
Net Asset Value End of Year ($)	–	–	–	–	15.13	16.42
Ratio of Expenses to Net Assets (%)	–	–	–	–	1.05	.29
Portfolio Turnover Rate (%)	–	–	–	–	389	167
Total Assets: End of Year (Millions $)	–	–	–	–	2.9	19.8
Annual Rate of Return (%) Years Ending 12/31	–	–	–	–	23.4	15.0

Five-Year Total Return	NA	Degree of Diversification	NA	Beta	NA	Bull NA	Bear NA

Objective: Seeks to maximize total return from capital appreciation and current income through investment of at least 75% of its portfolio in debt securities rated BBB (Baa) or lower of varying maturities. May convert entirely to short-term debt securities as defensive move.

Portfolio: (8/31/86) Bonds 94%, cash 4%, short-term securities 2%.

Distributions: **Income:** Monthly   **Capital Gains:** Annually

12b-1: Yes   **Amount:** .10%

Minimum: **Initial:** $1,000   **Subsequent:** $100

Min IRA: **Initial:** $750   **Subsequent:** None

Services: IRA, Keogh, SEP, Withdraw, Deduct

Tel Exchange: Yes   **With MMF:** Yes

Registered: All states except AR, MO, OH, WI

PARTNERS
Growth & Income

Neuberger and Berman
Management Inc.
342 Madison Ave.
New York, NY 10173
(800) 367-0770/(212) 850-8300

	Years Ending 6/30					
	1981	1982	1983	1984	1985	1986
Net Investment Income ($)	.96	1.20	.83	.74	.65	.42
Dividends from Net Investment Income ($)	.69	.95	1.11	.84	.72	.65
Net Gains (Losses) on Investments ($)	2.66	(.74)	4.47	(1.02)	3.63	4.71
Distributions from Net Realized Capital Gains ($)	3.01	3.30	—	1.96	.27	1.27
Net Asset Value End of Year ($)	16.81	13.02	17.21	14.13	17.42	20.63
Ratio of Expenses to Net Assets (%)	1.32	1.08	.97	.91	.93	.89
Portfolio Turnover Rate (%)	242	244	232	227	146	181
Total Assets: End of Year (Millions $)	61.1	74.4	139.3	146.3	221.9	433.3
Annual Rate of Return (%) Years Ending 12/31	6.1	26.6	19.1	8.2	29.8	17.3

Five-Year Total Return	148.3%	Degree of Diversification	A	Beta	.79	Bull	B	Bear	B

Objective: Seeks capital growth by investing primarily in securities of large, established, dividend-paying companies which are believed to offer appreciation potential. Seeks short-term gains. May invest in investment-grade debt securities, repurchase agreements and foreign securities, and may write covered call options.

Portfolio: (9/30/86) Common stocks 73%, U.S. government obligations 25%, corporate notes 2%, repos 1%. Largest stock holdings: chemicals 8%, insurance 7%.

Distributions: Income: Aug   **Capital Gains:** Aug

12b-1: Yes   **Amount:** .25%

Minimum: Initial: $500   **Subsequent:** $50

Min IRA: Initial: $250   **Subsequent:** $50

Services: IRA, Keogh, Corp, Withdraw, Deduct

Tel Exchange: Yes   **With MMF:** Yes

Registered: All states except NH

PAX WORLD
International

Pax World Management Corp.
224 State St.
Portsmouth, NH 03801
(603) 431-8022

	Years Ending 12/31					
	1981	1982	1983	1984	1985	1986
Net Investment Income ($)	.45	.46	.49	.56	.53	.46
Dividends from Net Investment Income ($)	.48	.41	.49	.51	.52	.50
Net Gains (Losses) on Investments ($)	(.35)	1.13	1.88	.22	2.23	.60
Distributions from Net Realized Capital Gains ($)	.32	.21	.28	.77	.37	.71
Net Asset Value End of Year ($)	9.40	10.37	11.97	11.47	13.34	13.19
Ratio of Expenses to Net Assets (%)	1.60	1.50	1.40	1.50	1.40	1.20
Portfolio Turnover Rate (%)	56	38	29	34	48	57
Total Assets: End of Year (Millions $)	5.1	7.1	12.2	16.9	32.7	53.8
Annual Rate of Return (%) Years Ending 12/31	1.2	18.4	24.1	7.5	25.5	8.4

Five-Year Total Return 114.9%	Degree of Diversification B	Beta .71	Bull C	Bear C

Objective: Primarily seeks income and secondarily long-term capital growth. Endeavors to contribute to world peace through investment in companies producing life-supportive goods and services. Will not invest in companies engaging in or contributing to military activities nor those in the liquor, gambling or tobacco industries.

Portfolio: (12/31/86) Common stocks 75%, government bonds 16%, CDs 8%, cash 1%. Largest stock holdings: natural gas 13%, consumer goods 12%.

Distributions: Income: Jan, July   **Capital Gains:** Jan

12b-1: Yes   **Amount:** .25%

Minimum: Initial: $250   Subsequent: $50

Min IRA: Initial: $250   Subsequent: $50

Services: IRA, Keogh, Withdraw

Tel Exchange: No

Registered: All states except NE

PENN SQUARE MUTUAL

Growth & Income

Penn Square Management Corp.
PO Box 1419
Reading, PA 19603
(800) 523-8440/(215) 670-1031

	Years Ending 12/31					
	1981	1982	1983	1984	1985	1986
Net Investment Income ($)	.49	.46	.41	.41	.38	.39
Dividends from Net Investment Income ($)	.49	.49	.43	.42	.37	.39
Net Gains (Losses) on Investments ($)	(.39)	.97	1.85	(.39)	1.72	.76
Distributions from Net Realized Capital Gains ($)	.53	.56	.61	.70	.53	1.25
Net Asset Value End of Year ($)	8.00	8.38	9.60	8.50	9.70	9.21
Ratio of Expenses to Net Assets (%)	.65	.66	.63	.65	.74	.80
Portfolio Turnover Rate (%)	8	21	34	16	24	22
Total Assets: End of Year (Millions $)	142.5	155.3	182.2	171.3	198.8	198.9
Annual Rate of Return (%) Years Ending 12/31	1.2	20.7	29.3	0.5	26.6	12.9

Five-Year Total Return	124.4%	Degree of Diversification	A	Beta	.95	Bull	B	Bear	D

Objective: Seeks long-term capital growth through the common stocks of only 30 to 50 large, well-established companies from a cross-section of industries.

Portfolio: (12/31/86) Common stocks 84%, short-term securities 17%. Largest stock holdings: electronics and telecommunications 11%, consumer goods 11%.

Distributions: Income: Jan, April, July, Oct   **Capital Gains:** Jan

12b-1: No

Minimum: Initial: $500   Subsequent: $100

Min IRA: Initial: $250   Subsequent: None

Services: IRA, Keogh, Corp, SEP, Withdraw

Tel Exchange: No

Registered: All states

PERMANENT PORTFOLIO
Growth

World Money Managers
7 Fourth Street, Suite 14
Petaluma, CA 94952
(800) 531-5142/(512) 453-7558

	Years Ending 12/31			1/31		
	1981	1982	1983	1984* (1 mo.)	1985	1986
Net Investment Income ($)	—	1.26	.38	.02	.39	.33
Dividends from Net Investment Income ($)	—	—	—	Nil	—	—
Net Gains (Losses) on Investments ($)	—	—	.24	(.15)	(1.32)	.73
Distributions from Net Realized Capital Gains ($)	—	—	—	Nil	—	—
Net Asset Value End of Year ($)	—	11.26	11.88	11.75	10.82	11.88
Ratio of Expenses to Net Assets (%)	—	.82	.92	.92	.90	.90
Portfolio Turnover Rate (%)	—	0	2	0	11	17
Total Assets: End of Year (Millions $)	—	5.5	69.9	68.9	71.1	73.0

Changed fiscal year-end from 12/31 to 1/31.

Annual Rate of Return (%) Years Ending 12/31	—	—	5.5	(12.9)	12.2	13.6

Five-Year Total Return	NA	Degree of Diversification	E	Beta .30	Bull NA	Bear NA

Objective: Invests a fixed "target percentage" of its net assets in gold, silver, Swiss francs, real estate and natural resource company stocks, and other stocks with the aim of preserving and increasing "purchasing power." Strives for long-term asset appreciation.

Portfolio: (7/31/86) U.S. government securities 34%, common stocks 28%, gold 22%, Swiss franc assets 11%, silver 5%. Largest stock holdings: natural resources 7%, real estate 7%.

Distributions:	Income: Jan	**Capital Gains:** Jan
12b-1:	Yes	Amount: .25%
Minimum:	Initial: $1,000	Subsequent: $100
Min IRA:	Initial: $1,000	Subsequent: $100
Services:	IRA, Withdraw, Corp	
Tel Exchange:	None	
Registered:	All states	

PINE STREET
Growth & Income

Wood, Struthers & Winthrop
Management Corp.
140 Broadway
New York, NY 10005
(800) 221-5672/(212) 902-4396

	Years Ending 6/30					
	1981	**1982**	**1983**	**1984**	**1985**	**1986**
Net Investment Income ($)	.60	.62	.56	.46	.56	.56
Dividends from Net Investment Income ($)	.60	.62	.56	.47	.56	.55
Net Gains (Losses) on Investments ($)	1.51	(2.05)	5.25	(1.74)	3.39	3.23
Distributions from Net Realized Capital Gains ($)	.48	.28	1.33	1.45	1.26	1.96
Net Asset Value End of Year ($)	12.57	10.25	14.17	10.97	13.10	14.38
Ratio of Expenses to Net Assets (%)	1.12	1.22	1.15	1.15	1.09	1.17
Portfolio Turnover Rate (%)	48	59	103	104	65	90
Total Assets: End of Year (Millions $)	43.2	34.5	45.0	39.3	52.1	65.9
Annual Rate of Return (%) Years Ending 12/31	(7.7)	20.4	19.1	5.1	30.7	14.3

Five-Year Total Return	125.1%	Degree of Diversification	A	Beta	.92	Bull	B	Bear	C

Objective: Seeks to combine continuity of income with opportunity for growth through investment in common stocks of well-established companies. May invest in debt or equity securities of foreign countries.

Portfolio: (9/30/86) Common stocks 79%, convertible bonds 12%, commercial paper 5%, convertible preferred stock 2%, U.S. government obligations 2%. Largest stock holdings: basic industries 24%, consumer products & services 20%.

Distributions: Income: Mar, June, Sept, Dec   **Capital Gains:** June
12b-1: Yes   **Amount:** .30%
Minimum: Initial: $1,000   Subsequent: $100
Min IRA: Initial: $1,000   Subsequent: $100
Services: IRA, Keogh, Withdraw
Tel Exchange: No
Registered: All states except: DC, HI, ME, MO, NJ, NV, WI

T. ROWE PRICE EQUITY INCOME
Growth & Income

T. Rowe Price
100 East Pratt Street
Baltimore, MD 21202
(800) 638-5660/(301) 547-2308

	Years Ending 12/31					
	1981	1982	1983	1984	1985 (2 mos.)	1986
Net Investment Income ($)	–	–	–	–	.14	.66
Dividends from Net Investment Income ($)	–	–	–	–	–	.65
Net Gains (Losses) on Investments ($)	–	–	–	–	.86	2.21
Distributions from Net Realized Capital Gains ($)	–	–	–	–	–	.26
Net Asset Value End of Year ($)	–	–	–	–	11.00	12.96
Ratio of Expenses to Net Assets (%)	–	–	–	–	1.00	1.00
Portfolio Turnover Rate (%)	–	–	–	–	37	73
Total Assets: End of Year (Millions $)	–	–	–	–	16.6	94.0

Annual Rate of Return (%) Years Ending 12/31	–	–	–	–	–	26.6

Five-Year Total Return	NA	Degree of Diversification	NA	Beta	NA	Bull	NA	Bear	NA

Objective: Seeks high income through investment in dividend-paying common stocks of established companies that also have capital appreciation potential. May invest in investment-grade (BBB or higher) debt securities without limit. Will invest at least 65% of fund's assets in income-producing common stocks.

Portfolio: (12/31/86) Common and preferred stocks 64%, convertible bonds 9%, corporate bonds 10%, short-term securities 16%. Largest stock holdings: automobiles and related 7%, insurance 6%.

Distributions: **Income:** Quarterly   **Capital Gains:** Annually

12b-1: No

Minimum: **Initial:** $1,000   **Subsequent:** $100

Min IRA: **Initial:** $500   **Subsequent:** $50

Services: IRA, Keogh, Corp, 403(b), Withdraw, Deduct

Tel Exchange: Yes   **With MMF:** Yes

Registered: All states

T. ROWE PRICE GNMA
Bond

T. Rowe Price Associates
100 E. Pratt St.
Baltimore, MD 21202
(800) 638-5660/(301) 547-2308

	Years Ending 2/28					
	1981	1982	1983	1984	1985	1986 (3 mos.)
Net Investment Income ($)	–	–	–	–	–	.26
Dividends from Net Investment Income ($)	–	–	–	–	–	.26
Net Gains (Losses) on Investments ($)	–	–	–	–	–	.12
Distributions from Net Realized Capital Gains ($)	–	–	–	–	–	–
Net Asset Value End of Year ($)	–	–	–	–	–	10.12
Ratio of Expenses to Net Assets (%)	–	–	–	–	–	1.00
Portfolio Turnover Rate (%)	–	–	–	–	–	51
Total Assets: End of Year (Millions $)	–	–	–	–	–	123.6

Annual Rate of Return (%) Years Ending 12/31	–	–	–	–	–	11.0

Five-Year Total Return	NA	Degree of Diversification	NA	Beta	NA	Bull NA	Bear NA

Objective: Seeks high level of current income consistent with preservation of capital. Invests in securities backed by the U.S. government, principally GNMAs.

Portfolio: (11/30/86) GNMA securities 85%, U.S. Treasury notes & bonds 18%, repos 2%.

Distributions: **Income:** Monthly   **Capital Gains:** Annually

12b-1: No

Minimum: **Initial:** $1,000   **Subsequent:** $100

Min IRA: **Initial:** $500   **Subsequent:** $50

Services: IRA, Keogh, Corp, 403(b), Withdraw, Deduct

Tel Exchange: Yes   **With MMF:** Yes

Registered: All states

T. ROWE PRICE GROWTH & INCOME

Growth & Income

T. Rowe Price Associates
100 E. Pratt St.
Baltimore, MD 21202
(800) 638-5660/(301) 547-2308

	Years Ending 12/31					
	1981	**1982**	**1983**	**1984**	**1985**	**1986**
Net Investment Income ($)	–	–	.77	.81	.59	.75
Dividends from Net Investment Income ($)	–	–	.60	.79	.61	.71
Net Gains (Losses) on Investments ($)	–	–	2.88	(.57)	1.76	.33
Distributions from Net Realized Capital Gains ($)	–	–	–	.06	–	1.57
Net Asset Value End of Year ($)	–	–	13.05	12.44	14.18	12.98
Ratio of Expenses to Net Assets (%)	–	–	.90	.94	.94	.96
Portfolio Turnover Rate (%)	–	–	48	52	121	100
Total Assets: End of Year (Millions $)	–	–	234.5	309.1	356.8	388.6
Annual Rate of Return (%) Years Ending 12/31	–	–	32.6	1.9	19.7	7.9

Five-Year Total Return	NA	Degree of Diversification	C	Beta .87	Bull NA	Bear NA

Objective: Seeks long-term growth of capital, a reasonable level of current income and an increase in future income through investment primarily in income-producing equity securities which have prospects for both capital growth and dividend income.

Portfolio: (12/31/86) Common stocks 77%, corporate bonds 15%, short-term securities 3%, preferred stocks 2%. Largest holdings: utilities & telephone 23%, petroleum 12%.

Distributions: Income: Jan, April, July, Oct   **Capital Gains:** Jan

12b-1: No

Minimum: Initial: $1,000   Subsequent: $100

Min IRA: Initial: $500   Subsequent: $50

Services: IRA, Keogh, 403(b), Corp, Withdraw, Deduct

Tel Exchange: Yes   **With MMF:** Yes

Registered: All states

T. ROWE PRICE GROWTH STOCK
Growth

T. Rowe Price Associates
100 E. Pratt St.
Baltimore, MD 21202
(800) 638-5660/(301) 547-2308

	Years Ending 12/31					
	1981	1982	1983	1984	1985	1986
Net Investment Income ($)	.55	.49	.34	.34	.38	.31
Dividends from Net Investment Income ($)	.50	.53	.50	.36	.34	.38
Net Gains (Losses) on Investments ($)	(2.37)	1.48	1.30	(.54)	4.35	3.26
Distributions from Net Realized Capital Gains ($)	.04	.09	—	.45	.64	4.18
Net Asset Value End of Year ($)	12.72	14.07	15.21	14.20	17.95	16.96
Ratio of Expenses to Net Assets (%)	.49	.51	.50	.52	.52	.59
Portfolio Turnover Rate (%)	38	54	63	60	69	60
Total Assets: End of Year (Millions $)	919.2	1,007.4	1,013.0	965.5	1,158.4	1,273.2

Annual Rate of Return (%) Years Ending 12/31	(12.5)	16.3	12.3	(0.7)	35.1	21.7

Five-Year Total Return 113.1%	Degree of Diversification D	Beta .89	Bull B	Bear E

Objective:	Seeks long-term capital appreciation primarily through investment in common stocks of well-established growth companies. May invest up to 25% of assets in foreign securities, write covered call options, and may loan its portfolio securities up to 30% of its assets.
Portfolio:	(12/31/86) Common stocks 90%, short-term securities 10%, convertible bonds 1%. Largest stock holdings: foreign 25%, technology 18%.

Distributions: Income: Jan   **Capital Gains:** Jan
12b-1: No
Minimum: Initial: $1,000   Subsequent: $100
Min IRA: Initial: $500   Subsequent: $50
Services: IRA, Keogh, Corp, 403(b), Withdraw, Deduct
Tel Exchange: Yes   **With MMF:** Yes
Registered: All states

T. ROWE PRICE HIGH YIELD
Bond

T. Rowe Price Associates
100 E. Pratt St.
Baltimore, MD 21202
(800) 638-5660/(301) 547-2308

	Years Ending 2/28					
	1981	**1982**	**1983**	**1984**	**1985** (2 mos.)	**1986**
Net Investment Income ($)	–	–	–	–	.22	1.37
Dividends from Net Investment Income ($)	–	–	–	–	.22	1.37
Net Gains (Losses) on Investments ($)	–	–	–	–	(.01)	1.00
Distributions from Net Realized Capital Gains ($)	–	–	–	–	–	–
Net Asset Value End of Year ($)	–	–	–	–	9.99	10.99
Ratio of Expenses to Net Assets (%)	–	–	–	–	1.00	1.00
Portfolio Turnover Rate (%)	–	–	–	–	6	164
Total Assets: End of Year (Millions $)	–	–	–	–	22.5	456.7
Annual Rate of Return (%) Years Ending 12/31	–	–	–	–	22.5	15.1

Five-Year Total Return	NA	Degree of Diversification	NA	Beta	NA	Bull NA	Bear NA

Objective: Seeks high level of current income by investing in long-term, high-yielding, lower and medium quality fixed-income securities. May lend its securities, write options, and purchase foreign debt securities.

Portfolio: (11/30/86) Corporate bonds 86%, U.S. government obligations 6%, commercial paper 4%, common & preferred stocks 3%.

Distributions: **Income:** Monthly   **Capital Gains:** February

12b-1: No

Minimum: **Initial:** $1,000   **Subsequent:** $100

Min IRA: **Initial:** $500   **Subsequent:** $100

Services: IRA, Keogh, Corp, 403(b), Withdraw, Deduct

Tel Exchange: Yes   **With MMF:** Yes

Registered: All states

T. ROWE PRICE INTERNATIONAL
International

T. Rowe Price Associates
100 E. Pratt St.
Baltimore, MD 21202
(800) 638-5660/(301) 547-2308

	Years Ending 12/31					
	1981	1982	1983	1984	1985	1986
Net Investment Income ($)	.30	.32	15	.30	.22	.21
Dividends from Net Investment Income ($)	.43	.29	.21	.15	.30	.22
Net Gains (Losses) on Investments ($)	(.49)	.32	3.03	(1.12)	5.43	10.46
Distributions from Net Realized Capital Gains ($)	.08	—	—	.16	.45	2.75
Net Asset Value End of Year ($)	10.99	11.34	14.31	13.18	18.08	25.78
Ratio of Expenses to Net Assets (%)	1.10	1.16	1.14	1.11	1.11	1.10
Portfolio Turnover Rate (%)	65	79	69	38	62	56
Total Assets: End of Year (Millions $)	78.5	101.0	130.0	180.6	376.9	790.0
Annual Rate of Return (%) Years Ending 12/31	(1.8)	6.2	28.4	(5.6)	45.2	60.5

Five-Year Total Return	199.9%	Degree of Diversification	E	Beta	.51	Bull	A	Bear	D

Objective: Seeks long-term capital growth and income by investing in a diversified portfolio of marketable securities of established non-U.S. issuers.

Portfolio: (12/31/86) Japan 30%, United Kingdom 12%, Germany 9%.

Distributions: **Income:** Jan   **Capital Gains:** Jan

12b-1: No

Minimum: **Initial:** $1,000   **Subsequent:** $100

Min IRA: **Initial:** $500   **Subsequent:** $50

Services: IRA, Keogh, Corp, 403(b), Withdraw, Deduct

Tel Exchange: Yes   **With MMF:** Yes

Registered: All states

T. ROWE PRICE NEW AMERICA GROWTH
Growth

T. Rowe Price
100 East Pratt Street
Baltimore, MD 21202
(800) 638-5660/(301) 547-2308

	Years Ending 12/31					
	1981	**1982**	**1983**	**1984**	**1985** (3 mos.)	**1986**
Net Investment Income ($)	—	—	—	—	.10	.06
Dividends from Net Investment Income ($)	—	—	—	—	—	.10
Net Gains (Losses) on Investments ($)	—	—	—	—	1.75	1.63
Distributions from Net Realized Capital Gains ($)	—	—	—	—	—	.30
Net Asset Value End of Year ($)	—	—	—	—	11.85	13.14
Ratio of Expenses to Net Assets (%)	—	—	—	—	1.00	1.00
Portfolio Turnover Rate (%)	—	—	—	—	49	81
Total Assets: End of Year (Millions $)	—	—	—	—	30.5	83.4

Annual Rate of Return (%) Years Ending 12/31	—	—	—	—	—	14.3

Five-Year Total Return	NA	Degree of Diversification	NA	Beta	NA	Bull NA	Bear NA

Objective: Seeks long-term growth of capital through investment primarily in common stocks of companies which operate in the service sector of the economy. Will invest at least 75% of net assets in service sector stocks. May also write covered call options and buy puts.

Portfolio: (12/31/86) Common stocks 98%, short-term securities 3%. Largest stock holdings: consumer services 40%, financial services 35%.

Distributions: **Income:** Annually   **Capital Gains:** Annually
12b-1: No
Minimum: **Initial:** $1,000   **Subsequent:** $100
Min IRA: **Initial:** $500   **Subsequent:** $50
Services: IRA, Keogh, Withdraw, Corp, 403(b), Deduct
Tel Exchange: Yes   **With MMF:** Yes
Registered: All states

T. ROWE PRICE NEW ERA
Growth

T. Rowe Price Associates
100 E. Pratt St.
Baltimore, MD 21202
(800) 638-5660/(301) 547-2308

	Years Ending 12/31					
	1981	1982	1983	1984	1985	1986
Net Investment Income ($)	.91	.84	.58	.67	.49	.38
Dividends from Net Investment Income ($)	.68	.86	.81	.61	.68	.50
Net Gains (Losses) on Investments ($)	(4.68)	(.74)	3.21	(.08)	3.14	2.46
Distributions from Net Realized Capital Gains ($)	1.48	3.05	.07	1.29	1.41	3.25
Net Asset Value End of Year ($)	19.34	15.53	18.44	17.13	18.67	17.76
Ratio of Expenses to Net Assets (%)	.64	.71	.68	.68	.69	.73
Portfolio Turnover Rate (%)	18	62	37	39	37	32
Total Assets: End of Year (Millions $)	436.3	411.5	485.1	472.1	529.4	496.2

Annual Rate of Return (%) Years Ending 12/31	(15.5)	1.7	26.4	3.5	22.9	16.2

Five-Year Total Return	90.2%	Degree of Diversification	B	Beta .88	Bull B	Bear E

Objective: Seeks long-term growth of capital through investment primarily in common stocks of companies which own or develop natural resources and selected growth companies with capable management, sound financial and accounting policies, effective R & D, and efficient service. May invest in foreign securities, loan its portfolio securities (up to 30% of assets) and write covered call options.

Portfolio: (12/31/86) Common stocks 85%, short-term securities 11%. Largest stock holdings: natural resource related companies 59%, science & technology 13%.

Distributions: Income: Jan   **Capital Gains:** Jan
12b-1: No
Minimum: Initial: $1,000   Subsequent: $100
Min IRA: Initial: $500   Subsequent: $50
Services: IRA, Keogh, Corp, 403(b), Withdraw, Deduct
Tel Exchange: Yes   **With MMF:** Yes
Registered: All states

T. ROWE PRICE NEW HORIZONS
Aggressive Growth

T. Rowe Price Associates
100 E. Pratt St.
Baltimore, MD 21202
(800) 638-5660/(301) 547-2308

	Years Ending 12/31					
	1981	**1982**	**1983**	**1984**	**1985**	**1986**
Net Investment Income ($)	.35	.19	.16	.14	.09	.02
Dividends from Net Investment Income ($)	.32	.35	.20	.16	.14	.09
Net Gains (Losses) on Investments ($)	(1.82)	2.62	2.80	(1.38)	2.92	(.04)
Distributions from Net Realized Capital Gains ($)	1.68	2.62	.76	3.72	.52	2.64
Net Asset Value End of Year ($)	16.06	15.90	17.90	12.78	15.13	12.38
Ratio of Expenses to Net Assets (%)	.53	.56	.61	0.71	.70	.73
Portfolio Turnover Rate (%)	35	36	45	32	31	35
Total Assets: End of Year (Millions $)	876.0	1,198.7	1,355.1	1,273.2	1,474.9	1,033.9
Annual Rate of Return (%) Years Ending 12/31	(7.9)	22.5	19.7	(11.8)	24.0	(0.2)

Five-Year Total Return	60.1%	Degree of Diversification	E	Beta	1.08	Bull	D	Bear	E

Objective: Seeks long-term growth of capital through investment primarily in common stocks of small growth companies which have the potential to become major companies in the future.

Portfolio: (12/31/86) Common stocks 94%, short-term investments 6%. Largest stock holdings: technology 23%, consumer services 22%.

Distributions: Income: Annually   **Capital Gains:** Annually
12b-1: No
Minimum: Initial: $1,000   Subsequent: $100
Min IRA: Initial: $500   Subsequent: $50
Services: IRA, Keogh, Corp, 403(b), Withdraw, Deduct
Tel Exchange: Yes   **With MMF:** Yes
Registered: All states

T. ROWE PRICE NEW INCOME
Bond

T. Rowe Price Associates
100 E. Pratt St.
Baltimore, MD 21202
(800) 638-5660/(301) 547-2308

	Years Ending 12/31		Years Ending 2/28		
	1981	1982	1984*	1985	1986
Net Investment Income ($)	1.09	1.07	.94	.94	.88
Dividends from Net Investment Income ($)	1.07	1.07	.95	.94	.88
Net Gains (Losses) on Investments ($)	(.58)	.67	(.31)	(.06)	.77
Distributions from Net Realized Capital Gains ($)	—	—	—	—	—
Net Asset Value End of Year ($)	7.79	8.46	8.24	8.18	8.95
Ratio of Expenses to Net Assets (%)	.62	.59	.62	.64	.66
Portfolio Turnover Rate (%)	110	96	84	155	185
Total Assets: End of Year (Millions $)	377.2	611.3	695.5	707.8	936.0

Fiscal year-end changed from 12/31 to 2/28; the 2 resulting months have been skipped.

Annual Rate of Return (%) Years Ending 12/31	6.9	24.1	11.9	17.6	14.0

Five-Year Total Return	104.2%	Degree of Diversification	NA	Beta —.06	Bull E	Bear A

Objective: Seeks high current income with reasonable stability through investment in high grade fixed-income securities.

Portfolio: (8/31/86) Corporate bonds and notes 42%, U.S. governments 37%, commercial paper 12%, other foreign securities 4%, Canadian securities 2%, bankers' acceptances 1%, CDs 1%.

Distributions: Income: Monthly   **Capital Gains:** Mar

12b-1: No

Minimum: Initial: $1,000   Subsequent: $100

Min IRA: Initial: $500   Subsequent: $50

Services: IRA, Keogh, Corp, 403(b), Withdraw, Deduct

Tel Exchange: Yes   **With MMF:** Yes

Registered: All states

T. ROWE PRICE SHORT-TERM BOND
Bond

T. Rowe Price Assoc.
100 E. Pratt St.
Baltimore, MD 21202
(800) 638-5660/(301) 547-2308

			Years Ending 2/28			
	1981	1982	1983	1984	1985 (10 mos.)	1986
Net Investment Income ($)	–	–	–	–	.53	.47
Dividends from Net Investment Income ($)	–	–	–	–	.53	.47
Net Gains (Losses) on Investments ($)	–	–	–	–	(.03)	.20
Distributions from Net Realized Capital Gains ($)	–	–	–	–	–	–
Net Asset Value End of Year ($)	–	–	–	–	4.97	5.17
Ratio of Expenses to Net Assets (%)	–	–	–	–	.90	1.31
Portfolio Turnover Rate (%)	–	–	–	–	73	21
Total Assets: End of Year (Millions $)	–	–	–	–	42.0	96.1

	1981	1982	1983	1984	1985	1986
Annual Rate of Return (%) Years Ending 12/31	–	–	–	–	12.8	9.0

Five-Year Total Return	NA	Degree of Diversification	NA	Beta NA	Bull NA	Bear NA

Objective: Seeks high level of income with minimum fluctuation of principal value and liquidity. Portfolio will consist of short- and intermediate-term securities.

Portfolio: (8/31/86) Corporate bonds & notes 53%, commercial paper 25%, CDs 12%, U.S. government securities 10%.

Distributions: Income: Monthly　　　　Capital Gains: Mar

12b-1: No

Minimum: Initial: $1,000　　Subsequent: $100

Min IRA: Initial: $500　　Subsequent: $50

Services: IRA, Keogh, Corp, 403(b), Withdraw, Deduct

Tel Exchange: Yes　　　　With MMF: Yes

Registered: All states

QUEST FOR VALUE
Aggressive Growth

Oppenheimer Capital Corp.
Oppenheimer Tower
World Financial Center
37th Floor
New York, NY 10281
(212) 667-7000

	Years Ending 4/30					
	1981	1982	1983	1984	1985	1986
Net Investment Income ($)	.09	.28	.54	.30	.29	.19
Dividends from Net Investment Income ($)	–	.05	.30	.52	.34	.27
Net Gains (Losses) on Investments ($)	5.47	1.23	10.63	1.45	2.99	6.99
Distributions from Net Realized Capital Gains ($)	–	.60	.60	4.84	3.82	.70
Net Asset Value End of Year ($)	15.56	16.42	26.69	23.08	22.20	28.41
Ratio of Expenses to Net Assets (%)	4.33	2.77	2.48	2.29	2.34	2.18
Portfolio Turnover Rate (%)	79	53	93	74	42	68
Total Assets: End of Year (Millions $)	1.5	5.0	8.9	13.4	28.1	64.3
Annual Rate of Return (%) Years Ending 12/31	30.3	40.8	38.2	4.8	27.4	14.3

Five-Year Total Return	196.8%	Degree of Diversification	B	Beta	.66	Bull	A	Bear	A

Objective: Seeks capital appreciation through investment in common stocks of small, unseasoned companies as well as established companies believed to be undervalued on the basis of companies' assets, earnings or growth potentials. May employ leverage and invest in warrants, restricted securities and foreign securities. Defensively, may convert to long- and short-term debt securities.

Portfolio: (10/31/86) Common and preferred stock 75%, short-term corporate notes 24%, cash 1%. Largest stock holdings: retail & wholesale 10%, electronics 8%.

Distributions: Income: May   **Capital Gains:** May

12b-1: No

Minimum: Initial: $2,000   Subsequent: $25

Min IRA: Initial: $250   Subsequent: $25

Services: IRA, Keogh, Corp, 403(b), Withdraw

Tel Exchange: No

Registered: All states except AL, AR, HI, IA, KS, LA, ME, MO, MS, MT, ND, NE, NH, OK, OH, SD, TN, WV, WY

RAINBOW
Growth

Furman, Anderson & Co.
19 Rector St.
New York, NY 10006
(212) 509-8532

	Years Ending 5/31					
	1981	1982	1983	1984	1985	1986
Net Investment Income ($)	.14	.03	(.01)	.02	.11	.01
Dividends from Net Investment Income ($)	–	–	–	–	–	–
Net Gains (Losses) on Investments ($)	.58	(.89)	1.04	(.32)	.44	1.18
Distributions from Net Realized Capital Gains ($)	–	–	–	–	–	–
Net Asset Value End of Year ($)	3.84	2.98	4.01	3.71	4.26	5.45
Ratio of Expenses to Net Assets (%)	3.21	3.42	4.65	4.32	3.02	3.46
Portfolio Turnover Rate (%)	185	127	291	247	164	190
Total Assets: End of Year (Millions $)	2.0	1.6	1.8	1.5	1.7	2.0

Annual Rate of Return (%) Years Ending 12/31	(3.1)	(3.2)	22.2	(4.9)	20.7	15.8

Five-Year Total Return	57.3%	Degree of Diversification	D	Beta	.76	Bull	D	Bear	E

Objective: Seeks capital appreciation through investment in common stocks of established companies. Employs speculative market techniques such as listed put and call options. May write covered and uncovered put and call options, buy and write options on stock indexes. May sell securities short, invest up to 20% of its assets in warrants and up to 25% in foreign securities.

Portfolio: (11/30/86) Common stock 90%, U.S. government obligations 4%. Largest stock holdings: drugs & beauty products 25%, banking & finance 10%.

Distributions: Income: NA   **Capital Gains:** NA
12b-1: No
Minimum: Initial: $300   Subsequent: $50
Min IRA: Initial: $250   Subsequent: $50
Services: IRA, Withdraw
Tel Exchange: No
Registered: NJ, NY

REICH & TANG EQUITY
Aggressive Growth

Reich & Tang, Inc.
100 Park Avenue
New York, NY 10017
(212) 370-1240

	Years Ending 12/31					
	1981	1982	1983	1984	1985 (11 mos.)	1986
Net Investment Income ($)	–	–	–	–	.31	.35
Dividends from Net Investment Income ($)	–	–	–	–	.30	.28
Net Gains (Losses) on Investments ($)	–	–	–	–	3.43	1.62
Distributions from Net Realized Capital Gains ($)	–	–	–	–	–	.63
Net Asset Value End of Year ($)	–	–	–	–	13.44	14.50
Ratio of Expenses to Net Assets (%)	–	–	–	–	.99	1.21
Portfolio Turnover Rate (%)	–	–	–	–	20	35
Total Assets: End of Year (Millions $)	–	–	–	–	54.2	110.5
Annual Rate of Return (%) Years Ending 12/31	–	–	–	–	–	14.7

Five-Year Total Return	NA	Degree of Diversification	NA	Beta	NA	Bull NA	Bear NA

Objective: Seeks long-term capital appreciation; current income is a secondary consideration. Invests in common stocks of undervalued companies showing good growth potential. May convert entirely to debt securities and money market instruments for defensive purposes. May enter into repos, buy warrants, invest in foreign securities and restricted securities.

Portfolio: (12/31/86) Common stocks 84%, short-term securities 14%, bonds 2%. Largest stock holdings: consumer products 11%, aerospace 9%.

Distributions: Income: Semi-Annually   **Capital Gains:** Annually
12b-1: Yes   Amount: .05%
Minimum: Initial: $5,000   Subsequent: None
Min IRA: Initial: $250   Subsequent: None
Services: IRA, Keogh, Corp, Withdraw
Tel Exchange: Yes   With MMF: Yes
Registered: AL, CA, CT, DC, DE, FL, HI, IL, MA, MD, MI, MN, MT, NC, NJ, NM, NV, NY, OH, PA, TX, VA, VT

RIGHTIME
Growth

Rightime Econometrics
The Benson East Office Plaza
Jenkintown, PA 19046
(800) 242-1421/(215) 927-7880

	Years Ending 10/31					
	1981	**1982**	**1983**	**1984**	**1985** (2 mos.)	**1986**
Net Investment Income ($)	—	—	—	—	(.01)	(.53)
Dividends from Net Investment Income ($)	—	—	—	—	—	.05
Net Gains (Losses) on Investments ($)	—	—	—	—	.88	6.96
Distributions from Net Realized Capital Gains ($)	—	—	—	—	—	.20
Net Asset Value End of Year ($)	—	—	—	—	25.87	32.05
Ratio of Expenses to Net Assets (%)	—	—	—	—	1.99	1.57
Portfolio Turnover Rate (%)	—	—	—	—	—	231
Total Assets: End of Year (Millions $)	—	—	—	—	14.7	145.2

Annual Rate of Return (%) Years Ending 12/31	—	—	—	—	—	11.0

Five-Year Total Return	NA	Degree of Diversification	NA	Beta	NA	Bull NA	Bear NA

Objective: Seeks high total return through investment in other investment companies. Looks at past performance and investment structure. Investment companies may be open- or closed-end, load or no load.

Portfolio: (10/31/86) Equity funds 100%. Largest fund holdings: Putnam Fund for Growth and Income 11%, Decatur Income Fund 9%.

Distributions: Income: Annually   **Capital Gains:** Annually

12b-1: Yes   **Amount:** 1.20%

Minimum: Initial: $2,000   Subsequent: $250

Min IRA: Initial: None   Subsequent: None

Services: IRA, Keogh, 403(b), Withdraw

Tel Exchange: Yes   **With MMF:** No

Registered: All states except AL, CA, ME, NC, NH, OK, TN, TX, WI

SAFECO EQUITY
Growth & Income

Safeco Asset Management Co.
Safeco Plaza
Seattle, WA 98185
(800) 426-6730/(206) 545-5530

	Years Ending 9/30					
	1981	1982	1983	1984	1985	1986
Net Investment Income ($)	.65	.66	.48	.45	.40	.29
Dividends from Net Investment Income ($)	.62	.68	.52	.45	.41	.34
Net Gains (Losses) on Investments ($)	(.81)	(.59)	2.63	(.26)	1.19	2.46
Distributions from Net Realized Capital Gains ($)	.75	.81	.83	.58	.72	1.22
Net Asset Value End of Year ($)	10.28	8.86	10.62	9.79	10.25	11.44
Ratio of Expenses to Net Assets (%)	.63	.65	.65	.64	.68	.88
Portfolio Turnover Rate (%)	10	22	16	20	56	86
Total Assets: End of Year (Millions $)	31.5	28.3	34.5	31.4	34.9	46.7
Annual Rate of Return (%) Years Ending 12/31	(5.1)	11.4	21.1	2.8	32.6	12.6

Five-Year Total Return	107.2%	Degree of Diversification	A	Beta	.96	Bull	B	Bear	E

Objective: Seeks reasonable balance of long-term growth of capital and reasonable current income for shareholders. Fund invests primarily in common stocks or convertibles of well-established, dividend-paying companies.

Portfolio: (9/30/86) Common stocks 94%, bonds 3%, short-term securities 3%. Largest stock holdings: health care 13%, chemicals 9%.

Distributions: **Income:** Feb, May, Aug, Nov   **Capital Gains:** Nov

12b-1: No

Minimum: **Initial:** $1,000   **Subsequent:** $100

Min IRA: **Initial:** $250   **Subsequent:** $100

Services: IRA, Keogh, Corp, Withdraw, Deduct

Tel Exchange: Yes   **With MMF:** Yes

Registered: All states except ME, NH, VT

SAFECO GROWTH
Growth

Safeco Asset Management Co.
Safeco Plaza
Seattle, WA 98185
(800) 426-6730/(206) 545-5530

	Years Ending 9/30					
	1981	1982	1983	1984	1985	1986
Net Investment Income ($)	.59	.52	.42	.51	.51	.31
Dividends from Net Investment Income ($)	.55	.59	.44	.46	.56	.42
Net Gains (Losses) on Investments ($)	(.95)	.43	7.56	(2.37)	1.19	1.62
Distributions from Net Realized Capital Gains ($)	.99	1.22	.67	1.20	1.16	2.98
Net Asset Value End of Year ($)	14.36	13.50	20.38	16.87	16.86	15.40
Ratio of Expenses to Net Assets (%)	.61	.64	.61	.61	.63	.85
Portfolio Turnover Rate (%)	17	13	19	23	29	46
Total Assets: End of Year (Millions $)	39.1	40.6	64.5	63.5	66.3	68.4

Annual Rate of Return (%) Years Ending 12/31	(2.3)	19.0	31.8	(7.0)	19.6	1.8

Five-Year Total Return 77.5%	Degree of Diversification B	Beta .98	Bull C	Bear E

Objective: Seeks capital growth and increased shareholder income through investment in large, well-established, dividend-paying companies. Short-term investments are only made when deemed beneficial. The aim is to keep portfolio turnover rates low.

Portfolio: (9/30/86) Common stocks 84%, short-term securities 13%, bonds 3%. Largest stock holdings: drugs 8%, office equipment 7%.

Distributions: Income: Semiannually   **Capital Gains:** Nov

12b-1: No

Minimum: Initial: $1,000   Subsequent: $100

Min IRA: Initial: $250   Subsequent: $100

Services: IRA, Keogh, Corp, 403(b), Withdraw, Deduct

Tel Exchange: Yes   **With MMF:** Yes

Registered: All states except ME, NH, VT

SAFECO INCOME
Balanced

Safeco Asset Management Co.
Safeco Plaza
Seattle, WA 98185
(800) 426-6730/(206) 545-5530

	Years Ending 9/30					
	1981	**1982**	**1983**	**1984**	**1985**	**1986**
Net Investment Income ($)	.83	.86	.83	.87	.77	.78
Dividends from Net Investment Income ($)	.82	.86	.83	.85	.80	.79
Net Gains (Losses) on Investments ($)	(.41)	.41	3.62	.04	1.53	3.12
Distributions from Net Realized Capital Gains ($)	.74	.44	.44	.87	1.17	.56
Net Asset Value End of Year ($)	10.30	10.26	13.44	12.63	12.96	15.52
Ratio of Expenses to Net Assets (%)	.67	.63	.63	.63	.73	.95
Portfolio Turnover Rate (%)	20	28	32	34	29	29
Total Assets: End of Year (Millions $)	15.1	15.4	21.5	19.8	31.5	102.3
Annual Rate of Return (%) Years Ending 12/31	6.5	22.0	28.3	10.7	31.4	19.9

Five-Year Total Return	172.9%	Degree of Diversification	A	Beta	.74	Bull	A	Bear	C

Objective: Seeks high current income and capital growth through investments in common stocks and convertible securities of medium- to large-sized companies that pay dividends.

Portfolio: (9/30/86) Common stocks 61%, corporate bonds 27%, preferred stocks 10%, short-term securities 4%. Largest stock holdings: utilities 17%, banks 6%.

Distributions: Income: Feb, May, Aug, Nov   **Capital Gains:** Nov

12b-1: No

Minimum: Initial: $1,000   Subsequent: $100

Min IRA: Initial: $250   Subsequent: $100

Services: IRA, Keogh, Withdraw, Deduct

Tel Exchange: Yes   **With MMF:** Yes

Registered: All states except ME, NH, VT

SALEM GROWTH
Growth

Salem Funds
99 High Street
Boston, MA 02110
(800) 343-3424/(704) 331-0710

	Years Ending 3/31					
	1981	**1982**	**1983**	**1984**	**1985**	**1986**
Net Investment Income ($)	–	–	–	–	–	19
Dividends from Net Investment Income ($)	–	–	–	–	–	.20
Net Gains (Losses) on Investments ($)	–	–	–	–	–	2.32
Distributions from Net Realized Capital Gains ($)	–	–	–	–	–	–
Net Asset Value End of Year ($)	–	–	–	–	–	12.35
Ratio of Expenses to Net Assets (%)	–	–	–	–	–	2.00
Portfolio Turnover Rate (%)	–	–	–	–	–	20
Total Assets: End of Year (Millions $)	–	–	–	–	–	5.6

Annual Rate of Return (%) Years Ending 12/31	–	–	–	–	–	16.6

Five-Year Total Return	NA	Degree of Diversification	NA	Beta	NA	Bull NA	Bear NA

Objective: Primary objective is long-term capital growth; income is a secondary objective. Invests in companies with at least $100 million in equity. Will also invest in convertible securities rated at least BBB by S&P.

Portfolio: (9/30/86) Common stocks 86%, short-term securities 10%. Largest stock holdings: public utilities 9%, transportation 8%

Distributions: Income: Quarterly   **Capital Gains:** Annually

12b-1: Yes   Amount: .35%

Minimum: Initial: $1,000   Subsequent: None

Min IRA: Initial: NA   Subsequent: NA

Tel Exchange: No

Registered: DC, FL, GA, KY, MS, NC, NJ, NY, SC, VA

SBSF FUND
Growth

Spears, Benzak, Salomon &
Farrell, Inc.
10 Rockefeller Plaza
New York, NY 10020
(212) 903-1200

	Years Ending 11/30					
	1981	1982	1983	1984	1985	1986
Net Investment Income ($)	–	–	–	.44	.31	.37
Dividends from Net Investment Income ($)	–	–	–	.18	.40	.32
Net Gains (Losses) on Investments ($)	–	–	–	.55	2.81	1.13
Distributions from Net Realized Capital Gains ($)	–	–	–	–	–	.55
Net Asset Value End of Year ($)	–	–	–	10.81	13.53	14.16
Ratio of Expenses to Net Assets (%)	–	–	–	1.37	1.40	1.17
Portfolio Turnover Rate (%)	–	–	–	87	80	65
Total Assets: End of Year (Millions $)	–	–	–	23.5	60.7	90.1
Annual Rate of Return (%) Years Ending 12/31	–	–	–	11.8	28.3	8.1

Five-Year Total Return	NA	Degree of Diversification	B	Beta	.63	Bull NA	Bear NA

Objective: Seeks high total return over the long term consistent with reasonable risk. Using common stocks, bonds and convertible securities, the fund looks for above-average capital appreciation during up markets and capital preservation during down markets.

Portfolio: (11/30/86) Common stocks 74%, short-term securities 14%, government bonds 11%, convertible bonds 1%. Largest stock holdings: insurance 19%, communications, 8%.

Distributions: Income: Semi-Annually   **Capital Gains:** Annually

12b-1: Yes   **Amount:** .25%

Minimum: Initial: None   **Subsequent:** None

Min IRA: Initial: $500   **Subsequent:** None

Services: IRA, Keogh, Withdraw

Tel Exchange: Yes   **With MMF:** Yes

Registered: All states except NC

SCUDDER CAPITAL GROWTH
Growth

Scudder, Stevens & Clark
175 Federal St.
Boston, MA 02110
(800) 453-3305/(617) 426-8300

	Years Ending 9/30					
	1981	1982	1983	1984	1985	1986
Net Investment Income ($)	.34	.34	.28	.29	.26	.26
Dividends from Net Investment Income ($)	.25	.67	–	.26	.29	.23
Net Gains (Losses) on Investments ($)	(1.08)	.82	4.93	(.83)	2.19	3.67
Distributions from Net Realized Capital Gains ($)	–	–	–	.72	.51	1.88
Net Asset Value End of Year ($)	9.52	10.01	15.22	13.70	15.35	17.17
Ratio of Expenses to Net Assets (%)	.77	1.00	.82	.90	.86	.84
Portfolio Turnover Rate (%)	27	57	48	36	58	56
Total Assets: End of Year (Millions $)	100.6	110.5	237.5	236.3	302.4	413.9
Annual Rate of Return (%) Years Ending 12/31	(6.2)	28.6	22.1	0.5	36.2	16.5

Five-Year Total Return	150.2%	Degree of Diversification	B	Beta 1.01	Bull B	Bear C

Objective: Seeks to maximize long-term growth of capital by investing in common stocks with growth potential, in special situations and in foreign companies. The fund may also invest in debt securities for defensive purposes and foreign securities.

Portfolio: (12/31/86) Common stocks 90%, short-term securities 8%, preferred stocks 2%. Largest stock holdings: media & service 31%, utilities 13%.

Distributions: Income: Oct **Capital Gains:** Oct
12b-1: No
Minimum: Initial: $1,000 **Subsequent:** None
Min IRA: Initial: $240 **Subsequent:** None
Services: IRA, Keogh, 403(b), Corp, Withdraw, Deduct
Tel Exchange: Yes **With MMF:** Yes
Registered: All states

SCUDDER DEVELOPMENT
Aggressive Growth

Scudder, Stevens & Clark
175 Federal St.
Boston, MA 02110
(800) 453-3305/(617) 426-8300

	Years Ending 6/30					
	1981	**1982**	**1983**	**1984**	**1985**	**1986**
Net Investment Income ($)	.79	1.55	.96	.94	.42	(.02)
Dividends from Net Investment Income ($)	.56	.79	1.36	1.03	.85	.51
Net Gains (Losses) on Investments ($)	19.74	(10.34)	27.99	(13.41)	7.00	17.43
Distributions from Net Realized Capital Gains ($)	–	4.35	–	1.31	1.06	2.76
Net Asset Value End of Year ($)	56.85	42.92	70.51	55.70	61.21	73.35
Ratio of Expenses to Net Assets (%)	1.20	1.22	1.26	1.31	1.29	1.25
Portfolio Turnover Rate (%)	25	19	22	20	26	29
Total Assets: End of Year (Millions $)	80.0	89.0	253.0	206.4	254.0	358.7
Annual Rate of Return (%) Years Ending 12/31	9.6	15.6	18.2	(10.3)	19.8	7.6

Five-Year Total Return	58.0%	Degree of Diversification	C	Beta 1.13	Bull E	Bear C

Objective: Seeks long-term capital growth by investing in marketable equity securities of small or little-known companies with promise of expanding in size and profitability and/or of gaining increased market recognition for their securities. May invest in restricted securities and foreign securities. May convert to debt instruments as defensive measure.

Portfolio: (6/30/86) Common stocks 86%, short-term securities 13%. Largest stock holdings: consumer nondurable 24%, technology 22%.

Distributions: Income: Aug   **Capital Gains:** Aug

12b-1: No

Minimum: Initial: $1,000   Subsequent: None

Min IRA: Initial: $240   Subsequent: None

Services: IRA, Keogh, 403(b), Corp, Withdraw, Deduct

Tel Exchange: Yes   **With MMF:** Yes

Registered: All states

SCUDDER GOVERNMENT MORTGAGE SECURITIES
Bond

Scudder, Stevens & Clark
175 Federal St.
Boston, MA 02110
(800) 453-3305/(617) 426-8300

	Years Ending 3/31					
	1981	1982	1983	1984	1985	1986 (8 mos.)
Net Investment Income ($)	–	–	–	–	–	1.12
Dividends from Net Investment Income ($)	–	–	–	–	–	1.12
Net Gains (Losses) on Investments ($)	–	–	–	–	–	.41
Distributions from Net Realized Capital Gains ($)	–	–	–	–	–	–
Net Asset Value End of Year ($)	–	–	–	–	–	15.41
Ratio of Expenses to Net Assets (%)	–	–	–	–	–	1.02
Portfolio Turnover Rate (%)	–	–	–	–	–	124
Total Assets: End of Year (Millions $)	–	–	–	–	–	153.8

Annual Rate of Return (%) Years Ending 12/31	–	–	–	–	–	11.3

Five-Year Total Return	NA	Degree of Diversification	NA	Beta	NA	Bull	NA	Bear	NA

Objective: Seeks high current income and safety of principal through investment of at least 65% of its net assets in GNMA securities. Invests in other U.S. government-backed securities. May also buy and sell options and futures contracts.

Portfolio: (9/30/86) GNMAs 82%, U.S. treasury obligations 16%, repos 2%.

Distributions: Income: Monthly   **Capital Gains:** Apr
12b-1: No
Minimum: Initial: $1,000   Subsequent: None
Min IRA: Initial: $240   Subsequent: None
Services: IRA, Keogh, Corp. 403(b), Withdraw, Deduct
Tel Exchange: Yes   **With MMF:** Yes
Registered: All states

SCUDDER GROWTH & INCOME

Growth & Income

Scudder, Stevens & Clark
175 Federal St.
Boston, MA 02110-2267
(800) 453-3305/(617) 426-8300

	Years Ending 12/31					
	1981	1982	1983	1984*	1985	1986
Net Investment Income ($)	.50	.50	.44	.41	.59	.67
Dividends from Net Investment Income ($)	.50	.49	.43	.40	.58	.68
Net Gains (Losses) on Investments ($)	(1.41)	1.99	1.38	(1.12)	3.44	1.96
Distributions from Net Realized Capital Gains ($)	.90	1.36	.49	1.78	–	2.28
Net Asset Value End of Year ($)	13.25	13.89	14.79	11.90	15.35	15.02
Ratio of Expenses to Net Assets (%)	.73	.86	.92	.89	.84	.83
Portfolio Turnover Rate (%)	57	52	84	79	73	45
Total Assets: End of Year (Millions $)	147.9	188.6	260.1	223.6	302.1	384.5

Changed name and objectives.

Annual Rate of Return (%) Years Ending 12/31	(6.2)	22.6	13.3	(3.7)	34.5	17.8

Five-Year Total Return 111.9%	Degree of Diversification B	Beta .95	Bull C	Bear C

Objective: Seeks long-term capital growth and current income by purchasing seasoned and readily marketable dividend-paying securities of leading companies. May invest in foreign securities and sell covered call options and futures contracts. May also lend portfolio securities and enter into repos.

Portfolio: (12/31/86) Common stocks 61%, convertible securities 32%, short-term securities 7%, preferred stocks 1%. Largest stock holdings: utilities 16%, financial 11%.

Distributions: Income: Feb, May, Aug, Nov   **Capital Gains:** Feb

12b-1: No

Minimum: Initial: $1,000   **Subsequent:** None

Min IRA: Initial: $240   **Subsequent:** None

Services: IRA, Keogh, Corp, 403(b), Withdraw, Deduct

Tel Exchange: Yes   **With MMF:** Yes

Registered: All states

SCUDDER INCOME
Bond

Scudder, Stevens & Clark
175 Federal St.
Boston, MA 02110-2267
(800) 453-3305/(617) 426-8300

	Years Ending 12/31					
	1981	1982	1983	1984	1985	1986
Net Investment Income ($)	1.34	1.27	1.26	1.25	1.29	1.22
Dividends from Net Investment Income ($)	1.36	1.27	1.25	1.25	1.29	1.22
Net Gains (Losses) on Investments ($)	(.94)	1.55	(.04)	.06	1.12	.59
Distributions from Net Realized Capital Gains ($)	–	–	–	–	–	–
Net Asset Value End of Year ($)	10.12	11.67	11.64	11.70	12.82	13.41
Ratio of Expenses to Net Assets (%)	.83	.93	.97	1.02	.91	.88
Portfolio Turnover Rate (%)	59	41	40	40	30	24
Total Assets: End of Year (Millions $)	58.1	91.2	110.5	122.9	171.7	248.5
Annual Rate of Return (%) Years Ending 12/31	4.0	30.0	10.8	12.3	21.7	14.6

Five-Year Total Return	125.6%	Degree of Diversification	NA	Beta	.25	Bull	C	Bear	A

Objective: Seeks current income through investment in fixed-income securities, dividend-paying common stocks and government obligations. May invest in foreign securities and CDs of both foreign and domestic banks, and may sell covered call options and enter into repos.

Portfolio: (12/31/86) Long-term bonds 62%, intermediate-term bonds 17%, common stocks 12%, short-term securities 7%, preferred stocks 2%, convertible bonds 1%.

Distributions: Income: Feb, May, Aug, Nov   **Capital Gains:** Feb

12b-1: No

Minimum: Initial: $1,000   **Subsequent:** None

Min IRA: Initial: $240   **Subsequent:** None

Services: IRA, Keogh, Corp, 403(b), Withdraw, Deduct

Tel Exchange: Yes   **With MMF:** Yes

Registered: All states

SCUDDER
INTERNATIONAL
International

Scudder, Stevens & Clark
175 Federal St.
Boston, MA 02110
(800) 453-3305/(617) 426-8300

	Years ending 7/31			3/31		
	1981	1982	1983	1984* (8 mos.)	1985	1986
Net Investment Income ($)	.58	.54	.40	.15	.51	.74
Dividends from Net Investment Income ($)	.57	.40	.54	.31	.10	.41
Net Gains (Losses) on Investments ($)	(.07)	(2.69)	6.37	3.24	(1.09)	13.70
Distributions from Net Realized Capital Gains ($)	1.23	.03	—	—	.58	.13
Net Asset Value End of Year ($)	17.56	14.98	21.21	24.29	23.03	36.93
Ratio of Expenses to Net Assets (%)	1.10	1.16	1.13	1.05	1.04	.99
Portfolio Turnover Rate (%)	33	42	39	17	20	36
Total Assets: End of Year (Millions $)	55.7	56.7	110.8	188.9	222.9	597

Fiscal year changed from 7/31 to 3/31. The above figures are for the eight-month period ending 3/31/84.

Annual Rate of Return (%) Years Ending 12/31	(2.7)	1.2	29.2	(0.7)	48.9	50.5

Five-Year Total Return 191.1%	Degree of Diversification E	Beta .50	Bull A	Bear D

Objective: Seeks long-term capital growth through investment in marketable equity securities selected primarily to permit participation in established non-U.S. companies and economies with prospects for growth. Also invests in fixed-income securities of foreign governments and companies with a view toward total investment return.

Portfolio: (9/30/86) Common stocks 86%, bonds 6%, convertible bonds 4%. Largest holdings: Japan 22%, Germany 11%.

Distributions: Income: April   **Capital Gains:** April

12b-1: No

Minimum: Initial: $1,000   **Subsequent:** None

Min IRA: Initial: $240   **Subsequent:** None

Services: IRA, Keogh, 403(b), Corp, Withdraw, Deduct

Tel Exchange: Yes   **With MMF:** Yes

Registered: All states

SCUDDER TARGET GENERAL 1990
Bond

Scudder, Stevens & Clark
175 Federal St.
Boston, MA 02110-2267
(800) 453-3305/(617) 426-8300

	Years Ending 12/31					
	1981	1982	1983	1984	1985	1986
Net Investment Income ($)	—	—	.59	.82	.83	.66
Dividends from Net Investment Income ($)	—	—	.59	.82	.83	.66
Net Gains (Losses) on Investments ($)	—	—	(.67)	.05	.85	.54
Distributions from Net Realized Capital Gains ($)	—	—	—	—	—	.39
Net Asset Value End of Year ($)	—	—	9.33	9.38	10.38	10.53
Ratio of Expenses to Net Assets (%)	—	—	1.00	1.06	1.00	1.25
Portfolio Turnover Rate (%)	—	—	4	13	49	35
Total Assets: End of Year (Millions $)	—	—	6.0	8.8	12.5	16.2
Annual Rate of Return (%) Years Ending 12/31	—	—	(0.4)	12.9	18.3	12.0

Five-Year Total Return	NA	Degree of Diversification	NA	Beta	.14	Bull NA	Bear NA

Objective: Seeks current income plus preservation of capital. Invests in high-grade corporate bonds and notes plus U.S. Treasury securities. The portfolio is designed to be liquidated in 1990.

Portfolio: (12/31/86) Corporate bonds 69%, U.S. Treasury obligations 23%, U.S. government-backed obligations 5%, repos 2%.

Distributions: **Income:** Monthly   **Capital Gains:** Annually
12b-1: No
Minimum: **Initial:** $1,000   **Subsequent:** None
Min IRA: **Initial:** $240   **Subsequent:** None
Services: IRA, Keogh, Corp, SEP, Withdraw, Deduct
Tel Exchange: Yes   **With MMF:** Yes
Registered: All states

SELECTED AMERICAN SHARES
Growth & Income

Prescott Asset Mgmt., Inc.
230 W. Monroe St. 28th Flr.
Chicago, IL 60606
(800) 621-7321/(312) 641-7862

	Years Ending 12/31					
	1981	1982	1983	1984	1985	1986
Net Investment Income ($)	.52	.58	.56	.46	.48	.42
Dividends from Net Investment Income ($)	.48	.56	.56	.48	.40	.48
Net Gains (Losses) on Investments ($)	(.60)	1.08	1.19	.93	2.90	1.65
Distributions from Net Realized Capital Gains ($)	—	—	—	.05	.17	2.29
Net Asset Value End of Year ($)	7.39	8.49	9.68	10.54	13.35	12.65
Ratio of Expenses to Net Assets (%)	.94	1.02	.94	.99	.87	.85
Portfolio Turnover Rate (%)	21	15	66	49	33	40
Total Assets: End of Year (Millions $)	72.3	76.6	81.3	84.3	122.6	160.5
Annual Rate of Return (%) Years Ending 12/31	(0.9)	24.3	22.6	13.9	33.2	17.0

Five-Year Total Return	170.3%	Degree of Diversification	C	Beta	.68	Bull	A	Bear	B

Objective: To provide a combination of growth of capital and income. The fund invests in common stocks and fixed-income securities in varying proportions of companies with large capitalizations and long records of earnings growth and dividends. May lend portfolio securities and write covered call options.

Portfolio: (12/31/86) Common stocks 88%, short-term securities 7%, preferred stock 5%. Largest stock holdings: tobacco 11%, banking 10%.

Distributions: Income: Jan, Mar, June, Sept   **Capital Gains:** Jan

12b-1: Yes   **Amount:** 1.00%

Minimum: Initial: $1,000   **Subsequent:** $100

Min IRA: Initial: $1,000   **Subsequent:** $100

Services: IRA, Keogh, Corp, SEP, Withdraw

Tel Exchange: Yes   **With MMF:** Yes

Registered: All states

SELECTED SPECIAL SHARES
Growth

Prescott Asset Mgmt., Inc.
230 W. Monroe St. 28th Flr.
Chicago, IL 60606
(800) 621-7321/(312) 641-7862

	Years Ending 12/31					
	1981	1982	1983	1984	1985	1986
Net Investment Income ($)	.45	.43	.65	.40	.67	.49
Dividends from Net Investment Income ($)	.65	.42	.38	.56	.49	.64
Net Gains (Losses) on Investments ($)	(1.77)	2.22	4.45	(1.14)	3.32	.88
Distributions from Net Realized Capital Gains ($)	—	—	—	4.28	.65	3.45
Net Asset Value End of Year ($)	16.33	18.56	23.28	17.70	20.55	17.83
Ratio of Expenses to Net Assets (%)	1.10	1.32	1.21	1.38	1.23	1.08
Portfolio Turnover Rate (%)	65	62	101	68	73	133
Total Assets: End of Year (Millions $)	30.6	31.0	36.6	32.7	35.9	32.8
Annual Rate of Return (%) Years Ending 12/31	(7.3)	16.8	28.0	(4.2)	23.5	7.2

Five-Year Total Return	89.6%	Degree of Diversification	C	Beta	.84	Bull	C	Bear	E

Objective:	Seeks growth of capital through investment in common stocks and convertible securities of growing companies that are undervalued. Looks for strong management and growth record. Current income is incidental to this objective.
Portfolio:	(12/31/86) Common stocks 89%, short-term securities 6%, convertible bonds 5%, preferred stock 4%. Largest stock holdings: distribution 12%, manufacturing 10%.
Distributions:	Income: Jan **Capital Gains:** Jan
12b-1:	Yes **Amount:** 1.00%
Minimum:	Initial: $1,000 Subsequent: $100
Min IRA:	Initial: $1,000 Subsequent: $100
Services:	IRA, Keogh, Corp, SEP, Withdraw
Tel Exchange:	Yes **With MMF:** Yes
Registered:	All states

SHERMAN, DEAN

Aggressive Growth

Sherman, Dean
Management and Research Corp.
6061 N.W. Expressway
Suite 465
San Antonio, TX 78201
(512) 735-7700

	Years Ending 5/31					
	1981	1982	1983	1984	1985	1986
Net Investment Income ($)	.05	.06	.05	.02	.00	(.11)
Dividends from Net Investment Income ($)	–	–	.12	.03	.01	.04
Net Gains (Losses) on Investments ($)	2.28	(3.49)	2.88	(2.25)	(.74)	(.75)
Distributions from Net Realized Capital Gains ($)	–	–	–	–	–	–
Net Asset Value End of Year ($)	9.74	6.31	9.12	6.86	6.11	5.21
Ratio of Expenses to Net Assets (%)	1.61	1.91	1.91	2.01	2.04	2.36
Portfolio Turnover Rate (%)	22	10	4	12	21	13
Total Assets: End of Year (Millions $)	8.4	4.9	5.1	4.3	3.8	2.3

Annual Rate of Return (%) Years Ending 12/31	(0.1)	(3.9)	(3.8)	(32.0)	13.1	(4.7)

Five-Year Total Return	(32.3)%	Degree of Diversification	E	Beta .59	Bull E	Bear E

Objective: Seeks long-term capital appreciation through investment in common stocks of companies with apparently unusually favorable prospects including small, unseasoned and special situation companies. May concentrate 50% of assets in two companies—25% each.

Portfolio: (11/30/86) Common stocks 98%, bonds 1%. Largest stock holdings: mining 65%, energy 25%.

Distributions: Income: June   **Capital Gains:** June

12b-1: Yes   **Amount:** .25%

Minimum: Initial: $1,000   **Subsequent:** $100

Min IRA: Initial: $500   **Subsequent:** $100

Services: IRA

Tel Exchange: No

Registered: All states except CA, CO, DC, DE, HI, IN, MI, MO, NJ, NV, NY, OR, PA, TX, WA

STEADMAN AMERICAN INDUSTRY
Growth

Steadman Security Corp.
1730 K St., NW
Washington, DC 20006
(800) 424-8570/(202) 223-1000

	Years Ending 1/31					
	1981	1982	1983	1984	1985	1986
Net Investment Income ($)	(.01)	.14	.05	(.02)	(.04)	(.04)
Dividends from Net Investment Income ($)	.01	—	.15	.03	—	—
Net Gains (Losses) on Investments ($)	.37	(.46)	.26	.04	(.36)	—
Distributions from Net Realized Capital Gains ($)	—	—	—	.02	—	—
Net Asset Value End of Year ($)	3.52	3.20	3.36	3.33	2.93	2.89
Ratio of Expenses to Net Assets (%)	3.30	3.61	4.33	3.75	4.83	5.03
Portfolio Turnover Rate (%)	40	81	143	78	227	249
Total Assets: End of Year (Millions $)	16.4	13.1	12.8	11.2	9.3	9.3
Annual Rate of Return (%) Years Ending 12/31	(14.5)	4.7	6.7	(23.2)	7.8	(19.7)

Five-Year Total Return (25.7)%	Degree of Diversification D	Beta .99	Bull E	Bear D

Objective: Seeks to provide long-term capital growth through investment in common stocks of large, established companies, debt securities, precious metals, oil and gas leases and limited partnerships, and real estate. Realization of current income is secondary. May employ leverage, effect short sales, write options and enter into repos.

Portfolio: (7/31/86) Common stocks 74%, short-term securities 24%, call options 2%. Largest stock holdings: basic industry 30%, consumer goods 27%.

Distributions: Income: Annually   **Capital Gains:** Annually

12b-1: Yes   **Amount:** .25%

Minimum: Initial: $100   **Subsequent:** $25

Min IRA: Initial: $100   **Subsequent:** $25

Services: IRA, Keogh, 403(b), Withdraw

Tel Exchange: Yes   **With MMF:** No

Registered: All states

STEADMAN
ASSOCIATED
Growth & Income

Steadman Security Corp.
1730 K St., NW
Washington, DC 20006
(800) 424-8570/(202) 223-1000

	Years Ending 9/30					
	1981	**1982**	**1983***	**1984**	**1985**	**1986**
Net Investment Income ($)	.07	.07	.06	.05	Nil	(.01)
Dividends from Net Investment Income ($)	.07	.07	.06	.05	.01	—
Net Gains (Losses) on Investments ($)	(.10)	.08	.15	(.14)	.01	.11
Distributions from Net Realized Capital Gains ($)	.04	—	.02	—	.04	.08
Net Asset Value End of Year ($)	.78	.87	1.00	.86	.82	.85
Ratio of Expenses to Net Assets (%)	2.03	2.18	1.99	2.6	2.85	2.88
Portfolio Turnover Rate (%)	48	41	78	304	211	375
Total Assets: End of Year (Millions $)	29.8	30.9	32.7	25.2	20.5	19.8

Was an income (bond) fund. Changed 10/83 to growth fund.

Annual Rate of Return (%) Years Ending 12/31	(3.7)	27.3	6.0	(8.6)	21.5	2.8
Five-Year Total Return **54.0%**	Degree of Diversification **C**	Beta **1.01**	Bull **E**	Bear **B**		

Objective: Seeks capital growth through use of a broad range of investments and techniques including purchase and sale of put and call options. Income is secondary goal. Emphasis is on large, well-established, dividend-paying companies.

Portfolio: (9/30/86) Common stocks 57%, short-term investments 39%, restricted securities 3%. Largest stock holdings: paper 11%, oil 10%.

Distributions: Income: Mar, June, Sept, Dec   **Capital Gains:** Sept

12b-1: Yes   **Amount:** .25%

Minimum: **Initial:** $100   **Subsequent:** $25

Min IRA: **Initial:** $100   **Subsequent:** $25

Services: IRA, Keogh, 403(b), Withdraw

Tel Exchange: Yes   **With MMF:** No

Registered: All states

STEADMAN INVESTMENT
Growth

Steadman Security Corp.
1730 K St., NW
Washington, DC 20006
(800) 424-8570/(202) 223-1000

	Years Ending 12/31					
	1981	**1982**	**1983**	**1984**	**1985**	**1986**
Net Investment Income ($)	.10	.07	.01	.03	.13	.06
Dividends from Net Investment Income ($)	.05	.09	.04	.02	.02	—
Net Gains (Losses) on Investments ($)	(.29)	.03	.11	(.20)	(.05)	.09
Distributions from Net Realized Capital Gains ($)	—	—	—	—	—	—
Net Asset Value End of Year ($)	1.48	1.49	1.58	1.39	1.46	1.61
Ratio of Expenses to Net Assets (%)	2.43	2.71	2.61	3.52	5.15	3.97
Portfolio Turnover Rate (%)	164	162	186	262	406	129
Total Assets: End of Year (Millions $)	14.9	14.1	13.6	9.7	9.0	8.1
Annual Rate of Return (%) Years Ending 12/31	(11.5)	7.4	8.0	(10.9)	5.3	10.3

Five-Year Total Return	20.1%	Degree of Diversification	D	Beta	.85	Bull	E	Bear	D

Objective: Long-term capital appreciation through investing in common stocks and other equity-related securities. May invest up to 10% of assets in foreign securities and use option techniques.

Portfolio: (12/31/86) Common stocks 44%, convertible bonds 29%, convertible preferred stocks 16%, preferred stocks 5%, restricted stocks 4%, short-term securities 1%. Largest stock holdings: Occidental Petroleum 9%, Philadelphia Electric 7%.

Distributions: **Income:** Annually   **Capital Gains:** Annually
12b-1: Yes   **Amount:** .25%
Minimum: **Initial:** $100   **Subsequent:** $25
Min IRA: **Initial:** $100   **Subsequent:** $25
Services: IRA, Keogh, 403(b), Withdraw
Tel Exchange: Yes   **With MMF:** No
Registered: All states

STEADMAN OCEANOGRAPHIC, TECHNOLOGY & GROWTH

Aggressive Growth

Steadman Security Corp.
1730 K St., NW
Washington, DC 20006
(800) 424-8570/(202) 223-1000

	Years Ending 12/31					
	1981	1982	1983	1984	1985	1986
Net Investment Income ($)	.17	.13	(.06)	(.09)	(.22)	(.33)
Dividends from Net Investment Income ($)	.24	.15	.07	—	—	—
Net Gains (Losses) on Investments ($)	(2.63)	(.24)	.68	(.64)	(.61)	(.25)
Distributions from Net Realized Capital Gains ($)	2.17	—	.06	—	—	—
Net Asset Value End of Year ($)	6.39	6.13	6.62	5.89	5.06	4.48
Ratio of Expenses to Net Assets (%)	3.91	4.13	3.67	4.43	5.30	5.81
Portfolio Turnover Rate (%)	190	214	225	270	260	197
Total Assets: End of Year (Millions $)	8.7	8.0	8.0	6.5	4.9	3.8
Annual Rate of Return (%) Years Ending 12/31	(24.2)	(1.7)	10.2	(10.9)	(14.3)	(11.3)

Five-Year Total Return (26.5)%	Degree of Diversification D	Beta 1.26	Bull E	Bear E

Objective: Seeks capital growth through investment in common stocks of companies primarily engaged in basic industries. May employ leverage, short-selling, may invest in foreign securities, may buy and sell option contracts.

Portfolio: (12/31/86) Common stocks 79%, short-term securities 10%, restricted stocks 10%. Largest stock holdings: oil and oil services 26%, technology 16%.

Distributions: Income: Annually   **Capital Gains:** Annually

12b-1: Yes   Amount: .25%

Minimum: Initial: $100   Subsequent: $25

Min IRA: Initial: $100   Subsequent: $25

Services: IRA, Keogh, 403(b), Withdraw

Tel Exchange: Yes   **With MMF:** No

Registered: All states

STEINROE & FARNHAM CAPITAL OPPORTUNITIES

Aggressive Growth

Stein Roe & Farnham
PO Box 1143
Chicago, IL 60690
(800) 621-0320/(312) 368-7826

	Years Ending 12/31					
	1981	1982	1983	1984	1985	1986
Net Investment Income ($)	.35	.24	.11	.30	.20	.06
Dividends from Net Investment Income ($)	.20	.33	.19	.12	.29	.20
Net Gains (Losses) on Investments ($)	(4.23)	4.57	2.80	(4.69)	4.53	3.93
Distributions from Net Realized Capital Gains ($)	1.45	.64	.65	2.55	–	.85
Net Asset Value End of Year ($)	20.52	24.36	26.43	19.37	23.81	26.75
Ratio of Expenses to Net Assets (%)	.91	.95	.89	.92	.95	.95
Portfolio Turnover Rate (%)	69	95	72	85	90	116
Total Assets: End of Year (Millions $)	126.6	197.9	292.5	176.1	176.1	191.4
Annual Rate of Return (%) Years Ending 12/31	(15.3)	24.9	11.9	(16.8)	24.6	16.8

Five-Year Total Return	69.2%	Degree of Diversification	D	Beta 1.22	Bull D	Bear E

Objective: To provide long-term capital appreciation by investing in selected common stocks of both seasoned and smaller companies which have potential for success with new products or services, technological developments or management shifts. May invest in foreign securities.

Portfolio: (12/31/86) Common stocks 87%, convertible subordinated debentures 5%, short-term obligations 9%. Largest stock holdings: business services 23%, technology 22%.

Distributions: Income: Annually   **Capital Gains:** Annually

12b-1: No

Minimum: Initial: $2,500   Subsequent: $100

Min IRA: Initial: $500   Subsequent: $50

Services: IRA, Keogh, Corp, SEP, Withdraw

Tel Exchange: Yes   **With MMF:** Yes

Registered: All states

STEINROE & FARNHAM STOCK

Aggressive Growth

Stein Roe & Farnham
PO Box 1143
Chicago, IL 60690
(800) 621-0320/(312) 368-7826

	Years Ending 12/31					
	1981	1982	1983	1984	1985	1986
Net Investment Income ($)	.40	.48	.25	.36	.31	.26
Dividends from Net Investment Income ($)	.37	.45	.28	.38	.30	.25
Net Gains (Losses) on Investments ($)	(4.69)	4.62	2.41	(2.60)	3.38	2.75
Distributions from Net Realized Capital Gains ($)	1.89	1.48	1.43	4.70	–	3.22
Net Asset Value End of Year ($)	17.24	20.41	21.36	14.04	17.43	16.97
Ratio of Expenses to Net Assets (%)	.62	.66	.63	.67	.67	.67
Portfolio Turnover Rate (%)	94	116	173	195	114	137
Total Assets: End of Year (Millions $)	178.4	234.9	269.3	216.5	224.4	226.6
Annual Rate of Return (%) Years Ending 12/31	(19.0)	33.4	14.0	(9.8)	26.5	17.3

Five-Year Total Return	103.7%	Degree of Diversification	C	Beta	1.13	Bull	C	Bear	D

Objective: Seeks long-term capital appreciation through investment primarily in common stocks and convertible securities of established companies. May write covered call options on up to 25% of assets.

Portfolio: (12/31/86) Common stocks 98%, short-term notes 1%, other 1%. Largest stock holdings: food, beverages & tobacco 8%, distribution 8%.

Distributions: Income: Feb, May, Aug, Nov   **Capital Gains:** Feb

12b-1: No

Minimum: Initial: $2,500   Subsequent: $100

Min IRA: Initial: $500   Subsequent: $50

Services: IRA, Keogh, Corp, SEP, Withdraw

Tel Exchange: Yes   **With MMF:** Yes

Registered: All states except NH

STEINROE DISCOVERY

Aggressive Growth

Stein Roe & Farnham
PO Box 1143
Chicago, IL 60690
(800) 621-0320/(312) 368-7826

	Years Ending 6/30					
	1981	1982	1983	1984 (11 mos.)	1985	1986
Net Investment Income ($)	–	–	–	.02	.04	.03
Dividends from Net Investment Income ($)	–	–	–	–	.03	.04
Net Gains (Losses) on Investments ($)	–	–	–	(2.53)	2.72	3.55
Distributions from Net Realized Capital Gains ($)	–	–	–	–	–	–
Net Asset Value End of Year ($)	–	–	–	7.49	10.22	13.76
Ratio of Expenses to Net Assets (%)	–	–	–	1.49	1.42	1.29
Portfolio Turnover Rate (%)	–	–	–	64	101	157
Total Assets: End of Year (Millions $)	–	–	–	33.2	97.2	133.4

Annual Rate of Return (%) Years Ending 12/31	–	–	–	(12.2)	45.3	(5.3)

Five-Year Total Return	NA	Degree of Diversification	D	Beta 1.44	Bull NA	Bear NA

Objective: Seeks long-term capital appreciation by investing in the common stock of smaller companies with less than $250 million in market capitalization and in larger companies with new products or technological developments or other favorable business developments. May include new issues. May write covered call options and enter into repurchase agreements.

Portfolio: (9/30/86) Common stocks 87%, short-term obligations 15%. Largest stock holdings: business services 21%, entertainment 15%.

Distributions: Income: Aug   Capital Gains: Aug
12b-1: No
Minimum: Initial: $2,500   Subsequent: $100
Min IRA: Initial: $500   Subsequent: $50
Services: IRA, Keogh, Corp, SEP, Withdraw
Tel Exchange: Yes   With MMF: Yes
Registered: All states except CA, NH

STEINROE
MANAGED BONDS
Bond

Stein Roe & Farnham
PO Box 1143
Chicago, IL 60690
(800) 621-0320/(312) 368-7826

	Years Ending 6/30					
	1981	1982	1983	1984	1985	1986
Net Investment Income ($)	1.03	1.10	.97	.94	.89	.84
Dividends from Net Investment Income ($)	1.03	1.10	.97	.94	.89	.84
Net Gains (Losses) on Investments ($)	(1.41)	(.20)	1.08	(1.04)	1.14	1.03
Distributions from Net Realized Capital Gains ($)	–	–	–	.21	–	–
Net Asset Value End of Year ($)	8.12	7.92	9.00	7.75	8.89	9.92
Ratio of Expenses to Net Assets (%)	1.22	1.07	.81	.78	.70	.69
Portfolio Turnover Rate (%)	66	241	185	152	286	334
Total Assets: End of Year (Millions $)	15.4	28.3	84.1	86.5	134.6	183.4

Annual Rate of Return (%) Years Ending 12/31	5.4	27.4	6.9	11.8	22.9	16.3

Five-Year Total Return 117.6%	Degree of Diversification NA	Beta .20	Bull D	Bear A

Objective: Seeks high current income through investment in marketable, investment-grade debt securities. May enter into interest rate futures contracts and covered call options as a hedge. May invest in foreign debt securities. Any common stock investment would be in dividend-paying companies.

Portfolio: (9/30/86) U.S. government obligations 55%, corporate bonds 36%, short-term obligations 13%.

Distributions: **Income:** Jan, April, July, Oct   **Capital Gains:** July

12b-1: No

Minimum: **Initial:** $2,500   **Subsequent:** $100

Min IRA: **Initial:** $500   **Subsequent:** $50

Services: IRA, Keogh, Corp, SEP, Withdraw

Tel Exchange: Yes   **With MMF:** Yes

Registered: All states except NH.

STEINROE SPECIAL
Aggressive Growth

Stein Roe & Farnham
PO Box 1143
Chicago, IL 60690
(800) 621-0320/(312) 368-7826

	Years Ending 12/31					
	1981	**1982**	**1983**	**1984**	**1985**	**1986**
Net Investment Income ($)	.31	.23	.23	.28	.25	.35
Dividends from Net Investment Income ($)	.21	.29	.23	.23	.19	.34
Net Gains (Losses) on Investments ($)	(1.89)	3.50	4.21	(.61)	4.01	2.33
Distributions from Net Realized Capital Gains ($)	.95	1.26	.57	2.29	.54	3.80
Net Asset Value End of Year ($)	11.91	14.09	17.73	14.88	18.41	16.95
Ratio of Expenses to Net Assets (%)	.93	.96	.93	.96	.92	.92
Portfolio Turnover Rate (%)	75	61	81	89	96	116
Total Assets: End of Year (Millions $)	56.2	78.2	145.2	152.0	278.0	253.7
Annual Rate of Return (%) Years Ending 12/31	(11.1)	36.7	32.9	0.0	29.4	14.8

Five-Year Total Return 169.8%	Degree of Diversification B	Beta 1.08	Bull A	Bear E

Objective: Seeks capital appreciation through investment in the common stocks of companies expected to benefit from special factors or trends or having unusual capital appreciation potential, including new issues.

Portfolio: (12/31/86) Common stocks 85%, bonds and notes 10%, short-term securities 4%. Largest stock holdings: technology 20%, media 10%.

Distributions: Income: Annually **Capital Gains:** Annually

12b-1: No

Minimum: Initial: $2,500 **Subsequent:** $100

Min IRA: Initial: $500 **Subsequent:** $50

Services: IRA, Keogh, Corp, SEP, Withdraw

Tel Exchange: Yes **With MMF:** Yes

Registered: All states except NH

STEINROE TOTAL RETURN
Balanced

Stein Roe & Farnham
PO Box 1143
Chicago, IL 60690
(800) 621-0320/(312) 368-7826

	Years Ending 12/31					
	1981	**1982**	**1983**	**1984**	**1985**	**1986**
Net Investment Income ($)	.90	1.23	1.30	1.41	1.41	1.33
Dividends from Net Investment Income ($)	.81	1.15	1.26	1.41	1.42	1.35
Net Gains (Losses) on Investments ($)	(3.98)	3.03	1.61	(.48)	3.87	2.75
Distributions from Net Realized Capital Gains ($)	.61	.43	–	1.55	.19	2.70
Net Asset Value End of Year ($)	19.07	21.75	23.40	21.37	25.04	25.07
Ratio of Expenses to Net Assets (%)	.70	.73	.73	.73	.77	.79
Portfolio Turnover Rate (%)	67	84	79	50	100	108
Total Assets: End of Year (Millions $)	76.2	84.7	93.0	95.7	128.7	149.8
Annual Rate of Return (%) Years Ending 12/31	(13.4)	24.3	13.5	5.2	25.6	16.9

Five-Year Total Return 117.9%	Degree of Diversification B	Beta .64	Bull C	Bear C

Objective: To maintain and increase the purchasing power of invested capital while providing income by investing in high-quality bonds, preferred stocks and common stocks of established companies. Stocks will comprise no more than 75% of assets. May write (sell) covered call options.

Portfolio: (12/31/86) Common stocks 34%, convertible debentures 22%, bonds & notes 23%, short-term securities 14%, convertible preferred 9%. Largest stock holdings: electric utilities 4%, financial 3%.

Distributions: Income: Feb, May, Aug, Nov   **Capital Gains:** Feb
12b-1: No
Minimum: Initial: $2,500   Subsequent: $100
Min IRA: Initial: $500   Subsequent: $50
Services: IRA, Keogh, Corp, 403(b), SEP, Withdraw
Tel Exchange: Yes   **With MMF:** Yes
Registered: All states except NH

STEINROE UNIVERSE
Growth

Stein Roe & Farnham
PO Box 1143
Chicago, IL 60690
(800) 621-0320/(312) 368-7826

	Years Ending 6/30					
	1981	1982*	1983	1984	1985	1986
Net Investment Income ($)	–	.36	.16	.28	.29	.21
Dividends from Net Investment Income ($)	–	.14	.36	.17	.28	.27
Net Gains (Losses) on Investments ($)	–	(2.12)	10.86	(6.94)	3.06	6.35
Distributions from Net Realized Capital Gains ($)	–	–	–	.64	–	–
Net Asset Value End of Year ($)	–	11.79	22.45	14.98	18.05	24.34
Ratio of Expenses to Net Assets (%)	–	1.16	1.10	1.09	1.19	1.20
Portfolio Turnover Rate (%)	–	81	75	130	179	147
Total Assets: End of Year (Millions $)	–	115.0	336.4	182.5	116.8	114.7

4 for 1 stock split 6/83. Prices reflect adjustment.

Annual Rate of Return (%) Years Ending 12/31	–	31.6	20.6	(18.8)	28.3	13.2

Five-Year Total Return	87.1%	Degree of Diversification	C	Beta 1.08	Bull D	Bear D

Objective: Seeks capital appreciation primarily through investment in common stocks of growth companies including small and unseasoned companies or securities convertible into common stocks selected by its computerized database which includes financial forecasts and estimates of indicated market value. May write covered call options, invest in foreign securities and enter into repos.

Portfolio: (9/30/86) Common stocks 72%, short-term obligations 28%, other 1%. Largest stock holdings: food, beverages and tobacco 7%, natural gas companies 7%.

Distributions: Income: Aug   **Capital Gains:** Aug

12b-1: No

Minimum: Initial: $2,500   Subsequent: $100

Min IRA: Initial: $500   Subsequent: $50

Services: IRA, Keogh, Corp, SEP, Withdraw

Tel Exchange: Yes   **With MMF:** Yes

Registered: All states except CA, NH

STRATTON GROWTH

Growth

Stratton Management Co.
PO Box 550
Blue Bell, PA 19422
(215) 542-8025

	Years Ending 5/31					
	1981	**1982**	**1983**	**1984**	**1985**	**1986**
Net Investment Income ($)	.25	.25	.18	.15	.20	.28
Dividends from Net Investment Income ($)	.31	.28	.29	.13	.14	.20
Net Gains (Losses) on Investments ($)	3.16	(1.36)	7.09	(2.27)	3.82	5.93
Distributions from Net Realized Capital Gains ($)	–	–	–	–	.70	.61
Net Asset Value End of Year ($)	12.33	10.94	17.92	15.67	18.85	24.25
Ratio of Expenses to Net Assets (%)	1.76	1.90	1.80	1.61	1.61	1.49
Portfolio Turnover Rate (%)	59	47	70	36	35	29
Total Assets: End of Year (Millions $)	7.6	6.7	11.8	11.4	14.3	19.3
Annual Rate of Return (%) Years Ending 12/31	(6.5)	32.6	26.3	(4.6)	27.2	10.7

Five-Year Total Return 125.0%	Degree of Diversification C	Beta 1.08	Bull B	Bear C

Objective:	Seeks growth of capital with current income as a secondary consideration. The fund will normally invest in common stocks and convertible securities of medium to large, well-established, dividend-paying companies.
Portfolio:	(11/30/86) Common stocks 87%, cash 6%, convertible debentures 6%, convertible preferred stocks 1%. Largest stock holdings: banking 19%, business services 13%.
Distributions:	**Income:** June **Capital Gains:** June
12b-1:	No
Minimum:	**Initial:** $1,000 **Subsequent:** $100
Min IRA:	**Initial:** None **Subsequent:** None
Services:	IRA, Keogh, Corp, 403(b), Withdraw
Tel Exchange:	Yes **With MMF:** No
Registered:	CA, CO, CT, DC, DE, FL, GA, HI, IL, IN, MA, MD, MI, MN, NE, NJ, NY, OH, OR, PA, RI, TX, VA, WA, WY

STRATTON MONTHLY DIVIDEND SHARES
Bond

Stratton Management Co.
Butler & Skippack Pikes
PO Box 550
Blue Bell, PA 19422
(215) 542-8025

	Years Ending 1/31					
	1981	1982	1983	1984	1985	1986
Net Investment Income ($)	1.71	2.01	2.08	1.85	1.96	1.83
Dividends from Net Investment Income ($)	1.69	1.76	1.83	1.93	2.05	2.17
Net Gains (Losses) on Investments ($)	(.31)	.21	2.52	(.19)	2.24	5.69
Distributions from Net Realized Capital Gains ($)	—	—	—	—	—	—
Net Asset Value End of Year ($)	17.36	17.82	20.59	20.32	22.47	27.82
Ratio of Expenses to Net Assets (%)	1.55	1.99	1.98	1.74	1.72	1.49
Portfolio Turnover Rate (%)	42	30	33	30	28	14
Total Assets: End of Year (Millions $)	9.8	7.5	8.5	9.0	10.4	21.3

Annual Rate of Return (%) Years Ending 12/31	—	20.4	11.8	21.0	29.7	20.4

Five-Year Total Return	154.3%	Degree of Diversification	NA	Beta	.49	Bull	A	Bear	NA

Objective: Seeks high dividend and interest income from common stocks and convertible securities. Of these investments, 25% must be in public utility companies engaged in production, transmission or distribution of electric energy, gas, water or telephone service. May convert to cash equivalents for defensive purposes.

Portfolio: (7/31/86) Common stocks 57%, convertible debenture 31%, convertible preferred stocks 6%, cash 6%. Largest stock holdings: electric utilities 33%, electric and gas utilities 23%.

Distributions: **Income:** Monthly   **Capital Gains:** Annually

12b-1: No

Minimum: **Initial:** $1,000   **Subsequent:** $100

Min IRA: **Initial:** None   **Subsequent:** None

Services: IRA, Keogh, 403(b), Withdraw

Tel Exchange: Yes   **With MMF:** No

Registered: AZ, CA, CT, DC, DE, FL, GA, HI, IL, KS, KY, MA, MD, MI, MO, NJ, NY, OH, PA, RI, TX, VA, WA, WI, WY

STRONG INCOME
Balanced

Strong/Corneliuson Capital Mgmt.
815 E. Mason St.
Milwaukee, WI 53202
(800) 368-3863/(414) 765-0620

	Years Ending 12/31					
	1981	1982	1983	1984	1985 (1 mo.)	1986
Net Investment Income ($)	–	–	–	–	.03	.98
Dividends from Net Investment Income ($)	–	–	–	–	–	.71
Net Gains (Losses) on Investments ($)	–	–	–	–	.27	2.08
Distributions from Net Realized Capital Gains ($)	–	–	–	–	–	–
Net Asset Value End of Year ($)	–	–	–	–	10.30	12.65
Ratio of Expenses to Net Assets (%)	–	–	–	–	1.1	1.0
Portfolio Turnover Rate (%)	–	–	–	–	7	205
Total Assets: End of Year (Millions $)	–	–	–	–	2.5	118.7

Annual Rate of Return (%) Years Ending 12/31	–	–	–	–	–	29.9

Five-Year Total Return	NA	Degree of Diversification	NA	Beta	NA	Bull NA	Bear NA

Objective: Seeks high level of current income from investments in a diversified portfolio of fixed-income securities and dividend-paying common stocks. The fixed-income securities may be unrated or as low as CC. May also enter into repos, invest in foreign securities, convertibles and preferred stocks.

Portfolio: (12/31/86) Corporate bonds 96%, preferred stock 4%.

Distributions: **Income:** Quarterly   **Capital Gains:** Jan

12b-1: No

Minimum: **Initial:** $1,000   **Subsequent:** $200

Min IRA: **Initial:** $250   **Subsequent:** None

Services: IRA, Keogh, Corp, SEP, 403(b), Withdraw

Tel Exchange: Yes   **With MMF:** Yes

Registered: All states

TRANSATLANTIC FUND

International

Kleinwort Benson International
200 Park Ave. Suite 5610
New York, NY 10166
(800) 237-4218/(212) 687-2515

	Years Ending 12/31					
	1981	1982	1983	1984	1985	1986
Net Investment Income ($)	.25	.32	.18	.07	.09	.06
Dividends from Net Investment Income ($)	.14	.30	.17	.03	.06	–
Net Gains (Losses) on Investments ($)	(2.94)	(2.66)	3.53	(2.03)	6.21	9.09
Distributions from Net Realized Capital Gains ($)	.92	1.54	.06	1.00	.16	4.18
Net Asset Value End of Year ($)	15.56	11.38	14.86	11.87	17.95	22.92
Ratio of Expenses to Net Assets (%)	1.24	1.44	1.28	1.53	1.94	1.49
Portfolio Turnover Rate (%)	40	45	96	60	73	76
Total Assets: End of Year (Millions $)	38.9	27.8	35.4	28.0	41.3	92.6
Annual Rate of Return (%) Years Ending 12/31	(14.5)	(15.3)	32.9	(14.4)	54.2	51.7

Five-Year Total Return	125.5%	Degree of Diversification	E	Beta	.53	Bull	A	Bear	E

Objective: Seeks long-term capital growth through investment in equity securities of companies domiciled in countries other than the United States. For defensive purposes, can invest all or a portion of assets in U.S. government securities or other domestic issues.

Portfolio: (12/31/86) Common stocks and convertible securities 100%. Largest stock holdings: Japan 41%, United Kingdom 14%.

Distributions: Income: Semi-Annually   **Capital Gains:** Annually

12b-1: Yes   **Amount:** .20%

Minimum: Initial: $1,000   **Subsequent:** $500

Min IRA: Initial: $1,000   **Subsequent:** $500

Services: IRA

Tel Exchange: No

Registered: AK, CA, CO, CT, DC, DE, FL, GA, HI, IL, IN, LA, MA, MD, MI, MN, NV, NY, OH, OR, PA, RI, TX, VA, WA

TUDOR

Aggressive Growth

Tudor Mgmt. Co.
One New York Plaza
New York, NY 10004
(800) 223-3332/(212) 908-9582

	Years Ending 3/31		Years Ending 12/31			
	1982	**1983**	**1983*** (9 mos.)	**1984**	**1985**	**1986**
Net Investment Income ($)	.29	.30	.13	.40	.08	(.04)
Dividends from Net Investment Income ($)	.10	.22	.28	.11	.37	.07
Net Gains (Losses) on Investments ($)	(.66)	8.72	1.67	(1.98)	5.37	2.92
Distributions from Net Realized Capital Gains ($)	–	–	.54	1.56	–	5.48
Net Asset Value End of Year ($)	11.14	19.94	20.92	17.67	22.75	20.08
Ratio of Expenses to Net Assets (%)	1.58	1.35	1.01	1.01	.95	1.01
Portfolio Turnover Rate (%)	134	99	55	83	123	128
Total Assets: End of Year (Millions $)	18.4	53.3	91.5	94.0	155.9	163.8

Fiscal year changed to 12/31 from 3/31.

Annual Rate of Return (%) Years Ending 12/31	45.3	28.4	–	(7.2)	31.2	12.3

Five-Year Total Return	155.2%	Degree of Diversification	B	Beta	1.15	Bull	B	Bear	B

Objective: Seeks capital appreciation through investment in common stocks. The fund invests approximately 50% of its assets in "special situations" and may write covered call options. May enter into repos.

Portfolio: (12/31/86) Common stocks 96%, repos 5%. Largest stock holdings: media 10%, basic industries 10%.

Distributions: **Income:** March, Aug **Capital Gains:** March

12b-1: No

Minimum: Initial: $1,000 Subsequent: $50

Min IRA: Initial: $250 Subsequent: $50

Services: IRA, Keogh, Withdraw

Tel Exchange: Yes **With MMF:** Yes

Registered: All states except ID, ND

20th CENTURY GROWTH

Aggressive Growth

Investors Research Corp.
PO Box 200
Kansas City, MO 64141
(816) 531-5575

	Years Ending 10/31					
	1981	1982	1983	1984	1985	1986
Net Investment Income ($)	(.01)	.06	.06	.16	.17	.12
Dividends from Net Investment Income ($)	–	–	.05	.05	.15	.18
Net Gains (Losses) on Investments ($)	1.29	(.45)	4.03	(1.77)	1.85	5.37
Distributions from Net Realized Capital Gains ($)	1.15	.60	–	1.82	–	–
Net Asset Value End of Year ($)	12.72	11.73	15.77	12.29	14.16	19.47
Ratio of Expenses to Net Assets (%)	1.09	1.08	1.02	1.01	1.01	1.01
Portfolio Turnover Rate (%)	87	132	98	132	116	105
Total Assets: End of Year (Millions $)	277.0	388.5	659.1	678.2	759.9	964.5

Annual Rate of Return (%) Years Ending 12/31	(5.5)	9.3	24.5	(10.2)	33.9	19.4

Five-Year Total Return 95.3%	Degree of Diversification B	Beta 1.21	Bull B	Bear E

Objective: Capital growth through investment in common stocks of smaller companies which management considers to possess better than average growth prospects based on fundamental and technical analysis and three-year history.

Portfolio: (10/31/86) Common stocks 100%. Largest stock holdings: leisure 11%, computer systems 11%.

Distributions: Income: Jan   **Capital Gains:** Jan

12b-1: No

Minimum: Initial: None   Subsequent: None

Min IRA: Initial: None   Subsequent: None

Services: IRA, Keogh Corp, 403(b), Withdraw, Deduct

Tel Exchange: Yes   **With MMF:** Yes

Registered: All states

20th CENTURY SELECT
Aggressive Growth

Investors Research Corp.
PO Box 200
Kansas City, MO 64141
(816) 531-5575

	Years Ending 10/31					
	1981	1982	1983	1984	1985	1986
Net Investment Income ($)	.29	.08	.11	.45	.56	.43
Dividends from Net Investment Income ($)	.10	.12	.14	.14	.47	.52
Net Gains (Losses) on Investments ($)	.39	3.68	7.98	(2.74)	4.04	9.01
Distributions from Net Realized Capital Gains ($)	1.50	.31	—	.69	—	—
Net Asset Value End of Year ($)	14.18	17.51	25.46	22.35	26.48	35.40
Ratio of Expenses to Net Assets (%)	1.09	1.08	1.02	1.01	1.01	1.01
Portfolio Turnover Rate (%)	126	145	57	112	119	85
Total Assets: End of Year (Millions $)	33.2	93.4	648.9	840.5	1,143.1	1,978.4
Annual Rate of Return (%) Years Ending 12/31	1.4	42.4	30.0	(7.6)	33.8	20.7

Five-Year Total Return	176.2%	Degree of Diversification	A	Beta	1.19	Bull	A	Bear	C

Objective: Primarily capital growth but designed for investors also interested in income. Invests in securities of companies with above-average growth prospects and which also pay dividends or interest.

Portfolio: (10/31/86) Common stocks 100%. Largest stock holdings: pharmaceuticals 12%, consumer products (non-durables) 9%.

Distributions: Income: Jan   **Capital Gains:** Jan

12b-1: No

Minimum: **Initial:** None   **Subsequent:** None

Min IRA: **Initial:** None   **Subsequent:** None

Services: IRA, Keogh, Corp, 403(b), Withdraw, Deduct

Tel Exchange: Yes   **With MMF:** Yes

Registered: All states

20TH CENTURY U.S. GOVERNMENTS
Bond

Investors Research Corp.
PO Box 200
Kansas City, MO 64141
(816) 531-5575

	Years Ending 10/31					
	1981	**1982**	**1983** (10 mos.)	**1984**	**1985**	**1986**
Net Investment Income ($)	–	–	8.02	10.25	9.97	8.71
Dividends from Net Investment Income ($)	–	–	8.02	10.25	9.97	8.71
Net Gains (Losses) on Investments ($)	–	–	(2.42)	(.80)	2.72	2.63
Distributions from Net Realized Capital Gains ($)	–	–	–	–	–	.56
Net Asset Value End of Year ($)	–	–	97.58	96.79	99.51	101.58
Ratio of Expenses to Net Assets (%)	–	–	1.02	1.01	1.01	1.01
Portfolio Turnover Rate (%)	–	–	403	352	573	464
Total Assets: End of Year (Millions $)	–	–	34.7	58.8	98.8	254.7
Annual Rate of Return (%) Years Ending 12/31	–	–	7.0	12.3	12.9	9.9

Five-Year Total Return	NA	Degree of Diversification	NA	Beta .08	Bull NA	Bear NA

Objective: Seeks income through investment in U.S. government securities, with its portfolio averaging four years or less maturity.

Portfolio: (10/31/86) U.S. government securities 90%, other 8%.

Distributions: **Income:** Monthly   **Capital Gains:** Annually

12b-1: No

Minimum: **Initial:** None   **Subsequent:** None

Min IRA: **Initial:** None   **Subsequent:** None

Services: IRA, Keogh, Corp, 403(b), Withdraw, Deduct

Tel Exchange: Yes   **With MMF:** Yes

Registered: All states

UMB BOND
Bond

Jones & Babson, Inc.
Three Crown Center
2440 Pershing Road
Kansas City, MO 64108
(800) 821-5591/(816) 471-5200

	Years Ending 6/30					
	1981	1982	1983 (7 mos.)	1984	1985	1986
Net Investment Income ($)	–	–	.35	1.02	.93	.88
Dividends from Net Investment Income ($)	–	–	.36	1.06	.46	1.29
Net Gains (Losses) on Investments ($)	–	–	(.01)	(.87)	1.25	.56
Distributions from Net Realized Capital Gains ($)	–	–	–	–	–	.08
Net Asset Value End of Year ($)	–	–	9.98	9.07	10.79	10.86
Ratio of Expenses to Net Assets (%)	–	–	.85	.87	.88	.88
Portfolio Turnover Rate (%)	–	–	–	–	51	23
Total Assets: End of Year (Millions $)	–	–	4.6	6.0	9.8	19.0
Annual Rate of Return (%) Years Ending 12/31	–	–	4.8	13.5	16.2	12.3

Five-Year Total Return	NA	Degree of Diversification	NA	Beta	.09	Bull NA	Bear NA

Objective: To provide maximum current income while preserving capital. Invests in the guaranteed obligations of the U.S. government and its agencies, including Treasury securities and GNMAs. Will also invest in corporate debt rated A or better by S&P.

Portfolio: (9/30/86) U.S. government-backed securities 37%, corporate bonds 34%, U.S. government securities 16%, short-term corporate notes 9%, U.S. government agencies 3%, repos 2%.

Distributions: Income: Semi-Annually   **Capital Gains:** Annually

12b-1: No

Minimum: Initial: $1,000   Subsequent: $100

Min IRA: Initial: $250   Subsequent: None

Services: IRA, Keogh, Corp, Withdraw

Tel Exchange: Yes   **With MMF:** Yes

Registered: CA, FL, IA, IN, MT, NE, OH, PA, SD

UMB STOCK
Growth & Income

Jones & Babson, Inc.
Three Crown Center
2440 Pershing Road
Kansas City, MO 64108
(800) 821-5591/(816) 471-5200

	1981	1982	1983 (7 mos.)	1984	1985	1986
Net Investment Income ($)	–	–	.15	.48	.49	.48
Dividends from Net Investment Income ($)	–	–	.19	.60	.25	.71
Net Gains (Losses) on Investments ($)	–	–	1.96	(.75)	1.96	2.57
Distributions from Net Realized Capital Gains ($)	–	–	.42	.54	–	1.11
Net Asset Value End of Year ($)	–	–	11.50	10.09	12.29	13.52
Ratio of Expenses to Net Assets (%)	–	–	.85	.87	.88	.87
Portfolio Turnover Rate (%)	–	–	76	80	65	38
Total Assets: End of Year (Millions $)	–	–	6.8	11.2	18.3	31.7

Years Ending 6/30

Annual Rate of Return (%) Years Ending 12/31	–	–	23.7	5.9	23.1	12.3

Five-Year Total Return	NA	Degree of Diversification	A	Beta .84	Bull NA	Bear NA

Objective: Seeks long-term growth of both capital and dividend income. Normally will invest 80% of its assets in common stocks which have demonstrated a consistent and above-average ability to increase earnings and dividends.

Portfolio: (9/30/86) Common stocks 78%, short-term corporate notes 14%, convertible corporate bonds 5%, convertible preferred stocks 3%, repos 1%. Largest stock holdings: paper and forest products 5%, health care 5%.

Distributions: Income: Semi-Annually **Capital Gains:** Annually
12b-1: No
Minimum: Initial: $1,000 Subsequent: $100
Min IRA: Initial: $250 Subsequent: None
Services: IRA, Keogh, Corp, Withdraw
Tel Exchange: Yes **With MMF:** Yes
Registered: CA, FL, IA, IN, MT, NE, OH, PA, SD

UNIFIED GROWTH
Growth

Unified Management Corp.
600 Guaranty Bldg.
Indianapolis, IN 46204
(800) 862-7283/(317) 634-3300

	Years Ending 4/30					
	1981	**1982**	**1983**	**1984**	**1985**	**1986**
Net Investment Income ($)	.51	.46	.33	.54	.40	.36
Dividends from Net Investment Income ($)	.50	.46	.33	.55	.40	.35
Net Gains (Losses) on Investments ($)	3.91	(2.29)	5.45	(1.39)	3.25	5.64
Distributions from Net Realized Capital Gains ($)	—	—	1.08	—	—	—
Net Asset Value End of Year ($)	14.63	12.34	16.71	15.31	18.56	24.21
Ratio of Expenses to Net Assets (%)	1.39	1.34	1.28	1.16	1.10	1.00
Portfolio Turnover Rate (%)	22	33	99	16	37	27
Total Assets: End of Year (Millions $)	4.7	3.8	8.5	10.9	15.0	25.5
Annual Rate of Return (%) Years Ending 12/31	(7.5)	28.2	11.3	7.5	26.0	13.5

Five-Year Total Return	119.3%	Degree of Diversification	B	Beta	.97	Bull	B	Bear	D

Objective: Seeks long-term appreciation by investing primarily in common stocks and convertible securities of medium and smaller companies with attractive profit margins and high return on equity. Current income is a secondary consideration. May take defensive posture with debt instruments.

Portfolio: (10/31/86) Common stocks 84%, commercial paper 14%, short-term note 2%. Largest stock holdings: banking 8%, publication services 8%.

Distributions: Income: April   **Capital Gains:** April

12b-1: No

Minimum: Initial: $200   Subsequent: $25

Min IRA: Initial: $25   Subsequent: $25

Services: IRA, Keogh, Corp, 403(b), Withdraw, Deduct

Tel Exchange: Yes   **With MMF:** Yes

Registered: All states

UNIFIED INCOME
Balanced

Unified Management Corp.
Guaranty Bldg.
Indianapolis, IN 46204
(800) 862-7283/(317) 634-3300

	Years Ending 10/31					
	1981	**1982**	**1983**	**1984**	**1985**	**1986**
Net Investment Income ($)	1.06	.88	.89	1.17	1.10	.89
Dividends from Net Investment Income ($)	1.07	.89	.90	1.16	1.10	.89
Net Gains (Losses) on Investments ($)	(.60)	2.06	1.41	(1.00)	.58	1.00
Distributions from Net Realized Capital Gains ($)	.10	–	.44	–	–	–
Net Asset Value End of Year ($)	9.15	11.20	12.16	11.17	11.75	12.75
Ratio of Expenses to Net Assets (%)	1.74	1.86	1.33	1.30	1.22	1.12
Portfolio Turnover Rate (%)	23	15	19	25	18	49
Total Assets: End of Year (Millions $)	1.5	2.5	7.5	7.1	8.7	13.6
Annual Rate of Return (%) Years Ending 12/31	8.9	32.2	17.9	(0.5)	20.5	9.8

Five-Year Total Return	105.4%	Degree of Diversification	D	Beta	.51	Bull	D	Bear	B

Objective: Seeks current income and preservation of capital by investing in fixed and convertible corporate debt, common and preferred stock, and short-term instruments.

Portfolio: (10/31/86) Corporate and convertible bonds 39%, common stocks 31%, commercial paper 17%, convertible preferred stocks 11%, short-term notes 3%. Largest stock holdings: utilities 5%, banking and financial services 5%.

Distributions: Income: April, Oct   **Capital Gains:** Oct

12b-1: No

Minimum: Initial: $500   Subsequent: $25

Min IRA: Initial: $25   Subsequent: $25

Services: IRA, Keogh, Corp, 403(b), Deduct, Withdraw

Tel Exchange: Yes   **With MMF:** Yes

Registered: All states

UNIFIED MUTUAL SHARES
Growth & Income

Unified Management Corp.
Guaranty Bldg.
Indianapolis, IN 46204-3057
(800) 862-7283/(317) 634-3300

	Years Ending 7/31					
	1981	1982	1983	1984	1985	1986
Net Investment Income ($)	.66	.63	.50	.59	.55	.62
Dividends from Net Investment Income ($)	.66	.64	.50	.59	.55	.59
Net Gains (Losses) on Investments ($)	.01	(1.88)	3.74	(1.12)	3.51	2.55
Distributions from Net Realized Capital Gains ($)	—	—	—	—	—	.17
Net Asset Value End of Year ($)	10.15	8.26	12.00	10.88	14.39	16.80
Ratio of Expenses to Net Assets (%)	1.24	1.32	1.23	1.21	1.11	1.02
Portfolio Turnover Rate (%)	12	7	51	12	5	41
Total Assets: End of Year (Millions $)	7.9	6.1	9.8	8.8	12.6	18.9
Annual Rate of Return (%) Years Ending 12/31	(7.0)	17.6	21.7	8.5	30.8	11.6

Five-Year Total Return	126.6%	Degree of Diversification	A	Beta	.81	Bull	B	Bear	D

Objective: The fund seeks capital growth and current income principally through the purchase of high-quality, income-producing common stocks and convertible securities whose markets, profit margins and rates of return indicate future growth potentials. May write covered options.

Portfolio: (7/31/86) Common stocks 64%, commercial paper 24%, short-term notes 9%, convertible corporate bonds 2%, convertible preferred stocks 1%. Largest stock holdings: banking and financial services 16%, drugs 10%.

Distributions: Income: Jan, July   **Capital Gains:** July
12b-1: No
Minimum: Initial: $200   Subsequent: $25
Min IRA: Initial: $25   Subsequent: $25
Services: IRA, Keogh, Corp, 403(b), Withdraw, Deduct
Tel Exchange: Yes   **With MMF:** Yes
Registered: All states

US GOLD SHARES
Precious Metals

United Services Advisors
PO Box 29467
San Antonio, TX 78229
(800) 824-4653/(512) 696-1234

	Years Ending 6/30					
	1981	1982	1983	1984	1985	1986
Net Investment Income ($)	.92	.43	.37	.33	.24	.30
Dividends from Net Investment Income ($)	.90	.64	.34	.41	.29	.26
Net Gains (Losses) on Investments ($)	(1.88)	(1.46)	5.63	(.97)	(2.48)	(2.05)
Distributions from Net Realized Capital Gains ($)	–	–	–	–	.06	–
Net Asset Value End of Year ($)	4.98	3.31	8.97	7.92	5.33	3.32
Ratio of Expenses to Net Assets (%)	1.00	1.15	1.11	1.06	1.15	1.27
Portfolio Turnover Rate (%)	0	7	4	11	10	14
Total Assets: End of Year (Millions $)	78.0	61.4	314.9	443.1	389.6	214.8

Annual Rate of Return (%) Years Ending 12/31	(27.9)	71.5	1.2	(29.7)	(26.9)	37.5

Five-Year Total Return	22.7%	Degree of Diversification	E	Beta −.03	Bull E	Bear E

Objective: Seeks long-term capital growth as well as protection against inflation and monetary instability. Fund concentrates its investments in common stocks of companies involved in exploration for, mining of, processing of, or dealing in gold, with emphasis on stocks of foreign companies.

Portfolio: (9/30/86) Common stocks 98%, U.S. government obligations 1%, other 1%. Largest holdings: gold-uranium mines 30%, long-life gold mines 29%.

Distributions: Income: Feb, Aug   **Capital Gains:** Aug

12b-1: No

Minimum: Initial: $100   Subsequent: $50

Min IRA: Initial: None   Subsequent: None

Services: IRA, Keogh, Corp, 403(b), SEP, Withdraw, Deduct

Tel Exchange: Yes   **With MMF:** No

Registered: All states

US GOOD AND BAD TIMES
Growth

United Services Advisors
PO Box 29467
San Antonio, TX 78229
(800) 824-4653/(512) 696-1234

	Years Ending 6/30					
	1981 (9 mos.)	1982 (6 mos.)	1983	1984	1985	1986
Net Investment Income ($)	.19	.16	.10	.34	.24	.35
Dividends from Net Investment Income ($)	–	.18	.15	.11	.49	.17
Net Gains (Losses) on Investments ($)	(.55)	(.16)	3.52	(1.20)	2.84	3.65
Distributions from Net Realized Capital Gains ($)	–	–	–	–	–	–
Net Asset Value End of Year ($)	9.64	9.46	12.93	11.96	14.55	18.38
Ratio of Expenses to Net Assets (%)	1.00	2.18	2.20	1.45	1.50	1.40
Portfolio Turnover Rate (%)	55	47	156	92	99	91
Total Assets: End of Year (Millions $)	1.8	1.8	15.3	12.8	36.1	32.7
Annual Rate of Return (%) Years Ending 12/31	–	23.4	11.1	2.7	23.9	11.3

Five-Year Total Return	94.0%	Degree of Diversification	B	Beta	.90	Bull	D	Bear	C

Objective: Invests in common stock of industrial corporations with little or no debt believed to be able to have capital appreciation in good economic times and preservation of capital in bad economic times. May invest up to 50% of assets in debt instruments as a defensive tactic.

Portfolio: (9/30/86) Common stocks 83%, government obligations 16%, other 1%. Largest stock holdings: miscellaneous 46%, aircraft 11%.

Distributions: Income: Aug   **Capital Gains:** Aug

12b-1: No

Minimum: Initial: $100   Subsequent: $50

Min IRA: Initial: None   Subsequent: None

Services: IRA, Keogh, Corp, 403(b), SEP, Withdraw, Deduct

Tel Exchange: Yes   **With MMF:** No

Registered: All states

US GROWTH
Aggressive Growth

United Services Advisors
PO Box 29467
San Antonio, TX 78229
(800) 824-4653/(512) 696-1234

	Years Ending 6/30					
	1981	1982	1983	1984	1985	1986
Net Investment Income ($)	–	–	–	.09	.03	.06
Dividends from Net Investment Income ($)	–	–	–	–	.07	.06
Net Gains (Losses) on Investments ($)	–	–	–	(2.47)	.02	2.27
Distributions from Net Realized Capital Gains ($)	–	–	–	–	–	–
Net Asset Value End of Year ($)	–	–	–	7.62	7.60	9.87
Ratio of Expenses to Net Assets (%)	–	–	–	1.45	1.67	1.52
Portfolio Turnover Rate (%)	–	–	–	161	163	60
Total Assets: End of Year (Millions $)	–	–	–	6.3	12.7	11.9

Annual Rate of Return (%) Years Ending 12/31	–	–	–	(25.6)	21.0	11.5

Five-Year Total Return	NA	Degree of Diversification	C	Beta	1.09	Bull NA	Bear NA

Objective: Seeks capital appreciation through investment in common stocks of established, well-known and newer, less-seasoned companies. Fundamental analysis is employed to identify underpriced stocks, cyclical companies and companies changing for what looks like the better. May invest up to 25% of assets in foreign securities traded on U.S. exchanges.

Portfolio: (9/30/86) Common stocks 72%, U.S. government obligations 27%, other assets 1%. Largest stock holdings: miscellaneous 43%, steel 9%.

Distributions: Income: Aug   **Capital Gains:** Aug
12b-1: No
Minimum: Initial: $100   Subsequent: $50
Min IRA: Initial: None   Subsequent: None
Services: IRA, Keogh, SEP, Corp, 403(b), Withdraw, Deduct
Tel Exchange: Yes   **With MMF:** No
Registered: All states

US INCOME
Balanced

United Services Advisors
PO Box 29467
San Antonio, TX 78229
(800) 824-4653/(512) 696-1234

	Years Ending 6/30					
	1981	**1982**	**1983**	**1984** (8 mos.)	**1985**	**1986**
Net Investment Income ($)	–	–	–	.14	.55	.34
Dividends from Net Investment Income ($)	–	–	–	.11	.61	.38
Net Gains (Losses) on Investments ($)	–	–	–	(.84)	1.29	.89
Distributions from Net Realized Capital Gains ($)	–	–	–	–	–	.07
Net Asset Value End of Year ($)	–	–	–	9.19	10.42	11.20
Ratio of Expenses to Net Assets (%)	–	–	–	1.80	1.66	1.63
Portfolio Turnover Rate (%)	–	–	–	279	271	179
Total Assets: End of Year (Millions $)	–	–	–	1.2	2.5	2.9
Annual Rate of Return (%) Years Ending 12/31	–	–	–	3.9	15.3	5.5

Five-Year Total Return	NA	Degree of Diversification	D	Beta	.50	Bull NA	Bear NA

Objective: Seeks preservation of capital and current income. Secondarily, seeks capital appreciation through investment in common stocks of companies with a long record of paying cash dividends and U.S. Treasury debt securities and convertibles. May write covered call options.

Portfolio: (9/30/86) Common stocks 84%, convertible bonds 15%, convertible preferred stock 5%, government obligations 5%. Largest stock holdings: miscellaneous 31%, electric and other services combined 22%.

Distributions: **Income:** Mar, June, Sep, Dec   **Capital Gains:** Annually

12b-1: No

Minimum: **Initial:** $100   **Subsequent:** $50

Min IRA: **Initial:** None   **Subsequent:** None

Services: IRA, Keogh, Corp, 403(b), SEP, Withdraw, Deduct

Tel Exchange: Yes   **With MMF:** No

Registered: All states

US LOCAP
Aggressive Growth

United Services Advisors
PO Box 29467
San Antonio, TX 78229
(800) 824-4653/(512) 696-1234

	Years Ending 6/30					
	1981	**1982**	**1983**	**1984**	**1985** (5 mos.)	**1986**
Net Investment Income ($)	–	–	–	–	.02	.02
Dividends from Net Investment Income ($)	–	–	–	–	–	.02
Net Gains (Losses) on Investments ($)	–	–	–	–	(2.38)	.79
Distributions from Net Realized Capital Gains ($)	–	–	–	–	–	–
Net Asset Value End of Year ($)	–	–	–	–	7.64	8.43
Ratio of Expenses to Net Assets (%)	–	–	–	–	1.67	1.84
Portfolio Turnover Rate (%)	–	–	–	–	6	70
Total Assets: End of Year (Millions $)	–	–	–	–	2.1	3.2

Annual Rate of Return (%) Years Ending 12/31	–	–	–	–	–	(6.6)

Five-Year Total Return	NA	Degree of Diversification	NA	Beta	NA	Bull NA	Bear NA

Objective: To provide above-average capital appreciation. Current income is not a consideration. Invests in companies with a market capitalization in the bottom 10% of the combined group of common stocks listed on the New York and American stock exchanges.

Portfolio: (9/30/86) Common stocks 100%. Largest stock holdings: electronics/electrical 15%, energy 10%.

Distributions: **Income:** Annually   **Capital Gains:** Annually

12b-1: No

Minimum: **Initial:** $100   **Subsequent:** $50

Min IRA: **Initial:** None   **Subsequent:** None

Services: IRA, Keogh, Corp, 403(b), Deduct, Withdraw

Tel Exchange: Yes   **With MMF:** No

Registered: All states

US NEW PROSPECTOR
Precious Metals

United Services Advisors
PO Box 29467
San Antonio, TX 78229
(800) 824-4653/(512) 696-1234

	Years Ending 6/30					
	1981	**1982**	**1983**	**1984**	**1985**	**1986** (7 mos.)
Net Investment Income ($)	–	–	–	–	–	.01
Dividends from Net Investment Income ($)	–	–	–	–	–	–
Net Gains (Losses) on Investments ($)	–	–	–	–	–	(.04)
Distributions from Net Realized Capital Gains ($)	–	–	–	–	–	–
Net Asset Value End of Year ($)	–	–	–	–	–	.96
Ratio of Expenses to Net Assets (%)	–	–	–	–	–	1.51
Portfolio Turnover Rate (%)	–	–	–	–	–	31
Total Assets: End of Year (Millions $)	–	–	–	–	–	27.3
Annual Rate of Return (%) Years Ending 12/31	–	–	–	–	–	38.5

Five-Year Total Return	NA	Degree of Diversification	NA	Beta	NA	Bull	NA	Bear	NA

Objective: Seeks long-term growth of capital as well as protection against inflation and monetary instability. Current income is not a consideration. Invests in companies involved in the natural resource industry, including gold, silver, timber and oil.

Portfolio: (9/30/86) Common stocks 88%, convertible securities 2%, short-term securities 10%. Largest stock holdings: gold 79%, silver 5%

Distributions: **Income:** Annually   **Capital Gains:** Annually

12b-1: No

Minimum: **Initial:** $100   **Subsequent:** $50

Min IRA: **Initial:** None   **Subsequent:** None

Services: IRA, Keogh, Corp, 403(b), Deduct, Withdraw

Tel Exchange: Yes   **With MMF:** No

Registered: All states

USAA CORNERSTONE
Balanced

USAA Investment Mgmt. Co.
9800 Fredericksburg Rd.
San Antonio, TX 78288
(800) 531-8000/(512) 498-8000

	Years Ending 9/30					
	1981	1982	1983	1984 (1 mo.)	1985	1986
Net Investment Income ($)	–	–	–	.09	.51	.45
Dividends from Net Investment Income ($)	–	–	–	–	.04	.32
Net Gains (Losses) on Investments ($)	–	–	–	(.11)	.16	3.83
Distributions from Net Realized Capital Gains ($)	–	–	–	–	.02	.06
Net Asset Value End of Year ($)	–	–	–	9.98	10.58	14.49
Ratio of Expenses to Net Assets (%)	–	–	–	1.90	1.50	1.50
Portfolio Turnover Rate (%)	–	–	–	9	15	70
Total Assets: End of Year (Millions $)	–	–	–	3.3	13.6	29.0

Annual Rate of Return (%) Years Ending 12/31	–	–	–	–	14.7	40.1

Five-Year Total Return	NA	Degree of Diversification	NA	Beta	NA	Bull	NA	Bear	NA

Objective: Seeks to preserve purchasing power of capital and achieve reasonably stable value of fund shares and positive, inflation-adjusted rate of return despite shifting inflation and volatility in markets. Will invest 20% in each of five asset categories: gold stocks, foreign stocks, real estate stocks, basic value stocks and U.S. government securities.

Portfolio: (9/30/86) Common stocks 81%, U.S. government and agency issues 24%. Largest stock holdings: gold 20%, real estate 21%.

Distributions: Income: Oct   **Capital Gains:** Oct

12b-1: No

Minimum: Initial: $1,000   Subsequent: $100

Min IRA: Initial: $250   Subsequent: $25

Services: IRA, Keogh, SEP, 403(b), Withdraw, Deduct

Tel Exchange: Yes   **With MMF:** Yes

Registered: All states

USAA GOLD
Precious Metals

USAA Investment Mgmt. Co.
9800 Fredericksburg Rd.
San Antonio, TX 78288
(800) 531-8000/(512) 498-8000

	Years Ending 9/30					
	1981	**1982**	**1983**	**1984** (1 mo.)	**1985**	**1986**
Net Investment Income ($)	–	–	–	.06	.28	.10
Dividends from Net Investment Income ($)	–	–	–	–	.02	.12
Net Gains (Losses) on Investments ($)	–	–	–	(.86)	(2.63)	1.46
Distributions from Net Realized Capital Gains ($)	–	–	–	–	–	–
Net Asset Value End of Year ($)	–	–	–	9.20	6.83	8.27
Ratio of Expenses to Net Assets (%)	–	–	–	1.93	1.50	1.50
Portfolio Turnover Rate (%)	–	–	–	–	–	62
Total Assets: End of Year (Millions $)	–	–	–	3.3	15.1	29.5

Annual Rate of Return (%) Years Ending 12/31	–	–	–	–	(20.7)	53.3

Five-Year Total Return	NA	Degree of Diversification	NA	Beta	NA	Bull	NA	Bear	NA

Objective: Seeks long-term capital appreciation and protection of capital against inflation through investment in common stock of companies engaged in gold exploration, mining or processing. Up to 20% of assets may be in other precious metals, diamonds or minerals.

Portfolio: (9/30/86) Common stocks 85%, U.S. government security 22%. Largest stock holdings: North American gold mines 43%, Australian gold mines 40%.

Distributions: Income: Oct   **Capital Gains:** Oct
12b-1: No
Minimum: Initial: $1,000   **Subsequent:** $100
Min IRA: Initial: $250   **Subsequent:** $25
Services: IRA, Keogh, SEP, 403(b), Withdraw, Deduct
Tel Exchange: Yes   **With MMF:** Yes
Registered: All states

USAA GROWTH
Growth

USAA Investment Mgmt. Co.
9800 Fredericksburg Rd.
San Antonio, TX 78288
(800) 531-8000/(512) 498-8000

	Years Ending 9/30					
	1981	1982	1983	1984	1985	1986
Net Investment Income ($)	.29	.34	.19	.29	.26	.22
Dividends from Net Investment Income ($)	.32	.29	.32	.14	.23	.28
Net Gains (Losses) on Investments ($)	(.54)	.25	5.43	(2.51)	.65	2.54
Distributions from Net Realized Capital Gains ($)	–	.29	–	.47	–	.31
Net Asset Value End of Year ($)	10.60	10.62	15.91	13.08	13.76	15.94
Ratio of Expenses to Net Assets (%)	1.00	1.23	1.03	1.00	1.06	1.09
Portfolio Turnover Rate (%)	56	91	94	69	128	110
Total Assets: End of Year (Millions $)	56.1	60.7	107.2	128.6	145.2	173.8

Annual Rate of Return (%) Years Ending 12/31	(8.1)	20.9	15.8	(7.5)	19.9	10.1

Five-Year Total Return	71.0%	Degree of Diversification	A	Beta 1.07	Bull D	Bear D

Objective: Long-term growth of capital. Invests in common stocks of companies that are established and have substantial capitalizations with exceptional prospects for growth in earnings. May invest up to 10% of its assets in foreign securities listed on U.S. exchanges.

Portfolio: (9/30/86) Common stocks 88%, short-term notes 7%, bonds 4%. Largest stock holdings: regional banking 14%, health care 11%.

Distributions: Income: Oct   **Capital Gains:** Oct
12b-1: No
Minimum: Initial: $1,000   Subsequent: $25
Min IRA: Initial: $250   Subsequent: $25
Services: IRA, Keogh, 403(b), SEP, Withdraw, Deduct
Tel Exchange: Yes   **With MMF:** Yes
Registered: All states

USAA INCOME
Balanced

USAA Investment Mgmt. Co.
9800 Fredericksburg Rd.
San Antonio, TX 78288
(800) 531-8000/(512) 498-8000

	Years Ending 9/30					
	1981	1982	1983	1984	1985	1986
Net Investment Income ($)	.99	1.08	1.14	1.16	1.23	1.15
Dividends from Net Investment Income ($)	.84	1.00	1.05	1.06	1.21	1.12
Net Gains (Losses) on Investments ($)	(.95)	1.51	.51	(.22)	.76	.61
Distributions from Net Realized Capital Gains ($)	–	.01	–	.12	–	.02
Net Asset Value End of Year ($)	8.76	10.34	10.93	10.68	11.46	12.08
Ratio of Expenses to Net Assets (%)	.97	1.13	1.09	.75	.68	.65
Portfolio Turnover Rate (%)	52	116	166	116	79	38
Total Assets: End of Year (Millions $)	12.9	19.7	39.0	92.1	138.8	213.6
Annual Rate of Return (%) Years Ending 12/31	9.1	28.9	10.7	13.9	19.0	12.6

Five-Year Total Return	117.8%	Degree of Diversification	E	Beta	.19	Bull	D	Bear	A

Objective: Seeks high yields from marketable income-producing securities with a mix of maturities and qualities. May invest in restricted securities.

Portfolio: (9/30/86) U.S. government 48%, common stocks 16%, corporate bonds 31%, short-term corporate notes 1%.

Distributions: Income: Jan, April, July, Oct   **Capital Gains:** Oct

12b-1: No

Minimum: Initial: $1,000   Subsequent: $25

Min IRA: Initial: $250   Subsequent: $25

Services: IRA, Keogh, SEP, 403(b), Withdraw, Deduct

Tel Exchange: Yes   **With MMF:** Yes

Registered: All states

USAA SUNBELT ERA
Aggressive Growth

USAA Investment Mgmt. Co.
9800 Fredericksburg Rd.
San Antonio, TX 78288
(800) 531-8000/(512) 498-8000

	Years Ending 9/30					
	1981 (2 mos.)	1982	1983	1984	1985	1986
Net Investment Income ($)	.09	.10	.10	.07	.10	.07
Dividends from Net Investment Income ($)	–	.09	.04	.06	.08	.11
Net Gains (Losses) on Investments ($)	(.40)	1.04	7.46	(3.83)	.56	2.55
Distributions from Net Realized Capital Gains ($)	–	–	–	.25	–	–
Net Asset Value End of Year ($)	9.69	10.74	18.27	14.20	14.78	17.29
Ratio of Expenses to Net Assets (%)	1.50	1.45	1.06	1.06	1.11	1.05
Portfolio Turnover Rate (%)	–	76	49	52	74	57
Total Assets: End of Year (Millions $)	1.0	9.8	79.9	98.2	108.9	119.0

Annual Rate of Return (%) Years Ending 12/31	–	24.6	23.9	(18.1)	23.0	5.5

Five-Year Total Return 64.0%	Degree of Diversification C	Beta 1.24	Bull D	Bear NA

Objective: Seeks appreciation of capital through investment primarily in common stocks of smaller, emerging companies located in or doing business in the sunbelt region of the United States.

Portfolio: (9/30/86) Common stocks 86%, bonds 6%, short-term notes 6%. Largest stock holdings: electronics 9%, retail stores 9%.

Distributions: Income: Oct   **Capital Gains:** Oct

12b-1: No

Minimum: Initial: $1,000   Subsequent: $25

Min IRA: Initial: $250   Subsequent: $25

Services: IRA, Keogh, SEP, 403(b), Withdraw, Deduct

Tel Exchange: Yes   **With MMF:** Yes

Registered: All states

VALLEY FORGE
Growth & Income

Valley Forge Mgmt. Corp.
PO Box 262
Valley Forge, PA 19481
(215) 688-6839

	Years Ending 12/31					
	1981	**1982**	**1983**	**1984**	**1985**	**1986**
Net Investment Income ($)	1.12	.63	.72	.67	.58	.66
Dividends from Net Investment Income ($)	.45	.73	.42	.54	.47	.69
Net Gains (Losses) on Investments ($)	(.05)	1.47	1.05	.01	.40	(.05)
Distributions from Net Realized Capital Gains ($)	1.37	.06	.78	.96	.06	.41
Net Asset Value End of Year ($)	9.65	10.96	11.53	10.71	11.16	10.67
Ratio of Expenses to Net Assets (%)	1.90	2.00	1.60	1.70	1.40	1.40
Portfolio Turnover Rate (%)	13	38	39	70	87	40
Total Assets: End of Year (Millions $)	1.5	2.2	3.2	7.8	10.1	9.2
Annual Rate of Return (%) Years Ending 12/31	12.4	28.7	17.9	6.7	10.5	5.5

Five-Year Total Return	88.6%	Degree of Diversification	E	Beta	.14	Bull	E	Bear	A

Objective: Seeks capital appreciation and secondarily current income through investment in common stocks of established companies chosen on the basis of fundamental analysis and technical market considerations. May convert to short-term debt securities during adverse stock market conditions.

Portfolio: (12/31/86) Short-term money market securities 81%, common stocks 10%, bonds 6%, preferred stocks 3%. Largest stock holdings: industrial machinery 30%, housing 25%, energy 10%.

Distributions: Income: Jan   **Capital Gains:** Jan
12b-1: No
Minimum: Initial: $2,500   Subsequent: $100
Min IRA: Initial: $1,000   Subsequent: $100
Services: IRA
Tel Exchange: No
Registered: Call regarding registration

VALUE LINE CONVERTIBLE
Growth & Income

Value Line Inc.
711 Third Avenue
New York, NY 10017
(800) 223-0818/(212) 687-3965

	Years Ending 4/30					
	1981	1982	1983	1984	1985	1986 (10 mos.)
Net Investment Income ($)	–	–	–	–	–	.38
Dividends from Net Investment Income ($)	–	–	–	–	–	.24
Net Gains (Losses) on Investments ($)	–	–	–	–	–	2.28
Distributions from Net Realized Capital Gains ($)	–	–	–	–	–	–
Net Asset Value End of Year ($)	–	–	–	–	–	12.45
Ratio of Expenses to Net Assets (%)	–	–	–	–	–	1.31
Portfolio Turnover Rate (%)	–	–	–	–	–	164
Total Assets: End of Year (Millions $)	–	–	–	–	–	49.8

Annual Rate of Return (%) Years Ending 12/31	–	–	–	–	–	16.1

Five-Year Total Return	NA	Degree of Diversification	NA	Beta	NA	Bull	NA	Bear	NA

Objective: Seeks high current income and capital appreciation through investment primarily in convertible securities. May also invest in non-convertible debt and equity securities.

Portfolio: (10/31/86) Convertible bonds & notes 75%, convertible preferred stock 18%, U.S. treasury obligations 4%, cash 2%, repos 1%. Largest holdings: savings & loans 9%, food processing 9%.

Distributions: Income: Quarterly   **Capital Gains:** Annually

12b-1: No

Minimum: Initial: $1,000   Subsequent: $250

Min IRA: Initial: $1,000   Subsequent: $250

Services: IRA, Keogh, Corp, 403(b), SEP, Withdraw, Deduct

Tel Exchange: Yes   **With MMF:** Yes

Registered: All states

VALUE LINE FUND
Growth

Value Line, Inc.
711 Third Ave.
New York, NY 10017
(800) 223-0818/(212) 687-3965

	Years Ending 12/31					
	1981	1982	1983	1984	1985	1986
Net Investment Income ($)	.66	1.00	.32	.18	.20	.22
Dividends from Net Investment Income ($)	.52	.80	.55	.20	.20	.23
Net Gains (Losses) on Investments ($)	(.38)	2.21	(.43)	(2.08)	3.50	2.17
Distributions from Net Realized Capital Gains ($)	2.10	3.20	.75	—	—	1.75
Net Asset Value End of Year ($)	15.07	14.28	12.87	10.77	14.27	14.68
Ratio of Expenses to Net Assets (%)	.63	.67	.77	.83	.81	.73
Portfolio Turnover Rate (%)	57	87	97	110	129	145
Total Assets: End of Year (Millions $)	72.8	109.0	203.2	166.5	206.0	212.6

Annual Rate of Return (%) Years Ending 12/31	1.5	28.5	(1.3)	(14.7)	34.6	16.7

Five-Year Total Return	69.8%	Degree of Diversification	B	Beta 1.27	Bull E	Bear B

Objective: Primary objective is long-term growth of capital by investing in common stocks chosen on the basis of the Value Line Ranking System for timeliness. May write covered call options, invest in restricted securities and enter into repurchase agreements. May take defensive posture in debt investments.

Portfolio: (12/31/86) Common stocks 88%, U.S. Treasury obligations 11%, preferred stocks 1%, repurchase agreements 1%. Largest stock holdings: industrial services 10%, computer software & service 10%.

Distributions: Income: Quarterly   **Capital Gains:** Annually
12b-1: No
Minimum: Initial: $1,000   Subsequent: $100
Min IRA: Initial: $1,000   Subsequent: $100
Services: IRA, Keogh, 403(b), SEP, Corp, Withdraw, Deduct
Tel Exchange: Yes   **With MMF:** Yes
Registered: All states

VALUE LINE INCOME
Balanced

Value Line, Inc.
711 Third Ave.
New York, NY 10017
(800) 223-0818/(212) 687-3965

	Years Ending 12/31					
	1981	1982	1983	1984	1985	1986
Net Investment Income ($)	.58	.60	.39	.43	.50	.47
Dividends from Net Investment Income ($)	.46	.56	.56	.48	.48	.48
Net Gains (Losses) on Investments ($)	.49	1.05	.07	(.30)	.91	.64
Distributions from Net Realized Capital Gains ($)	.71	1.45	.14	.26	–	.91
Net Asset Value End of Year ($)	7.37	7.01	6.77	6.16	7.09	6.81
Ratio of Expenses to Net Assets (%)	.75	.78	.78	.89	.83	.77
Portfolio Turnover Rate (%)	42	82	72	114	148	167
Total Assets: End of Year (Millions $)	73.3	94.7	125.9	117.9	134.4	162.8
Annual Rate of Return (%) Years Ending 12/31	16.2	29.8	6.7	2.9	23.7	16.3

Five-Year Total Return	104.9%	Degree of Diversification	C	Beta	.71	Bull	D	Bear	A

Objective: Seeks current income but considers capital appreciation to be an important secondary objective. Substantially all its investments are in common stocks or convertibles chosen on the basis of the Value Line Ranking System for timeliness. May shift portfolio to debt investments as defensive posture. May invest in repurchase agreements and restricted securities and write covered call options.

Portfolio: (12/31/86) Common stocks 45%, corporate bonds 34%, foreign currency bonds 8%, U.S. government agency obligations 7%, U.S. Treasury obligations 5%. Largest stock holdings: banks 9%, drugs 6%.

Distributions: **Income:** Quarterly   **Capital Gains:** Annually
12b-1: No
Minimum: **Initial:** $1,000   **Subsequent:** $100
Min IRA: **Initial:** $1,000   **Subsequent:** $100
Services: IRA, Keogh, SEP, Corp, 403(b), Withdraw, Deduct
Tel Exchange: Yes   **With MMF:** Yes
Registered: All states

VALUE LINE LEVERAGED GROWTH
Growth

Value Line, Inc.
711 Third Ave.
New York, NY 10017
(800) 223-0818/(212) 687-3965

	Years Ending 12/31					
	1981	1982	1983	1984	1985	1986
Net Investment Income ($)	.56	.71	.36	.16	.29	.20
Dividends from Net Investment Income ($)	.30	.65	.65	.31	.13	.34
Net Gains (Losses) on Investments ($)	1.99	3.48	1.15	(1.96)	4.18	4.64
Distributions from Net Realized Capital Gains ($)	3.15	3.25	.02	.99	—	2.60
Net Asset Value End of Year ($)	18.53	18.82	19.66	16.56	20.90	22.80
Ratio of Expenses to Net Assets (%)	.77	.84	.80	.86	.80	.96
Portfolio Turnover Rate (%)	105	95	105	89	121	115
Total Assets: End of Year (Millions $)	25.3	115.1	216.1	181.5	228.6	290.0
Annual Rate of Return (%) Years Ending 12/31	15.9	28.6	7.9	(8.8)	27.1	23.3

Five-Year Total Return	98.5%	Degree of Diversification	A	Beta	1.22	Bull	D	Bear	A

Objective: Capital growth through investment in common stocks chosen on the basis of Value Line Ranking System for timeliness. No consideration is given to current income in the choice of investments. May employ leverage from banks and may write covered call options. May enter into repurchase agreements.

Portfolio: (12/31/86) Common stocks 102%, repurchase agreements 2%. Largest stock holdings: paper/forest products 9%, air transport 7%.

Distributions: Income: Annually   **Capital Gains:** Annually

12b-1: No

Minimum: Initial: $1,000   Subsequent: $100

Min IRA: Initial: $1,000   Subsequent: $100

Services: IRA, Keogh, 403(b), SEP, Corp, Withdraw, Deduct

Tel Exchange: Yes   **With MMF:** Yes

Registered: All states except ME

VALUE LINE SPECIAL SITUATIONS
Aggressive Growth

Value Line, Inc.
711 Third Ave.
New York, NY 10017
(800) 223-0818/(212) 687-3965

	Years Ending 12/31					
	1981	1982	1983	1984	1985	1986
Net Investment Income ($)	.30	.46	.12	.09	.04	.06
Dividends from Net Investment Income ($)	.11	.30	.45	.02	.05	.04
Net Gains (Losses) on Investments ($)	(.57)	2.13	2.61	(4.19)	2.47	.68
Distributions from Net Realized Capital Gains ($)	–	–	–	.08	–	–
Net Asset Value End of Year ($)	11.54	13.83	16.11	11.91	14.37	15.07
Ratio of Expenses to Net Assets (%)	.97	1.02	1.00	1.06	1.07	1.02
Portfolio Turnover Rate (%)	34	50	63	75	88	73
Total Assets: End of Year (Millions $)	136.3	199.5	337.9	240.1	242.7	193.6

Annual Rate of Return (%) Years Ending 12/31	(2.3)	23.1	19.4	(25.5)	21.1	5.1

Five-Year Total Return	39.4%	Degree of Diversification	B	Beta 1.37	Bull E	Bear D

Objective: Seeks long-term capital growth. Experiences wider than average price fluctuations and a period of years without substantial current investment income; 80% of its assets are invested in securities of companies in special situations (unusual developments in the operations of the company such as a new product or a merger). Uses Value Line Ranking System of timeliness for determining possible undervaluation.

Portfolio: (12/31/86) Common stocks 88%, U.S. Treasury obligations 8%, repurchase agreements 2%. Largest stock holdings: savings & loans 10%, industrial services 9%.

Distributions: **Income:** Annually   **Capital Gains:** Annually

12b-1: No

Minimum: Initial: $1,000   Subsequent: $100

Min IRA: Initial: $1,000   Subsequent: $100

Services: IRA, Keogh, 403(b), SEP, Corp, Withdraw, Deduct

Tel Exchange: Yes   **With MMF:** Yes

Registered: All states

VALUE LINE U.S. GOVERNMENT SECURITIES
Bond

Value Line, Inc.
711 Third Ave.
New York, NY 10017
(800) 223-0818/(212) 687-3965

	Years Ending 8/31					
	1981	1982	1983	1984	1985	1986
Net Investment Income ($)	—	1.33	1.35	1.33	1.32	1.30
Dividends from Net Investment Income ($)	—	.96	1.36	1.28	1.30	1.32
Net Gains (Losses) on Investments ($)	—	1.44	.22	(.36)	1.41	.51
Distributions from Net Realized Capital Gains ($)	—	—	—	.28	—	.15
Net Asset Value End of Year ($)	—	11.56	11.77	11.18	12.61	12.95
Ratio of Expenses to Net Assets (%)	—	.98	.82	.92	.86	.76
Portfolio Turnover Rate (%)	—	0.0	7	31	64	73
Total Assets: End of Year (Millions $)	—	35.9	48.6	51.4	68.3	112.4

Annual Rate of Return (%) Years Ending 12/31	—	32.9	6.0	13.7	21.2	10.7

Five-Year Total Return	115.0%	Degree of Diversification	NA	Beta	.15	Bull	D	Bear	NA

Objective: Seeks income as high and dependable as is consistent with reasonable risk through investment of 80% of its net assets in investment grade bonds rated B++ or better by Value Line. Capital preservation and possible capital appreciation are secondary objectives. May invest up to 10% of its assets in unregistered securities. May lend its portfolio's securities and engage in repos.

Portfolio: (8/31/86) U.S. government agency obligations 77%, corporate bonds and notes 6%, U.S. Treasury obligations 14%, repos 3%.

Distributions: **Income:** Quarterly   **Capital Gains:** Annually

12b-1: No

Minimum: **Initial:** $1,000   **Subsequent:** $250

Min IRA: **Initial:** $1,000   **Subsequent:** $250

Services: IRA, Keogh, Corp, 403(b), SEP, Withdraw, Deduct

Tel Exchange: Yes   **With MMF:** Yes

Registered: All states

VANGUARD EXPLORER II

Aggressive Growth

Vanguard Group
Vanguard Financial Ctr.
Valley Forge, PA 19482
(800) 662-7447/(215) 648-6000

	Years Ending 10/31					
	1981	1982	1983	1984	1985 (4 mos.)	1986
Net Investment Income ($)	–	–	–	–	.08	.04
Dividends from Net Investment Income ($)	–	–	–	–	–	.08
Net Gains (Losses) on Investments ($)	–	–	–	–	(.83)	.87
Distributions from Net Realized Capital Gains ($)	–	–	–	–	–	–
Net Asset Value End of Year ($)	–	–	–	–	19.25	20.08
Ratio of Expenses to Net Assets (%)	–	–	–	–	1.06	1.17
Portfolio Turnover Rate (%)	–	–	–	–	3	27
Total Assets: End of Year (Millions $)	–	–	–	–	13.8	36.5

Annual Rate of Return (%) Years Ending 12/31	–	–	–	–	–	(7.3)

Five-Year Total Return	NA	Degree of Diversification	NA	Beta	NA	Bull	NA	Bear	NA

Objective: Seeks long-term growth of capital by investing in common stocks of small unseasoned companies with less than $100 million in annual revenues and more than three years of operating history.

Portfolio: (10/31/86) Common stocks 96%, cash 10%. Largest stock holdings: automation and controls 23%, medical and biotechnology 19%.

Distributions: **Income:** Annually   **Capital Gains:** Annually

12b-1: No

Minimum: **Initial:** $3,000   **Subsequent:** $100

Min IRA: **Initial:** $500   **Subsequent:** None

Services: IRA, Keogh, Corp, 403(b), SEP, Withdraw, Deduct

Tel Exchange: No

Registered: All states

VANGUARD GNMA
Bond

Vanguard Group
Vanguard Financial Ctr.
Valley Forge, PA 19482
(800) 662-7447/(215) 648-6000

	Years Ending 1/31					
	1981 (7 mos.)	1982	1983	1984	1985	1986
Net Investment Income ($)	.61	1.12	1.11	1.07	1.08	1.04
Dividends from Net Investment Income ($)	.61	1.12	1.11	1.07	1.08	1.04
Net Gains (Losses) on Investments ($)	(1.25)	(.83)	1.29	(.01)	.05	.67
Distributions from Net Realized Capital Gains ($)	–	–	–	–	–	–
Net Asset Value End of Year ($)	8.75	7.92	9.21	9.20	9.25	9.92
Ratio of Expenses to Net Assets (%)	.65	.89	.57	.58	.58	.50
Portfolio Turnover Rate (%)	4	17	41	21	23	32
Total Assets: End of Year (Millions $)	26.8	25.0	84.7	172.4	298.9	1,262.1

Annual Rate of Return (%) Years Ending 12/31	4.7	31.5	9.7	14.0	20.6	11.5

Five-Year Total Return	121.3%	Degree of Diversification	NA	Beta	.13	Bull	D	Bear	A

Objective: Seeks current income through investing at least 80% of assets in GNMA mortgage-backed securities whose interest and principal payment is guaranteed by the U.S. government. Balance invested in other U.S. government guaranteed securities.

Portfolio: (7/31/86) GNMA obligations 100%.

Distributions: Income: Monthly   **Capital Gains:** Annually

12b-1: No

Minimum: Initial: $3,000   **Subsequent:** $100

Min IRA: Initial: $500   **Subsequent:** $100

Services: IRA, Keogh, SEP, Corp, 403(b), Withdraw, Deduct

Tel Exchange: Yes   **With MMF:** Yes

Registered: All states

VANGUARD HIGH YIELD BOND

Bond

Vanguard Group
Vanguard Financial Ctr.
Valley Forge, PA 19482
(800) 662-7447/(215) 648-6000

	Years Ending 1/31					
	1981	1982	1983	1984	1985	1986
Net Investment Income ($)	1.18	1.24	1.28	1.20	1.18	1.13
Dividends from Net Investment Income ($)	1.18	1.24	1.28	1.20	1.18	1.14
Net Gains (Losses) on Investments ($)	(.76)	(.62)	1.08	.01	(.45)	.33
Distributions from Net Realized Capital Gains ($)	–	–	–	–	–	–
Net Asset Value End of Year ($)	8.50	7.88	8.96	8.97	8.52	8.84
Ratio of Expenses to Net Assets (%)	.74	.93	.71	.68	.65	.60
Portfolio Turnover Rate (%)	47	87	52	82	71	61
Total Assets: End of Year (Millions $)	12.0	13.0	51.2	116.8	252.5	634.6
Annual Rate of Return (%) Years Ending 12/31	9.4	27.2	15.7	7.5	21.9	16.9

Five-Year Total Return	125.5%	Degree of Diversification	NA	Beta	.22	Bull	C	Bear	A

Objective: Seeks current income primarily from investment in high yielding, medium and lower quality bonds. Normally only 20% can be in debt securities rated below B, convertibles, preferred stocks or short-term investments. May invest in foreign securities and restricted securities. Fund performs own credit analysis.

Portfolio: (7/31/86) Corporate bonds 91%, government obligations 7%, preferred stocks 1%.

Distributions: **Income:** Monthly   **Capital Gains:** Annually

12b-1: No

Minimum: **Initial:** $3,000   **Subsequent:** $100

Min IRA: **Initial:** $500   **Subsequent:** $100

Services: IRA, Keogh, SEP, Corp, 403(b), Withdraw, Deduct

Tel Exchange: Yes   **With MMF:** Yes

Registered: All states

VANGUARD INDEX TRUST

Growth & Income

Vanguard Group
Vanguard Financial Ctr.
Valley Forge, PA 19482
(800) 662-7447/(215) 648-6000

	Years Ending 12/31					
	1981	1982	1983	1984	1985	1986
Net Investment Income ($)	.83	.83	.87	.88	.91	.89
Dividends from Net Investment Income ($)	.83	.83	.87	.88	.91	.89
Net Gains (Losses) on Investments ($)	(1.76)	2.29	2.85	.30	5.08	3.30
Distributions from Net Realized Capital Gains ($)	.56	.25	.71	.48	1.61	2.02
Net Asset Value End of Year ($)	15.52	17.56	19.70	19.52	22.99	24.27
Ratio of Expenses to Net Assets (%)	.42	.39	.28	.27	.28	.28
Portfolio Turnover Rate (%)	12	11	35	14	36	29
Total Assets: End of Year (Millions $)	91.2	110.0	233.7	289.7	394.2	485.0

Annual Rate of Return (%) Years Ending 12/31	(5.3)	19.3	21.3	6.2	31.1	18.3

Five-Year Total Return 138.5%	Degree of Diversification A	Beta 1.00	Bull A	Bear C

Objective: Seeks to duplicate stock market price and yield performance by owning all stocks in the Standard & Poor's 500 stock index. Established fund shareholders may exchange their shares of S&P 500 stocks for fund shares.

Portfolio: (12/31/86) Common stocks 100%, repos 1%. Owns all S&P 500 companies.

Distributions: Income: Mar, June, Sept, Dec   Capital Gains: Dec

12b-1: No

Minimum: Initial: $1,500   Subsequent: $100

Min IRA: Initial: $500   Subsequent: $50

Services: IRA, Keogh, Corp, SEP, 403(b), Withdraw, Deduct

Tel Exchange: No

Registered: All states

VANGUARD INVESTMENT GRADE BOND

Bond

Vanguard Group
Vanguard Financial Ctr.
Valley Forge, PA 19482
(800) 662-7447/(215) 648-6000

	Years Ending 1/31					
	1981	**1982**	**1983**	**1984**	**1985**	**1986**
Net Investment Income ($)	.88	.93	.96	.95	.96	.92
Dividends from Net Investment Income ($)	.88	.93	.96	.95	.96	.92
Net Gains (Losses) on Investments ($)	(.27)	(.35)	.94	(.16)	–	.58
Distributions from Net Realized Capital Gains ($)	–	–	–	–	–	–
Net Asset Value End of Year ($)	7.41	7.06	8.00	7.84	7.84	8.42
Ratio of Expenses to Net Assets (%)	.74	.93	.75	.67	.62	.55
Portfolio Turnover Rate (%)	271	156	122	62	55	56
Total Assets: End of Year (Millions $)	37.0	36.4	62.5	68.6	106.5	318.3
Annual Rate of Return (%) Years Ending 12/31	9.0	28.5	6.7	14.2	21.9	14.3

Five-Year Total Return	118.3%	Degree of Diversification	NA	Beta	.20	Bull	D	Bear	A

Objective: Seeks current income through investment primarily in long-term corporate bonds with high coupons of Baa or higher grade. Fund performs own credit analysis. May invest in foreign securities, restricted securities and engage in repos of similar quality.

Portfolio: (7/31/86) Corporate bonds 74%, government obligations 24%.

Distributions: **Income:** Monthly   **Capital Gains:** Annually

12b-1: No

Minimum: **Initial:** $3,000   **Subsequent:** $100

Min IRA: **Initial:** $500   **Subsequent:** $100

Services: IRA, Keogh, SEP, Corp, 403(b), Withdraw, Deduct

Tel Exchange: Yes   **With MMF:** Yes

Registered: All states

VANGUARD
SHORT-TERM BOND
Bond

Vanguard Group
Vanguard Financial Ctr.
Valley Forge, PA 19482
(800) 662-7447/(215) 648-6000

	1981	1982	1983 (3 mos.)	1984	1985	1986
			Years Ending 1/31			
Net Investment Income ($)	—	—	.27	1.02	1.07	1.00
Dividends from Net Investment Income ($)	—	—	.27	1.02	1.07	1.00
Net Gains (Losses) on Investments ($)	—	—	.05	(.11)	.23	.38
Distributions from Net Realized Capital Gains ($)	—	—	—	—	—	—
Net Asset Value End of Year ($)	—	—	10.05	9.94	10.17	10.55
Ratio of Expenses to Net Assets (%)	—	—	.51	.56	.62	.49
Portfolio Turnover Rate (%)	—	—	65	121	270	460
Total Assets: End of Year (Millions $)	—	—	64.1	135.8	119.1	198.5

Annual Rate of Return (%) Years Ending 12/31	—	—	9.1	14.2	14.9	11.3

Five-Year Total Return	NA	Degree of Diversification	NA	Beta .08	Bull NA	Bear NA

Objective: The fund invests primarily in short-term investment grade bonds with maturities ranging from less than 1 year to 4 years. Has objective of obtaining the highest possible income consistent with minimum fluctuation in principal. May engage in repos and invest up to 20% of assets in foreign securities.

Portfolio: (7/31/86) Corporate bonds 46%, government obligations 36%, temporary cash investments 10%, foreign securities 7%.

Distributions: Income: Monthly   Capital Gains: Annually
12b-1: No
Minimum: Initial: $3,000   Subsequent: $100
Min IRA: Initial: $500   Subsequent: $100
Services: IRA, Keogh, SEP, Corp, 403(b), Withdraw, Deduct
Tel Exchange: Yes   With MMF: Yes
Registered: All states

VANGUARD STAR
Growth

Vanguard Group
Vanguard Financial Center
Valley Forge, PA 19482
(800) 662-7447/(215) 648-6000

	Years Ending 12/31					
	1981	**1982**	**1983**	**1984**	**1985** (9 mos.)	**1986**
Net Investment Income ($)	–	–	–	–	.93	1.15
Dividends from Net Investment Income ($)	–	–	–	–	.05	.86
Net Gains (Losses) on Investments ($)	–	–	–	–	.57	.31
Distributions from Net Realized Capital Gains ($)	–	–	–	–	–	.71
Net Asset Value End of Year ($)	–	–	–	–	11.45	11.34
Ratio of Expenses to Net Assets (%)	–	–	–	–	0	0
Portfolio Turnover Rate (%)	–	–	–	–	–	–
Total Assets: End of Year (Millions $)	–	–	–	–	112.3	454.7

Annual Rate of Return (%) Years Ending 12/31	–	–	–	–	–	13.8

Five-Year Total Return	NA	Degree of Diversification	NA	Beta	NA	Bull	NA	Bear	NA

Objective: Designed as a retirement portfolio. The fund invests in other Vanguard mutual funds, which in turn invest in common stocks and bonds. Seeks maximum total investment return. Will invest at least 60% in equity funds and not more than 40% in bond funds. May also invest in repurchase agreements.

Portfolio: (12/31/86) Growth and income 56%, fixed-income 25%, money market 13%, aggressive growth 6%.

Distributions: **Income:** Semi-Annually **Capital Gains:** Annually

12b-1: No

Minimum: **Initial:** $500 **Subsequent:** $100

Min IRA: **Initial:** $500 **Subsequent:** $100

Services: IRA, Keogh, SEP, 403(b), Corp, Withdraw, Deduct

Tel Exchange: Yes **With MMF:** Yes

Registered: All states

VANGUARD/ TRUSTEES' COMMINGLED— International Portfolio
International

Vanguard Group
Vanguard Financial Center
Valley Forge, PA 19482
(800) 662-7447/(215) 648-6000

	Years Ending 12/31					
	1981	1982	1983 (7 mos.)	1984	1985	1986
Net Investment Income ($)	–	–	.51	1.02	.93	1.03
Dividends from Net Investment Income ($)	–	–	.44	1.09	.93	1.03
Net Gains (Losses) on Investments ($)	–	–	.93	(1.21)	8.86	14.32
Distributions from Net Realized Capital Gains ($)	–	–	.02	.11	2.54	6.55
Net Asset Value End of Year ($)	–	–	25.98	24.59	30.91	38.68
Ratio of Expenses to Net Assets (%)	–	–	.90	.63	.56	.52
Portfolio Turnover Rate (%)	–	–	-0-	8	29	24
Total Assets: End of Year (Millions $)	–	–	65.3	317.1	581.6	718.7

Annual Rate of Return (%) Years Ending 12/31	–	–	–	(0.7)	40.2	49.9

Five-Year Total Return	NA	Degree of Diversification	E	Beta	.39	Bull NA	Bear NA

Objective: Invests primarily in non-U.S. securities concentrating on areas apparently undervalued to achieve long-term total return. The contrarian approach is employed as well as computer modeling. May lend its portfolio securities.

Portfolio: (12/31/86) Common stocks 96%, temporary cash investments 4%. Largest stock holdings: Australia 17%, Japan 17%.

Distributions: Income: Quarterly   **Capital Gains:** Annually

12b-1: No

Minimum: Initial: $25,000   Subsequent: $1,000

Min IRA: Initial: $500   Subsequent: $50

Services: IRA, Keogh, Corp, 403(b), Withdraw, Deduct

Tel Exchange: Yes   **With MMF:** Yes

Registered: All states

VANGUARD/ TRUSTEES' COMMINGLED— U.S. Portfolio

Growth & Income

Vanguard Group
Vanguard Financial Ctr.
Valley Forge, PA 19482
(800) 662-7447/(215) 648-6000

	Years Ending 12/31					
	1981	1982	1983	1984	1985	1986
Net Investment Income ($)	1.80	1.75	1.52	1.57	1.45	1.16
Dividends from Net Investment Income ($)	1.80	1.75	1.52	1.57	1.45	1.16
Net Gains (Losses) on Investments ($)	.97	4.70	7.31	(2.65)	4.69	3.69
Distributions from Net Realized Capital Gains ($)	.87	1.19	2.15	2.51	4.10	6.15
Net Asset Value End of Year ($)	27.05	30.56	35.72	30.56	31.15	28.69
Ratio of Expenses to Net Assets (%)	.67	.63	.50	.53	.48	.52
Portfolio Turnover Rate (%)	21	43	30	33	25	19
Total Assets: End of Year (Millions $)	91.2	190.6	269.9	271.6	201.6	162.5

Annual Rate of Return (%) Years Ending 12/31	10.3	24.9	29.1	(2.9)	20.4	15.6

Five-Year Total Return	117.9%	Degree of Diversification	B	Beta 1.01	Bull C	Bear C

Objective: Seeks long-term total return. Looks for securities of industries or companies unpopular in the marketplace, stocks not widely held by other institutions with low price-to-book value, and undervalued companies with under-utilized borrowing power.

Portfolio: (12/31/86) Common stocks 88%, cash 9%. Largest stock holdings: IBM 3%, Mobile Corp. 3%.

Distributions: **Income:** Quarterly   **Capital Gains:** Annually
12b-1: No
Minimum: Initial: $25,000   Subsequent: $1,000
Min IRA: Initial: $500   Subsequent: $50
Services: IRA, Keogh, Corp, 403(b), Withdraw, Deduct
Tel Exchange: Yes   **With MMF:** Yes
Registered: All states

VANGUARD/W.L. MORGAN GROWTH
Growth

Vanguard Group
Vanguard Financial Ctr.
Valley Forge, PA 19482
(800) 662-7447/(215) 648-6000

	Years Ending 12/31					
	1981	1982	1983	1984	1985	1986
Net Investment Income ($)	.30	.25	.31	.25	.23	.21
Dividends from Net Investment Income ($)	.29	.30	.25	.31	.25	.43
Net Gains (Losses) on Investments ($)	(.87)	2.32	2.81	(.94)	2.99	.78
Distributions from Net Realized Capital Gains ($)	.45	1.31	1.04	1.39	.60	2.88
Net Asset Value End of Year ($)	11.05	12.01	13.84	11.45	13.82	11.50
Ratio of Expenses to Net Assets (%)	.90	1.04	.85	.68	.60	.54
Portfolio Turnover Rate (%)	39	43	31	38	41	31
Total Assets: End of Year (Millions $)	229.7	288.5	401.7	467.8	665.0	594.3
Annual Rate of Return (%) Years Ending 12/31	(4.7)	27.2	28.0	(5.1)	29.5	7.8

Five-Year Total Return	116.0%	Degree of Diversification	C	Beta 1.03	Bull C	Bear D

Objective: Primarily long-term capital growth. Fund follows a "three-tier" strategy of investing in established growth, emerging growth and cyclical growth companies chosen on the basis of greater than average earnings growth potential and quality of management.

Portfolio: (12/31/86) Common stocks 97%, cash 4%. Largest stock holdings: emerging growth 39%, established growth companies 30%.

Distributions: Income: Annually   **Capital Gains:** Annually

12b-1: No

Minimum: Initial: $1,500   Subsequent: $100

Min IRA: Initial: $500   Subsequent: $50

Services: IRA, Keogh, Corp, 403(b), SEP, Withdraw, Deduct

Tel Exchange: Yes   **With MMF:** Yes

Registered: All states

VANGUARD/ WELLESLEY
Balanced

Vanguard Group
Vanguard Financial Ctr.
Valley Forge, PA 19482
(800) 662-7447/(215) 648-6000

	Years Ending 12/31					
	1981	1982	1983	1984	1985	1986
Net Investment Income ($)	1.27	1.26	1.31	1.37	1.38	1.33
Dividends from Net Investment Income ($)	1.25	1.26	1.31	1.37	1.38	1.33
Net Gains (Losses) on Investments ($)	(.36)	1.08	.84	.62	2.13	1.43
Distributions from Net Realized Capital Gains ($)	–	–	–	–	.10	.47
Net Asset Value End of Year ($)	10.74	11.82	12.66	13.28	15.31	16.27
Ratio of Expenses to Net Assets (%)	.72	.71	.70	.71	.60	.58
Portfolio Turnover Rate (%)	92	60	38	36	21	31
Total Assets: End of Year (Millions $)	88.2	94.1	105.4	114.6	224.1	510.2

Annual Rate of Return (%) Years Ending 12/31	8.6	23.3	18.6	16.6	27.4	18.4

Five-Year Total Return	157.0%	Degree of Diversification	D	Beta	.46	Bull	B	Bear	A

Objective: Seeks to provide as much current income as management believes is consistent with reasonable risk. Invests approximately 70% of assets in investment-grade fixed-income securities, with the balance invested in high-yielding common stocks. May lend its portfolio securities and engage in repos.

Portfolio: (12/31/86) Corporate bonds 52%, common stocks 36%, U.S. government agency obligations 8%. Largest stock holdings: General Motors 2%, GTE Corp 2%.

Distributions: **Income:** Quarterly   **Capital Gains:** Annually

12b-1: No

Minimum: **Initial:** $1,500   **Subsequent:** $100

Min IRA: **Initial:** $500   **Subsequent:** $50

Services: IRA, Keogh, Corp, 403(b), SEP, Withdraw, Deduct

Tel Exchange: Yes   **With MMF:** Yes

Registered: All states

VANGUARD/ WELLINGTON
Balanced

Vanguard Group
Vanguard Financial Ctr.
Valley Forge, PA 19482
(800) 662-7447/(215) 648-6000

	Years Ending 11/30					
	1981	1982	1983	1984	1985	1986
Net Investment Income ($)	.84	.87	.91	.93	.91	.94
Dividends from Net Investment Income ($)	.84	.87	.91	.92	.92	.94
Net Gains (Losses) on Investments ($)	(.60)	1.01	1.88	.06	2.22	2.41
Distributions from Net Realized Capital Gains ($)	–	–	.44	.48	.30	.34
Net Asset Value End of Year ($)	10.04	11.05	12.49	12.08	13.99	16.06
Ratio of Expenses to Net Assets (%)	.62	.69	.64	.59	.64	.53
Portfolio Turnover Rate (%)	53	38	30	27	27	25
Total Assets: End of Year (Millions $)	541.5	555.0	617.3	604.2	783.8	1,102.1
Annual Rate of Return (%) Years Ending 12/31	2.9	23.0	24.6	10.7	28.4	18.2

Five-Year Total Return 157.4%	Degree of Diversification A	Beta .70	Bull A	Bear B

Objective: Seeks to provide conservation of principal, reasonable income return and profits without undue risk through balanced investments in common stocks, bonds and preferred stocks of well-established, dividend-paying companies. Common stocks generally amount to 60% to 70% of total portfolio.

Portfolio: (11/30/86) Common stocks 64%, bonds 23%, U.S. government & agency obligations 11%, cash 3%, convertible securities 1%. Largest stock holdings: basic industries 26%, utilities 11%.

Distributions: Income: Feb, May, Aug, Nov   **Capital Gains:** Nov

12b-1: No

Minimum: Initial: $1,500   Subsequent: $100

Min IRA: Initial: $500   Subsequent: $50

Services: IRA, Keogh, Corp, 403(b), SEP, Withdraw, Deduct

Tel Exchange: Yes   **With MMF:** Yes

Registered: All states

VANGUARD WINDSOR II
Growth & Income

Vanguard Group
Vanguard Financial Ctr.
Valley Forge, PA 19482
(800) 662-7447/(215) 648-6000

	Years Ending 10/31					
	1981	**1982**	**1983**	**1984**	**1985** (4 mos.)	**1986**
Net Investment Income ($)	–	–	–	–	.11	.43
Dividends from Net Investment Income ($)	–	–	–	–	.11	.43
Net Gains (Losses) on Investments ($)	–	–	–	–	(.09)	3.09
Distributions from Net Realized Capital Gains ($)	–	–	–	–	–	.52
Net Asset Value End of Year ($)	–	–	–	–	9.91	12.48
Ratio of Expenses to Net Assets (%)	–	–	–	–	.80	.65
Portfolio Turnover Rate (%)	–	–	–	–	1	50
Total Assets: End of Year (Millions $)	–	–	–	–	133.0	814.0

Annual Rate of Return (%) Years Ending 12/31	–	–	–	–	–	21.4

Five-Year Total Return	NA	Degree of Diversification	NA	Beta	NA	Bull NA	Bear NA

Objective: Seeks long-term growth of capital and income through investment in common stocks characterized by above-average income yields and below-average price-earnings ratios. May hold cash or fixed-income securities for defensive purposes and engage in repos or lend its securities.

Portfolio: (10/31/86) Common stocks 94%, cash 9%. Largest stock holdings: financial 24%, utilities 22%.

Distributions: Income: May and Dec   **Capital Gains:** Dec

12b-1: No

Minimum: Initial: $1,500   Subsequent: $100

Min IRA: Initial: $500   Subsequent: $100

Services: IRA, Keogh, Corp, SEP, 403(b), Withdraw, Deduct

Tel Exchange: Yes   **With MMF:** Yes

Registered: All states

VANGUARD WORLD-INTERNATIONAL GROWTH

International

Vanguard Group
Vanguard Financial Ctr.
Valley Forge, PA 19482
(800) 662-7447/(215) 648-6000

	Years Ending 8/31					
	1981	1982	1983	1984	1985	1986
Net Investment Income ($)	–	–	–	–	–	.07
Dividends from Net Investment Income ($)	–	–	–	–	–	–
Net Gains (Losses) on Investments ($)	–	–	–	–	–	5.41
Distributions from Net Realized Capital Gains ($)	–	–	–	–	–	–
Net Asset Value End of Year ($)	–	–	–	–	–	11.67
Ratio of Expenses to Net Assets (%)	–	–	–	–	–	.78
Portfolio Turnover Rate (%)	–	–	–	–	–	39
Total Assets: End of Year (Millions $)	–	–	–	–	–	451.3

Annual Rate of Return (%) Years Ending 12/31	–	–	–	–	–	56.6

Five-Year Total Return	NA	Degree of Diversification	NA	Beta	NA	Bull	NA	Bear	NA

Objective: Seeks long-term capital appreciation through investment in common stocks of seasoned foreign companies in a wide diversity of countries. May enter into foreign currency futures contracts and may lend its securities.

Portfolio: (8/31/86) Common stocks 94%, cash 6%. Largest country holdings: Japan 35%, West Germany 14%.

Distributions: Income: Oct   **Capital Gains:** Oct

12b-1: No

Minimum: Initial: $1,500   Subsequent: $100

Min IRA: Initial: $500   Subsequent: $50

Services: IRA, Keogh, Corp, SEP, 403(b), Withdraw, Deduct

Tel Exchange: Yes   **With MMF:** Yes

Registered: All states

VANGUARD WORLD-
U.S. GROWTH
Growth

Vanguard Group
Vanguard Financial Ctr.
Valley Forge, PA 19482
(800) 662-7447/(215) 648-6000

	Years Ending 8/31					
	1981	1982	1983	1984	1985	1986
Net Investment Income ($)	–	–	–	–	–	.24
Dividends from Net Investment Income ($)	–	–	–	–	–	–
Net Gains (Losses) on Investments ($)	–	–	–	–	–	3.03
Distributions from Net Realized Capital Gains ($)	–	–	–	–	–	–
Net Asset Value End of Year ($)	–	–	–	–	–	13.21
Ratio of Expenses to Net Assets (%)	–	–	–	–	–	.80
Portfolio Turnover Rate (%)	–	–	–	–	–	77
Total Assets: End of Year (Millions $)	–	–	–	–	–	188.0

Annual Rate of Return (%) Years Ending 12/31	–	–	–	–	–	7.6

Five-Year Total Return	NA	Degree of Diversification	NA	Beta	NA	Bull NA	Bear NA

Objective: Seeks long-term capital appreciation through investment in common stock of primarily seasoned companies. May also invest in special situations and newer companies, and for defensive purposes, debt securities.

Portfolio: (8/31/86) Common stocks 81%, convertible securities 15%, cash 7%. Largest stock holdings: basic industry 30%, applied science and research 25%.

Distributions: Income: Oct   **Capital Gains:** Oct

12b-1: No

Minimum: Initial: $1,500   Subsequent: $100

Min IRA: Initial: $500   Subsequent: $50

Services: IRA, Keogh, Corp, SEP, (403)b, Withdraw, Deduct

Tel Exchange: Yes   **With MMF:** Yes

Registered: All states

VIKING EQUITY INDEX—GENERAL

Growth & Income

Viking Equity Index Fund, Inc.
232 Lakeside Drive
Horsham, PA 19044
(800) 441-3885

	Years Ending 1/31					
	1981	1982	1983	1984	1985	1986
Net Investment Income ($)	–	–	–	–	–	.38
Dividends from Net Investment Income ($)	–	–	–	–	–	.37
Net Gains (Losses) on Investments ($)	–	–	–	–	–	1.76
Distributions from Net Realized Capital Gains ($)	–	–	–	–	–	.13
Net Asset Value End of Year ($)	–	–	–	–	–	11.64
Ratio of Expenses to Net Assets (%)	–	–	–	–	–	.95
Portfolio Turnover Rate (%)	–	–	–	–	–	9
Total Assets: End of Year (Millions $)	–	–	–	–	–	2.2

Annual Rate of Return (%) Years Ending 12/31	–	–	–	–	–	16.7

Five-Year Total Return	NA	Degree of Diversification	NA	Beta	NA	Bull NA	Bear NA

Objective: Designed to track the investment results of an equity index prepared by First Pennsylvania Bank. The index is substantially similar to the S&P 500 Index.

Portfolio: (7/31/86) Common stocks 94%, short-term securities 4%. Largest stock holdings: drugs and medical 8%, business machines 7%.

Distributions: **Income:** Quarterly   **Capital Gains:** Annually

12b-1: No

Minimum: **Initial:** $250   **Subsequent:** None

Min IRA: **Initial:** $250   **Subsequent:** None

Services: IRA

Tel Exchange: Yes   **With MMF:** Yes

Registered: DE, NJ, PA

WAYNE HUMMER GROWTH

Growth & Income

Wayne Hummer Mgmt. Co.
175 W. Jackson Blvd.
Chicago, IL 60604
(800) 621-4477/(312) 431-1700

	Years Ending 3/31					
	1981	1982	1983	1984 (3 mos.)	1985	1986
Net Investment Income ($)	–	–	–	.12	.44	.29
Dividends from Net Investment Income ($)	–	–	–	–	.33	.30
Net Gains (Losses) on Investments ($)	–	–	–	(.29)	.73	3.20
Distributions from Net Realized Capital Gains ($)	–	–	–	–	–	.01
Net Asset Value End of Year ($)	–	–	–	9.83	10.67	13.85
Ratio of Expenses to Net Assets (%)	–	–	–	1.50	1.50	1.50
Portfolio Turnover Rate (%)	–	–	–	0	26	27
Total Assets: End of Year (Millions $)	–	–	–	1.7	4.3	10.1
Annual Rate of Return (%) Years Ending 12/31	–	–	–	4.0	24.4	13.8

Five-Year Total Return	NA	Degree of Diversification	A	Beta	.98	Bull NA	Bear NA

Objective: Seeks long-term capital growth and secondarily current income through investment in established dividend-paying companies' common stock, preferred stock, bonds or convertibles. May temporarily invest in investment grade debt securities as defensive move.

Portfolio: (9/30/86) Common stocks 91%, commercial paper 9%. Largest stock holdings: consumer non-durables 25%, basic industry 17%.

Distributions: Income: Jan, April, July, Oct   **Capital Gains:** April

12b-1: Yes   Amount: .25%

Minimum: Initial: $1,000   Subsequent: $500

Min IRA: Initial: $500   Subsequent: $200

Services: IRA, Keogh, SEP, Corp

Tel Exchange: No

Registered: All states except DE, ID, NH, OK

WORLD OF TECHNOLOGY
International

Financial Programs
PO Box 2040
Denver, CO 80201
(800) 525-8085/(303) 779-1233

	Years Ending 2/28					
	1981	1982	1983	1984 (11 mos.)	1985	1986
Net Investment Income ($)	—	—	—	.09	(.04)	(0.7)
Dividends from Net Investment Income ($)	—	—	—	.09	—	—
Net Gains (Losses) on Investments ($)	—	—	—	(1.43)	.32	.72
Distributions from Net Realized Capital Gains ($)	—	—	—	—	—	—
Net Asset Value End of Year ($)	—	—	—	7.69	7.97	8.61
Ratio of Expenses to Net Assets (%)	—	—	—	1.44	1.50	1.50
Portfolio Turnover Rate (%)	—	—	—	56	99	121
Total Assets: End of Year (Millions $)	—	—	—	11.5	9.6	8.1
Annual Rate of Return (%) Years Ending 12/31	—	—	—	(17.5)	16.5	16.5

Five-Year Total Return	NA	Degree of Diversification	D	Beta 1.06	Bull NA	Bear NA

Objective: Seeks capital appreciation through investment in common stocks of smaller emerging companies involved in high technology. Invests worldwide but major portion of holdings are in U.S. companies.

Portfolio: (8/31/86) Common stocks 91%, fixed-income securities 7%, preferred stocks 2%. Largest stock holdings: electric equipment 15%, computer services & software 13%.

Distributions: Income: Feb   **Capital Gains:** Feb

12b-1: No

Minimum: Initial: $250   Subsequent: $50

Min IRA: Initial: $250   Subsequent: $50

Services: IRA, Keogh, Corp, 403(b), SEP, Withdraw, Deduct

Tel Exchange: Yes   **With MMF:** Yes

Registered: All states

WPG
Growth

Weiss, Peck & Greer
One New York Plaza, 30th Flr
New York, NY 10004
(800) 223-3332/(212) 908-9582

	Years Ending 12/31					
	1981	**1982**	**1983**	**1984**	**1985**	**1986**
Net Investment Income ($)	.50	.62	.31	.70	.49	.16
Dividends from Net Investment Income ($)	.46	.51	.47	.57	.65	.68
Net Gains (Losses) on Investments ($)	(1.39)	3.63	3.01	(1.11)	5.26	2.76
Distributions from Net Realized Capital Gains ($)	–	–	.01	.54	–	6.02
Net Asset Value End of Year ($)	14.26	18.00	20.84	19.32	24.42	20.64
Ratio of Expenses to Net Assets (%)	1.78	1.78	1.32	1.17	1.21	1.23
Portfolio Turnover Rate (%)	118	212	63	104	108	71
Total Assets: End of Year (Millions $)	14.9	21.5	33.0	32.7	42.1	36.1
Annual Rate of Return (%) Years Ending 12/31	(5.6)	30.6	18.5	(1.6)	30.5	11.2

Five-Year Total Return	121.0%	Degree of Diversification	A	Beta	.99	Bull	C	Bear	C

Objective: Seeks both current income and capital growth. Portfolio generally consists of 75% equity securities and 25% debt securities of well-known, seasoned, established, dividend-paying companies. May write covered call options, buy options, lend its portfolio securities, and enter into repos.

Portfolio: (12/31/86) Common stocks 98%, repos 2%, preferred stocks 1%. Largest stock holdings: basic industries 13%, computer hardware 12%.

Distributions: Income: Mar, June, Sept, Dec   **Capital Gains:** Mar

12b-1: No

Minimum: Initial: $1,000   Subsequent: $50

Min IRA: Initial: $250   Subsequent: $50

Services: IRA, Keogh, Withdraw

Tel Exchange: Yes   **With MMF:** Yes

Registered: All states except ID, ND

Tax-Exempt Bond Funds

On the following pages, we present 60 tax-exempt bond funds, listed alphabetically. All return figures are based on a calendar year-end, and assume monthly reinvestment of distributions. We did not calculate beta figures or degrees of diversification for tax-exempt bond funds, since they are measures relative to the stock market and are thus less meaningful for these funds.

AARP INSURED TAX FREE BOND

Scudder Fund Distributors
175 Federal Street
Boston, MA 02110-2267
(800) 253-2277

			Years Ending 9/30			
	1981	1982	1983	1984	1985 (10 mos.)	1986
Dividends from Net Investment Income ($)	—	—	—	—	.64	1.01
Distributions from Net Realized Capital Gains ($)	—	—	—	—	—	.06
Net Asset Value End of Year ($)	—	—	—	—	15.12	16.69
Ratio of Expenses to Net Assets (%)	—	—	—	—	1.29	1.13
Portfolio Turnover Rate (%)	—	—	—	—	91	36
Total Assets: End of Year (Millions $)	—	—	—	—	62.3	129.3
Annual Rate of Return (%) Years Ending 12/31	—	—	—	—	—	16.9

Distr: Income: Monthly
    Capital Gains: Annually
Minimum: Initial: $250
    Subsequent: None

Telephone Exchange: Yes
    With MMF: Yes
Registered In: All states
12b-1: No

AARP INSURED TAX FREE SHORT TERM

Scudder Fund Distributors
175 Federal Street
Boston, MA 02110-2267
(800) 253-2277

			Years Ending 9/30			
	1981	1982	1983	1984	1985 (10 mos.)	1986
Dividends from Net Investment Income ($)	—	—	—	—	.47	.73
Distributions from Net Realized Capital Gains ($)	—	—	—	—	—	—
Net Asset Value End of Year ($)	—	—	—	—	15.11	15.58
Ratio of Expenses to Net Assets (%)	—	—	—	—	1.50	1.48
Portfolio Turnover Rate (%)	—	—	—	—	—	23
Total Assets: End of Year (Millions $)	—	—	—	—	30.1	48.1
Annual Rate of Return (%) Years Ending 12/31	—	—	—	—	—	8.3

Distr: Income: Monthly
    Capital Gains: Annually
Minimum: Initial: $250
    Subsequent: None

Telephone Exchange: Yes
    With MMF: Yes
Registered In: All states
12b-1: No

BABSON TAX-FREE INCOME—Portfolio L

Jones & Babson
3 Crown Ctr.
2440 Pershing Rd.
Kansas City, MO 64108
(800) 821-5591/(816) 471-5200

	Years Ending 6/30					
	1981	**1982**	**1983**	**1984**	**1985**	**1986**
Dividends from Net Investment Income ($)	.71	.74	.74	.73	.72	.71
Distributions from Net Realized Capital Gains ($)	–	–	–	–	–	–
Net Asset Value End of Year ($)	7.84	6.94	8.30	7.66	8.76	9.45
Ratio of Expenses to Net Assets (%)	.75	.75	.75	.92	1.00	1.00
Portfolio Turnover Rate (%)	19	9	27	27	32	46
Total Assets: End of Year (Millions $)	2.1	3.5	10.6	11.9	16.0	20.9
Annual Rate of Return (%) Years Ending 12/31	(13.4)	39.6	9.0	9.1	20.4	18.2

Distr: Income: Monthly
    Capital Gains: Annually
Minimum: Initial: $1,000
    Subsequent: $100

Telephone Exchange: Yes
    With MMF: Yes
Registered In: All states
12b-1: No

BENHAM CALIFORNIA TAX-FREE INTERMEDIATE

Benham Management Corp.
755 Page Mill Road
Palo Alto, CA 94304
(800) 227-8380/(415) 858-3600

	Years Ending 8/31					
	1981	**1982**	**1983**	**1984**	**1985**	**1986**
Dividends from Net Investment Income ($)	–	–	–	.58	.69	.69
Distributions from Net Realized Capital Gains ($)	–	–	–	–	–	–
Net Asset Value End of Year ($)	–	–	–	9.56	9.86	10.56
Ratio of Expenses to Net Assets (%)	–	–	–	.97	.96	.74
Portfolio Turnover Rate (%)	–	–	–	93	48	23
Total Assets: End of Year (Millions $)	–	–	–	30.4	56.3	124.9
Annual Rate of Return (%) Years Ending 12/31	–	–	–	5.3	13.8	12.7

Distr: Income: Monthly
    Capital Gains: Annually
Minimum: Initial: $1,000
    Subsequent: $100

Telephone Exchange: Yes
    With MMF: Yes
Registered In: AZ, CA, NV, OR, WA
12b-1: No

BENHAM CALIFORNIA TAX FREE LONG TERM

Benham Management Corp.
755 Page Mill Road
Palo Alto, CA 94304
(800) 227-8380/(415) 858-3600

	Years Ending 8/31					
	1981	1982	1983	1984	1985	1986
Dividends from Net Investment Income ($)	–	–	–	.71	.84	.83
Distributions from Net Realized Capital Gains ($)	–	–	–	–	–	–
Net Asset Value End of Year ($)	–	–	–	9.54	10.15	11.42
Ratio of Expenses to Net Assets (%)	–	–	–	.97	.95	.74
Portfolio Turnover Rate (%)	–	–	–	107	91	48
Total Assets: End of Year (Millions $)	–	–	–	27.5	83.9	196.6
Annual Rate of Return (%) Years Ending 12/31	–	–	–	5.7	17.6	18.7

Distr: Income: Monthly
    Capital Gains: Annually
Minimum: Initial: $1,000
    Subsequent: $100

Telephone Exchange: Yes
    With MMF: Yes
Registered In: AZ, CA, NV, OR, WA
12b-1: No

BENHAM NATIONAL TAX-FREE TRUST LONG TERM

Benham Management Corp.
755 Page Mill Road
Palo Alto, CA 94304
(800) 227-8380/(415) 858-3600

	Years Ending 5/31					
	1981	1982	1983	1984	1985 (10 mos.)	1986
Dividends from Net Investment Income ($)	–	–	–	–	.82	.94
Distributions from Net Realized Capital Gains ($)	–	–	–	–	–	–
Net Asset Value End of Year ($)	–	–	–	–	10.56	11.37
Ratio of Expenses to Net Assets (%)	–	–	–	–	–	.26
Portfolio Turnover Rate (%)	–	–	–	–	33	57
Total Assets: End of Year (Millions $)	–	–	–	–	7.1	22.8
Annual Rate of Return (%) Years Ending 12/31	–	–	–	–	19.2	18.7

Distr: Income: Monthly
    Capital Gains: Annually
Minimum: Initial: $1,000
    Subsequent: $100

Telephone Exchange: Yes
    With MMF: Yes
Registered In: All states
12b-1: No

BULL & BEAR TAX-FREE INCOME

Bull & Bear Advisors
11 Hanover Square
New York, NY 10005
(800) 847-4200/(215) 786-6535

	Years Ending 12/31					
	1981	1982	1983	1984 (10 mos.)	1985	1986
Dividends from Net Investment Income ($)	–	–	–	1.10	1.39	1.32
Distributions from Net Realized Capital Gains ($)	–	–	–	–	–	.58
Net Asset Value End of Year ($)	–	–	–	15.04	16.88	18.17
Ratio of Expenses to Net Assets (%)	–	–	–	.82	1.02	1.18
Portfolio Turnover Rate (%)	–	–	–	–	58	60
Total Assets: End of Year (Millions $)	–	–	–	4.2	11.0	21.8
Annual Rate of Return (%) Years Ending 12/31	–	–	–	–	22.4	19.6

Distr: Income: Monthly
    Capital Gains: Annually
Minimum: Initial: $1,000
    Subsequent: $100

Telephone Exchange: Yes
    With MMF: Yes
Registered In: All states except ME
12b-1: Yes **Amount:** .50%

CALIFORNIA TAX-FREE INCOME

CCM Partners
44 Montgomery Street
San Franciso, CA 94104
(415) 398-2727

	Years Ending 8/31					
	1981	1982	1983	1984	1985	1986 (9 mos.)
Dividends from Net Investment Income ($)	–	–	–	–	–	.50
Distributions from Net Realized Capital Gains ($)	–	–	–	–	–	–
Net Asset Value End of Year ($)	–	–	–	–	–	11.72
Ratio of Expenses to Net Assets (%)	–	–	–	–	–	.03
Portfolio Turnover Rate (%)	–	–	–	–	–	50
Total Assets: End of Year (Millions $)	–	–	–	–	–	20.8
Annual Rate of Return (%) Years Ending 12/31	–	–	–	–	–	22.7

Distr: Income: Monthly
    Capital Gains: Annually
Minimum: Initial: $10,000
    Subsequent: $250

Telephone Exchange: Yes
    With MMF: Yes
Registered In: CA, HI, NV, OK
12b-1: No

CALVERT TAX-FREE RESERVES—Limited Term

Calvert Asset Management Co.
1700 Pennsylvania Ave., NW
Washington, DC 20006
(800) 368-2748/(301) 951-4820

	Years Ending 12/31					
	1981 (10 mos.)	1982	1983	1984	1985	1986
Dividends from Net Investment Income ($)	.63	.84	.67	.71	.73	.64
Distributions from Net Realized Capital Gains ($)	—	.03	.01	.01	.01	.04
Net Asset Value End of Year ($)	9.88	10.31	10.29	10.33	10.48	10.67
Ratio of Expenses to Net Assets (%)	.47	1.00	1.00	.96	.88	.81
Portfolio Turnover Rate (%)	120	86	79	155	90	67
Total Assets: End of Year (Millions $)	4.2	31.0	55.7	52.3	77.8	189.4
Annual Rate of Return (%) Years Ending 12/31	—	13.2	6.2	7.5	8.4	8.6

Distr: Income: Daily
   Capital Gains: Annually
Minimum: Initial: $2,000
   Subsequent: $250

Telephone Exchange: Yes
   With MMF: Yes
Registered In: All states
12b-1: No

CALVERT TAX-FREE RESERVES—Long Term

Calvert Asset Management Co.
1700 Pennsylvania Ave., NW
Washington, DC 20006
(800) 368-2748/(301) 951-4820

	Years Ending 12/31					
	1981	1982	1983 (4 mos.)	1984	1985	1986
Dividends from Net Investment Income ($)	—	—	.51	1.40	1.47	1.24
Distributions from Net Realized Capital Gains ($)	—	—	—	—	.23	.87
Net Asset Value End of Year ($)	—	—	14.96	14.70	15.80	16.36
Ratio of Expenses to Net Assets (%)	—	—	.60	.71	.84	.85
Portfolio Turnover Rate (%)	—	—	103	272	194	146
Total Assets: End of Year (Millions $)	—	—	13.1	31.5	56.8	81.8
Annual Rate of Return (%) Years Ending 12/31	—	—	—	8.1	18.8	17.4

Distr: Income: Daily
   Capital Gains: Annually
Minimum: Initial: $2,000
   Subsequent: $250

Telephone Exchange: Yes
   With MMF: Yes
Registered In: All states
12b-1: Yes **Amount:** .35%

DREYFUS CALIFORNIA TAX EXEMPT BOND

The Dreyfus Corp.
600 Madison Ave.
New York, NY 10022
(800) 645-6561/(718) 895-1206

			Years Ending 5/31		
	1981	1982	1983	1984 (10 mos.)	1985	1986

	1981	1982	1983	1984 (10 mos.)	1985	1986
Dividends from Net Investment Income ($)	–	–	–	1.02	1.15	1.12
Distributions from Net Realized Capital Gains ($)	–	–	–	–	–	–
Net Asset Value End of Year ($)	–	–	–	12.54	13.87	14.70
Ratio of Expenses to Net Assets (%)	–	–	–	.55	.75	.72
Portfolio Turnover Rate (%)	–	–	–	36	27	19
Total Assets: End of Year (Millions $)	–	–	–	216.1	529.3	973.2
Annual Rate of Return (%) Years Ending 12/31	–	–	–	–	18.0	17.7

Distr: Income: Monthly
    Capital Gains: June
Minimum: Initial: $2,500
    Subsequent: $100

Telephone Exchange: Yes
    With MMF: Yes
Registered In: CA
12b-1: No

DREYFUS INSURED TAX EXEMPT BOND

The Dreyfus Corp.
600 Madison Ave.
New York, NY 10022
(800) 645-6561/(718) 895-1206

			Years Ending 4/30		
	1981	1982	1983	1984	1985	1986 (10 mos.)

	1981	1982	1983	1984	1985	1986 (10 mos.)
Dividends from Net Investment Income ($)	–	–	–	–	–	1.14
Distributions from Net Realized Capital Gains ($)	–	–	–	–	–	–
Net Asset Value End of Year ($)	–	–	–	–	–	18.03
Ratio of Expenses to Net Assets (%)	–	–	–	–	–	.73
Portfolio Turnover Rate (%)	–	–	–	–	–	51
Total Assets: End of Year (Millions $)	–	–	–	–	–	144.3
Annual Rate of Return (%) Years Ending 12/31	–	–	–	–	–	17.1

Distr: Income: Monthly
    Capital Gains: Annually
Minimum: Initial: $2,500
    Subsequent: $100

Telephone Exchange: Yes
    With MMF: Yes
Registered In: All states
12b-1: Yes **Amount:** .20%

DREYFUS INTERMEDIATE TAX-EXEMPT

Dreyfus Corp.
600 Madison Ave.
New York, NY 10022
(800) 645-6561/(718) 895-1206

	Years Ending 5/31					
	1981	1982	1983	1984 (9 mos.)	1985	1986
Dividends from Net Investment Income ($)	–	–	–	.82	1.02	1.03
Distributions from Net Realized Capital Gains ($)	–	–	–	–	–	–
Net Asset Value End of Year ($)	–	–	–	11.84	12.93	13.47
Ratio of Expenses to Net Assets (%)	–	–	–	.69	.81	.75
Portfolio Turnover Rate (%)	–	–	–	29	21	34
Total Assets: End of Year (Millions $)	–	–	–	228.5	548.7	920.2
Annual Rate of Return (%) Years Ending 12/31	–	–	–	–	16.1	15.4

Distr: Income: Monthly
    Capital Gains: Annually
Minimum: Initial: $2,500
    Subsequent: $100

Telephone Exchange: Yes
    With MMF: Yes
Registered In: All states
12b-1: No

DREYFUS MASSACHUSETTS TAX EXEMPT BOND

The Dreyfus Corp.
600 Madison Ave.
New York, NY 10022
(800) 645-6561/(718) 895-1206

	Years Ending 5/31					
	1981	1982	1983	1984	1985	1986
Dividends from Net Investment Income ($)	–	–	–	–	–	1.17
Distributions from Net Realized Capital Gains ($)	–	–	–	–	–	–
Net Asset Value End of Year ($)	–	–	–	–	–	15.89
Ratio of Expenses to Net Assets (%)	–	–	–	–	–	.26
Portfolio Turnover Rate (%)	–	–	–	–	–	103
Total Assets: End of Year (Millions $)	–	–	–	–	–	54.7
Annual Rate of Return (%) Years Ending 12/31	–	–	–	–	–	17.9

Distr: Income: Monthly
    Capital Gains: Annually
Minimum: Initial: $2,500
    Subsequent: $100

Telephone Exchange: Yes
    With MMF: Yes
Registered In: All states
12b-1: No

DREYFUS NEW YORK TAX EXEMPT BOND

The Dreyfus Corp.
600 Madison Ave.
New York, NY 10022
(800) 645-6561/(718) 895-1206

	Years Ending 5/31					
	1981	1982	1983	1984 (10 mos.)	1985	1986
Dividends from Net Investment Income ($)	–	–	–	.97	1.16	1.15
Distributions from Net Realized Capital Gains ($)	–	–	–	–	–	–
Net Asset Value End of Year ($)	–	–	–	12.41	14.10	15.05
Ratio of Expenses to Net Assets (%)	–	–	–	.77	.76	.71
Portfolio Turnover Rate (%)	–	–	–	44	29	15
Total Assets: End of Year (Millions $)	–	–	–	252.1	652.9	1,246
Annual Rate of Return (%) Years Ending 12/31	–	–	–	–	20.6	17.1

Distr: Income: Monthly
    Capital Gains: June
Minimum: Initial: $2,500
    Subsequent: $100

Telephone Exchange: Yes
    With MMF: Yes
Registered In: NY
12b-1: No

DREYFUS TAX-EXEMPT

The Dreyfus Corporation
600 Madison Ave.
New York, NY 10022
(800) 645-6561/(718) 895-1206

	Years Ending 8/31					
	1981	1982	1983	1984	1985	1986
Dividends from Net Investment Income ($)	.96	.99	1.00	1.01	1.02	.99
Distributions from Net Realized Capital Gains ($)	–	–	–	–	–	–
Net Asset Value End of Year ($)	8.80	10.12	10.97	10.84	11.60	12.87
Ratio of Expenses to Net Assets (%)	.76	.77	.73	.71	.69	.69
Portfolio Turnover Rate (%)	26	40	37	22	28	53
Total Assets: End of Year (Millions $)	701.4	1,022.8	1,780.1	2,020.9	2,724.7	3,648.9
Annual Rate of Return (%) Years Ending 12/31	(10.0)	39.6	11.6	8.6	19.4	17.4

Distr: Income: Monthly
    Capital Gains: Annually
Minimum: Initial: $2,500
    Subsequent: $100

Telephone Exchange: Yes
    With MMF: Yes
Registered In: All states
12b-1: No

FEDERATED TAX-FREE INCOME (Liberty)

Federated Securities
421 Seventh Ave.
Pittsburgh, PA 15219
(800) 245-4770

	Years Ending 9/30				3/31	
	1981	**1982**	**1983**	**1984**	**1985** (6 mos.)	**1986**
Dividends from Net Investment Income ($)	.72	.73	.75	.80	.40	.80
Distributions from Net Realized Capital Gains ($)	—	—	—	—	—	—
Net Asset Value End of Year ($)	6.98	8.53	9.20	8.51	8.91	10.51
Ratio of Expenses to Net Assets (%)	1.47	1.60	1.46	1.14	1.04	.93
Portfolio Turnover Rate (%)	3	6	84	28	1	2
Total Assets: End of Year (Millions $)	34.3	43.1	47.9	47.6	105.7	248.7
Annual Rate of Return (%) Years Ending 12/31	(10.4)	45.3	10.7	6.2	18.3	20.4

Distr: Income: Monthly
Capital Gains: Annually
Minimum: Initial: $500
Subsequent: $100

Telephone Exchange: Yes
With MMF: Yes
Registered In: All states
12b-1: Yes **Amount:** Pd. by Advisor

FIDELITY AGGRESSIVE TAX-FREE PORTFOLIO

Fidelity Investments Co.
82 Devonshire St.
Boston, MA 02109
(800) 544-6666/(617) 523-1919

	Years Ending 12/31					
	1981	**1982**	**1983**	**1984**	**1985** (3 mos.)	**1986**
Dividends from Net Investment Income ($)	—	—	—	—	.31	.93
Distributions from Net Realized Capital Gains ($)	—	—	—	—	—	—
Net Asset Value End of Year ($)	—	—	—	—	10.66	11.56
Ratio of Expenses to Net Assets (%)	—	—	—	—	.60	.65
Portfolio Turnover Rate (%)	—	—	—	—	4	17
Total Assets: End of Year (Millions $)	—	—	—	—	101.4	394.1
Annual Rate of Return (%) Years Ending 12/31	—	—	—	—	—	17.6

Distr: Income: Monthly
Capital Gains: Annually
Minimum: Initial: $2,500
Subsequent: $250

Telephone Exchange: Yes
With MMF: Yes
Registered In: All states
12b-1: Yes **Amount:** Pd. by Advisor

FIDELITY CALIFORNIA TAX FREE HIGH YIELD

Fidelity Investments Co.
82 Devonshire Street
Boston, MA 02109
(800) 544-6666/(617) 523-1919

	Years Ending 4/30					
	1981	1982	1983	1984	1985 (10 mos.)	1986
Dividends from Net Investment Income ($)	–	–	–	–	.77	.88
Distributions from Net Realized Capital Gains ($)	–	–	–	–	–	–
Net Asset Value End of Year ($)	–	–	–	–	10.43	11.51
Ratio of Expenses to Net Assets (%)	–	–	–	–	1.00	.72
Portfolio Turnover Rate (%)	–	–	–	–	14	16
Total Assets: End of Year (Millions $)	–	–	–	–	30.2	323.5
Annual Rate of Return (%) Years Ending 12/31	–	–	–	–	16.6	17.7

Distr: Income: Monthly
Capital Gains: Annually
Minimum: Initial: $2,500
Subsequent: $250

Telephone Exchange: Yes
With MMF: Yes
Registered In: CA
12b-1: Yes **Amount:** Pd. by Advisor

FIDELITY HIGH-YIELD MUNICIPALS

Fidelity Investments Company
82 Devonshire St.
Boston, MA 02109
(800) 544-6666/(617) 523-1919

	Years Ending 11/30					
	1981	1982	1983	1984	1985	1986
Dividends from Net Investment Income ($)	1.03	1.13	1.07	1.07	1.04	1.0
Distributions from Net Realized Capital Gains ($)	–	–	–	–	–	.04
Net Asset Value End of Year ($)	9.52	10.62	11.17	11.0	12.29	13.77
Ratio of Expenses to Net Assets (%)	.67	.64	.65	.59	.56	.57
Portfolio Turnover Rate (%)	169	109	81	73	57	49
Total Assets: End of Year (Millions $)	177.9	356.7	750.2	1,040.2	1,600.8	2,449.3
Annual Rate of Return (%) Years Ending 12/31	(6.1)	36.0	15.9	9.9	21.4	18.9

Distr: Income: Monthly
Capital Gains: Dec
Minimum: Initial: $2,500
Subsequent: $250

Telephone Exchange: Yes
With MMF: Yes
Registered In: All states
12b-1: Yes **Amount:** Pd. by Advisor

FIDELITY INSURED TAX FREE

Fidelity Investments Co.
82 Devonshire Street
Boston, MA 02109
(800) 544-6666/(617) 523-1919

	Years Ending 12/31					
	1981	1982	1983	1984	1985 (2 mos.)	1986
Dividends from Net Investment Income ($)	–	–	–	–	.07	.73
Distributions from Net Realized Capital Gains ($)	–	–	–	–	–	–
Net Asset Value End of Year ($)	–	–	–	–	10.23	11.33
Ratio of Expenses to Net Assets (%)	–	–	–	–	.60	.60
Portfolio Turnover Rate (%)	–	–	–	–	–	23
Total Assets: End of Year (Millions $)	–	–	–	–	9.5	146.2
Annual Rate of Return (%) Years Ending 12/31	–	–	–	–	–	18.1

Distr: Income: Monthly
Capital Gains: Annually
Minimum: Initial: $2,500
Subsequent: $250

Telephone Exchange: Yes
With MMF: Yes
Registered In: All states
12b-1: Yes **Amount:** Pd. by Advisor

FIDELITY LIMITED TERM MUNICIPALS

Fidelity Investments Company
82 Devonshire St.
Boston, MA 02109
(800) 544-6666/(617) 523-1919

	Years Ending 12/31					
	1981	1982	1983	1984	1985	1986
Dividends from Net Investment Income ($)	.58	.69	.62	.64	.63	.62
Distributions from Net Realized Capital Gains ($)	–	–	–	–	–	–
Net Asset Value End of Year ($)	6.88	7.89	8.03	8.15	8.88	9.58
Ratio of Expenses to Net Assets (%)	.83	.99	.83	.79	.71	.68
Portfolio Turnover Rate (%)	332	210	146	152	73	30
Total Assets: End of Year (Millions $)	46.6	99.7	182.0	214.2	315.8	580.2
Annual Rate of Return (%) Years Ending 12/31	(2.9)	25.9	9.9	9.9	17.3	15.2

Distr: Income: Monthly
Capital Gains: Annually
Minimum: Initial: $2,500
Subsequent: $250

Telephone Exchange: Yes
With MMF: Yes
Registered In: All states
12b-1: No

FIDELITY MASSFREE
Muni Bond

Fidelity Investments Co.
82 Devonshire St.
Boston, MA 02109
(800) 544-6666/(617) 523-1919

	Years Ending 7/30					
	1981	1982	1983	1984 (8 mos.)	1985	1986
Dividends from Net Investment Income ($)	–	–	–	.72	.92	.87
Distributions from Net Realized Capital Gains ($)	–	–	–	–	–	–
Net Asset Value End of Year ($)	–	–	–	9.64	10.54	11.18
Ratio of Expenses to Net Assets (%)	–	–	–	.89	.76	.64
Portfolio Turnover Rate (%)	–	–	–	102	12	13
Total Assets: End of Year (Millions $)	–	–	–	56.2	203.1	500.2
Annual Rate of Return (%) Years Ending 12/31	–	–	–	–	19.6	16.9

Distr: Income: Monthly
    Capital Gains: Aug
Minimum: Initial: $2,500
    Subsequent: $250

Telephone Exchange: Yes
    With MMF: Yes
Registered In: MA
12b-1: Pending

FIDELITY MICHIGAN TAX-FREE

Fidelity Investments, Co.
82 Devonshire St.
Boston, MA 02109
(800) 544-6666/(617) 523-1919

	Years Ending 12/31					
	1981	1982	1983	1984	1985 (2 mos.)	1986
Dividends from Net Investment Income ($)	–	–	–	–	.09	.79
Distributions from Net Realized Capital Gains ($)	–	–	–	–	–	–
Net Asset Value End of Year ($)	–	–	–	–	10.27	11.38
Ratio of Expenses to Net Assets (%)	–	–	–	–	.60	.60
Portfolio Turnover Rate (%)	–	–	–	–	9	24
Total Assets: End of Year (Millions $)	–	–	–	–	6.6	127.6
Annual Rate of Return (%) Years Ending 12/31	–	–	–	–	–	18.7

Distr: Income: Monthly
    Capital Gains: Annually
Minimum: Initial: $2,500
    Subsequent: $250

Telephone Exchange: Yes
    With MMF: Yes
Registered In: MI
12b-1: Yes **Amount:** Pd. by Advisor

FIDELITY MINNESOTA TAX FREE

Fidelity Investments, Co.
82 Devonshire St.
Boston, MA 02109
(800) 544-6666/(617) 523-1919

	Years Ending 12/31					
	1981	**1982**	**1983**	**1984**	**1985** (1 mos.)	**1986**
Dividends from Net Investment Income ($)	–	–	–	–	.07	.77
Distributions from Net Realized Capital Gains ($)	–	–	–	–	–	–
Net Asset Value End of Year ($)	–	–	–	–	10.09	10.99
Ratio of Expenses to Net Assets (%)	–	–	–	–	.60	.60
Portfolio Turnover Rate (%)	–	–	–	–	–	23
Total Assets: End of Year (Millions $)	–	–	–	–	5.1	93.7
Annual Rate of Return (%) Years Ending 12/31	–	–	–	–	–	17.0

Distr: Income: Monthly
Capital Gains: Annually
Minimum: Initial: $2,500
Subsequent: $250

Telephone Exchange: Yes
With MMF: Yes
Registered In: MN
12b-1: Yes **Amount:** Pd. by Advisor

FIDELITY MUNICIPAL

Fidelity Investments Company
82 Devonshire St.
Boston, MA 02109
(800) 544-6666/(617) 523-1919

	Years Ending 12/31					
	1981	**1982**	**1983**	**1984**	**1985**	**1986**
Dividends from Net Investment Income ($)	.61	.62	.60	.59	.58	.55
Distributions from Net Realized Capital Gains ($)	–	–	–	–	–	–
Net Asset Value End of Year ($)	5.32	6.71	6.72	6.70	7.42	8.28
Ratio of Expenses to Net Assets (%)	.60	.62	.59	.53	.46	.51
Portfolio Turnover Rate (%)	138	95	52	93	145	72
Total Assets: End of Year (Millions $)	326.2	634.6	703.5	741.2	905.8	1,141.3
Annual Rate of Return (%) Years Ending 12/31	(10.2)	39.7	9.3	9.0	20.1	19.5

Distr: Income: Monthly
Capital Gains: Annually
Minimum: Initial: $2,500
Subsequent: $250

Telephone Exchange: Yes
With MMF: Yes
Registered In: All states
12b-1: No

FIDELITY NEW YORK TAX-FREE HIGH YIELD

Fidelity Investments, Co.
82 Devonshire St.
Boston, MA 02109
(800) 544-6666/(617) 523-1919

	Years Ending 4/30					
	1981	1982	1983	1984	1985 (10 mos.)	1986
Dividends from Net Investment Income ($)	–	–	–	–	.74	.89
Distributions from Net Realized Capital Gains ($)	–	–	–	–	–	–
Net Asset Value End of Year ($)	–	–	–	–	10.69	11.98
Ratio of Expenses to Net Assets (%)	–	–	–	–	1.00	.67
Portfolio Turnover Rate (%)	–	–	–	–	8	62
Total Assets: End of Year (Millions $)	–	–	–	–	28.0	202.7
Annual Rate of Return (%) Years Ending 12/31	–	–	–	–	20.8	16.8

Distr: Income: Monthly
    Capital Gains: Annually
Minimum: Initial: $2,500
    Subsequent: $250

Telephone Exchange: Yes
    With MMF: Yes
Registered In: NY
12b-1: No

FIDELITY NEW YORK TAX-FREE INSURED

Fidelity Investments, Co.
82 Devonshire St.
Boston, MA 02109
(800) 544-6666/(617) 523-1919

	Years Ending 4/30					
	1981	1982	1983	1984	1985	1986 (7 mos.)
Dividends from Net Investment Income ($)	–	–	–	–	–	.41
Distributions from Net Realized Capital Gains ($)	–	–	–	–	–	–
Net Asset Value End of Year ($)	–	–	–	–	–	10.96
Ratio of Expenses to Net Assets (%)	–	–	–	–	–	.60
Portfolio Turnover Rate (%)	–	–	–	–	–	8
Total Assets: End of Year (Millions $)	–	–	–	–	–	63.9
Annual Rate of Return (%) Years Ending 12/31	–	–	–	–	–	17.3

Distr: Income: Monthly
    Capital Gains: Annually
Minimum: Initial: $2,500
    Subsequent: $250

Telephone Exchange: Yes
    With MMF: Yes
Registered In: NY
12b-1: No

FIDELITY OHIO
TAX FREE

Fidelity Investments, Co.
82 Devonshire St.
Boston, MA 02109
(800) 544-6666/(617) 523-1919

	Years Ending 12/31					
	1981	1982	1983	1984	1985 (2 mos.)	1986
Dividends from Net Investment Income ($)	—	—	—	—	.09	.77
Distributions from Net Realized Capital Gains ($)	—	—	—	—	—	—
Net Asset Value End of Year ($)	—	—	—	—	10.12	10.97
Ratio of Expenses to Net Assets (%)	—	—	—	—	.60	.60
Portfolio Turnover Rate (%)	—	—	—	—	54	32
Total Assets: End of Year (Millions $)	—	—	—	—	4.4	107.1
Annual Rate of Return (%) Years Ending 12/31	—	—	—	—	—	16.4

Distr: Income: Monthly
    Capital Gains: Annually
Minimum: Initial: $2,500
    Subsequent: $250

Telephone Exchange: Yes
    With MMF: Yes
Registered In: OH
12b-1: Yes **Amount:** Pd. by Advisor

FINANCIAL TAX-FREE
INCOME SHARES

Financial Programs, Inc.
PO Box 2040
Denver, CO 80201
(800) 525-8085/(303) 779-1233

	Years Ending 6/30					
	1981	1982	1983	1984	1985	1986
Dividends from Net Investment Income ($)	—	1.21	1.31	1.24	1.27	1.21
Distributions from Net Realized Capital Gains ($)	—	.03	.15	.08	.70	.80
Net Asset Value End of Year ($)	—	12.46	14.47	13.07	14.32	15.20
Ratio of Expenses to Net Assets (%)	—	.40	.56	.59	.65	.68
Portfolio Turnover Rate (%)	—	56	52	88	156	92
Total Assets: End of Year (Millions $)	—	21.2	61.7	60.3	85.5	108.5
Annual Rate of Return (%) Years Ending 12/31	—	34.6	8.0	9.1	22.9	22.1

Distr: Income: Monthly
    Capital Gains: July
Minimum: Initial: $250
    Subsequent: $50

Telephone Exchange: Yes
    With MMF: Yes
Registered In: All states
12b-1: No

GIT TAX-FREE HIGH YIELD

Bankers Finance Investment Management
1655 N. Fort Myer Dr.
Arlington, VA 22209
(800) 336-3063/(703) 528-6500

		Years E	nding 9/30			
	1981	1982	1983 (10 mos.)	1984	1985	1986
Dividends from Net Investment Income ($)	–	–	.81	.89	.89	.86
Distributions from Net Realized Capital Gains ($)	–	–	–	–	–	.81
Net Asset Value End of Year ($)	–	–	10.32	9.87	10.49	11.20
Ratio of Expenses to Net Assets (%)	–	–	0.95	1.14	1.29	1.16
Portfolio Turnover Rate (%)	–	–	222	252	173	117
Total Assets: End of Year (Millions $)	–	–	25.4	27.1	34.3	43.2
Annual Rate of Return (%) Years Ending 12/31	–	–	–	9.8	19.2	19.4

Distr: Income: Monthly
    Capital Gains: Oct
Minimum: Initial: $2,000
    Subsequent: None

Telephone Exchange: Yes
    With MMF: Yes
Registered In: All states except IN, LA, MT, NH, OK
12b-1: Yes **Amount:** 1.00%

KENTUCKY TAX-FREE INCOME

Dupree & Co.
167 W. Main St.
Lexington, KY 40507
(800) 432-9518/(606) 254-7741

		Years Ending 6/30				
	1981	1982	1983	1984	1985	1986
Dividends from Net Investment Income ($)	.63	.61	.58	.58	.57	.55
Distributions from Net Realized Capital Gains ($)	–	–	–	–	–	–
Net Asset Value End of Year ($)	6.63	5.56	6.26	6.01	6.38	6.62
Ratio of Expenses to Net Assets (%)	.75	.81	.79	.81	.76	.78
Portfolio Turnover Rate (%)	58	152	59	57	30	28
Total Assets: End of Year (Millions $)	4.5	3.2	6.9	10.0	19.4	36.3
Annual Rate of Return (%) Years Ending 12/31	(7.4)	17.3	12.2	8.1	15.8	16.9

Distr: Income: Mar, June, Sep, Dec
    Capital Gains: Annually
Minimum: Initial: $2,500
    Subsequent: $100

Telephone Exchange: No
Registered In: KY
12b-1: No

NEW YORK MUNI

New York Muni Fund, Inc.
One World Trade Ctr., #8407
New York, NY 10048
(800) 528-6050/(212) 775-0043

	Years Ending 12/31					
	1981 (8 mos.)	1982	1983	1984	1985	1986
Dividends from Net Investment Income ($)	.07	.08	.09	.08	.09	.09
Distributions from Net Realized Capital Gains ($)	–	–	–	–	–	.06
Net Asset Value End of Year ($)	.94	1.04	1.07	1.07	1.19	1.25
Ratio of Expenses to Net Assets (%)	1.41	1.92	1.53	1.62	1.60	1.48
Portfolio Turnover Rate (%)	54	71	109	157	424	334
Total Assets: End of Year (Millions $)	3.5	14.4	79.4	129.2	174.4	261.2
Annual Rate of Return (%) Years Ending 12/31	–	NA	NA	8.1	20.3	17.7

Distr: Income: Monthly
    Capital Gains: Dec
Minimum: Initial: $1,000
    Subsequent: $100

Telephone Exchange: No
Registered In: CT, FL, NJ, NY, PA
12b-1: Yes **Amount:** .50%

PACIFIC HORIZON CALIFORNIA TAX-EXEMPT BOND

Pacific Horizon Funds
3550 Wilshire Blvd., Suite 1408
Los Angeles, CA 90010
(800) 645-3515

	Years Ending 2/28					
	1981	1982	1983	1984	1985 (11 mos.)	1986
Dividends from Net Investment Income ($)	–	–	–	–	1.02	1.04
Distributions from Net Realized Capital Gains ($)	–	–	–	–	–	–
Net Asset Value End of Year ($)	–	–	–	–	12.25	14.13
Ratio of Expenses to Net Assets (%)	–	–	–	–	.54	.99
Portfolio Turnover Rate (%)	–	–	–	–	144	42
Total Assets: End of Year (Millions $)	–	–	–	–	20.3	66.3
Annual Rate of Return (%) Years Ending 12/31	–	–	–	–	18.3	18.3

Distr: Income: Monthly
    Capital Gains: Annually
Minimum: Initial: $1,000
    Subsequent: $100

Telephone Exchange: Yes
    With MMF: Yes
Registered In: AR, CA, CO, HI, ID,
MT, NJ, NM, NV, OR, UT, WA,
WY
12b-1: Yes **Amount:** .10%

PARK AVENUE NEW YORK TAX EXEMPT—
Intermediate

Park Ave. N.Y. Tax Exempt
Intermediate Bond Fund,
Inc.
600 Madison Ave.
New York, NY 10022
(800) 848-4350/(718) 895-1219

	Years Ending 10/31					
	1981	1982	1983	1984	1985 (11 mos.)	1986
Dividends from Net Investment Income ($)	–	–	–	–	1.22	1.19
Distributions from Net Realized Capital Gains ($)	–	–	–	–	–	–
Net Asset Value End of Year ($)	–	–	–	–	17.39	18.97
Ratio of Expenses to Net Assets (%)	–	–	–	–	.21	.46
Portfolio Turnover Rate (%)	–	–	–	–	32	38
Total Assets: End of Year (Millions $)	–	–	–	–	13.9	57.0
Annual Rate of Return (%) Years Ending 12/31	–	–	–	–	14.9	14.2

Distr: Income: Monthly
　　　Capital Gains: Annually
Minimum: Initial: $2,500
　　　Subsequent: $100

Telephone Exchange: Yes
　　　With MMF: Yes
Registered In: CT, FL, NJ, NY
12b-1: Yes **Amount:** .20%

T. ROWE PRICE TAX-FREE HIGH YIELD

T. Rowe Price Associates, Inc.
100 East Pratt St.
Baltimore, MD 21202
(800) 638-5660/(301) 547-2308

	Years Ending 2/28					
	1981	1982	1983	1984	1985	1986
Dividends from Net Investment Income ($)	–	–	–	–	–	.87
Distributions from Net Realized Capital Gains ($)	–	–	–	–	–	–
Net Asset Value End of Year ($)	–	–	–	–	–	11.43
Ratio of Expenses to Net Assets (%)	–	–	–	–	–	1.00
Portfolio Turnover Rate (%)	–	–	–	–	–	157
Total Assets: End of Year (Millions $)	–	–	–	–	–	168.2
Annual Rate of Return (%) Years Ending 12/31	–	–	–	–	–	20.4

Distr: Income: Monthly
　　　Capital Gains: Annually
Minimum: Initial: $1,000
　　　Subsequent: $100

Telephone Exchange: Yes
　　　With MMF: Yes
Registered In: All states
12b-1: No

T. ROWE PRICE TAX-FREE INCOME

T. Rowe Price Associates
100 E. Pratt St.
Baltimore, MD 21202
(800) 638-5660/(301) 547-2308

	Years Ending 12/31			2/28		
	1980	1981	1982	1984*	1985	1986
Dividends from Net Investment Income ($)	.67	.73	.80	.72	.65	.71
Distributions from Net Realized Capital Gains ($)	—	—	—	—	—	—
Net Asset Value End of Year ($)	8.06	7.26	8.58	8.48	8.41	9.73
Ratio of Expenses to Net Assets (%)	.71	.71	.65	.66	.63	.63
Portfolio Turnover Rate (%)	132	136	224	221	277	188
Total Assets: End of Year (Millions $)	256.0	265.9	673.3	962.4	937.3	1,325.7

* *Year-end changed to Feb. 28. Data missing for 2 months: Jan. & Feb. 1983.*

Annual Rate of Return (%) Years Ending 12/31	(5.3)	(0.9)	30.8	7.1	16.9	19.8

Distr: Income: Monthly
 Capital Gains: Mar
Minimum: Initial: $1,000
 Subsequent: $100

Telephone Exchange: Yes
 With MMF: Yes
Registered In: All states
12b-1: No

T. ROWE PRICE TAX FREE SHORT INTERMEDIATE

T. Rowe Price Associates
100 E. Pratt Street
Baltimore, MD 21202
(800) 638-5660/(301) 547-2308

	Years Ending 2/28					
	1981	1982	1983	1984 (2 mos.)	1985	1986
Dividends from Net Investment Income ($)	—	—	—	.06	.32	.32
Distributions from Net Realized Capital Gains ($)	—	—	—	—	—	—
Net Asset Value End of Year ($)	—	—	—	4.97	5.02	5.20
Ratio of Expenses to Net Assets (%)	—	—	—	.90	.90	.90
Portfolio Turnover Rate (%)	—	—	—	111	301	129
Total Assets: End of Year (Millions $)	—	—	—	23.5	68.0	155.5

Annual Rate of Return (%) Years Ending 12/31	—	—	—	6.2	8.9	9.7

Distr: Income: Monthly
 Capital Gains: Annually
Minimum: Initial: $1,000
 Subsequent: $100

Telephone Exchange: Yes
 With MMF: Yes
Registered In: All states
12b-1: No

SAFECO CALIFORNIA TAX-FREE INCOME

Safeco Asset Management Co.
Safeco Plaza
Seattle, WA 98185
(800) 426-6730/(206) 545-5530

	Years Ending 3/31					
	1981	1982	1983	1984 (8 mos.)	1985	1986
Dividends from Net Investment Income ($)	–	–	–	.54	.78	.84
Distributions from Net Realized Capital Gains ($)	–	–	–	–	–	–
Net Asset Value End of Year ($)	–	–	–	9.90	9.99	11.68
Ratio of Expenses to Net Assets (%)	–	–	–	.90	.77	.76
Portfolio Turnover Rate (%)	–	–	–	44	23	41
Total Assets: End of Year (Millions $)	–	–	–	8.1	11.5	21.1
Annual Rate of Return (%) Years Ending 12/31	–	–	–	7.6	21.0	19.7

Distr: Income: Monthly
    Capital Gains: Annually
Minimum: Initial: $2,500
    Subsequent: $250

Telephone Exchange: Yes
    With MMF: Yes
Registered In: CA
12b-1: No

SAFECO MUNICIPAL

Safeco Asset Management Co.
Safeco Plaza
Seattle, WA 98185
(800) 426-6730/(206) 545-5530

	Years Ending 3/31					
	1981	1982	1983	1984	1985	1986
Dividends from Net Investment Income ($)	–	.53	1.05	1.05	1.07	1.06
Distributions from Net Realized Capital Gains ($)	–	–	–	–	–	.02
Net Asset Value End of Year ($)	–	9.36	11.87	11.38	11.69	13.74
Ratio of Expenses to Net Assets (%)	–	1.03	.72	.64	.63	.63
Portfolio Turnover Rate (%)	–	99	40	92	47	21
Total Assets: End of Year (Millions $)	–	4.9	22.6	50.6	84.3	161.0
Annual Rate of Return (%) Years Ending 12/31	–	42.1	10.4	10.1	21.4	19.8

Distr: Income: Monthly
    Capital Gains: Annually
Minimum: Initial: $2,500
    Subsequent: $250

Telephone Exchange: Yes
    With MMF: Yes
Registered In: All states except ME, NH, VT
12b-1: No

SCUDDER CALIFORNIA TAX FREE

Scudder, Stevens & Clark
175 Federal St.
Boston, MA 02110
(800) 453-3305/(617) 426-8300

	Years Ending 3/31					
	1981	1982	1983	1984 (8 mos.)	1985	1986
Dividends from Net Investment Income ($)	–	–	–	.50	.80	.73
Distributions from Net Realized Capital Gains ($)	–	–	–	–	–	–
Net Asset Value End of Year ($)	–	–	–	9.61	9.54	10.95
Ratio of Expenses to Net Assets (%)	–	–	–	1.00	.99	.88
Portfolio Turnover Rate (%)	–	–	–	92	168	267
Total Assets: End of Year (Millions $)	–	–	–	38.2	73.1	132.8
Annual Rate of Return (%) Years Ending 12/31	–	–	–	–	18.4	16.8

Distr: Income: Monthly
    Capital Gains: April
Minimum: Initial: $1,000
    Subsequent: None

Telephone Exchange: Yes
    With MMF: Yes
Registered In: CA
12b-1: No

SCUDDER MANAGED MUNICIPAL

Scudder, Stevens & Clark
175 Federal St.
Boston, MA 02110
(800) 453-3305/(617) 426-8300

	Years Ending 12/31					
	1981	1982	1983	1984	1985	1986
Dividends from Net Investment Income ($)	.70	.73	.70	.70	.59	.61
Distributions from Net Realized Capital Gains ($)	–	–	–	–	–	.24
Net Asset Value End of Year ($)	5.97	7.69	7.67	7.69	8.40	8.93
Ratio of Expenses to Net Assets (%)	.69	.65	.65	.61	.58	.58
Portfolio Turnover Rate (%)	213	146	83	120	98	78
Total Assets: End of Year (Millions $)	109.0	292.8	479.2	545.1	574.6	662.4
Annual Rate of Return (%) Years Ending 12/31	(10.8)	43.2	9.1	10.2	17.5	16.8

Distr: Income: Monthly
    Capital Gains: Feb
Minimum: Initial: $1,000
    Subsequent: None

Telephone Exchange: Yes
    With MMF: Yes
Registered In: All states
12b-1: No

SCUDDER NEW YORK TAX FREE

Scudder, Stevens & Clark
175 Federal St.
Boston, MA 02110
(800) 453-3305/(617) 426-8300

	Years Ending 3/31					
	1981	1982	1983	1984 (8 mos.)	1985	1986
Dividends from Net Investment Income ($)	—	—	—	.52	.83	.75
Distributions from Net Realized Capital Gains ($)	—	—	—	—	—	—
Net Asset Value End of Year ($)	—	—	—	9.97	10.11	11.19
Ratio of Expenses to Net Assets (%)	—	—	—	1.00	1.01	.88
Portfolio Turnover Rate (%)	—	—	—	1.51	167	40
Total Assets: End of Year (Millions $)	—	—	—	27.7	61.6	102
Annual Rate of Return (%) Years Ending 12/31	—	—	—	—	16.0	14.1

Distr: Income: Monthly
Capital Gains: April
Minimum: Initial: $1,000
Subsequent: None

Telephone Exchange: Yes
With MMF: Yes
Registered In: NY
12b-1: No

SCUDDER TAX FREE TARGET 1987

Scudder, Stevens & Clark
175 Federal Street
Boston, MA 02110
(800) 225-2470/(617) 482-3990

	Years Ending 12/31					
	1981	1982	1983 (9 mos.)	1984	1985	1986
Dividends from Net Investment Income ($)	—	—	.40	.63	.58	.52
Distributions from Net Realized Capital Gains ($)	—	—	—	—	—	.08
Net Asset Value End of Year ($)	—	—	9.70	9.88	9.99	10.03
Ratio of Expenses to Net Assets (%)	—	—	1.00	.93	.98	.94
Portfolio Turnover Rate (%)	—	—	90	112	158	37
Total Assets: End of Year (Millions $)	—	—	8.5	16.3	30.5	35.6
Annual Rate of Return (%) Years Ending 12/31	—	—	—	8.6	7.2	6.6

Distr: Income: Monthly
Capital Gains: Annually
Minimum: Initial: $1,000
Subsequent: None

Telephone Exchange: Yes
With MMF: Yes
Registered In: All states
12b-1: No

SCUDDER TAX FREE TARGET 1990

Scudder, Stevens & Clark
175 Federal Street
Boston, MA 02110
(800) 225-2470/(617) 482-3990

		Years Ending 12/31			
	1981	**1982**	**1983** (9 mos.)	**1984**	**1985**	**1986**
Dividends from Net Investment Income ($)	—	—	.45	.73	.68	.62
Distributions from Net Realized Capital Gains ($)	—	—	—	—	—	.10
Net Asset Value End of Year ($)	—	—	9.65	9.67	10.03	10.34
Ratio of Expenses to Net Assets (%)	—	—	1.00	.83	.85	.82
Portfolio Turnover Rate (%)	—	—	97	96	132	44
Total Assets: End of Year (Millions $)	—	—	13.5	30.8	59.1	104.0
Annual Rate of Return (%) Years Ending 12/31	—	—	—	8.0	11.1	10.5

Distr: Income: Monthly
Capital Gains: Annually
Minimum: Initial: $1,000
Subsequent: None

Telephone Exchange: Yes
With MMF: Yes
Registered In: All states
12b-1: No

SCUDDER TAX FREE TARGET 1993

Scudder, Stevens & Clark
175 Federal Street
Boston, MA 02110
(800) 225-2470/(617) 482-3990

		Years Ending 12/31			
	1981	**1982**	**1983** (9 mos.)	**1984**	**1985**	**1986**
Dividends from Net Investment Income ($)	—	—	.49	.80	.75	.67
Distributions from Net Realized Capital Gains ($)	—	—	—	—	—	.23
Net Asset Value End of Year ($)	—	—	9.95	9.95	10.59	11.04
Ratio of Expenses to Net Assets (%)	—	—	1.00	.89	.86	.81
Portfolio Turnover Rate (%)	—	—	190	78	265	80
Total Assets: End of Year (Millions $)	—	—	9.5	23.7	55.2	118.8
Annual Rate of Return (%) Years Ending 12/31	—	—	—	8.3	14.5	13.2

Distr: Income: Monthly
Capital Gains: Annually
Minimum: Initial: $1,000
Subsequent: None

Telephone Exchange: Yes
With MMF: Yes
Registered In: All states
12b-1: No

STEINROE HIGH-YIELD MUNICIPALS

Stein Roe & Farnham
PO Box 1143
Chicago, IL 60690
(800) 621-0320/(312) 368-7826

	Years Ending 12/31					
	1981	1982	1983	1984 (10 mos.)	1985	1986
Dividends from Net Investment Income ($)	−	−	−	.73	.94	.90
Distributions from Net Realized Capital Gains ($)	−	−	−	−	−	.15
Net Asset Value End of Year ($)	−	−	−	10.02	11.10	12.06
Ratio of Expenses to Net Assets (%)	−	−	−	1.43	.81	.76
Portfolio Turnover Rate (%)	−	−	−	68	46	34
Total Assets: End of Year (Millions $)	−	−	−	32.8	99.8	225.9
Annual Rate of Return (%) Years Ending 12/31	−	−	−	−	20.9	19.0

Distr: Income: Quarterly
    Capital Gains: Annually
Minimum: Initial: $2,500
    Subsequent: $100

Telephone Exchange: Yes
    With MMF: Yes
Registered In: All states except NH
12b-1: No

STEINROE INTERMEDIATE MUNICIPALS

SteinRoe & Farnham
PO Box 1143
Chicago, IL 60690
(800) 621-0320/(312) 368-7826

	Years Ending 12/31					
	1981	1982	1983	1984	1985 (3 mos.)	1986
Dividends from Net Investment Income ($)	−	−	−	−	.12	.58
Distributions from Net Realized Capital Gains ($)	−	−	−	−	−	−
Net Asset Value End of Year ($)	−	−	−	−	10.14	10.76
Ratio of Expenses to Net Assets (%)	−	−	−	−	2.38	.94
Portfolio Turnover Rate (%)	−	−	−	−	−	10
Total Assets: End of Year (Millions $)	−	−	−	−	23.0	104.7
Annual Rate of Return (%) Years Ending 12/31	−	−	−	−	−	12.1

Distr: Income: Quarterly
    Capital Gains: Annually
Minimum: Initial: $2,500
    Subsequent: $100

Telephone Exchange: Yes
    With MMF: Yes
Registered In: All states except NH
12b-1: No

STEINROE MANAGED MUNICIPALS

Stein Roe & Farnham
PO Box 1143
Chicago, IL 60690
(800) 621-0320/(312) 368-7826

	Years Ending 12/31					
	1981	1982	1983	1984	1985	1986
Dividends from Net Investment Income ($)	.68	.68	.64	.67	.68	.67
Distributions from Net Realized Capital Gains ($)	–	–	–	–	.03	.92
Net Asset Value End of Year ($)	5.75	7.56	7.71	7.89	8.93	9.22
Ratio of Expenses to Net Assets (%)	.85	.75	.65	.64	.65	.65
Portfolio Turnover Rate (%)	111	166	114	190	113	92
Total Assets: End of Year (Millions $)	42.9	142.6	214.9	242.8	357.2	524.0
Annual Rate of Return (%) Years Ending 12/31	(7.8)	46.0	10.8	11.2	22.8	21.7

Distr: Income: Quarterly
  Capital Gains: Annually
Minimum: Initial: $2,500
  Subsequent: $100

Telephone Exchange: Yes
  With MMF: Yes
Registered In: All states except NH
12b-1: No

UNIFIED MUNICIPAL– GENERAL SERIES

Unified Management
Corporation
Guaranty Building
Indianapolis, IN 46204-3057
(800) 862-7283/(317) 634-3300

	Years Ending 4/30					
	1981	1982	1983	1984	1985 (1 mo.)	1986
Dividends from Net Investment Income ($)	–	–	–	–	–	.58
Distributions from Net Realized Capital Gains ($)	–	–	–	–	–	.02
Net Asset Value End of Year ($)	–	–	–	–	7.88	8.77
Ratio of Expenses to Net Assets (%)	–	–	–	–	–	1.24
Portfolio Turnover Rate (%)	–	–	–	–	–	19
Total Assets: End of Year (Millions $)	–	–	–	–	4.0	5.4
Annual Rate of Return (%) Years Ending 12/31	–	–	–	–	–	18.3

Distr: Income: April, October
  Capital Gains: April
Minimum: Initial: $1,000
  Subsequent: $25

Telephone Exchange: Yes
  With MMF: Yes
Registered In: All states
12b-1: No

UNIFIED MUNICIPAL– INDIANA SERIES

Unified Management Corporation
Guaranty Building
Indianapolis, IN 46204-3057
(800) 862-7283/(317) 634-3300

	Years Ending 4/30					
	1981	1982	1983	1984	1985 (1 mo.)	1986
Dividends from Net Investment Income ($)	–	–	–	–	–	.49
Distributions from Net Realized Capital Gains ($)	–	–	–	–	–	–
Net Asset Value End of Year ($)	–	–	–	–	7.91	8.77
Ratio of Expenses to Net Assets (%)	–	–	–	–	–	1.18
Portfolio Turnover Rate (%)	–	–	–	–	–	17
Total Assets: End of Year (Millions $)	–	–	–	–	3.8	8.0
Annual Rate of Return (%) Years Ending 12/31	–	–	–	–	–	19.0

Distr: Income: April, October
    Capital Gains: April
Minimum: Initial: $1,000
    Subsequent: $25

Telephone Exchange: Yes
    With MMF: Yes
Registered In: All states
12b-1: No

USAA TAX EXEMPT
High-Yield

USAA Investment Mgmt. Co.
9800 Fredericksburg Rd.
San Antonio, TX 78288
(800) 531-8000/(512) 498-8000

	Years Ending 3/31					
	1981	1982 (4 mos.)	1983	1984	1985	1986
Dividends from Net Investment Income ($)	–	–	1.40	1.08	1.13	1.13
Distributions from Net Realized Capital Gains ($)	–	–	–	–	–	–
Net Asset Value End of Year ($)	–	10.38	12.02	11.76	11.88	13.52
Ratio of Expenses to Net Assets (%)	–	1.29	1.09	.68	.56	.50
Portfolio Turnover Rate (%)	–	15	18	64	150	122
Total Assets: End of Year (Millions $)	–	3.2	50.3	148.2	272.8	648.0
Annual Rate of Return (%) Years Ending 12/31	–	–	11.3	10.2	19.7	17.2

Distr: Income: Mar, June, Sep, Dec
    Capital Gains: April
Minimum: Initial: $3,000
    Subsequent: $100

Telephone Exchange: Yes
    With MMF: Yes
Registered In: All states
12b-1: No

Tax-Exempt Bond Funds **335**

USAA TAX EXEMPT
Intermediate-Term

USAA Investment Mgmt. Co.
9800 Fredericksburg Rd.
San Antonio, TX 78288
(800) 531-8000/(512) 498-8000

	1981	1982 (4 mos.)	1983	1984	1985	1986
Years Ending 3/31						
Dividends from Net Investment Income ($)	—	—	1.25	.98	1.00	.98
Distributions from Net Realized Capital Gains ($)	—	—	—	—	—	—
Net Asset Value End of Year ($)	—	10.24	11.39	11.15	11.19	12.27
Ratio of Expenses to Net Assets (%)	—	1.24	1.18	.73	.64	.57
Portfolio Turnover Rate (%)	—	—	38	49	127	80
Total Assets: End of Year (Millions $)	—	3.1	33.5	70.1	107.3	201.3
Annual Rate of Return (%) Years Ending 12/31	—	—	9.6	8.8	16.3	13.2

Distr: Income: Mar, June, Sep, Dec
   Capital Gains: April
Minimum: Initial: $3,000
   Subsequent: $100

Telephone Exchange: Yes
   With MMF: Yes
Registered In: All states
12b-1: No

USAA TAX EXEMPT
Short-Term

USAA Investment Mgmt. Co.
9800 Fredericksburg Rd.
San Antonio, TX 78288
(800) 531-8000/(512) 498-8000

	1981	1982 (4 mos.)	1983	1984	1985	1986
Years Ending 3/31						
Dividends from Net Investment Income ($)	—	—	1.01	.68	.74	.72
Distributions from Net Realized Capital Gains ($)	—	—	—	—	—	—
Net Asset Value End of Year ($)	—	10.24	10.35	10.27	10.36	10.66
Ratio of Expenses to Net Assets (%)	—	1.26	1.15	.85	.70	.65
Portfolio Turnover Rate (%)	—	—	57	56	159	101
Total Assets: End of Year (Millions $)	—	3.1	20.5	62.2	85.2	139.3
Annual Rate of Return (%) Years Ending 12/31	—	—	6.3	7.6	9.5	8.7

Distr: Income: Mar, June, Sep, Dec
   Capital Gains: April
Minimum: Initial: $3,000
   Subsequent: $100

Telephone Exchange: Yes
   With MMF: Yes
Registered In: All states
12b-1: No

VALUE LINE
TAX EXEMPT
High Yield

Value Line Securities
711 Third Ave.
New York, NY 10017
(800) 223-0818/(212) 687-3965

	Years Ending 2/28					
	1981	**1982**	**1983**	**1984**	**1985** (11 mos.)	**1986**
Dividends from Net Investment Income ($)	–	–	–	–	.94	.98
Distributions from Net Realized Capital Gains ($)	–	–	–	–	–	.02
Net Asset Value End of Year ($)	–	–	–	–	9.97	11.12
Ratio of Expenses to Net Assets (%)	–	–	–	–	.17	.66
Portfolio Turnover Rate (%)	–	–	–	–	187	254
Total Assets: End of Year (Millions $)	–	–	–	–	36.8	133.9
Annual Rate of Return (%) Years Ending 12/31	–	–	–	–	19.3	13.4

Distr: Income: Monthly
    Capital Gains: Annually
Minimum: Initial: $1,000
    Subsequent: $250

Telephone Exchange: Yes
    With MMF: Yes
Registered In: All states
12b-1: No

VANGUARD
HIGH-YIELD
MUNICIPAL BOND

Vanguard Group
Vanguard Financial Ctr.
Valley Forge, PA 19482
(800) 662-7447/(215) 648-6000

	Years Ending 8/31					
	1981	**1982**	**1983**	**1984**	**1985**	**1986**
Dividends from Net Investment Income ($)	.88	.91	.85	.87	.87	.85
Distributions from Net Realized Capital Gains ($)	–	–	–	–	–	.39
Net Asset Value End of Year ($)	7.55	8.44	9.03	8.94	9.56	10.55
Ratio of Expenses to Net Assets (%)	.47	.48	.46	.41	.39	.33
Portfolio Turnover Rate (%)	148	207	206	90	41	38
Total Assets: End of Year (Millions $)	31.8	71.4	156.2	238.9	451.9	794.1
Annual Rate of Return (%) Years Ending 12/31	(8.8)	35.9	10.4	9.7	21.7	19.7

Distr: Income: Monthly
    Capital Gains: Annually
Minimum: Initial: $3,000
    Subsequent: $100

Telephone Exchange: Yes
    With MMF: Yes
Registered In: All states
12b-1: No

Tax-Exempt Bond Funds **337**

VANGUARD INTERMEDIATE-TERM MUNICIPAL BOND

Vanguard Group
Vanguard Financial Ctr.
Valley Forge, PA 19482
(800) 662-7447/(215) 648-6000

| | Years Ending 8/31 | | | | | |
	1981	1982	1983	1984	1985	1986
Dividends from Net Investment Income ($)	.86	.91	.87	.90	.92	.89
Distributions from Net Realized Capital Gains ($)	—	—	—	—	—	.02
Net Asset Value End of Year ($)	9.05	10.14	10.54	10.44	10.98	12.15
Ratio of Expenses to Net Assets (%)	.47	.48	.46	.41	.39	.33
Portfolio Turnover Rate (%)	110	107	117	55	26	13
Total Assets: End of Year (Millions $)	22.9	49.1	150.1	209.1	411.8	811.8
Annual Rate of Return (%) Years Ending 12/31	(7.4)	31.1	6.5	9.5	17.3	16.2

Distr: Income: Monthly
Capital Gains: Annually
Minimum: Initial: $3,000
Subsequent: $100

Telephone Exchange: Yes
With MMF: Yes
Registered In: All states
12b-1: No

VANGUARD LONG-TERM MUNICIPAL BOND

Vanguard Group
Vanguard Financial Ctr.
Valley Forge, PA 19482
(800) 662-7447/(215) 648-6000

| | Years Ending 8/31 | | | | | |
	1981	1982	1983	1984	1985	1986
Dividends from Net Investment Income ($)	.88	.88	.84	.86	.87	.85
Distributions from Net Realized Capital Gains ($)	—	—	—	—	—	.19
Net Asset Value End of Year ($)	7.66	8.78	9.32	9.17	9.79	10.97
Ratio of Expenses to Net Assets (%)	.47	.48	.46	.41	.39	.33
Portfolio Turnover Rate (%)	130	191	211	99	72	32
Total Assets: End of Year (Millions $)	59.1	120.4	230.6	290.0	410.7	627.7
Annual Rate of Return (%) Years Ending 12/31	(11.2)	38.5	9.5	8.5	20.8	19.4

Distr: Income: Monthly
Capital Gains: Annually
Minimum: Initial: $3,000
Subsequent: $100

Telephone Exchange: Yes
With MMF: Yes
Registered In: All states
12b-1: No

VANGUARD
MUNICIPAL BOND
Insured Long-Term

Vanguard Group
Vanguard Financial Center
Valley Forge, PA 19482
(800) 662-7447/(215) 648-6000

			Years Ending 8/31			
	1981	1982	1983	1984	1985 (10 mos.)	1986
Dividends from Net Investment Income ($)	–	–	–	–	.83	.90
Distributions from Net Realized Capital Gains ($)	–	–	–	–	–	.17
Net Asset Value End of Year ($)	–	–	–	–	10.50	11.73
Ratio of Expenses to Net Assets (%)	–	–	–	–	.36	.33
Portfolio Turnover Rate (%)	–	–	–	–	16	20
Total Assets: End of Year (Millions $)	–	–	–	–	336.0	709.3
Annual Rate of Return (%) Years Ending 12/31	–	–	–	–	19.3	18.7

Distr: Income: Monthly
    Capital Gains: Annually
Minimum: Initial: $3,000
    Subsequent: $100

Telephone Exchange: Yes
    With MMF: Yes
Registered In: All states
12b-1: No

VANGUARD
SHORT-TERM
MUNICIPAL BOND

Vanguard Group
Vanguard Financial Ctr.
Valley Forge, PA 19482
(800) 662-7447/(215) 648-6000

			Years Ending 8/31			
	1981	1982	1983	1984	1985	1986
Dividends from Net Investment Income ($)	.91	1.16	.95	.92	.99	.90
Distributions from Net Realized Capital Gains ($)	–	–	–	–	–	.01
Net Asset Value End of Year ($)	14.80	15.18	15.15	15.08	15.24	15.39
Ratio of Expenses to Net Assets (%)	.47	.48	.46	.41	.39	.33
Portfolio Turnover Rate (%)	192	224	136	102	55	57
Total Assets: End of Year (Millions $)	192.0	179.9	346.8	353.9	536.3	906.1
Annual Rate of Return (%) Years Ending 12/31	8.3	10.1	5.1	6.8	7.0	7.4

Distr: Income: Monthly
    Capital Gains: Annually
Minimum: Initial: $3,000
    Subsequent: $100

Telephone Exchange: Yes
    With MMF: Yes
Registered In: All states
12b-1: No

New Funds

BARTLETT FIXED INCOME

Bond

Bartlett & Company
36 East Fourth Street
Cincinnati, Ohio 45202
(800) 543-0863/(513) 621-0066

Investment Objectives/Policy: Seeks high level of current income. Capital appreciation is of secondary importance. Invests in a broad range of fixed income securities, including U.S. government, corporate and mortgage-backed bonds. May also invest in high-yielding equity securities.
Year First Offered: 1986
Distr: Income: Monthly
    Capital Gains: Annually

Minimum: Initial: $5,000
    Subsequent: $100
Min IRA: Initial: $250
    Subsequent: $50
Investor Services: IRA, Keogh, Corp, 403(b)
Telephone Exchange: Yes
    With MMF: Yes
Registered In: AZ, CA, CO, DC, IN, KY, MA, MI, MN, MO, NY, OH, PA
12b-1: Yes   **Amount:** .25%

BOSTON CO. GNMA

Bond

The Boston Company Advisors
One Boston Place
Boston, MA 02108
(800) 343-6324/(617) 956-9745

Investment Objectives/Policy: Seeks high current income consistent with preservation of capital. Invests in U.S. government backed debt obligations—principally GNMA mortgage backed securities.
Year First Offered: 1986
Distr: Income: Monthly
    Capital Gains: Annually

Minimum: Initial: $1,000
    Subsequent: None
Min IRA: Initial: $500
    Subsequent: None
Investor Services: IRA, Keogh, Corp, Withdraw
Telephone Exchange: Yes
    With MMF: Yes
Registered In: All states
12b-1: Yes   **Amount:** .45%

BULL & BEAR U.S. GOVERNMENT GUARANTEED SECURITIES

Bond

Bull & Bear Advisors
11 Hanover Square
New York, NY 10005
(800) 847-4200/(212) 785-0900

Investment Objectives/Policy: Seeks high level of current income, liquidity, and safety of principal. Invests in U.S. Treasury and government agency securities including bills, notes, bonds, GNMAs, and Federal Housing Administration bonds. Can also write covered call options on securities it owns.
Year First Offered: 1986
Distr: Income: Monthly
    Capital Gains: August

Minimum: Initial: $1,000
    Subsequent: $100
Min IRA: Initial: $100
    Subsequent: $100
Investor Services: IRA, Keogh, SEP, 403(b), Withdraw
Telephone Exchange: Yes
    With MMF: Yes
Registered In: All states except ME
12b-1: Yes   **Amount:** .50%

FIDELITY SHORT TERM BOND

Bond

Fidelity Investments
82 Devonshire Street
Boston, MA 02109
(800) 544-6666/(617) 523-1919

Investment Objectives/Policy: Seeks high level of current income consistent with preservation of capital. Average maturity of portfolio cannot exceed 3 years. Invests in investment-grade fixed-income securities rated BBB or higher by S&P—including government notes, commercial paper and bankers' acceptances.
Year First Offered: 1986
Distr: Income: Monthly
    Capital Gains: Annually

Minimum: Initial: $1,000
    Subsequent: $250
Min IRA: Initial: $500
    Subsequent: $250
Investor Services: IRA, Keogh, 403(b), Corp
Telephone Exchange: Yes
    With MMF: Yes
Registered In: All states except AZ, WI
12b-1: Yes   **Amount:** Pd. by Advisor

FIDELITY TEXAS TAX-FREE

Tax-Exempt

Fidelity Investments
82 Devonshire Street
Boston, MA 02109
(800) 544-6666/(617) 523-1919

Investment Objectives/Policy: Seeks a high level of current income exempt from federal income tax. Invests primarily in Texas municipals. However, the fund may invest up to 20% of its assets in municipal securities issued outside of Texas.
Year First Offered: 1986

Distr: Income: Monthly
    Capital Gains: Annually
Minimum: Initial: $2,500
    Subsequent: $250
Investor Services: Withdraw, Deduct
Telephone Exchange: Yes
    With MMF: Yes
Registered In: TX
12b-1: Yes   **Amount:** Pd. by Advisor

FINANCIAL BOND SHARES—U.S. GOVERNMENT

Bond

Financial Programs, Inc.
PO Box 2040
Denver, CO 80201
(800) 525-8085/(303) 779-1233

Investment Objectives/Policy: Seeks high level of current income by investing in U.S. government and government agency debt obligations. These include bills, notes, bonds and GNMA mortgage-backed securities. May also buy and sell interest rate futures contracts to hedge the portfolio.
Year First Offered: 1986
Distr: Income: Quarterly
    Capital Gains: Annually

Minimum: Initial: $250
    Subsequent: $50
Min IRA: Initial: $250
    Subsequent: $50
Investor Services: IRA, SEP, Corp, Withdraw
Telephone Exchange: Yes
    With MMF: Yes
Registered In: All states except NH
12b-1: No

FINANCIAL STRATEGIC PORTFOLIO— EUROPEAN

International

Financial Programs, Inc.
P.O. Box 2040
Denver, CO 80201
(800) 525-9831/(303) 779-1233

Investment Objectives/Policy: Seeks capital appreciation through investment in foreign securities located on principal exchanges in Europe—including England, France, West Germany and Italy. May enter into forward foreign currency contracts to hedge against exchange rate fluctuations.
Year First Offered: 1986
Distr: Income: Annually
    Capital Gains: Annually

Minimum: Initial: $250
    Subsequent: $50
Min IRA: Initial: $250
    Subsequent: $50
Investor Services: IRA, Keogh, SEP, Corp, 403(h), Withdraw
Telephone Exchange: Yes
    With MMF: Yes
Registered In: All states except AZ, NH
12b-1: No

FINANCIAL STRATEGIC PORTFOLIO— FINANCIAL SERVICES

Aggressive Growth

Financial Programs, Inc.
PO Box 2040
Denver, CO 80201
(800) 525-9831/(303) 779-1233

Investment Objectives/Policy: Seeks capital appreciation through investment in companies in the financial services industry. These include banks, savings and loans, securities brokers and insurance companies.
Year First Offered: 1986
Distr: Income: Annually
    Capital Gains: Annually

Minimum: Initial: $250
    Subsequent: $50
Min IRA: Initial: $250
    Subsequent: $50
Investor Services: IRA, Keogh, SEP, Corp, 403(b), Withdraw
Telephone Exchange: Yes
    With MMF: Yes
Registered In: All states except AZ, NH
12b-1: No

FINANCIAL STRATEGIC PORTFOLIO— UTILITIES

Aggressive Growth

Financial Programs, Inc.
PO Box 2040
Denver, CO 80201
(800) 525-9831/(303) 779-1233

Investment Objectives/Policy: Seeks capital appreciation through investment in public utility companies. These include companies which manufacture, produce, generate, transmit or sell gas or electric energy. Also invests in telephone and other communication utilities.
Year First Offered: 1986
Distr: Income: Annually
    Capital Gains: Annually

Minimum: Initial: $250
    Subsequent: $50
Min IRA: Initial: $250
    Subsequent: $50
Investor Services: IRA, Keogh, SEP, Corp, 403(b), Withdraw
Telephone Exchange: Yes
    With MMF: Yes
Registered In: All states except AZ, NH
12b-1: No

GATEWAY GROWTH PLUS

Growth

Investment Objectives/Policy: Seeks long-term growth of capital with secondary objective of conserving capital. Normally will invest in New York or American Stock Exchange-listed issues which have market capitalizations above $50 million and revenues exceeding $100 million. Can also invest in index options.
Year First Offered: 1986
Distr: Income: Quarterly
    Capital Gains: Annually

Gateway Investment Advisors, Inc.
PO Box 458167
Cincinnati, OH 45245
(800) 354-6339/(513) 248-2700

Minimum: Initial: $500
    Subsequent: $100
Min IRA: Initial: $500
    Subsequent: $100
Investor Services: IRA, SEP, Corp, Withdraw
Telephone Exchange: Yes
    With MMF: No
Registered In: All states
12b-1: No

HARBOR GROWTH

Growth

Investment Objectives/Policy: Primary objective is to achieve long-term growth of capital through investment in common stocks. Uses computer-generated forecasts of earnings and return-on-investment to select above-average growth companies.
Year First Offered: 1986
Distr: Income: Quarterly
    Capital Gains: Annually

Harbor Capital Advisors, Inc.
One SeaGate
Toledo, OH 43666
(419) 247-1940

Minimum: Initial: $2,000
    Subsequent: $500
Min IRA: Initial: $2,000
    Subsequent: $500
Investor Services: IRA, Withdraw
Telephone Exchange: No
Registered In: All states except HI, MO, NE
12b-1: Yes   **Amount:** .25%

IVY INTERNATIONAL FUND

International

Investment Objectives/Policy: Seeks long-term capital appreciation through investment in foreign equity securities, primarily those traded in European and Pacific Basin markets. For defensive purposes the fund may invest in U.S. equity securities. Current income is a secondary objective.
Year First Offered: 1986
Distr: Income: Annually
    Capital Gains: Annually

Hingham Management Inc.
40 Industrial Park Rd.
Hingham, MA 02043
(800) 235-3322/(617) 749-1416

Minimum: Initial: $1,000
    Subsequent: $100
Min IRA: Initial: None
    Subsequent: None
Investor Services: IRA, Keogh, Corp, Withdraw
Telephone Exchange: No
Registered In: All states except CA, ME, TN
12b-1: No

NORTH STAR RESERVE FUND

Bond

Investment Objectives/Policy: Seeks a high level of capital stability and liquidity, with a secondary objective of high current income. Invests in investment-grade government and commercial paper. Will not purchase securities with a maturity date more than 25 months from the date of acquisition.
Year First Offered: 1986
Distr: Income: Quarterly
    Capital Gains: Annually

Investment Advisors, Inc.
1100 Dain Tower
PO Box 357
Minneapolis, MN 55440
(612) 371-2884

Minimum: Initial: $2,500
    Subsequent: $100
Min IRA: Initial: None
    Subsequent: None
Investor Services: IRA, Keogh, 403(b), Corp, Withdraw
Telephone Exchange: No
Registered In: AZ, CO, IA, IL, MD, MI, MN, MO, MT, ND, NY, PA, SD, TN, WA, WI
12b-1: No

T. ROWE PRICE CALIFORNIA TAX-FREE BOND

Tax-Exempt

Investment Objectives/Policy: Seeks high level of interest income which is exempt from federal and California state taxes. Invests in long-term municipal bonds rated BBB or higher by S&P. Can invest 5% of the fund's assets in below investment grade bonds.
Year First Offered: 1986

T. Rowe Price
100 East Pratt Street
Baltimore, MD 21202
(800) 638-5660/(301) 547-2308

Distr: Income: Monthly
    Capital Gains: Annually
Minimum: Initial: $1,000
    Subsequent: $100
Investor Services: Withdraw, Deduct
Telephone Exchange: Yes
    With MMF: Yes
Registered In: AZ, DC, HI, MD, NV, OR, WY
12b-1: No

T. ROWE PRICE CAPITAL APPRECIATION

Aggressive Growth

Investment Objectives/Policy: Seeks capital appreciation through investment primarily in common stocks. Portfolio consists of two categories 1) long-term "core" holdings of undervalued growth stocks and 2) short-term holdings, where the stock price is expected to rise over the short term. Can invest up to 35% of the fund's assets in corporate debt.
Year First Offered: 1986
Distr: Income: Annually
    Capital Gains: Annually

T. Rowe Price Associates
100 East Pratt Street
Baltimore, MD 21202
(800) 638-5660/(301) 547-2308

Minimum: Initial: $1,000
    Subsequent: $100
Min IRA: Initial: $500
    Subsequent: $50
Investor Services: IRA, Keogh, SEP, Corp, 403(b), Deduct, Withdraw
Telephone Exchange: Yes
    With MMF: Yes
Registered In: All states
12b-1: No

T. ROWE PRICE INTERNATIONAL BOND

International

T. Rowe Price
100 East Pratt Street
Baltimore, MD 21202
(800) 638-5660/(301) 547-2308

Investment Objectives/Policy: To achieve a high level of current income through investment in foreign bonds. Also seeks capital appreciation and protection of its principal through actively managing its maturity structure and currency exposure.
Year First Offered: 1986
Distr: Income: Monthly
 Capital Gains: Annually

Minimum: Initial: $1,000
 Subsequent: $100
Min IRA: Initial: $500
 Subsequent: $50
Investor Services: IRA, Keogh, Corp, 403(b), Deduct, Withdraw
Telephone Exchange: Yes
 With MMF: Yes
Registered In: All states
12b-1: No

PRIMARY TREND FUND

Balanced

Arnold Investment Counsel, Inc.
First Financial Centre
700 North Water Street
Milwaukee, WI 53202
(800) 443-6544/(414) 271-7870

Investment Objectives/Policy: Seeks to maximize total return without exposing capital to undue risk. Invests in common stock, convertible and fixed-income securities. Attempts to align the portfolio with primary market trends which can last for several quarters up to several years.
Year First Offered: 1986
Distr: Income: Annually
 Capital Gains: Annually

Minimum: Initial: $5,000
 Subsequent: $100
Min IRA: Initial: $2,000
 Subsequent: $100
Investor Services: IRA, Keogh, SEP, Corp, 403(b), Withdraw
Telephone Exchange: No
Registered In: All states except AR, IA, ID, ND, NH, NM, VT
12b-1: No

SCUDDER GLOBAL

International

Scudder, Stevens & Clark
175 Federal Street
Boston, MA 02110-2267
(800) 225-2470/(617) 426-8300

Investment Objectives/Policy: Seeks long-term growth of capital through worldwide investment in equity securities. Will be invested in at least three different countries, one of which will be the U.S. Income is an incidental consideration. Can buy and sell index and foreign currency futures as a hedge.
Year First Offered: 1986
Distr: Income: Annually
 Capital Gains: Annually

Minimum: Initial: $1,000
 Subsequent: None
Min IRA: Initial: $240
 Subsequent: None
Investor Services: IRA, Keogh, Corp, 403(b), Withdraw
Telephone Exchange: Yes
 With MMF: Yes
Registered In: All states
12b-1: No

STEINROE HIGH-YIELD BONDS

Bond

Stein Roe & Farnham
P.O. Box 1143
Chicago, IL 60690
(800) 621-0320/(312) 368-7826

Investment Objectives/Policy: Seeks high level of current income; capital appreciation is of secondary importance. Invests in below investment grade (BBB) bonds and convertible securities. May invest up to 35% of its assets in preferred and common stocks.
Year First Offered: 1986
Distr: Income: Quarterly
    Capital Gains: Annually

Minimum: Initial: $2,500
    Subsequent: $100
Min IRA: Initial: $500
    Subsequent: $100
Investor Services: IRA, Keogh, SEP, Withdraw
Telephone Exchange: Yes
    With MMF: Yes
Registered In: All states
12b-1: No

VALUE LINE AGGRESSIVE INCOME

Bond

Value Line, Inc.
711 Third Avenue
New York, NY 10017
(800) 223-0818/(212) 687-3965

Investment Objectives/Policy: Seeks to maximize current income; capital appreciation is of secondary importance. Invests primarily in high-yielding, fixed-income corporate securities issued by companies rated B++ or lower for relative strength in the Value Line Investment Survey.
Year First Offered: 1986
Distr: Income: Monthly
    Capital Gains: Annually

Minimum: Initial: $1,000
    Subsequent: $250
Min IRA: Initial: $1,000
    Subsequent: $250
Investor Services: IRA, Keogh, 403(b), Withdraw
Telephone Exchange: Yes
    With MMF: Yes
Registered In: All states
12b-1: No

VANGUARD CALIFORNIA INSURED TAX-FREE

Tax-Exempt

Vanguard Group
Vanguard Financial Ctr.
Valley Forge, PA 19482
(800) 662-7447/(215) 648-6000

Investment Objectives/Policy: Seeks high level of current income exempt from both federal and California state taxes. Invests primarily in insured long-term municipal bonds issued by California state and local municipalities. May invest 20% in uninsured taxable government and corporate securities.
Year First Offered: 1986

Distr: Income: Monthly
    Capital Gains: Annually
Minimum: Initial: $3,000
    Subsequent: $100
Investor Services: Withdraw
Telephone Exchange: Yes
    With MMF: Yes
Registered In: CA
12b-1: No

VANGUARD CONVERTIBLE SECURITIES

Growth & Income

Vanguard Group
Vanguard Financial Ctr.
Valley Forge, PA
(800) 662-7447/(215) 648-6000

Investment Objectives/Policy: Seeks high level of current income together with long-term capital appreciation. At least 80% of the fund's assets will be invested in convertible bonds, debentures, corporate notes, and preferred stocks. Can invest up to 20% of assets in non-convertible corporate or government debt securities.
Year First Offered: 1986
Distr: Income: Quarterly
   Capital Gains: April

Minimum: Initial: $3,000
   Subsequent: $100
Min IRA: Initial: $500
   Subsequent: $100
Investor Services: IRA, Keogh, SEP, Corp, 403(b), Withdraw
Telephone Exchange: Yes
   With MMF: Yes
Registered In: All states
12b-1: No

VANGUARD NEW YORK INSURED TAX-FREE

Tax-Exempt

Vanguard Group
Vanguard Financial Ctr.
Valley Forge, PA 19482
(800) 662-7447/(215) 648-6000

Investment Objectives/Policy: Seeks high level of current income exempt from both federal and New York state taxes. Invests primarily in insured long-term municipal bonds issued by New York state and local municipalities. May invest 20% in uninsured taxable government and corporate debt securities.
Year First Offered: 1986

Distr: Income: Monthly
   Capital Gains: Annually
Minimum: Initial: $3,000
   Subsequent: $100
Investor Services: Withdraw
Telephone Exchange: Yes
   With MMF: Yes
Registered In: NY
12b-1: No

VANGUARD PENNSYLVANIA INSURED TAX-FREE

Tax-Exempt

Vanguard Group
Vanguard Financial Ctr.
Valley Forge, PA 19482
(800) 662-7447/(215) 648-6000

Investment Objectives/Policy: Seeks high level of current income exempt from both federal and Pennsylvania state taxes. Invests primarily in insured long-term municipal bonds issued by Pennsylvania state and local municipalities. May invest 20% in uninsured taxable government and corporate debt securities.
Year First Offered: 1986

Distr: Income: Monthly
   Capital Gains: Annually
Minimum: Initial: $3,000
   Subsequent: $100
Investor Services: Withdraw
Telephone Exchange: Yes
   With MMF: Yes
Registered In: PA
12b-1: No

VANGUARD U.S. TREASURY BOND

Bond

Vanguard Group
Vanguard Financial Ctr.
Valley Forge, PA 19482
(800) 662-7447/(215) 648-6000

Investment Objectives/Policy: Seeks high level of current income consistent with safety of principal and liquidity. Invests at least 85% of its assets in long-term U.S. Treasury bonds and other "full faith and credit" obligations of the U.S. government. Can invest in zero coupon Treasury bonds and interest rate futures.
Year First Offered: 1986
Distr: Income: Monthly
    Capital Gains: Annually

Minimum: Initial: $3,000
    Subsequent: $100
Min IRA: Initial: $500
    Subsequent: $100
Investor Services: IRA, Keogh, SEP, Corp, 403(b), Withdraw
Telephone Exchange: Yes
    With MMF: Yes
Registered In: All states
12b-1: No

Funds Not Listed In Data Pages

We base our mutual fund guide on the listings that appear in the newspaper; we select only no-load funds. Some of the funds listed in the newspaper are not true no-loads despite their designation as "N.L.," while others are inappropriate for individuals or are not available to individuals for other reasons. In this section, we list the funds designated as no-loads in the financial press but not in the main part of this book, and we state the reasons why those funds are not included.

Key to reasons:
- **BB:** Can be bought only from a bank or broker.
- **C:** Closed to new investors.
- **I:** For institutional or corporate investors only.
- **L:** Limited to employees or members of a particular organization.
- **M:** Minimum investment is greater than $25,000.
- **NS:** Information not supplied in time for publication.
- **R:** Redemption fee does not disappear after 6 months.
- **SC:** Front-end sales charge.
- **X:** Refused to supply information.

R	Advest Advantage Government	R	Dean Witter Tax Advantaged
R	Advest Advantage Growth	R	Dean Witter U.S. Government
R	Advest Advantage Income	R	Dean Witter World Wide Inv.
R	Advest Advantage Special	C	Destiny I
L	AMA American Medical	BB	Destiny II
X	American Heritage	I	DFA Fixed Income Portfolio
R	American Investors Pension	I	DFA Small Stock
L	AMEV Special	L	DIT Capital Growth
M	Bartlett Corporate Cash	L	DIT Current Income
SC	Blanchard Strategic Growth	L	DIT OTC Growth
M	Brandywine Fund	SC	DIT U.S. Gov't Securities
C	California Muni Fund†	R	Drexel Fenimore Int'l.
R	Calvert Washington Growth	R	Drexel Series Trust Bond
L	Cheapside Dollar	R	Drexel Series Trust Convertible
C	Chestnut Street Exchange	R	Drexel Series Trust Emerg. Gr.
R	Clipper Fund	R	Drexel Series Trust Gov't. Sec.
R	Columbia Municipal	R	Drexel Series Trust Growth
R	Cowen Income & Growth	R	Drexel Series Trust Option Inc.
R	Dean Witter Calif. Tax-Free	R	E.F. Hutton Basic Value
R	Dean Witter Convertible	R	E.F. Hutton Bond
R	Dean Witter Develop. Growth	R	E.F. Hutton Gov't. Securities
R	Dean Witter Dividend Growth	R	E.F. Hutton Growth
R	Dean Witter Industry Valued	R	E.F. Hutton Option Income
R	Dean Witter Natural Resources	R	E.F. Hutton Precious Metals
R	Dean Witter N.Y. Tax-Free	R	E.F. Hutton Special Equity
R	Dean Witter Option Income	R	Eaton Vance Calif. Muni.
R	Dean Witter Sears Tax-Exempt	R	Eaton Vance High Income

†*Fund performance is included in table for closed funds in performance ranking section.*

R	Eaton Vance High Yield Muni.	R	Integrated Resources Cap. App.
R	Equitec Siebel Agg. Growth	R	Integrated Res. Home Investors
R	Equitec Siebel High Yield Bond	R	Investment Portfolios Equity
R	Equitec Siebel Total Return	R	Investment Port. Gov't. Plus
R	Equitec Siebel US Government	R	Investment Port. High Yield
I	Federated Cash Mgmt. Trust	R	Investment Port. Option Inc.
I	Federated Exchange	I	Ivy Institutional
I	Federated F.T. International	R	Kaufman
I	Federated Floating Rate	R	Keystone International
I	Federated GNMA Trust	R	Keystone Custodian B1, B2, B4
I	Federated Government Trust	R	Keystone Custodian K1, K2
I	Federated Growth Trust	R	Keystone Custodian S1, S3, S4
I	Federated High Yield	R	Keystone Precious Metals
I	Federated Income	R	Keystone Tax-Exempt
I	Federated Intermediate Gov't.	R	Keystone Tax-Free
I	Federated Intermediate Muni.	R	Kidder Peabody Equity Income
I	Federated Short Inter. Gov't.	R	Kidder Peabody Gov't. Income
I	Federated Short Inter. Muni	R	Kidder Peabody Special Gr.
I	Federated Stock & Bond	M	Ltd. Mat. Bd.: Neuberger Ber.
I	Federated Stock Trust	C	Lindner†
C	Fidelity Congress St.	C	Lindner Dividend†
I	Fidelity CT ARP	C	Loomis-Sayles Cap. Dev.†
C	Fidelity Exchange	R	MacKay Shields Capital App.
I	Fidelity Qualified Dividend	R	MacKay Shields Convertible
M	Flagship Corporate Cash	R	MacKay Shields Corporate Bd.
I	Flagship Corporate Mgmt.	R	MacKay Shields Gov't. Plus
R	Fortress Investors High Quality	R	MacKay Shields Tax Free Bd.
I	Franklin Corporate Cash	R	MacKay Shields Value Fund
R	Freedom Gold and Gov't.	R	Meeschaert Cap. Accum.
R	Freedom Government Plus	R	Merrill Lynch Calif. Tax-Ex.
R	Freedom Regional Bank Fund	R	Merrill Fd. for Tomorrow
M	Fund Trust—Agg. Growth	I	Merrill Lynch Inst. Inter.
M	Fund Trust—Growth	R	Merrill Lynch Muni Inc.
M	Fund Trust—Growth & Income	R	Merrill Lynch Natural Res.
M	Fund Trust—Income	R	Merrill Lynch New York Muni
R,M	Gabelli Asset Fund	R	Merrill Lynch Retirement
I	Geico Adj. Rate Preferred	R	Merrill Retire. Global Bd.
BB	General Aggressive Growth	R	Merrill Lynch Retire. Income
L	General Electric Elfun Income	L	MSB
L	G.E. Elfun Tax-Exempt	M	Mutual Beacon
L	G.E. Elfun Trust	R	Paine Webber Asset Allocation
L	G.E. S&S Long-Term Interest	R	Paine Webber Master Growth
L	General Electric S&S Program	R	Paine Webber Master Income
BB	General Tax Exempt Bond	C	Pennsylvania Mutual†
M	Gintel Fund	C	Phoenix Total Return
SC,R	Guardian Bond	R	Prudential-Bache Adj. Rate
SC,R	Guardian Stock	R	Prudential-Bache Calif. Muni
R	Horace Mann Growth Fund	R	Prudential-Bache Equity
R	IDS Aggressive	R	Prudential-Bache Global
R	IDS Income	R	Prudential-Bache GNMA
I	IFG Diversified	R	Prudential-Bache Gov't. Sec.
I	IFG Intermediate	R	Prudential-Bache Gov't. Plus
I	IFG International	R	Prudential-Bache Growth Opp.
X	Industry Fund of America	R	Prudential-Bache High Yield

†*Fund performance is included in table for closed funds in performance ranking section.*

R	Pru-Bache High Yield Muni	R	Thomson McKinnon Income
R	Pru-Bache Inc. Vertible Plus	R	Thomson McKinnon Opp.
R	Prudential-Bache Muni Arizona	R	Thomson McKinnon Tax-Ex.
R	Pru-Bache Muni Maryland	R	Thomson McK. U.S. Gov't.
R	Prudential-Bache Muni Mass.	I	Trust Fund Bond
R	Prudential-Bache Muni Minn.	I	Trust Fund Equity Index
R	Prudential-Bache Muni N.Y.	I	Trust Portfolios: Equity Gr.
R	Prudential-Bache Muni Ohio	I	Trust Portfolios: Equity Income
R	Pru-Bache Option Growth	I	Trust Portfolios: Fixed Income
R	Prudential-Bache Research	R	U.S. Boston—Boston I Series
R	Prudential-Bache Utility Shares	R	United Services Prospector
R	Putnam Capital	C	Vance Exchange—Capital Exch.
R	Putnam Tax-Free High Yield	C	.V.E.—Depositors of Boston
R	Putnam Tax-Free Insured	C	V.E.—Diversification
C	Quasar Associates†	C	V.E.—Exchange of Boston
R	Royce Value	C	V.E.—Fiduciary Exchange
C	Sequoia†	C	Vance Exchange—Fund
SC	Shearson ATT Growth Fund	C	V.E.—Second Fiduciary Exch.
SC	Shearson ATT Income Fund	C	Vanguard Explorer†
R	Shearson Special Portfolio	M	Vanguard PrimeCap
X	Sierra Growth Fund	I	Vanguard Qual. Dividend II
R	Southeast Growth	C	Vanguard Qual. Divi. Port. I†
L	State Farm Balanced	I	Vanguard Qual. Divi. Port. III
L	State Farm Growth	R	Vanguard Specialized Portfolios
L	State Farm Municipal Bond	C	Vanguard Windsor†
C	State Street Exchange	R	Venture Advisers Retire.—Bond
C	State Street Growth	R	Venture Retire.—Equity
R	Telephone Income Shares	R	Venture Municipal Plus Fund
R	Thomson McKinnon Global	R	WPG Government
R	Thomson McKinnon Growth	R	WPG Growth

†Fund performance is included in table for closed funds in performance ranking section.

Mutual Fund Families

Below we present a list of mutual fund families that are primarily no-load. We have listed all funds within a family, including those with loads and redemption fees.

AMA
5 Sentry Pkwy. W., Suite 120
PO Box 1111
Blue Bell, PA 19422
(800) 523-0864/(215) 825-0400

AMA Income
AMA Emerging Medical Technology
AMA Global Growth
Medical Technology
Money-Prime
Pro Money—Treasury

American Investors
777 W. Putnam Ave.
Greenwich, CT 06836
(800) 243-5353/(203) 531-5000

American Investors Growth
American Investors Income
American Investors Money
American Investors Option

Axe-Houghton Management, Inc.
400 Benedict Avenue
Tarrytown, NY 10591
(800) 431-1030/(914) 631-8131

Fund B
Income
Money Market
Stock

D.L. Babson
3 Crown Center
2440 Pershing Rd.
Kansas City, MO 64108
(800) 821-5591/(816) 471-5200

Bond Trust
Enterprise
Growth
Money Market—Federal
Money Market—Prime
Tax-Free Income Funds:
    Shorter-Term Portfolio
    Longer-Term Portfolio
    Money Market Portfolio
UMB Bond
UMB Money Market
UMB Qualified Dividend
UMB Stock

UMB Tax Free
Value

Bartlett & Company
36 E. Fourth St.
Cincinnati, OH 45202
(800) 543-0863/(513) 621-0066

Basic Value
Corporate Cash
Fixed Income

Benham
755 Page Mill Rd.
Palo Alto, CA 94304
(800) 227-8380/(415) 858-3600

California—High Yield
California—Insured
California—Intermediate
California—Long-Term
California—Money Market
Capital Preservation
Capital Preservation II
Capital Preservation Treasury Note
GNMA
National Tax-Free—Intermediate
National Tax-Free—Long-Term
National Tax-Free—Money Market
Target Maturities Trust

Boston Company
One Boston Place
Boston, MA 02106
(800) 343-6324/(617) 956-9740

Capital Appreciation
Cash Management
GNMA
Government Money
Managed Income
Massachusetts Tax-Free Bond
Massachusetts Tax-Free Money
Special Growth
Tax-Free—Bond
Tax-Free—Money

Bull & Bear Funds
11 Hanover Square
New York, NY 10005
(800) 431-6060/(212) 785-0900

Bull & Bear Capital Growth
Bull & Bear Dollar Reserves
Bull & Bear Equity Income
Bull & Bear Golconda Investors
Bull & Bear High Yield
Bull & Bear Special Equities
Bull & Bear Tax Free Income
Bull & Bear U.S. Gov't. Sec.

Calvert
1700 Pennsylvania Ave., N.W.
Washington, DC 20006
(800) 368-2748/(301) 951-4820

Cash Reserves
Equity
First Variable Rate
Income
Social Investment Managed Growth
Social Investment Money Market
Tax-Free Reserves:
    Limited-Term
    Long-Term
    Money Market
U.S. Government
Washington Area Growth

CCM Partners
44 Montgomery Street
San Francisco, CA 94104
(415) 398-2727

Calif. Ginnie Mae
Calif. Tax-Free Income
Calif. Tax-Free Money Market

Columbia
1301 SW Fifth Ave.
PO Box 1350
Portland, OR 97207
(800) 547-1037/(503) 222-3600

Daily Income
Fixed Income Securities
Growth
Municipal Bond
Special
U.S. Guaranteed Gov't. Sec.

Composite
Seafirst Financial Center, 9th Fl.
Spokane, WA 99201
(800) 541-0830/(509) 624-4101

Bond & Stock
Cash Management
Fund
Income
Select High-Yield

Select Northwest Portfolio
Select Value Portfolio
Tax-Exempt Bond
U.S. Government

Delaware Management Company
Ten Penn Center Plaza
Philadelphia, PA 19103
(800) 523-4640/(215) 988-1200

Cash Reserve
Decatur Fund—I Series
Decatur Fund—II Series
Delaware Fund
Delcap Concept I
Delchester Bond Fund
Delta Trend Fund
Gov't. Fund—GMNA Series
Gov't. Fund—U.S. Gov't. Series
Tax-Free Insured Series
Tax-Free Money Fund
Tax-Free New York
Tax-Free Pennsylvania
Tax-Free USA
Treasury Reserves Cashier Series
Treasury Reserves Investor Series

Dividend/Growth
107 N. Adams St.
Rockville, MD 20850
(800) 638-2042/(301) 251-1002

Dividend Series
Government Obligations
Laser & Advanced Technology

Dodge & Cox
One Post St., 35th Fl.
San Francisco, CA 94104
(415) 981-1710

Balanced
Stock

Dreyfus
600 Madison Avenue
New York, NY 10022
(800) 645-6561/(718) 895-1206

A Bonds Plus
Calif. Tax Exempt Bond
Calif. Tax-Exempt Money Market
Capital Value
Convertible Securities
Dreyfus Fund
GNMA
Growth Opportunity
Insured Tax-Exempt Bond
Intermediate Tax-Exempt Bond

Leverage
Liquid Assets
Massachusetts Tax Free
Money Market Instr.:
  Government
  Money Market
New Leaders
N.Y. Insured Tax Exempt Bond
N.Y. Tax Exempt Bond
Strategic Income Fund
Strategic Investment Fund
Tax-Exempt Bond
Tax-Exempt Money Market
Third Century

Evergreen
Saxon Woods Asset Mgmt. Corp.
550 Mamaroneck Ave.
Harrison, NY 10528
(914) 698-5711/(212) 828-7700

Evergreen
Evergreen Total Return

Fidelity
82 Devonshire St.
Boston, MA 02109
(800) 544-6666/(617) 523-1919

Aggressive Tax-Free
Balanced
CalFree—High Yield Port.
CalFree—Insured Port.
CalFree—Money Market
CalFree—Muni Bond
CalFree—Short-Term
Capital Appreciation
Cash Reserves
Congress Street
Contrafund
Convertible Securities
Daily Income Trust
Daily Money
Daily Tax-Exempt Money
Destiny
Equity-Income
Europe
Exchange
Freedom
Fidelity Fund
Flexible Bond
Ginnie Mae
Global Bond
Government Securities
Growth Company
Growth & Income Port.
High Income

High Yield Municipals
Insured Tax-Free Portfolio
International Growth & Income
Limited-Term Municipals
Magellan
MassFree:
  Money Market
  Muni Bond
Mercury
Michigan Tax-Free
Minnesota Tax-Free
Money Market Trust:
  Domestic
  U.S. Government
  U.S. Treasury
Mortgage Securities
Municipal Bond
N.Y. Tax-Free—High Yield
New York Tax-Free—Insured
New York Tax-Free—Muni Bond
New York Tax-Free—Money Market
Ohio Tax-Free Port
OTC Portfolio
Overseas
Pacific Basin
Penn. T-F High Yield Port.
Penn T-F—Money Market
Puritan
Real Estate Investment
Select Portfolios:
  Air Transportation
  American Gold
  Automation & Machinery
  Automotive
  Biotechnology
  Broadcast and Media
  Brokerage & Investment Cos.
  Capital Goods
  Chemicals
  Computers
  Defense & Aerospace
  Electric Utilities
  Electronics
  Energy
  Energy Services
  Financial Services
  Food & Agriculture
  Health Care
  Health Care Delivery
  Housing
  Industrial Materials
  Leisure & Entertainment
  Life Insurance
  Money Markets
  Paper & Forest Products

Precious Metals & Minerals
Property & Casualty Insurance
Regional Banks
Restaurant Industry
Retailing
Savings & Loan
Software & Computer Services
Technology
Telecommunications
Transportation
Utilities
Short-term Bond Portfolio
Short-term Tax-Free Portfolio
Special Situations
Tax-Exempt Money Market Trust
Texas Tax-Free
Thrift Trust
Trend
U.S. Government Reserves
Value

Fiduciary
222 E. Mason St.
Milwaukee, WI 53202
(414) 271-6666

Capital Growth
ValQuest

Financial Programs
PO Box 2040
Denver, CO 80201
(800) 525-8085/(303) 779-1233

Bond Shares:
  High Yield
  Select Income
  U.S. Government
Daily Income Shares
Dynamics
Industrial
Industrial Income
Tax-Free Income Shares
Tax-Free Money
World of Technology
Group Portfolios:
  Energy
  European
  Financial
  Gold
  Health Sciences
  Leisure
  Pacific Basin
  Technology
  Utilities

Flex-Fund
R. Meeder & Associates
6000 Memorial Dr.
Dublin, OH 43017
(800) 325-3539/(614) 766-7000

Bond
Capital Gains
Corporate Income
Money Market
Retirement Growth

44 Wall Street
One State St. Plaza
New York, NY 10004
(800) 221-7836/(212) 344-4224

44 Wall Street
44 Wall Street Equity

Founders
3033 E. First Ave., #810
Denver, CO 80206
(800) 525-2440/(303) 394-4404

Equity Income
Frontier
Growth
Money Market
Mutual
Special

FundTrust
Furman Selz
230 Park Ave.
New York, NY 10169
(800) 845-8406/(212) 309-8400

Aggressive Growth
Equity Trust
Growth
Growth & Income
High Yield Investment Trust
Income
International Equity Trust
Money Trust
Tax-Free Trust

Gateway Investment Advisors
PO Box 458167
Cincinnati, OH 45245
(800) 354-6339/(513) 248-2700

Growth Plus
Option Income

G.T. Capital Management
601 Montgomery St., #1400
San Francisco, CA 94111
(415) 392-6181

Europe Growth
Government Obligations
International Growth
Japan Growth
Pacific Growth

Gintel
Greenwich Office Park OP-6
Greenwich, CT 06830
(800) 243-5808/(203) 622-6400

Gintel
Gintel Capital Appreciation
Gintel Erisa
Parkway

GIT
Bankers Finance Investment Mgmt.
1655 N. Fort Myer Dr.
Arlington, VA 22209
(800) 336-3063/(703) 528-6500

Cash:
    Government
    Regular
Equity Income
Government Investors
Income:
    A-Rated
    Insured Money Market
    Maximum
Select Growth
Special Growth
Tax-Free High Yield
Tax-Free Money Market

Gradison
The 580 Bldg.
6th & Walnut St.
Cincinnati, OH 45202
(800) 543-1818/(513) 579-5700

Cash
Established Growth
Opportunity Growth
U.S. Government

Hartwell
515 Madison Ave., 31st Fl.
New York, NY 10022
(800) 645-6405/(212) 308-3355

Growth
Leverage

Ivy Funds
Hingham Management Inc.
40 Industrial Park Rd.
Hingham, MA 02043
(800) 235-3322/(617) 749-1416

Ivy General Money Mkt.
Ivy Growth
Ivy International
Ivy Tax-Exempt Money Mkt.

Janus
100 Filmore St. #300
Denver, CO 80206
(800) 525-3713/(303) 333-3863

Janus
Janus Value
Janus Venture

Kleinwort Benson International
200 Park Ave. Suite 5610
New York, NY 10166
(800) 237-4218/(212) 687-2515

Transatlantic Growth
Transatlantic Income

Legg Mason Wood Walker
7 E. Redwood St.
Baltimore, MD 21203
(800) 368-2558/(301) 539-3400

Cash Reserve
Special Investment
Tax Exempt
Total Return
Value Trust

Lehman
55 Water Street
New York, NY 10041
(800) 221-5350/(212) 668-4308

Capital
Corporation
Investors
Mangement Cash Reserves
Management Gov't. Reserves
Management Tax-Free Reserves
Opportunity

Lexington
Park 80 W. Plaza 2
Saddle Brook, NJ 07662
(800) 526-0056

GNMA Income
Goldfund
Government Securities Money Mkt.
Growth
Money Market Trust
Research
Tax-Exempt Bond
Tax Free Money

Liberty
Federated
421 Seventh Ave.
Pittsburgh, PA 15219
(800) 245-4770

American Leaders
Federated Tax-Free Income
Fund for U.S. Gov't. Securities
Money Market Instruments
Tax-Free Instruments
U.S. Government Money Market

Loomis-Sayles
PO Box 449
Back Bay Annex
Boston, MA 02117
(800) 345-4048

Capital Development
Mutual

Midwest Advisory Service
700 Dixie Terminal Bldg.
Cincinnati, OH 45202
(800) 543-8721/(513) 629-2000

ABT Emerging Growth
ABT Growth & Income
ABT Security Income
ABT Utilities Income
LG Investment Trust:
    LG Fund for Growth
    LG U.S. Gov't. Securities
Midwest Group Tax-Free Trust:
    Limited Term
    Long Term
    Money Market
Midwest Income Trust:
    Cash Management
    Short-Term Gov't.

Mutual Shares Corporation
26 Broadway
New York, NY 10004
(800) 344-4515/(212) 908-4048

Mutual Beacon
Mutual Qualified Income
Mutual Shares

Neuberger & Berman Management
342 Madison Ave.
New York, NY 10173
(800) 367-0770/(212) 850-8300

Energy
Guardian Mutual
Liberty
Limited Maturity Bond

Manhattan
Money Market Plus
Neuberger Gov't. Money Fund
Neuberger Tax-Free
Partners

Newton
330 E. Kilbourn Ave.
Two Plaza East, #1150
Milwaukee, WI 53202
(800) 247-7039/(414) 347-1141

Growth
Income
Money

Nicholas
700 N. Water St.
Milwaukee, WI 53202
(414) 272-6133

Nicholas
Nicholas II
Nicholas Income

Noddings-Calamos Asset Mgmt.
2001 Spring Road, #750
Oak Brook, IL 60521
(800) 251-2411/(312) 571-7100

Convertible Growth
Convertible Income

North Star
1100 Dain Tower
Box 1160
Minneapolis, MN 55440
(612) 371-7780

Apollo
Bond
Regional
Reserve
Stock

Northeast Mgmt. & Research Co.
50 Congress Street
Boston, MA 02109
(617) 523-3588/(800) 225-6704

Northeast Investors Growth
Northeast Investors Trust

100 Fund
Berger Associates
899 Logan St.
Denver, CO 80203
(303) 837-1020/(816) 474-8520

100 Fund
101 Fund

Pacific Horizon
3550 Wilshire Blvd., #932
Los Angeles, CA 90010
(800) 645-3515

Aggressive Growth
California Tax-Exempt Bond
Government Money Market
High Yield Bond
Money Market
Tax-Exempt Money Market

Park Avenue Inc.
600 Madison Ave.
New York, NY 10022
(800) 848-4350/(718) 895-1219

NY Tax-Exempt Intermediate Bond
NY Tax-Exempt Money Market

T. Rowe Price
100 E. Pratt St.
Baltimore, MD 21202
(800) 638-5660/(301) 547-2308

CalFree Bond
CalFree Money
Capital Appreciation
Equity Income
GNMA
Growth & Income
Growth Stock
High Yield
International Bond
International Stock
New America Growth
New Era
New Horizons
New Income
New York Tax-Free Bond
New York Tax-Free Money
Prime Reserves
Reality Income I
Reality Income II
Reality Income III
Short-Term Bond
Tax-Exempt Money
Tax-Free High Yield
Tax-Free Income
Tax-Free Short-Intermediate
U.S. Treasury Money

Safeco Securities
Safeco Plaza
Seattle, WA 98185
(800) 426-6730/(206) 545-5530

Calif. Tax-Free Income
Equity

Growth
Income
Money Market Mutual
Municipal Bond
Tax-Free Money Market

Scudder Fund Distributors
175 Federal St.
Boston, MA 02110
(800) 453-3305/(617) 426-8300

AARP Capital Growth
AARP General Bond
AARP GNMA & U.S. Treasury
AARP Growth & Income
AARP Insured Tax-Free Bond
AARP Insured Tax-Free Short-Term
AARP Money Fund
Calif. Tax Free
Capital Growth
Cash Investment
Development
Global
Government Money
Gov't. Mortgage Securities
Growth & Income
High-Yield Tax-Free
Income
International
Managed Municipal Bonds
N.Y. Tax Free
Target
Tax Free Money
Tax Free Target
Zero Coupon Target

Selected Funds
Vincent, Chesley Advisors
230 W. Monroe St. 28th Fl.
Chicago, IL 60606
(800) 621-7321/(312) 641-7862

American Shares
Money Market:
   General
   Government
Special Shares

Sit Investment Associates, Inc.
1714 First Bank Place West
Minneapolis, MN 55402
(612) 332-3223

New Beginning Growth
New Beginning Income & Growth
New Beginning Investment Reserve
New Beginning Yield

Steadman
1730 K. St., N.W.
Washington, DC 20006
(800) 424-8570/(202) 223-1000

American Industry
Associated
EhrenKrentz—Growth
EhrenKrentz—Undiscovered Equity
Financial
Investment
Oceanographic, Technology & Gr.

Stein Roe & Farnham
150 S. Wacker Dr.
Chicago, IL 60606
(800) 621-0320/(312) 368-7826

Capital Opportunities
Cash Reserves
Discovery
Government Plus
Government Reserves
High Yield Bond
High Yield Municipals
Intermediate Municipal Bond
Managed Bonds
Managed Municipals
Special
Stock
Tax-Exempt Money Mkt.
Total Return
Universe

Stratton
PO Box 550
Blue Bell, PA 19422
(215) 542-8025

Growth
Monthly Dividend Shares

Strong/Corneliuson Capital Mgmt.
815 E. Mason St.
Milwaukee, WI 53202
(800) 368-3863/(414) 765-0620

Government Securities
Income
Investment
Money Market
Opportunity
Tax-Free Income
Tax-Free Money Market
Total Return

20th Century
Investors Research Corp.
PO Box 200, 605 W. 47th St.
Kansas City, MO 64141

(816) 531-5575
Cash Reserve
Giftrust
Growth
Long-Term Bond
Select
Tax-Exempt Intermediate
Tax-Exempt Long-Term
Ultra
U.S. Governments
Vista

Unified Management Corporation
Guaranty Building
Indianapolis, IN 46204
(800) 862-7283/(317) 634-3300

Amana Income
Growth
Income
Liquid Green Trust
Liquid Green Tax-Free Trust
Municipal:
    General
    Indiana
Mutual Shares

United Services
PO Box 29467
San Antonio, TX 78229
(800) 824-4653/(512) 696-0253

US GNMA
US Gold Shares
US Good & Bad Times
US Growth
US Income
US LoCap
US New Prospector
US Prospector
US Tax Free
US U.S. Treasury Securities

USAA Funds
9800 Fredericksburg Rd.
USAA Building
San Antonio, TX 78288
(800) 531-8000/(512) 690-6062

Cornerstone
Gold
Growth
Income
Money Market
Sunbelt Era
Tax-Exempt Funds:
    High Yield
    Intermediate-Term

Money Market
Short-Term

Value Line
711 Third Ave.
New York, NY 10017
(800) 223-0818/(212) 687-3965

Aggressive Income
Cash
Centurion (Limited)
Convertible
Income
Leveraged Growth Investors
Special Situations
Tax Exempts:
  High Yield
  Money Market
  U.S. Government Securities
Value Line Fund

Vanguard Group
Vanguard Financial Center
Valley Forge, PA 19482
(800) 662-7447/(215) 648-6000

Bond Market
California Insured Tax Free
Convertible Securities
Explorer
Explorer II
Fixed Income Securities:
  GNMA
  High Yield Bond
  Investment Grade Bond
  Short-Term Bond
Gemini
Gemini II
Index Trust
Money Market Trusts:
  Federal
  Insured

Prime
Municipal Bond Funds:
  High Yield
  Insured Long-Term
  Intermediate-Term
  Long-Term
  N.Y. Insured Tax-Free
  Penn. Insured Tax-Free
  Short-Term
Money Market
Naess & Thomas Special
PrimeCap
Qualified Dividend I
Qualified Dividend II
Qualified Dividend III
Quantitative Portfolio
Specialized Portfolios:
  Energy
  Gold & Precious Metals
  Health Care
  Service Economy
  Technology
Star
Trustees' Commingled Equity Int'l.
Trustees' Commingled Equity U.S.
U.S. Treasury Bond
W.L. Morgan
Wellesley
Wellington
Windsor
Windsor II
World Portfolio—International
World Portfolio—U.S.

Viking Equity Index Fund, Inc.
232 Lakeside Drive
Horsham, PA 19044
(800) 441-3885

Equity Index
Money Market

INDEX

AARP Capital Growth, 40, 52
AARP General Bond, 44, 53
AARP GNMA & U.S. Treasury, 44, 54
AARP Growth & Income, 42, 55
AARP Insured Tax Free Bond, 46, 310
AARP Insured Tax Free Short Term, 47, 310
Acorn, 40, 56
ADTEK, 43, 57
Afuture, 36, 41, 58
AMA Growth, 42, 59
AMA Income, 44, 60
American Investors Growth, 36, 39, 61
American Investors Income, 45, 62
American Leaders (Liberty), 37, 42, 63
Analytic Optioned Equity, 42, 64
Armstrong Associates, 40, 65
Axe-Houghton Fund B, 37, 43, 66
Axe-Houghton Income, 37, 44, 67
Axe-Houghton Stock, 38, 68

Babson Bond Trust, 44, 69
Babson Enterprise, 38, 70
Babson Growth, 40, 71
Babson Tax-Free Income Portfolio L, 46, 311
Babson Value, 42, 72
Bartlett Basic Value, 42, 73
Bartlett Fixed Income, 341
Beacon Hill Mutual, 41, 74
Benham California Tax-Free Intermediate, 47, 311
Benham California Tax Free Long Term, 46, 312
Benham GNMA Income, 44, 75
Benham National Tax-Free Trust Long Term, 46, 312
Benham Target Maturities Trust Series 1990, 44, 76
Benham Target Maturities Trust Series 1995, 44, 77
Benham Target Maturities Trust Series 2000, 44, 78
Benham Target Maturities Trust Series 2010, 36, 44, 79
Boston Co. Capital Appreciation, 37, 40, 80
Boston Co. Managed Income, 44, 81
Boston Co. Special Growth, 41, 82
Boston Company GNMA, 341
Bowser Growth, 36, 41, 83
Bruce Fund, 38, 84
Bull & Bear Capital Growth, 36, 38, 85
Bull & Bear Equity-Income, 43, 86
Bull & Bear High Yield, 45, 87
Bull & Bear Tax-Free Income, 46, 313
Bull & Bear U.S. Government Guaranteed Securities, 341

California Tax-Free Income Fund, 46, 313
Calvert—Equity Portfolio, 40, 88
Calvert Tax-Free Reserves Limited Term, 47, 314
Calvert Tax-Free Reserves Long-Term, 46, 314
Capital Preservation Treasury Note Trust, 44, 89
Century Shares Trust, 37, 41, 90
Claremont Combined Portfolio, 43, 91
Columbia Fixed Income Securities, 44, 92
Columbia Growth, 41, 93
Columbia Special, 38, 94
Copley Tax-Managed, 37, 40, 95
Cumberland Growth, 40, 96

deVegh Mutual, 41, 97
Delaware Treasury Reserves Investors Series, 45, 98
Dividend/Growth—Dividend Series, 42, 99
Dodge & Cox Balanced, 37, 43, 100
Dodge & Cox Stock, 37, 42, 101
Dreyfus A Bonds Plus, 44, 102
Dreyfus California Tax Exempt Bond, 46, 315
Dreyfus Capital Value, 38, 103
Dreyfus Convertible Securities, 43, 104
Dreyfus GNMA, 45, 105
Dreyfus Growth Opportunity, 40, 106
Dreyfus Insured Tax Exempt Bond, 46, 315
Dreyfus Intermediate Tax-Exempt, 46, 316
Dreyfus Massachusetts Tax Exempt Bond, 46, 316
Dreyfus New Leaders, 38, 107
Dreyfus New York Tax Exempt Bond, 46, 317
Dreyfus Tax-Exempt, 37, 46, 317
Dreyfus Third Century, 36, 42, 108

Energy, 42, 109
Evergreen, 37, 38, 110
Evergreen Total Return, 37, 43, 111

Fairmont, 37, 38, 112
Farm Bureau Growth, 41, 113
Federated Tax-Free Income (Liberty), 37, 46, 318
Fidelity Aggressive Tax-Free Portfolio, 46, 318
Fidelity California Tax Free High Yield, 46, 319
Fidelity Contrafund, 40, 114
Fidelity Flexible Bond, 44, 115
Fidelity Freedom, 38, 116
Fidelity Fund, 37, 42, 117
Fidelity Ginnie Mae, 44, 118

Fidelity Government Securities, 44, 119
Fidelity High Income, 37, 44, 120
Fidelity High-Yield Municipals, 37, 46, 319
Fidelity Insured Tax Free, 46, 320
Fidelity Limited Term Municipals, 47, 320
Fidelity MassFree—Muni Bond, 46, 321
Fidelity Michigan Tax-Free, 46, 321
Fidelity Minnesota Tax-Free, 46, 322
Fidelity Mortgage Securities, 44, 121
Fidelity Municipal, 37, 46, 322
Fidelity New York Tax-Free High Yield, 46, 323
Fidelity New York Tax-Free Insured, 46, 323
Fidelity Ohio Tax Free, 46, 324
Fidelity Puritan, 37, 43, 122
Fidelity Short Term Bond, 342
Fidelity Texas Tax-Free, 342
Fidelity Thrift, 44, 123
Fidelity Trend, 40, 124
Fidelity Value, 40, 125
Fiduciary Capital Growth, 36, 39, 126
Financial Bond Shares—High Yield Portfolio, 44, 127
Financial Bond Shares—Select Income Portfolio, 44, 128
Financial Bond Shares—U.S. Government, 342
Financial Dynamics, 38, 129
Financial Industrial, 41, 130
Financial Industrial Income, 37, 43, 131
Financial Strategic Portfolio—Energy, 38, 132
Financial Strategic Portfolio—European, 343
Financial Strategic Portfolio—Financial Services, 343
Financial Strategic Portfolio—Gold, 36, 48, 133
Financial Strategic Portfolio—Health Sciences, 38, 134
Financial Strategic Portfolio—Leisure, 38, 135
Financial Strategic Portfolio—Pacific Basin, 36, 48, 136
Financial Strategic Portfolio—Technology, 38, 137
Financial Strategic Portfolio—Utilities, 343
Financial Tax-Free Income Shares, 37, 46, 324
Flex-Fund—Retirement Growth, 40, 138
Flex Bond, 44, 139
44 Wall Street, 36, 39, 140
Founders Equity Income, 43, 141
Founders Growth, 40, 142
Founders Mutual, 37, 42, 143
Founders Special, 38, 144
Fund for U.S. Government Securities (Liberty), 45, 145

G. T. Europe Growth, 36, 48, 146

G. T. International Growth, 36, 48, 147
G. T. Japan Growth, 36, 48, 148
G. T. Pacific Growth, 36, 48, 149
Gateway Growth Plus, 344
Gateway Option Income, 42, 150
General Securities, 42, 151
Gintel Capital Appreciation, 38, 152
Gintel ERISA, 42, 153
GIT Equity Special Growth, 38, 154
GIT Income—Maximum, 45, 155
GIT Tax-Free High Yield, 46, 325
Golconda Investors, 36, 48, 156
Gradison Established Growth, 40, 157
Gradison Opportunity Growth, 38, 158
Growth Industry Shares, 41, 159
Guardian Mutual, 37, 42, 160

Harbor Growth, 344
Hartwell Growth, 38, 161
Hartwell Leverage, 38, 162

International Equity Trust, 36, 48, 163
Istel (Lepercq), 42, 164
Ivy Growth, 37, 42, 165
Ivy International Fund, 344

Janus, 42, 166
Janus Value, 40, 167
Janus Venture, 38, 168

Kentucky Tax-Free Income, 46, 325

Legg Mason Special Investment Trust, 38, 169
Legg Mason Total Return Trust, 36, 43, 170
Legg Mason Value Trust, 41, 171
Lehman Capital, 37, 40, 172
Lehman Investors, 40, 173
Lehman Opportunity, 37, 43, 174
Leverage Fund of Boston, 36, 39, 175
Lexington GNMA, 44, 176
Lexington Goldfund, 36, 48, 177
Lexington Growth, 38, 178
Lexington Research, 40, 179
Liberty, 44, 180
LMH, 42, 181
Loomis-Sayles Mutual, 37, 43, 182

Manhattan, 37, 40, 183
Mathers, 40, 184
Medical Technology, 38, 185
Mutual of Omaha America, 44, 186
Mutual Qualified Income, 37, 43, 187
Mutual Shares, 37, 43, 188

Naess & Thomas Special, 36, 38, 189
National Industries Fund, 41, 190
Neuwirth, 38, 191
New Beginning Growth, 38, 192
New York Muni, 46, 326

Newton Growth, 41, 193
Newton Income, 45, 194
Nicholas, 37, 40, 195
Nicholas II, 40, 196
Nicholas Income, 44, 197
Nodding-Calamos Convertible Income, 42, 198
Nomura Pacific Basin, 36, 48, 199
North Star Apollo, 36, 41, 200
North Star Bond, 44, 201
North Star Regional, 37, 40, 202
North Star Reserve Fund, 345
North Star Stock, 40, 203
Northeast Investors Growth, 40, 204
Northeast Investors Trust, 37, 44, 205
Nova, 38, 206

Omega, 38, 207
100 Fund, 38, 208
101 Fund, 40, 209

Pacific Horizon Aggressive Growth, 38, 210
Pacific Horizon California Tax-Exempt Bond, 46, 326
Pacific Horizon High Yield Bond, 44, 211
Park Avenue New York Tax Exempt— Intermediate, 47, 327
Partners, 37, 42, 212
Pax World, 48, 213
Penn Square Mutual, 42, 214
Permanent Portfolio, 40, 215
Pine Street, 42, 216
T. Rowe Price California Tax-Free Bond, 345
T. Rowe Price Capital Appreciation, 345
T. Rowe Price Equity Income, 42, 217
T. Rowe Price GNMA, 44, 218
T. Rowe Price Growth & Income, 42, 219
T. Rowe Price Growth Stock, 40, 220
T. Rowe Price High Yield, 44, 221
T. Rowe Price International, 36, 37, 48, 222
T. Rowe Price International Bond, 346
T. Rowe Price New America Growth, 40, 223
T. Rowe Price New Era, 40, 224
T. Rowe Price New Horizons, 36, 38, 225
T. Rowe Price New Income, 44, 226
T. Rowe Price Short-Term Bond, 45, 227
T. Rowe Price Tax-Free High Yield, 46, 327
T. Rowe Price Tax-Free Income, 46, 328
T. Rowe Price Tax Free Short Intermediate, 47, 328
Primary Trend Fund, 346

Quest for Value, 37, 38, 228

Rainbow, 40, 229
Reich & Tang Equity, 38, 230

Rightime, 40, 231

Safeco California Tax-Free Income, 46, 329
Safeco Equity, 42, 232
Safeco Growth, 36, 41, 233
Safeco Income, 37, 43, 234
Safeco Municipal, 37, 46, 329
Salem Growth, 40, 235
SBSF Fund, 41, 236
Scudder California Tax Free, 46, 330
Scudder Capital Growth, 37, 40, 237
Scudder Development, 38, 238
Scudder Global, 346
Scudder Government Mortgage Securities, 44, 239
Scudder Growth & Income, 42, 240
Scudder Income, 44, 241
Scudder International, 36, 37, 48, 242
Scudder Managed Municipal, 46, 330
Scudder New York Tax Free, 47, 331
Scudder Target General 1990, 44, 243
Scudder Tax Free Target 1987, 47, 331
Scudder Tax Free Target 1990, 47, 332
Scudder Tax Free Target 1993, 47, 332
Selected American Shares, 37, 42, 244
Selected Special Shares, 41, 245
Sherman, Dean, 36, 39, 246
Steadman American Industry, 36, 41, 247
Steadman Associated, 36, 42, 248
Steadman Investment, 40, 249
Steadman Oceanographic, Technology & Growth, 36, 39, 250
SteinRoe & Farnham Capital Opportunities, 38, 251
SteinRoe & Farnham Stock, 38, 252
SteinRoe Discovery, 36, 39, 253
SteinRoe High-Yield Bonds, 347
SteinRoe High-Yield Municipals, 46, 333
SteinRoe Intermediate Municipals, 47, 333
SteinRoe Managed Bonds, 44, 254
SteinRoe Managed Municipals, 37, 46, 334
SteinRoe Special, 37, 38, 255
SteinRoe Total Return, 43, 256
SteinRoe Universe, 40, 257
Stratton Growth, 40, 258
Stratton Monthly Dividend Shares, 37, 44, 259
Strong Income, 43, 260

Transatlantic Fund, 36, 48, 261
Tudor, 37, 38, 262
20th Century Growth, 38, 263
20th Century Select, 37, 38, 264
20th Century U.S. Governments, 45, 265

UMB Bond, 44, 266
UMB Stock, 42, 267
Unified Growth, 40, 268
Unified Income, 43, 269
Unified Municipal—General Series, 46, 334

Unified Municipal—Indiana Series, 46, 335
Unified Mutual Shares, 42, 270
US Gold Shares, 36, 48, 271
US Good and Bad Times, 40, 272
US Growth, 38, 273
US Income, 43, 274
US LoCap, 36, 39, 275
US New Prospector, 36, 48, 276
USAA Cornerstone, 36, 43, 277
USAA Gold, 36, 48, 278
USAA Growth, 40, 279
USAA Income, 43, 280
USAA Sunbelt Era, 38, 281
USAA Tax Exempt High-Yield, 46, 335
USAA Tax Exempt Intermediate-Term,
47, 336
USAA Tax Exempt Short-Term, 47, 336

Valley Forge, 42, 282
Value Line Aggressive Income, 347
Value Line Convertible, 44, 283
Value Line Fund, 40, 284
Value Line Income, 43, 285
Value Line Leveraged Growth, 40, 286
Value Line Special Situations, 38, 287
Value Line Tax Exempt—High Yield, 47,
337
Value Line U.S. Government Securities,
44, 288
Vanguard California Insured Tax-Free,
347
Vanguard Convertible Securities, 348
Vanguard Explorer II, 36, 39, 289
Vanguard GNMA, 44, 290
Vanguard High Yield Bond, 44, 291

Vanguard High-Yield Municipal Bond, 37,
46, 337
Vanguard Index Trust, 37, 42, 292
Vanguard Intermediate-Term Municipal
Bond, 46, 338
Vanguard Investment Grade Bond, 44,
293
Vanguard Long-Term Municipal Bond, 37,
46, 338
Vanguard Municipal Bond—Insured Long
Term, 46, 339
Vanguard New York Insured Tax-Free,
348
Vanguard Pennsylvania Insured Tax-Free,
348
Vanguard Short-Term Bond, 44, 294
Vanguard Short-Term Municipal Bond,
47, 339
Vanguard Star, 40, 295
Vanguard/Trustees' Commingled—
International Portfolio, 36, 48, 296
Vanguard/Trustees' Commingled—U.S.
Portfolio, 42, 297
Vanguard U.S. Treasury Bond, 349
Vanguard/W.L. Morgan Growth, 41, 298
Vanguard/Wellesley, 37, 43, 299
Vanguard/Wellington, 37, 43, 300
Vanguard Windsor II, 42, 301
Vanguard World—International Growth,
36, 48, 302
Vanguard World—U.S. Growth, 41, 303
Viking Equity Index—General, 42, 304

Wayne Hummer Growth, 42, 305
World of Technology, 48, 306
WPG, 40, 307

EDUCATIONAL PROGRAMS
FROM THE
AMERICAN ASSOCIATION OF INDIVIDUAL INVESTORS

The American Association of Individual Investors offers a variety of products geared to educate individuals in becoming effective managers of their own assets. For further information on the following products, write to: American Association of Individual Investors, 612 N. Michigan Ave., Chicago, IL 60611, Dept. 502A.

The Individual Investor's Microcomputer Resource Guide, Fifth Edition. A complete reference source for investor software, databases and financial information services available for the microcomputer. Also included are discussions of computer hardware, developments in the industry and an easy-reference grid for product selection.

Individual Investor's Home Study Curriculum. This 10-lesson home study course for the serious investor explains investment theory and provides practical applications for constructing and managing an investment portfolio. Included is detailed discussion of investment alternatives.

Investing Fundamentals. A six-hour, three-tape videocourse on the fundamentals of investing. The tapes cover the basic financial concepts and theories needed to make informed, independent investment decisions. Presented are reading financial statements; using financial statements to determine stock value; evaluating investment vehicles; how unit trusts and other packaged investment products work; developing a financial plan; and much more. A workbook containing problems and examples supplementing the videocourse is included.